R. Gupta's®
Popular Master Guide

RAJKIYA PRATIBHA VIKAS VIDYALAYA

Entrance Test

CLASS IX

- Sufficient Theory & Solved Questions for Practice
- Strictly According to Current Exam Pattern

2019
EDITION

RAMESH PUBLISHING HOUSE, New Delhi

Published by
O.P. Gupta *for* Ramesh Publishing House

Admin. Office
12-H, New Daryaganj Road, Opp. Officers' Mess,
New Delhi-110002 ✆ 23261567, 23275224, 23275124

E-mail: info@rameshpublishinghouse.com
Website: www.rameshpublishinghouse.com

Showroom
● Balaji Market, Nai Sarak, Delhi-6 ✆ 23253720, 23282525
● 4457, Nai Sarak, Delhi-6, ✆ 23918938

Book Code: R-1809

ISBN: 978-93-5012-790-2

HSN Code: 49011010

SCHEME OF EXAMINATION

The main purpose to establish the Rajkiya Pratibha Vikas Vidyalaya is the allround development of Brilliant Students through sports, education & competitive exams. Rajkiya Pratibha Vikas Vidyalaya (R.P.V.Vs) are being run by Education department of Delhi Government.

Eligibility for Entrance Test

(i) Those students who have studied at least 2 years regularly in the school, conducted by Delhi Govt./Aided by Delhi Govt./M.C.D./N.D.M.C./Cantonment Board are eligible to sit for this Examination.

(ii) Students should not have studied in one class for two years & should have passed Class VII & VIII in continous two years.

(iii) Students should aggregated at least 60% marks in Class-VIII Examination

Entrance Test

Selection will be on the basis of Entrance Test. The paper will include objective type questions on Numerical Ability, Mental Ability, General Knowledge and Language Comprehension. In addition to objective type questions there will be Descriptive Parameters in Language Comprehension.

CONTENTS

———————

DELHI : AT A GLANCE

Union Territory	:	Delhi (NCR)
Capital	:	New Delhi
Date of establish ment	:	1st November, 1956
Constitutional Name	:	Delhi
Ancient Name	:	Indraprastha
Area	:	1483 square km.
Boundary	:	In north east lies Uttar Pradesh and North south and south east is surrounded by Haryana

Population (Census 2011) :

Total population	:	16,787,941
Male	:	8,987,326
Female	:	7,800,615
Population density	:	11,320 person per square kilometre
Decadenal growth rate (2001 – 2011)	:	21.2%
Rural population :		419042
Male	:	226,321
Female	:	192721
Urban population	:	16,368,899
Male	:	8,761,005
Female	:	7,607,894
Percentage of Urban population	:	97.5%
Literacy	:	86.2% (2011)
Male	:	90. 9%
Female	:	80.8%
Sex ratio	:	868 Females per 1000 males
Population of scheduled Castes (2011)	:	28,12,309 (16.8%)
Mountain	:	Aravali ridge
River	:	Yamuna river
Official language	:	Hindi
Other official language	:	Urdu
Districts	:	11
Legislative Assembly	:	Unicameral
Number of members in Legislative Assembly	:	70
Number of members in Lok Sabha	:	7
Number of members in Rajya Sabha	:	3
State flower	:	Rose
State Bird	:	House Sparrow
First Lieutenant Governor	:	A.N. Jha
First chief Minister	:	Brahma Prakash
First women Chief Minister	:	Sushma Swaraj

Delhi : Some Important Facts

- Tomars king built the city of **Dhillika** (Delhi) in A.D. 736.
- Prithviraj III was the last Hindu rular of Delhi.
- Mohammad Ghori defeated Prithviraj III in the second battle of Tarain in 1192.
- The earliest rulers of the Delhi sultanate was **Qutb-ud-din Aibak,** the general of Muhammad Ghori. Who established the slave dynasity.
- Qutb - ud - din Aibak constructed two mosques - Quwat-ul-Islam at Delhi and **Adhai din ka Jhopra** at Ajmer.
- He also began the construction of **Qutab Minar in** the houour of famous Sufi Sant Khawaja **Qutub-ud-din Bakhtiyar Kaki**

The Sultanate of Delhi was Comprised of Five Dynasties

The Ilbaries : A.D 1206 – 1290
The Khaljis : A.D 1290 –1320
The Tughlaqs : A.D 1320 –1413

The Saiyids : A.D 1414 –1451
The Lodis   : A.D 1451 – 1526

Architecture of Sultanate Period

Architect	Place	Builders
Quwat-ul-Islam Mosque	Delhi	Qutb-ud-din Aibak
Qutub Minar	Delhi	Qutb - ud-din Aibak
Jamaat Khan Masjid	Delhi	Alauddin khilji
Alai Darwaja	Delhi	Alauddin Khilji
Fort of Siri	Delhi	Alauddin Khilji
Hauj - i- Khas	Delhi	Alauddin Khilji
Hazr Situn	Delhi	Alauddin Khilji
City of Tughlaqabad	Delhi	Ghiyas-ud-din Tughlaq
Place on Twelve pillars	Delhi	Muhammed Bin Tughlaq
Kotla Firoz Shah Fort	Delhi	Firoz Shah Tughlaq
Sultangarhi tomb	Delhi	Iltutmish
Fort of Adilabad	Delhi	Muhammed Bin Tughlaq
City of Jahan Panah	Delhi	Muhammed Tughlaq
Begumpuri	Delhi	Firoz shah Tughlaq
Window Mosque	Delhi	Firoz Shah Tughlaq

- The capital of British India was shifed from **Kolkata** to **Delhi** in 12th December, 1911.
- At first Jantar-Manter was built in Delhi.
- The president House is situated at Raisina ridge of Aravali.
- The Heart of India is Delhi.
- The Highest Minar of India is situated in Dehli
- The biggest Mosque of India (Jama Maszid) is situated in Delhi
- Jawaharlal Nehru stadium is situated in Delhi.
- Firoz Shah Kotla stadium is located in Delhi.
- First Asian Games were held in Delhi in 1951.

- First National Games were held in Delhi in 1985.
- Indira Gandhi International Air port is located in Delhi.
- First computer Railway Reservation was started in Delhi.
- In 1st November, 1956, Delhi became Union Territory.
- First T.V. Centre was established in 15th November 1959 in Delhi.
- Operation Black Rose was started to finish the terrorists in Delhi.
- Delhi High Court was established in 1966.
- The construction of President House was started in 1913.
- The Architecture of New Delhi was famous Architect Sir Edwin Lutyens.
- In India, first time Commonweath Games (19th) were organized in Delhi in 2010.

OBJECTIVE QUESTIONS

1. The Area of National capital Territory is:
   A. 1483 sq. km
   B. 2483 sq. km.
   C. 1983 sq. km
   D. 2983 sq. km.

2. Sex ratio of Delhi is :
   A. 811   B. 868
   C. 831   D. 841

3. The population density of Delhi per km^2 is:
   A. 9140 person   B. 9240 person
   C. 11320 person   D. 9540 person

4. The literacy rate of Delhi (2011) is :
   A. 80. 7%   B. 86.2%
   C. 82.7%   D. 85.7%

5. The female literacy rate of Delhi (2011) is:
   A. 70. 7%   B. 72.2%
   C. 80.8%   D. 76.7%

6. Delhi became capital of British India in :
   A. 12th December, 1911
   B. 12th December,1911
   C. 12th December, 1913
   D. 12th December, 1914

7. The Ancient name of Delhi was :
   A. Indraprastha
   B. Krishraprastha
   C. Sonprastha
   D. Agarprastha

8. Rai Pithore was known as :
   A. Mohammed Gohri
   B. Prithvi Raj Chauhan
   C. Babar
   D. Akabar

9. Din Panah was established by :
   A. Hummayu   B. Babar
   C. Sher Shah   D. Akabar

10. Moti mosque of Red Fort (Lal Quila) in Delhi was built by :
    A. Akbar   B. Jahangir
    C. Shahjahan   D. Aurangzeb

11. The construction of Qutub Minar was started by :
    A. Qutb - ud - din Aibak
    B. Balban
    C. Rajiya Sultan
    D. Sher Shah

12. Janter - Manter was first built in :
    A. Varanasi   B. Jaipur
    C. Agra   D. Delhi

13. The height of Iron pillar, located in Delhi, is :
    A. 8.20 m   B. 7. 20 m
    C. 9.20 m   D. 11.20 m

14. The height of India gate is :
    A. 40 m   B. 42 m
    C. 45 m   D. 50 m

15. The president House is located at :
    A. Badar pur Ridge
    B. Raisina ridge

C. Delhi ridge
D. Arawali ridge

16. The Direction of Yamuna river in Delhi is :
  A. North - south   B. North - west
  C. North - east   D. South - west

17. The Height of Delhi from sea level is :
  A. 900 ft   B. 800 ft
  C. 700 ft   D. 600 ft

18. The number of members in Delhi legistative Assembly is :
  A. 90   B. 80
  C. 70   D. 60

19. River yamuna is entered in Delhi at :
  A. Sabha pur village
  B. Pala village
  C. Mongolpuri
  D. Gokulpuri

20. The number of districts in Delhi is :
  A. Seven   B. Eleven
  C. Ten   D. Twelve

21. The ring Railway service was started in Delhi in :
  A. 1982   B. 1985
  C. 1987   D. 1990

22. Master plan for development of Delhi was started in :
  A. 1965   B. 1964
  C. 1963   D. 1961

23. Delhi became Union Territory in :
  A. 1955   B. 1956
  C. 1957   D. 1960

24. Which one of the following game associated with Ambedkar stadium of Delhi?
  A. Hockey   B. Cricket
  C. Tennis   D. Football

25. Delhi police day is celebrated on :
  A. 25th January
  B. 30th January
  C. 16 th February
  D. 25th February

ANSWERS

1	2	3	4	5	6	7	8	9	10
A	B	C	B	C	B	A	B	A	D

11	12	13	14	15	16	17	18	19	20
A	D	B	B	B	A	C	C	B	B

21	22	23	24	25
A	D	B	D	C

Rajkiya Pratibha Vikash Vidyalaya
Entrance Test (Class-IX)

General Knowledge

1. With which field is the Oscar Award Associated?
   A. Literature   B. Music
   C. Movie   D. Sports

2. Which state is bounded by Bangladesh on three sides?
   A. Mizoram   B. Meghalaya
   C. Tripura   D. West Bengal

3. As per census 2011, total population of Delhi is:
   A. 12,860,945   B. 18,970,605
   C. 16,787,941   D. 13,270,780

4. Sun Temple is located at :
   A. Konark   B. Madurai
   C. Kashmir   D. Jaipur

5. Who invented revolver:
   A. E.G. Otis   B. Frank Whittle
   C. Samuel Colt   D. Charles Goodyear

6. 'Pedogenesis' refers to :
   A. the process of continuous erosion
   B. the process of production in plants
   C. the process of soil formation
   D. the process of reproduction in animals

7. The ozone layer in the atmosphere :
   A. causes rainfall
   B. creates pollution
   C. protects life on earth from ultraviolet radiation
   D. produces oxygen in the atmosphere

8. McMahon line is the line that divides :
   A. India and China
   B. India and Myanmar
   C. India and Nepal
   D. India and Bangladesh

9. Which is the longest river of the world?
   A. Nile   B. Ganga
   C. Amazon   D. Mississipi

10. The literacy rate of Delhi (2011) is :
    A. 80.7%   B. 85.7%
    C. 82.7%   D. 86.2%

11. In India the 26th January is:
    A. Independence Day   B. Revolution Day
    C. Republic Day   D. Parliament Day

12. Area-wise which is the biggest state of India?
    A. Rajasthan   B. Uttar Pradesh
    C. Madhya Pradesh   D. Maharashtra

13. Who is the author of the famous book "Republic"?
    A. Plato   B. Aristotle
    C. Rousseau   D. Hobbes

14. Ashok Mehta Committee was set up :
    A. to settle water disputes between the States
    B. to review Centre–State relations
    C. to review the working of Panchayats
    D. to settle boundary disputes between the States

15. The Sardar Sarovar Project is built on the river :
    A. Tapti   B. Godavari
    C. Narmada   D. Krishna

16. Which is the highest plateau in the world?
    A. Deccan Plateau   B. Tibetan Plateau
    C. Colorado Plateau   D. Bolivian Plateau

17. Who gave the slogan 'Jai Hind' to India?
    A. L.B. Shastri   B. S.C. Bose
    C. M.K. Gandhi   D. J.L. Nehru

18. The members of the Rajya Sabha are elected for
    A. whole life   B. six years
    C. five years   D. two years

19. Who called Gandhiji as "Mahatma"?
    A. Jawahar Lal Nehru
    B. G.D. Birla
    C. Rabindra Nath Tagore
    D. Gopal Krishna Gokhale

20. With which sport is Aagha Khan Cup associated?
    A. Football   B. Table Tennis
    C. Volly ball   D. Hockey

21. Jallianwala Bagh massacre took place in the city :
A. Meerut   B. Agra
C. Amritsar   D. Lahore

22. The first railway line in India was started in the year :
A. 1853   B. 1850
C. 1840   D. 1890

23. The battle field of Plassey is situated in :
A. Bihar   B. Andhra Pradesh
C. Odisha   D. West Bengal

24. Which of the following is the oldest Veda?
A. Samveda   B. Yajurveda
C. Rigveda   D. Atharaveda

25. Influenza is caused by a :
A. Virus   B. Fungus
C. Algae   D. Bacterium

Mental Ability

26. Find out the pair of numbers which does **not** belong to the group for lack of common property.
A. 15 – 105   B. 16 – 112
C. 17 – 102   D. 18 – 126

27. Find out a set of numbers amongst the four sets of numbers given in the alternatives which is most like the set given in the question.
Given set : (6, 19, 43)
A. 4, 16, 40   B. 8, 22, 45
C. 9, 22, 45   D. 7, 18, 40

Directions : In questions no. 28 to 34, a series is given, with one term missing. Choose the correct alternative from the given ones that will complete the series.

28. 30, 24, 18, 12, ?
A. 8   B. 6
C. 5   D. 4

29. 5, 10, 13, 26, 29, 58, 61, ?
A. 122   B. 64
C. 125   D. 128

30. 5000, 1000, ? , 40, 8
A. 2000   B. 200
C. 400   D. 500

31. Question Figures :

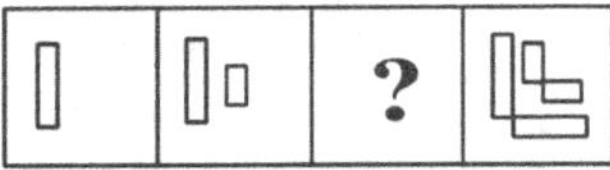

Answer Figures :

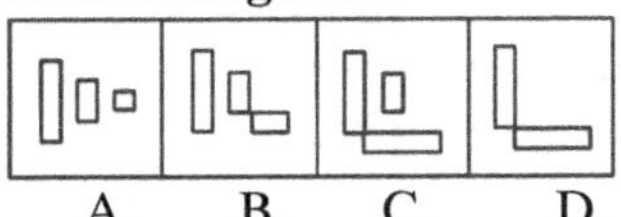

A.   B.   C.   D.

32. Y, Z, B, A, W, ? , D, C
A. X   B. U
C. V   D. F

33. ZXV, USQ, PNL, ?
A. MJH   B. JHF
C. KIG   D. KJI

34. Question Figures :

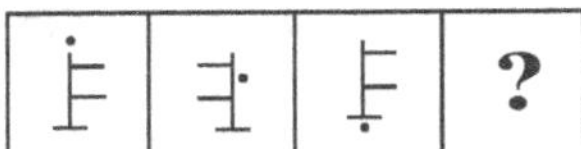

Answer Figures :

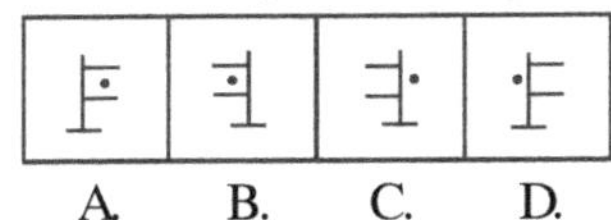

A.   B.   C.   D.

35. Which one set of letters when sequentially placed at the gaps in the given letter series shall complete it?
a_bbcc_abbc_aa_bcc
A. aacb   B. acac
C. bcac   D. cabc

Directions : In questions no. 36 to 41, select the one which is different from the other three responses.

36. A. DGJMP   B. HKNQT
C. LORUW   D. PSVYB

37. A. 6   B. 21
C. 24   D. 40

38. 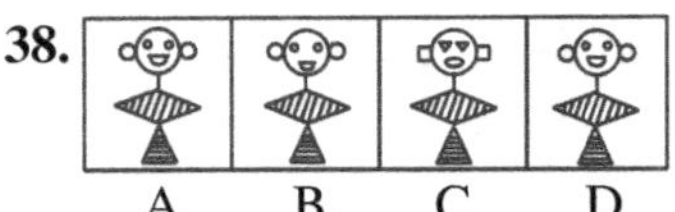

A.   B.   C.   D.

39. 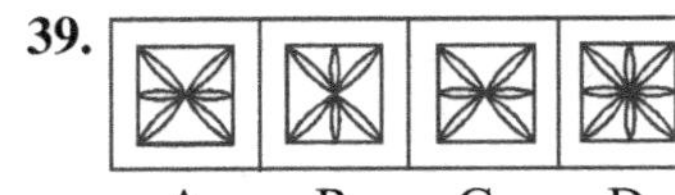

A.   B.   C.   D.

40. A. Amazon   B. Nile
C. Thames   D. Kabul

41. A. Milk   B. Curd
C. Petrol   D. Butter

42. If (–) stands for division, (+) for multiplication, (÷) for subtraction and (×) stands for addition, which one of the following answers is correct to the given equation?
$1 - (5 - 50) + 10 \div 60 \times 10 = \underline{?}$
A. 30   B. 40
C. 50   D. 20

43. Robin says, " If Jai gives me Rs. 40, he will have half as much as Atul, but if Atul gives me Rs. 40, then the three of us will all have the same amount." What is the total amount of money (in Rs.) that Robin, Jai and Atul have between them?
A. 240   B. 320
C. 360   D. 420

44. A is the son of B and C, B's sister has a son D and daughter E; F is the maternal uncle of D. How is E related to F?
A. Sister   B. Daughter
C. Niece   D. Wife

45. Mohan and Sohan started from the same point. Mohan moved 10 km north, then turned right and moved 5 km, again turned south, and moved 5 km. Sohan moved 10 km south, turned left, moved 5 km, turned north, and moved 5 km. What will be the distance between Mohan and Sohan?
A. 14 km   B. 10 km
C. 12 km   D. 8 km

46. In a certain code language, EDUCATION is written as BGRFXWFRK. How is TEACHER is written in that code?
A. HQFXEHO   B. WHXGKHU
C. QHXFEHO   D. SBEAGFU

47. If in a certain code TWENTY is written as 958193 and ELEVEN is written as 848681. How is TWELVE written in that code?

A. 846845   B. 985684
C. 896458   D. 958468

48. Which one of the answer figures shall complete the given question figure?
Question Figure:

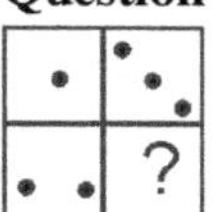

Answer Figures:

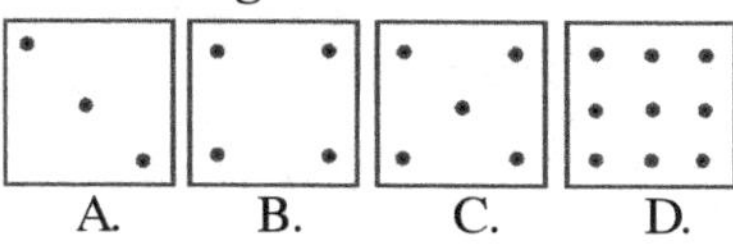

49. From the given answer figures, select the one in which the question figure is hidden/ embedded.
Question Figure:

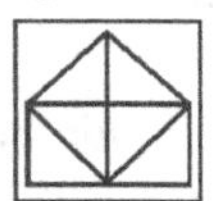

Answer Figures:

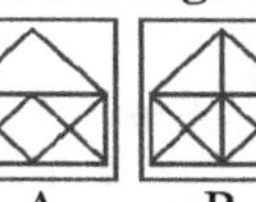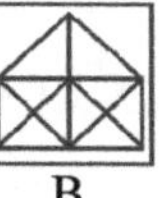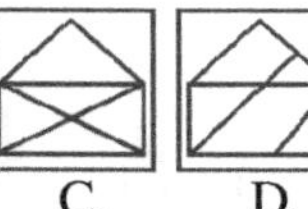

50. A piece of paper is fold and cut as shown below in the question figures. From the given answer figures, indicate how it will appear when opened.

Question Figures:

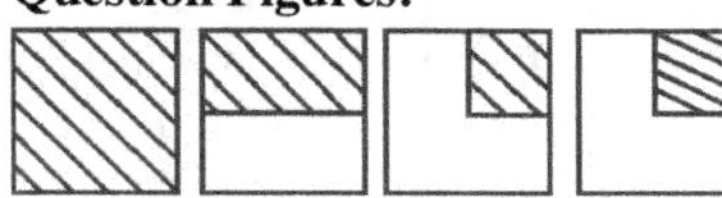

Answer Figures:

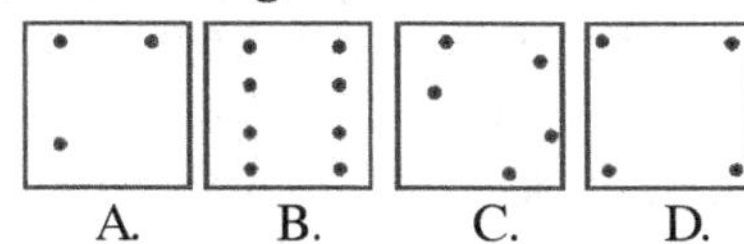

Numerical Ability

51. What will principal amount be ₹ 496 in 6 years at the rate of simple interest of 4% per annum?
A. ₹ 456   B. ₹ 500
C. ₹ 400   D. ₹ 460

52. A car covers a distance of 420 km at a certain speed. If its speed 4 km/hr more, it will take one hour less to cover the same distance. What was its speed?
A. 60 km/hr   B. 50 km/hr
C. 40 km/hr   D. 55 km/hr

53. A train 110 m long is running at 60 km/hr. A platform is 240 m long, what time will it take to cross the platform?

A. 21 secs   B. $5\dfrac{5}{6}$ secs

C. $14\dfrac{2}{5}$ secs   D. 4 secs

54. On the river, a man covers a distance of 3 km against the flow of stream or 15 km in the direction of stream flow in 3 hours, what is the speed of the stream flow?
A. 9 km/hr   B. 2 km/hr
C. 4 km/hr   D. 6 km/hr

55. In a race of 200 metres A and B can complete the race in 22 secs and 25 secs respectively. When A complete the race then B will be at how much distance from the finishing line?
A. 54 m   B. 30 m
C. 48 m   D. 24 m

56. If the difference between the circumference and the radius of a circle is 37 m, what is its radius?
A. 14 m   B. 5 m
C. 7 m   D. 12 m

57. A room is 12 m long, 9 m broad and 8 m high, what will be the length of its diagonal?

A. 17 m   B. $6\sqrt{3}$ m

C. $4\sqrt{6}$ m   D. 12 m

58. Two electronic music system were purchased for ₹ 8000. The first was sold at a profit of 40% and the other at a loss of 40%, if the selling prices of the both were same, then what were the cost prices of both the music systems?
A. ₹ 2400, ₹ 5600   B. ₹ 3000, ₹ 5000
C. ₹ 4000, ₹ 4000   D. ₹ 3500, ₹ 4500

59. If the marked price is 30% more than C.P. and there is a discount of 10% at the marked price, what is the profit?

A. $18\dfrac{1}{2}\%$ B. 20%

C. $15\dfrac{1}{2}\%$ D. 17%

60. A man had Rs. 2000, some part of this he lends at 5% per annum and rest of this at 4% per annum on simple interest. The whole annual interest was ₹ 96. How much did he lend at 4% per annum?
A. ₹ 1600   B. ₹ 1200
C. ₹ 600   D. ₹ 400

61. The sum of the present ages of A, B and C is 90 years. Six years ago, their ages were in the ratio of 1 : 2 : 3. What is the present age of C?
A. 45 years   B. 36 years
C. 42 years   D. 40 years

62. The sum of salaries of 'A' and 'B' is ₹ 2100. 'A' spends 80% of his salary and 'B' spends 70%. If their savings are in the proportion of 4 : 3, then what is the salary of A?
A. ₹ 700   B. ₹ 1400
C. ₹ 1200   D. ₹ 900

63. ₹ 1290 is divided among A, B and C such that A's share is $1\dfrac{1}{2}$ times that of B and B's share is $1\dfrac{3}{4}$ times that of C what is C's share?
A. ₹ 350   B. ₹ 240
C. ₹ 420   D. ₹ 630

64. Five litres of water is added to a certain quantity of pure milk, which costs Rs. 3 per litre. If the mixture is sold at same price of Rs. 3 per litre, a profit of 20% is made (ignore the cost of water). What is the amount of pure milk in the mixture?
A. 30 litres   B. 20 litres
C. 28 litres   D. 25 litres

65. Fifteen men working 8 hours a day, take 21 days to complete a work. How many days will be taken by 21 women to complete the same work, working 6 hours a day?
(3 women do as much work as 2 men)
A. 28 days   B. 25 days
C. 30 days   D. 33 days

66. 'A' can knit a pair of socks in 3 days. 'B' can knit the same pair in 9 days. If they are knitting together, in how many days will they knit two pairs of socks?
A. 3 days   B. 4 days

C. 5 days   D. $4\dfrac{1}{2}$ days

67. A reduction of ₹ 2 per kg in the price of sugar enables a man to now purchase 4 kg more sugar in ₹ 16. What was the original price of sugar?
A. ₹ 2 per kg
B. ₹ 16 per kg
C. ₹ 8 per kg
D. ₹ 4 per kg

68. 33% marks are required to pass an examination. A candidate who gets 210 marks fails by 21 marks. What are the total marks for the examination?
A. 550
B. 700
C. 650
D. 600

69. The ticket for admission to an exhibition was Rs. 5 and it was later reduced by 20%. As a result, the sale proceeds of tickets increased by 44%. What was the percentage increase in number of visitors?
A. 80%
B. 50%
C. 25%
D. 75%

70. The average weight of 8 men is increased by 2 kg when one man of 50 kg is replaced by a new man. What is the weight of the new man?
A. 66 kg
B. 58 kg
C. 68 kg
D. 60 kg

71. Cost of nine pencils is equal to the cost of four pens. Cost of thirteen pencils and six pens is ₹ 159. What is the cost of twenty one pencils and seventeen pens together?
A. ₹ 345.50
B. ₹ 354.50
C. ₹ 342
D. ₹ 355.50

72. Ramesh is five years older than Suresh. Respective ratio between Suresh's age and Madan's age is 3 : 8. Raju is 8 years younger than Madan. Raju's present age is 48 years. What is Ramesh's present age?
A. 16 years
B. 21 years
C. 26 years
D. 35 years

73. In a test, minimum passing percentage for girls and boys are 45% and 60% respectively. A boy scored 767 marks and failed by 313 marks. What are the minimum passing marks for girls?
A. 910
B. 920
C. 840
D. 810

74. Train–A crossed a stationary train in 39 seconds. It also crossed a man standing on a platform in 19 seconds. The length of the train–A is 456 metre. What is the length of the stationary train?
A. 460 metre
B. 480 metre
C. 490 metre
D. 430 metre

75. In a metro train there are 600 passengers out of which 34 per cent are females. Fare of each male is ₹ 20 and each female's fare is 25 per cent less than each male. What is the total revenue generated by all the passengers together?
A. ₹ 10,880
B. ₹ 10,980
C. ₹ 10,740
D. ₹ 10,680

Language Comprehension
(English)

Directions (Qs. 76-80): *Read the following passage and answer the questions.*

Antarctica is Earth's southern most continent, containing the geographic South Pole. Antarctica, on average, is the coldest, driest, and windiest continent, and has the highest average elevation of all the continents. Antarctica is the coldest of Earth's continents. The coldest natural temperature ever recorded on Earth was −89.2 °C at the Russian Vostok Station in Antarctica on 21 July 1983. East Antarctica is colder than its western counterpart because of its higher elevation. Antarctica is colder than the Arctic. Antarctica has no government, although various countries claim sovereignty in certain regions. New claims have not been allowed and now Antarctica is considered politically neutral. The Antarctic Treaty prohibits any military activity in the continent including establishing military bases and weapons testing. It prohibits mineral mining but supports scientific research. The climate does not allow extensive vegetation to form. A combination of freezing temperatures, poor soil quality, lack of moisture, and lack of sunlight inhibit plant growth. About 98% of Antarctica is covered by an ice sheet averaging thickness of 1.6 km. New techniques such as remote sensing and satellite imagery have begun to reveal the structures beneath the ice. The continent as about 90% of the world's ice and 70% of the world's water. Antarctic sea life includes penguins blue whales, orcas, squids etc.

76. Antarctica contains which of the following:
A. Equator
B. North Pole
C. South Pole
D. None of these

77. Which of the following is present in Antarctica?
A. Weapons testing
B. Military bases
C. Central govt
D. Research stations

78. Which of the following is true?
A. West Antarctica is warmer than East
B. Arctic is warmer than the Antarctic
C. Both A and B
D. None of these

79. Which of the following, according to the passage, are not seen in Antarctica?
A. Sealion
B. Penguin
C. Orca
D. Squid

80. What is used to study the structures beneath the ice sheet in Antarctica?
A. Remote sensing
B. Nuclear fusion
C. Both of these
D. None of these

81. Choose from the list below the permissing from the word in brackets in the following sentence—
You can't wear this dress to a party. It is old and ... (coloured)...
A. un....
B. dis...
C. re...
D. None of these

82. Choose the correct phrase to complete the sentence grammatically. They were talking very loudly. I couldn't help .... them.
A. to overhear
B. to overhearing
C. over hearing
D. None of these

83. Fill in the word that best fits the context in the given sentence—
She is fond of me but visits me.
A. seldom
B. often
C. frequently
D. None of these

84. Choose the correct helping verb to complete the sentence grammatically—
The population of the world ___ risen very fast.
A. have
B. has
C. were
D. None of these

85. Choose the phrase which best completes the sentence—
He has had to ____ smoking since his illness.
A. cut out
B. cut down
C. cut off
D. None of these

86. Choose the correct alternative to complete the sentence—
The man _____ I was sitting next to on the plane talked all the time.
A. whom
B. that
C. who
D. whose

87. Fill in the blank with the correct connective.
_____ all our careful plans, a lot of things went wrong.
A. Although
B. In spite of
C. Because of
D. None of these

88. Choose the correct preposition to complete the sentence—
She is not well. She often suffers _______ very bad headaches.
A. in
B. from
C. on
D. None of these

89. Choose the word that best completes the given sentence—
My companion was a very _____ fellow who bored me with his endless chatter.
A. tiring
B. tireless
C. tiresome
D. None of these

90. Pick out the correct alternative to complete the sentence grammatically .... she is injured, she should win easily.
A. As long as
B. Unless
C. Supposing
D. None of these

Directions (Qs. 91 to 95): *In the following items, some parts of the sentence have been jumbled up. You are required to re-arrange these parts which are labelled P, Q, R and S to produce the correct sentence. Choose the proper sequence.*

91. Many (P) way to fuel growth (Q) economists argue that (R) and alleviate poverty (S) free trade is a magic bullet—the quickest
Which one of the following is the correct sequence?
A. Q-P-S-R
B. R-S-P-Q
C. Q-S-P-R
D. R-P-S-Q

92. As a (P) maestro appeared to be enjoying every bit of it (Q) and followed every composition the (R) thunderous applause from (S) an appreciative audience preceded
Which one of the following is the correct sequence?

A. P-Q-S-R   B. R-S-Q-P
C. P-S-Q-R   D. R-Q-S-P

93. Keeping (P) farmers to smoke their fields during (Q) in view the prevailing weather conditions (R) agricultural experts have advised (S) the night to protect vegetables from cold
Which one of the following is the correct sequence?

A. S-R-P-Q   B. Q-P-R-S
C. S-P-R-Q   D. Q-R-P-S

94. It is (P) stressful or joyful (Q) with the belief in the evanescence of life itself (R) necessary to rise above the situations, (S) and in the philosophical quest of the purpose of life
Which one of the following is the correct sequence?

A. R-P-Q-S   B. Q-S-R-P
C. R-S-Q-P   D. Q-P-R-S

95. The difference (P) and development on the other affects (Q) in the relationship between death and birth rates on the one hand (R) but the age structure of the population (S) not just the rate of population growth
Which one of the following is the correct sequence?

A. S-R-Q-P   B. Q-P-S-R
C. S-P-Q-R   D. Q-R-S-P

Directions (Q.N. 96-97): *Choose the most suitable 'one word' for each of the following expressions given below.*

96. The belief that good must prevail over evil in the end
A. Optimism   B. Sophtism
C. Truism   D. Radicalism

97. Hater of women
A. Misochist   B. Misogamist
C. Misogynist   D. Misanthropist

Directions (Q. N. 98): *Read the sentence carefully and choose suitable preposition for the purpose.*

98. She is proud .... her beauty.
A. at   B. on
C. of   D. about

99. Write an essay on any one of the following topics:
A. Clean India Drive
B. Corruption in India
C. The Value of Sports

100. Write a letter to your grandfather who has been suffering from frequent ill health for the last six month.

ANSWERS

1	2	3	4	5	6	7	8	9	10
C	C	C	A	C	C	C	A	A	D
11	**12**	**13**	**14**	**15**	**16**	**17**	**18**	**19**	**20**
C	A	A	C	C	B	B	B	C	D
21	**22**	**23**	**24**	**25**	**26**	**27**	**28**	**29**	**30**
C	A	D	C	A	C	C	B	A	B
31	**32**	**33**	**34**	**35**	**36**	**37**	**38**	**39**	**40**
D	A	C	B	A	C	B	C	D	D
41	**42**	**43**	**44**	**45**	**46**	**47**	**48**	**49**	**50**
C	C	C	C	B	C	D	B	B	B
51	**52**	**53**	**54**	**55**	**56**	**57**	**58**	**59**	**60**
C	A	A	B	D	C	A	A	D	D
61	**62**	**63**	**64**	**65**	**66**	**67**	**68**	**69**	**70**
C	B	D	D	C	D	D	B	A	A
71	**72**	**73**	**74**	**75**	**76**	**77**	**78**	**79**	**80**
D	C	D	B	B	C	D	C	A	A

81	82	83	84	85	86	87	88	89	90
B	C	A	B	C	C	B	B	C	D

91	92	93	94	95	96	97	98
C	B	D	A	B	A	C	C

99. (B) Corruption in India

Corruption is one of the burning topics of today. It is also one of the most serious problems of society these days.

Corruption is there in all the government departments. It is there from the lowest to the highest level. If you want to get any work done in any department, you have to grease the palms of many officials there. The peons, the clerks and the officers, all are corrupt. It has, however, to be admitted that some exceptions are also there. Those who do not take bribes can be counted on fingers.

Corruption is there in many countries. But it is not so common in developed countries. India is one of the most corrupt countries in the world. In this respect, her place is with Pakistan, Bangladesh, Nigeria, etc. The European countries are the least corrupt in the world.

In India, it is said, nobody can get a government job without paying bribe. This became clear when the biggest recruitment scam was unearthed a few years ago in Punjab. Only the UPSC and the like may be an exception. As far as the state public service commissions are concerned, nothing can be said with certainty unless their working is thoroughly scrutinised by some investigative agency.

India has become a land of scams. During the last few decades, we have seen a number of scams unearthed. Some of them are 2G Spectrum scam, Coalgate, Railways scam, Securities scam, Hawala scam, Fodder scam, Bofors scam, Housing scam, Sugar scam, Wheat scam, Urea scam, Recruitment scam, Petrol pump scam, Coffingate, etc. Indeed, the list is endless. So many frauds are committed in banks. The money meant for the pension to the aged, widows, orphans and the handicapped is swindled. Unfortunately, this virus of corruption has spread even in the judiciary, at least at the lower level. It is heartening to note that the Supreme Court and the High Court are trying to root it out from judiciary. Let us hope for the best.

The biggest den of corruption is the political field. There is criminalisation of politics at the highest level. A fairly large number of our central and state legislators have a criminal background. The cases of corruption against many of them are going on in courts. The courts and the Election Commission are doing their best to end this criminalisation of politics.

If the democratic process has to be continued in the country and if the people are to be saved from losing all faith in the government, investigative agencies and the judiciary, something serious will have to be done. Otherwise, this country will go to the dogs, sooner or later.

100.

Examination Hall,
XYZ
February ....

My dear Grandpa,

I received a letter from uncle yesterday stating about your health. I am very disappointed to know that you have been suffering from frequent ill health for the last six months. I pray for your early recovery.

Grandpa, uncle's letter shows that you are not paying attention to the doctor's advise. So, it is my request to take proper rest and do as the doctor says. Take care because we all love you dearly and need you.

I am coming to visit you and Grandma early next month. So, be ready and out of bed to come back here with me. The weather here is pleasant and I am sure you will regain your lost health.

Get well soon. Convey my best regard to Grandma.

Yours affectionately

ABC

(Full name and address of the recipient)

Numerical Ability

Number System

In our System of numeration, numbers are written by using the symbols 0, 1, 2, 3, 4, 5, 6, 7, 8 and 9 with each symbol getting a value depending on the place it occupies. These symbols are called digits. A number related to the objects in a collection gives an idea of how many objects are there in the collection. We thus see that a number represents one or more numerals or indicates one or more different articles of the same type, e.g., *five* pens, *eight* inkpots, *twenty* books, *thirty* rupees etc. The italicized words represent the number of objects in the particular collection.

1. **Natural Numbers or Positive Integers (N = 1, 2, 3, 4, 5 .....):** These are also called counting numbers. When two natural numbers are added or multiplied together, the result is always a natural number. Therefore, all positive integers, used for counting objects, are always **natural numbers** whereas zero together with negative integers and fractional numbers are not natural numbers.

2. **Whole Numbers: (W = 0, 1, 2, 3, 4, 5, ...):** The number '0' together with the natural numbers gives us the numbers which are called **whole numbers,** e.g., 0, 1, 2, 3, 4 ..... etc. whereas -10, -15, -12 ..... or $\dfrac{1}{5}, \dfrac{2}{9}, \dfrac{4}{5}$ ..... etc. are not whole Numbers.

3. **Integers: (I = ..., -5, -4, -3, -2, -1, 0, 1, 2, 3, 4, 5, ...):** The negative numbers together with the whole numbers are called integers. The numbers -1, -2, -3, -4, -5, ... are called negative integers and 1, 2, 3, 4, 5, ..., *i.e.,* natural numbers are called positive integers. The number 0 is simply an integer, *i.e.,* it is neither positive nor negative.

4. **Rational Numbers:** A rational number is a number that can be put in the form $\dfrac{p}{q}$ where p and q are both integers and $q \neq 0$, e.g., 8, $-\dfrac{7}{5}$, $-\dfrac{3}{4}$, $\dfrac{1}{7}$, 0 .... are all rational numbers *i.e.* a rational number may be positive, zero or negative.

5. **Irrational Numbers:** An irrational number is a number that can not be put in the form $\dfrac{p}{q}$ where P and q are both integers and $q \neq 0$, e.g., $\sqrt{5}, \sqrt{11}, \sqrt{15}, 3 + \sqrt{5}$ .... etc. are all irrational numbers.

6. **Real Numbers:** All those numbers which are either rational or irrational, are called real numbers, e.g., $\dfrac{11}{17}, \dfrac{19}{21}, -\dfrac{7}{8}, \sqrt{7}, 8 + \sqrt{3}$ etc. are real numbers.

7. **Even Numbers:** All those numbers which are exactly divisible by 2, are called 'even numbers', e.g., 2, 8, 14, 28, 52 etc. are even numbers.

8. **Odd Numbers:** All those numbers which are not exactly divisible by 2, are called 'Odd Numbers', e.g., 1, 3, 5, 7, 9, 19 etc. are odd numbers.

9. **Composite Numbers:** The numbers which are divisible not only by 1 or themselves, but by some other numbers also, are called the 'Composite numbers'. In other words, the numbers which have more than two factors are called 'Composite Numbers.', e.g., 4, 9, 15, 18, 27, ... etc. are composite numbers.

10. **Prime Numbers:** The numbers which have only two factors, 1 and the number itself are called 'prime numbers', e.g., 2, 5, 11, 19, 23, 31, ... etc. are prime numbers.

11. **Co-primes:** Two numbers which have only 1 as the common factor are called 'co-primes'. 5 and 7 are coprimes. So are 15 and 16.

12. **Twin Primes:** Two prime numbers which differ by 2, are called 'twin primes', e.g., 3, 5; 5, 7; 11, 13; 71, 73 are some pairs of twin primes.

13. **Consecutive Numbers:** The numbers which are following or coming after other numbers in regular order, are called consecutive numbers. 4, 6, 8, 10 are consecutive even numbers and 9, 11, 13, 15 are consecutive odd numbers. 3, 4, 5, 6, 7 ..... etc. are consecutive numbers in the natural order of the number series.

Tests for Divisibility of Numbers

1. **Divisibility by 2:** A number is divisible by 2 if its units digit is 0, 2, 4, 6 or 8. For example each of the numbers 130, 244, 566, 278, ... etc. is divisible by 2.

2. **Divisibility by 3:** A number is divisible by 3 if the sum of its digits is a multiple of 3. For example each of the numbers 312, 213, 456 is divisible by 3 since sum of digits in each of these numbers is $(3 + 1 + 2 = 6)$, $(2 + 1 + 3 = 6)$ and $(4 + 5 + 6 = 15)$ respectively, each of which is a multiple of 3.

3. **Divisibility by 4:** A number is divisible by 4 if the number formed by its digits in ten's and unit's places is divisible by 4. For example numbers formed by ten's and unit's digits of 1132, 1312, 1400 and 1348 are 32, 12, 00 and 48 respectively which are divisible by 4. Hence these numbers also are divisible by 4.

4. **Divisibility by 5:** A number is divisible by 5 if its unit's digit is either 0 or 5. For example, each of the numbers 100, 205, 315, 435 is divisible by 5 since unit's digit in each of these numbers is either 0 or 5.

5. **Divisibility by 6:** A number is divisible by 6 if it is divisible by both 2 and 3.

6. **Divisiblity by 8:** A number is divisible by 8 if the number formed by its digits in hundred's, ten's and unit's places is divisible by 8. For example numbers formed by hundred's, ten's and unit's digits of 1864, 1024, 2008 and 5000 are 864, 024, 008 and 000 respectively which are divisible by 8. Hence these numbers also are divisible by 8.

7. **Divisibility by 9:** A number is divisible by 9 if the sum of its digits is a multiple of 9. For example each of the numbers 23409, 454554, 66636 is divisible by 9 since sum of digits in each of these numbers is $(2 + 3 + 4 + 0 + 9 = 18)$, $(4 + 5 + 4 + 5 + 5 + 4 = 27)$ and $(6 + 6 + 6 + 3 + 6 = 27)$ respectively each of which is a multiple of 9.

8. **Divisibility by 10:** A number is divisible by 10 if its unit's digit is zero. For example each of the numbers 50, 80, 1310, 1400 is divisible by 10 since unit's digit in each of these numbers is 0.

9. **Divisibility by 11:** A number is divisible by 11 if the difference of the sum of its digits in even places and the sum of its digits in odd places (starting from unit's place) is either 0 or a multiple of 11. For example each of the numbers 909183, 540045 and 184712 is divisible by 11 since in each of the numbers difference of the sum of digits in even places and sum of the digits in odd places is $[(9 + 9 + 8) - (0 + 1 + 3) = 22]$, $[(5 + 0 + 4) - (4 + 0 + 5) = 0]$ and $[(8 + 7 + 2) - (1 + 4 + 1) = 11]$ respectively each of which is either '0' or a multiple of '11'

Place Value and Face Value of a digit:

Place Value: Numbers are written by using the symbols 0, 1, 2, 3, 4, 5, 6, 7, 8 and 9, called digits, with each digit getting a value depending on the place it occupies. This value assigned to the digit due to its placement is called place value. For example, in the number 56, digit 6 is placed in unit's place and 5 in ten's place. Therefore place value of 6 in 56 is $6 \times 1 = 6$ and that of 5 is $5 \times 10 = 50$.

Face Value: In a number face value of a digit is the digit itself. For example, in 42, the face value of digit 2 is 2 and that of digit 4 is 4.

Additive Inverse: If sum of two numbers is zero, then each of the numbers (called addends) is called additive inverse of the other. For example, if $a + b = 0$, then '*b*' is additive inverse of '*a*' and *vice versa*.

Multiplicative Inverse: If a and b are two rational numbers such that $a \times b = 1$, then each is called the multiplicative inverse of the other.

Note: $\dfrac{p}{q}$ and $\dfrac{q}{p}$ are also called multiplicative inverse of each other. The multiplicative inverse of zero does not exist.

An important formula in respect of division of whole numbers

Dividend = Divisor × Quotient + Remainder

$$\text{or} \quad \text{Divisor} = \frac{\text{Dividend} - \text{Remainder}}{\text{Quotient}}$$

$$\text{or} \quad \text{Quotient} = \frac{\text{Dividend} - \text{Remainder}}{\text{Divisor}}$$

Some Important Notes

(*i*) The smallest natural number or positive integer is (+1).

(*ii*) The greatest negative integer is –1

(*iii*) The number '0' is neither positive nor negative integer.

(*iv*) 1 is only such number which is neither a prime number nor a composite number.

(*v*) 2 is only such number which is an even number as well as a prime number.

(*vi*) 2 is the smallest prime number.

(*vii*) The number of prime numbers between 1 to 100 is 25.

(*viii*) Any number is a perfect square number, if the unit's digit of the number is 0, 1, 4, 5, 6, or 9.

(*ix*) A cubic number may have any digit from 0 to 9 in its unit's place.

Things to remember while solving problems on whole numbers

(*a*) Sum of numbers from 1 to $n = \dfrac{n(n+1)}{2}$
(where n is the number of terms)

(*b*) Number of odd numbers from 1 to n

$$= \left(\frac{\text{Last odd number} + 1}{2}\right)$$

(*c*) Sum of odd numbers from 1 to n = (Number of odd numbers)^2

(*d*) Number of even numbers from 1 to n

$$= \left(\frac{\text{Last even number}}{2}\right)$$

(*e*) Sum of even numbers from 1 to n
= Number of even numbers × (Number of even numbers + 1)

EXAMPLES

Example 1 : What is the sum of first four prime numbers?
Solution: Sum of first four prime numbers = 2 + 3 + 5 + 7 = 17.

Example 2 : Is 979 a prime number?
Solution: The approximate square root of 979 is 32.
Prime numbers less than 32 are 2, 3, 5, 7, 11, 13, 17, 19, 23, 29, 31. We observe that 979 is divisible by 11, so it is not a prime number.

Example 3 : Prime factors of a number are 2, 2, 3, 7. Find the number.
Solution: The number is equal to the product of prime factors.
∴ 2 × 2 × 3 × 7 = 84 is the required number.

Example 4 : What is the sum of all primes between 70 and 100?
Solution: Prime numbers between 70 and 100 are 71, 73, 79, 83, 89 and 97.
∴ Sum of 71 + 73 + 79 + 83 + 89 + 97 = 492.

Example 5 : What is the difference in face value and local value of 5 in 7501?
Solution: The local value of 5 in 7501 = 500 and intrinsic value of 5 in 7501 = 5.
∴ Required difference = 500 – 5 = 495.

Example 6 : What will be the sum of even numbers between 1 to 40?

Solution: Number of even numbers between 1 to 40 = $\dfrac{40}{2}$ = 20

∴ Sum of even numbers between 1 to 40 = 20(20 + 1)

$$= 20 \times 21 = 420$$

Example 7 : A number when divided by 899 gives a remainder of 63. If the same number is divided by 29, then what will be the remainder?

Solution: Number $= D \times Q + R = 899 \times K + 63$
$$= 31 \times 29 \times K + 29 \times 2 + 5$$
$$= 29\,(31K + 2) + 5$$
∴ The remainder when the number is divided by 29 is 5 Ans.

Example 8 : What least number must be subtracted from 1294, so that the remainder when divided by 9, 11, 13 will leave in each case the same remainder 6?

Solution: The number when divided by 9, 11, 13 leaving remainder 6
= (L.C.M. of 9, 11, 13) + 6 = 1287 + 6 = 1293
∴ Required number = 1294 – 1293 = 1.

Example 9 : What is additive inverse of $\dfrac{3}{7}$?

Solution: We know that if sum of two numbers is 0, then each of the numbers is additive inverse of the other.

Therefore additive inverse of $\dfrac{3}{7}$ is $-\dfrac{3}{7}$, because $\dfrac{3}{7} - \dfrac{3}{7} = 0$

Example 10: What will be the multiplicative inverse of $-\dfrac{7}{8}$?

Solution: Multiplicative inverse (reciprocal) of $-\dfrac{7}{8}$ is $-\dfrac{8}{7}$ because $\left(-\dfrac{7}{8}\right) \times \left(-\dfrac{8}{7}\right) = 1$

MULTIPLE CHOICE QUESTIONS

Directions: *Each of the questions given below is followed by four alternatives of which one is correct. Candidates are required to go through the question and the following alternatives carefully and select the correct answer.*

1. Which of the following is a rational number?
   A. $\sqrt{6}$
   B. $2 + \sqrt{3}$
   C. $\sqrt{9}$
   D. $\sqrt{5}$

2. Which of the following is an irrational number?
   A. 0
   B. $\sqrt[3]{27}$
   C. $2 + \sqrt{16}$
   D. $2 + \sqrt{7}$

3. Additive inverse of 1 is:
   A. -1
   B. $+1$
   C. $-\dfrac{1}{2}$
   D. -2

4. Multiplicative inverse of $-\dfrac{8}{15}$ is:

    A. $+\dfrac{15}{8}$ B. $-\dfrac{15}{8}$ C. $\dfrac{3}{15}$ D. $-\dfrac{5}{8}$

5. How many prime numbers are there between 1 to 100?

    A. 22   B. 18   C. 25   D. 24

6. What is the difference between place value and face value of 9 in the number 9075?

    A. 8891   B. 9891   C. 8991   D. 8981

7. The largest negative integer is:

    A. −5   B. −10   C. −1   D. −20

8. How many two-digit numbers are completely divisible by 3?

    A. 30   B. 28   C. 32   D. 33

9. Difference between the squares of two consecutive numbers is 23. These numbers are:

    A. 13, 14   B. 8, 9   C. 12, 13   D. 11, 12

10. A number when divided by 119 leaves 19 as remainder. If the number is divided by 17 then the remainder will be:

    A. 1   B. 15   C. 2   D. 13

11. The only even prime number is

    A. 2   B. 67   C. 79   D. 98

12. Which of the following is not a prime number?

    A. 79   B. 83   C. 87   D. 97

13. The next number in the sequence 1, 7, 3, 9, 5, 11, ... is—

    A. 7   B. 13   C. 15   D. 17

14. In the sequence 4, 9, ..., 25, 36 the missing number is—

    A. 14   B. 16   C. 20   D. 21

15. In the sequence 17, ..., 18, 15, 19, 14, 20, 13 the missing number is—

    A. 5   B. 10   C. 12   D. 16

16. The product of two prime numbers is a—

    A. prime number   B. even number

    C. odd number   D. composite number

17. Prime factors of a number are 2, 2, 3, 7. The number is—

    A. 14   B. 41   C. 48   D. 84

18. Think of a number, divide it by 9 and add 9 to it, if the result is 27, the number is—

    A. 18   B. 21   C. 100   D. 162

19. The number which when added to itself 10 times gives 264. The number is—

    A. 20   B. 22   C. 24   D. 26

20. If $a = 16$ and $b = 15$, then what is the value of $\dfrac{a^2 + b^2 + ab}{a^3 - b^3} = ?$

    A. $\dfrac{1}{2}$ B. $\dfrac{1}{3}$ C. 1   D. 2

21. Find the number which when multiplied by 16 is increased by 225.

    A. 13   B. 14   C. 15   D. 16

22. A wine seller had three types of wine, 403 gallon of 1st type, 434 gallon of 2nd type, 465 gallon of 3rd type. Find the least possible number of casks of equal size in which different type of wine can be filled without mixing.
 A. 41 B. 42 C. 0 D. 43

23. A boy multiplies 987 by a certain number and obtains 559981 as his answer. If in the answer, both 9's are wrong, but the other digits are correct, then correct answer will be—
 A. 556581 B. 555681 C. 555181 D. 553681

24. A number when divided by 114 leaves the remainder 21. When the same number is divided by 19, then the remainder will be
 A. 21 B. 7 C. 2 D. 1

ANSWERS

1	2	3	4	5	6	7	8	9	10
C	D	A	B	C	C	C	A	D	C
11	**12**	**13**	**14**	**15**	**16**	**17**	**18**	**19**	**20**
A	C	A	B	D	D	D	D	C	C
21	**22**	**23**	**24**						
C	B	B	C						

Explanatory Answers

1. A rational number is a number that can be put in the form $\dfrac{p}{q}$ where p and q are both integers and $q \neq 0$. Thus it is clear that $\sqrt{9} = \sqrt{3 \times 3} = 3$ is a rational number which can be put in the form $\dfrac{p}{q}$. Therefore 'C' is the correct alternative.

2. An irrational number is a number that can not be written in the form $\dfrac{p}{q}$ where P and Q are both integers and $q \neq 0$. Thus it is clear that $\left(2 + \sqrt{7}\right)$ given in alternative 'D' is an irrational number.

3. Additive inverse of $+1$ is -1 because $+1 - 1 = 0$. Therefore alternative 'A' is the correct answer.

4. Multiplicative inverse of $-\dfrac{8}{15}$ is $-\dfrac{15}{8}$ because $-\dfrac{8}{15} \times -\dfrac{15}{8} = 1$. Therefore alternative 'B' is the correct answer.

5. The number of prime numbers between 1 to 100 is 25. Therefore alternative 'C' is the correct answer.

6. In 9075, place value of the digit $9 = 9 \times 1000 = 9000$ and its face value $= 9$
 $\therefore$ Difference between these two values $= 9000 - 9 = 8991$.
 Therefore alternative 'C' is the correct answer.

7. The greatest negative integer is -1. Therefore alternative 'C' is the correct answer.

8. The greatest two-digit number is 99.
 $\therefore$ Number of integers between 1 to 99 which are completely divisible by $3 = \dfrac{99}{3} = 33$
 Number of integers between 1 to 9 which are completely divisible by $3 = \dfrac{9}{3} = 3$
 $\therefore$ Number of integers between 10 to 99 which are completely divisible by $3 = 33 - 3 = 30$.
 Hence A is the correct alternative.

9. Let these numbers be x and $(x + 1)$. According to the condition of the problem,
$$(x + 1)^2 - x^2 = 23$$
$$\therefore \quad x^2 + 2x + 1 - x^2 = 23$$
$$2x = 22$$
$$x = 22/2 = 11$$

Therefore these numbers are 11 and 12. Hence alternative 'D' is the correct answer.

10. ∴ Number (dividend) = Divisor × Quotient + Remainder

In the first case,

Number = 119 × Quotient + 19 (Whatever the quotient may be)

In the second case,

∵ The number is divided by 17,

∴ Number = 17 × 7 quotient + 17 × 1 quotient + 2

$$= 17 \times 8 \text{ quotient} + 2 \left(\because \frac{119}{7} = 7, \frac{19}{17} = 1\right).$$

Hence it is clear that on dividing that number by 17, remainder 2 will be left. Therefore alternative 'C' is the correct alternative.

11. 2 is the only even prime number.

12. 87 is divisible by 3, therefore it is not a prime number.

13. In the sequence 1, 7, 3, 9, 5, 11 ... the alternate numbers differ by 2, *i.e.,* first and third number differ by 2, similarly the difference of second and fourth number is 2. Thus, next number in the series should be 5 + 2 = 7.

14. The sequence 4, 9, ..., 25, 36 contains the square of natural numbers, *i.e.,* $2^2, 3^2, 4^2, 5^2, 6^2$. Thus the missing number is 4^2, *i.e.,* 16.

15. In the sequence 17, ..., 18, 15, 19, 14, 20, 13, the next alternate number is one more than the previous alternate number, *i.e.,* 17 + 1 = 18, 18 + 1 = 19, 19 + 1 = 20. Also the second number and fourth number differ by 1, *i.e.,* 13 + 1 = 14, 14 + 1 = 15, 15 + 1 = 16 is the required missing number).

[* *means add the first number to the twice of the second number*].

16. Product of two prime numbers is never a prime number but it is either an odd number or an even number.

17. The number is equal to the product of prime factors.

∴ 2 × 2 × 3 × 7 = 84 is the required number.

18. Let the number is x.

$$\therefore \ \frac{x}{9} + 9 = 27 \quad \text{or,} \quad \frac{x}{9} = 27 - 9 = 18$$

$$\therefore \ x = 18 \times 9 = 162.$$

19. Let the number is x.

Then, $\qquad x + 10x = 264$

$\Rightarrow \qquad\qquad 11x = 264$

$$\therefore \quad x = \frac{264}{11} = 24$$

20. Given $a = 16$ and $b = 15$, then $\dfrac{a^2 + b^2 + ab}{a^3 - b^3}$

$$= \frac{a^2 + b^2 + ab}{(a-b)(a^2 + b^2 + ab)} = \frac{1}{a-b} = \frac{1}{16-15} = 1$$

21. Let the required no. $= x$

then, $\qquad\qquad 16x - x = 225$

$\Rightarrow \qquad\qquad\qquad 15x = 225$

$\therefore \qquad\qquad\qquad\quad x = 15$

22.

```
   403) 434 (1              31) 465 (15
        403                     31
        31) 403 (13             155
            31                  155
            93                   ×
            93
             ×
```

For least possible number of casks of equal size, the size of the casks must be the greatest and it is 31 gallon.

$$\therefore \text{ Required number } = \frac{403}{31} + \frac{434}{31} + \frac{465}{31}$$

$$= 13 + 14 + 15 = 42$$

23. Here, 947 = 3 × 7 × 47

Hence, the required number must be divisible by each of 3, 7 and 47.

Here, (C) and (D) are not divisible by 3 and (A) is also not divisible by 7.

Hence, required answer is (B).

24. The number $\quad = 114x + 21$

$= 19 \times 6x + 19 + 2$

$= 19(6x + 1) + 2$

Hence, the required remainder = 2

H.C.F. and L.C.M.

HIGHEST COMMON FACTOR (H.C.F.)

The Highest Common Factor of two or more given numbers is the largest or the highest among common factors of the given numbers. In other words H.C.F. of the given numbers is the greatest common divisor of the given numbers.

There are two methods of finding the Highest Common Factor of two or more given numbers.

1. Prime factorization method
2. Continued division method

1. Finding H.C.F. by Prime factorization method: Suppose we have to find the H.C.F. of 44, 45, and 55.

Then on writing prime factors of each of the given numbers:

$40 = 2 \times 2 \times 2 \times 5$

$45 = 3 \times 3 \times 5$

$55 = 11 \times 5$

We note that 5 occurs as a prime factor once in prime factorization of each of the given numbers. Therefore 5 is the common factor of the given numbers.

Hence, the required H.C.F. of the given numbers is 5.

2. Finding the H.C.F. by Continued division method: Prime factorization method of finding HCF is convenient only when the numbers are small. For larger numbers we use continued division method.

For example if H.C.F. of 40, 45 and 55 is to be found out then following method of finding H.C.F. by continued division is more appropriate:

$$40 \overline{)45}(1$$
$$\underline{40}$$
$$5 \overline{)40}(8$$
$$\underline{40}$$
$$\times$$

Here required H.C.F. of 40 and 45 is 5.

Now H.C.F. of 5 and 55 will be found out.

$$5 \overline{)55}(11$$
$$\underline{55}$$
$$\times$$

Hence H.C.F. of 5 and 55 is 5.

$\therefore$ H.C.F. of 40, 45 and 55 is 5.

LEAST COMMON MULTIPLE (L.C.M.)

Least common Multiple (L.C.M.) of two or more numbers is the smallest number which is a multiple of each of the given numbers.

L.C.M. of two or more given numbers is determined by following two methods:

1. By prime factorization method
2. By division method.

1. Finding L.C.M. of given numbers by prime factorization method

Suppose we have to find out L.C.M. of 40, 50, 60 and 80, then prime factors of these numbers:

$40 = 2 \times 2 \times 2 \times 5$

$50 = 2 \times 5 \times 5$

$60 = 2 \times 2 \times 3 \times 5$

$80 = 2 \times 2 \times 2 \times 2 \times 5$

We note that 2 occurs as a prime factor maximum 4 times, 3 one time and 5 two times.

$\therefore$ required L.C.M. $= 2 \times 2 \times 2 \times 2 \times 3 \times 5 \times 5 = 1200$.

2. Finding LCM by Division Method:

For determining LCM of the numbers 40, 50, 60 and 80, following process of division is adopted:

```
2 | 40, 50, 60, 80
2 | 20, 25, 30, 40
2 | 10, 25, 15, 20
5 |  5, 25, 15, 10
  |  1,  5,  3,  2
```

Now required L.C.M. $= 2 \times 2 \times 2 \times 5 \times 5 \times 3 \times 2$
$= 1200$.

As seen above, in the division method for finding L.C.M., all common factors of the given numbers have been set aside by division. The product of all the common factors set aside and of those that remain is the required L.C.M. of the given numbers.

RELATIONSHIP BETWEEN TWO NUMBERS AND THEIR L.C.M. AND H.C.F.

Product of the H.C.F. and the L.C.M. of two numbers is equal to the product of the given numbers.

i.e., 1st number $\times$ 2nd number $=$ H.C.F. $\times$ L.C.M.

EXAMPLES

Example 1: Determine the H.C.F. of 32, 64, 96 and 128.

Solution: $32 = 2 \times 2 \times 2 \times 2 \times 2$
$64 = \underline{2 \times 2 \times 2 \times 2 \times 2} \times 2$
$96 = \underline{2 \times 2 \times 2 \times 2 \times 2} \times 3$
$128 = \underline{2 \times 2 \times 2 \times 2 \times 2} \times 2 \times 2$
$\therefore$ Required H.C.F. $= 2 \times 2 \times 2 \times 2 \times 2 = 32$

Example 2: Find the H.C.F. of 8, 9 and 16.

Solution:

```
8) 9 (1
   8
   1) 8 (8
      8
      ×
```

$\therefore$ H.C.F. of 8 and 9 is 1

Now we will have to find out the H.C.F. of 1 and 16.

```
1) 16 (16
   16
    ×
```

$\therefore$ H.C.F. of 1 and 16 is 1

$\therefore$ the reqired H.C.F. of 8, 9 and 16 is 1

Example 3: Find the L.C.M. of 11, 33, 77 and 121.

Solution:

```
11 | 11, 33, 77, 121
   |  1,  3,  7,  11
```

$\therefore$ required L.C.M. $= 11 \times 3 \times 7 \times 11 = 2541$

Example 4: Find the smallest number between 300 and 400 which is exactly divisible by 6, 15 and 18.

Solution: That smallest number will be divisible by the L.C.M. of the given numbers. Hence, L.C.M. of 6, 15 and 18:

```
2 | 6, 15, 18
3 | 3, 15,  9
  | 1,  5,  3
```

$\therefore$ L.C.M. $= 2 \times 3 \times 5 \times 3 = 90$.

According to the condition of the problem, we have to find out such number between 300 and 400.

$\therefore$ The required number $= 90 \times 4 = 360$.

Example 5: Find the smallest number which when divided by 25, 35, 45 and 60, leaves a remainder of 18 in each case.

Solution: It is obvious from the given problem that the required smallest number will be 18 more than the L.C.M. of the given numbers.

$\therefore$ LCM of the given numbers.

$$\begin{array}{r|llll} 5 & 25, & 35, & 45, & 60 \\ \hline 3 & 5, & 7, & 9, & 12 \\ \hline & 5, & 7, & 3, & 4 \end{array}$$

$\therefore$ LCM $= 5 \times 3 \times 5 \times 7 \times 3 \times 4 = 6300$

$\therefore$ the requied number $= 6300 + 18 = 6318$

Example 6: Find the smallest number which when added to 7, the sum is exactly divisible by 18, 24, 48 and 80.

Solution: It is clear from the given problem that the required smallest number is 7 less than the L.C.M. of the given numbers 18, 24, 48 and 80.

$\therefore$ L.C.M of 18, 24, 48 and 80:

$$\begin{array}{r|llll} 2 & 18, & 24, & 48, & 80 \\ \hline 2 & 9, & 12, & 24, & 40 \\ \hline 2 & 9, & 6, & 12, & 20 \\ \hline 2 & 9, & 3, & 6, & 10 \\ \hline 3 & 9, & 3, & 3, & 5 \\ \hline & 3, & 1, & 1, & 5 \end{array}$$

$\therefore$ L.C.M $= 2 \times 2 \times 2 \times 2 \times 3 \times 3 \times 5 = 720$

$\therefore$ required number $= 720 - 7 = 713$

Example 7: The H.C.F. and the L.C.M. of two numbers are 18 and 252 respectively. If one of the numbers is 126, determine the other.

Solution: $\because$ 1st number $\times$ 2nd number $=$ H.C.F. $\times$ L.C.M.

$\therefore$ $126 \times$ 2nd number $= 18 \times 252$ $\qquad$ $\therefore$ 2nd number $= \dfrac{18 \times 252}{126} = 36.$

Example 8: The H.C.F. and the L.C.M. of two numbers are 12 and 120 respectively. If the two numbers are in the ratio of 2:5, determine the numbers.

Solution: Let the numbers be $2x$ and $5x$,

$\because$ 1st number $\times$ 2nd number $=$ H.C.F. $\times$ L.C.M.

$\therefore$ $2x \times 5x = 12 \times 120$ $\qquad$ or, $10x^2 = 12 \times 120$

or $x^2 = \dfrac{12 \times 120}{10} = 12 \times 12$ $\quad$ or $x = 12$

Therefore the two numbers are $2 \times 12 = 24$ and $5 \times 12 = 60$ respectively.

Example 9: Four bells ring respectively at an interval of 6 seconds, 8 seconds, 12 seconds and 18 seconds. They ring together at 12.00 O'clock, then at what time will they ring together again? Also state as to how many times will they ring together during 6 minutes.

Solution: In order to find out the time interval after which they will ring together, we will have to find out the L.C.M. of 6, 8, 12 and 18.

$$\begin{array}{r|llll} 2 & 6, & 8, & 12, & 18 \\ \hline 2 & 3, & 4, & 6, & 9 \\ \hline 3 & 3, & 2, & 3, & 9 \\ \hline 3 & 1, & 2, & 1, & 3 \end{array}$$

$\therefore$ L.C.M. of 6, 8, 12 and 18 $=$

$\therefore$ L.C.M. $= 2 \times 2 \times 3 \times 2 \times 3 = 72$ seconds $= 1$ minute 12 seconds.

Hence the four bells will ring together again at 12 hrs. 1 minute, 12 seconds.

$\because$ 6 minutes $= 6 \times 60 = 360$ seconds

$\therefore$ Number of times the bells will ring together during 6 minutes $= \dfrac{360}{72} = 5$ times.

MULTIPLE CHOICE QUESTIONS

1. The L.C.M. of two numbers is 85 and their product is 1020. Their H.C.F. will be
   A. 16
   B. 27
   C. 12
   D. 22

2. The L.C.M. and H.C.F. of two numbers are 4284 and 32 respectively. If one of the numbers is 204, the other is
   A. 672
   B. 576
   C. 676
   D. 572

3. The largest four-digit number divisible by 48, 60 and 64 will be
   A. 7200
   B. 9600
   C. 8400
   D. 10,000

4. The smallest number exactly divisible by 3, 4, 6 and 8 is
   A. 26
   B. 24
   C. 25
   D. 28

5. Two numbers are in the ratio of 8 : 15. If their H.C.F. is 4, the numbers are
   A. 32 and 60
   B. 16 and 30
   C. 80 and 150
   D. 64 and 120

6. The largest number that will divide 226 and 272 leaving 1 and 2 as remainders respectively, is
   A. 36
   B. 45
   C. 55
   D. 59

7. The greatest number that will divide 366, 513 and 324 leaving the same remainder in each case is
   A. 21
   B. 18
   C. 27
   D. 42

8. The greatest number that will divide 33, 64 and 80 leaving 3, 4 and 5 as remainders respectively, is
   A. 10
   B. 20
   C. 15
   D. 22

9. Three bells ring respectively at an interval of 15 seconds, 20 seconds and 24 seconds. If they ring continuously for 12 minutes then how many times, during this period, will they ring together?
   A. 2 times
   B. 6 times
   C. 5 times
   D. 3 times

10. If the sum of two numbers is 55 and the H.C.F. and L.C.M. of these numbers are 5 and 120 respectively. Find the sum of their reciprocals.
    A. $\dfrac{120}{11}$
    B. $\dfrac{11}{120}$
    C. $\dfrac{601}{55}$
    D. $\dfrac{55}{601}$

11. The L.C.M. of two numbers is 495 and their HCF is 5. If the sum of the numbers is 100, then find their difference.
    A. 90
    B. 70
    C. 46
    D. 10

12. The HCF of two numbers is 11 and their LCM is 7700. If one of the number is 275, then find the second number.
    A. 318
    B. 308
    C. 283
    D. 279

13. The greatest possible length which can be used to measure exactly the length 7 m, 3 m 85 cm, 12 m 95 cm is
    A. 42 cm
    B. 35 cm
    C. 25 cm
    D. 15 cm

14. The HCF of two numbers is 8. Which one of the following can never be their LCM?
    A. 60
    B. 56
    C. 48
    D. 24

15. The least number, which when divided by 12, 15, 20 and 54 leaves in each case a remainder of 8, is
    A. 548
    B. 544
    C. 536
    D. 504

ANSWERS

1	2	3	4	5	6	7	8	9	10
C	A	B	B	A	B	A	C	B	B

11	12	13	14	15
D	B	B	A	A

Explanatory Answers

1. L.C.M. of two numbers × H.C.F. of the numbers = Product of the numbers

$$\therefore \quad 85 \times \text{H.C.F.} = 1020$$

$$\therefore \quad \text{H.C.F.} = \frac{1020}{85} = 12$$

2. 1st number × 2nd number = LCM × HCF

$$\therefore \quad 204 \times \text{2nd number} = 4284 \times 32$$

$$\therefore \quad \text{2nd number} = \frac{4284 \times 32}{204} = 672$$

$$\therefore \quad \text{2nd number} = 672$$

3. In this question LCM of the given numbers 48, 60, 64 has to be found out.

$$48 = 2 \times 2 \times 2 \times 2 \times 3;$$
$$60 = 2 \times 2 \times 3 \times 5$$
$$64 = 2 \times 2 \times 2 \times 2 \times 2 \times 2$$
$$\therefore \text{LCM} = 2 \times 2 \times 2 \times 2 \times 2 \times 2 \times 3 \times 5 = 960$$

$\because$ Largest 4-digit number = 9999

$$\therefore \qquad 960 \,)\, 9999 \,(\, 10$$
$$\underline{9600}$$
$$399$$

$\therefore$ Required number = 9999 − 399 = 9600

4. L.C.M. of 3, 4, 6 and 8

2	3,	4,	6,	8
2	3,	2,	3,	4
3	3,	1,	3,	2
	1,	1,	1,	2

$\therefore$ The required number = LCM of the given numbers = $2 \times 2 \times 3 \times 2 = 24$.

5. Let the numbers be $8x$ and $15x$

$$8x = 2 \times 2 \times 2 \times x$$
$$15x = 3 \times 5 \times x$$

$\therefore$ LCM of $8x$ and $15x$

$$= 2 \times 2 \times 2 \times x \times 3 \times 5$$
$$= 120x$$

Now, 1st number × 2nd number = HCF × LCM

$$\Rightarrow \quad 8x \times 15x = 4 \times 120x$$
$$\Rightarrow \quad 120x^2 = 4 \times 120x$$
$$\Rightarrow \quad x = 4$$

$\therefore$ Numbers are $8 \times 4 = 32$ and $15 \times 4 = 60$

6. $226 - 1 = 225$ and $272 - 2 = 270$

Now, HCF of 225 and 270

$$225 \,)\, 270 \,(\, 1$$
$$\underline{225}$$
$$45 \,)\, 225 \,(\, 5$$
$$\underline{225}$$
$$\times$$

$\therefore$ The required number is 45.

7. Difference between 366 and 513

$$= 513 - 366 = 147$$

and difference between 513 and 324 = $513 - 324 = 189$

$\therefore$ HCF of 147 and 189

$$147 \,)\, 189 \,(\, 1$$
$$\underline{147}$$
$$\times \ 42 \,)\, 147 \,(\, 3$$
$$\underline{126}$$
$$\times \ 21 \,)\, 42 \,(\, 2$$
$$\underline{42}$$
$$\times$$

$\therefore$ The required largest number is 21.

8. $33 - 3 = 30$, $64 - 4 = 60$ and $80 - 5 = 75$

Now, HCF of 30, 60 and 75:

$$30 = 2 \times \underline{3 \times 5}$$
$$60 = 2 \times 2 \times \underline{3 \times 5}$$
$$75 = \underline{3 \times 5} \times 5$$

$\because \qquad$ Common factor = $3 \times 5 = 15$

$\therefore$ Required largest number = 15.

9. LCM of 15, 20 and 24

$$
\begin{array}{r|lll}
5 & 15, & 20, & 24 \\
\hline
4 & 3, & 4, & 24 \\
\hline
3 & 3, & 1, & 6 \\
\hline
 & 1, & 1, & 2
\end{array}
$$

LCM = $5 \times 4 \times 3 \times 2 = 120$

$\because$ 12 minutes $= 12 \times 60 = 720$ seconds

$\therefore$ Number of times the bells will ring together

during 12 minutes $= \dfrac{720}{120} = 6$ times.

10. Let the number be x and y.

Then, $x + y = 55$; $xy = $ HCF $\times$ LCM $= 5 \times 120$

$\therefore$ Sum of their reciprocals

$$
= \frac{1}{x} + \frac{1}{y} = \frac{x+y}{xy} = \frac{55}{5 \times 120} = \frac{11}{120}
$$

11. Let the number be x and $(100 - x)$

Now, $x(100 - x) = 5 \times 495$

$\Rightarrow x^2 - 100x + 2475 = 0$

$\Rightarrow x^2 - 55x - 45x + 2475 = 0$

$\Rightarrow x(x - 55) - 45(x - 55) = 0$

$\Rightarrow (x - 45)(x - 55) = 0$

Either, $x = 45$ or, $x = 55$

Hence, the numbers are 45 and 55

So, their difference $= 55 - 45 = 10$

12. Second number $= \dfrac{11 \times 7700}{275} = 308$

13. 7 m = 700 cm;

3 m 85 cm = 385 cm;

12 m 95 cm = 1295 cm

$$
\begin{array}{ll}
385)\ 700\ (1 & \qquad 35)\ 1295\ (37 \\
\underline{385} & \qquad\quad \underline{105} \\
315)\ 385\ (1 & \qquad\quad\ 245 \\
\underline{315} & \qquad\quad\ \underline{245} \\
70)\ 315\ (4 & \qquad\qquad\ \times \\
\underline{280} & \\
35\ )\ 70\ (\ 2 & \\
\underline{70} & \\
\times & \\
\end{array}
$$

Hence, required length = HCF of 700 cm, 385 cm, 1295 cm = 35 cm.

14. LCM of two numbers is always divisible by their HCF.

Here, 60 is not divisible by 8. Hence, 60 can never be their LCM.

15.

$$
\begin{array}{r|llll}
2 & 12, & 15, & 20, & 54 \\
\hline
2 & 6, & 15, & 10, & 27 \\
\hline
3 & 3, & 15, & 5, & 27 \\
\hline
5 & 1, & 5, & 5, & 9 \\
\hline
 & 1, & 1, & 1, & 9
\end{array}
$$

$= 2 \times 2 \times 3 \times 5 \times 9 = 540$

Hence, LCM of 12, 15, 20 and 54 is 540.

Since, required number $= 540 + 8 = 548$.

Average

The average is the estimation of arithmetical mean value of a number of quantities of the same kind.

To find out average of given quantities, sum of quantities is divided by the number of quantities.

IMPORTANT FORMULAE

$\text{Average} = \dfrac{\text{Sum of quantities}}{\text{number of quantities}}$	$\text{Number of quantities} = \dfrac{\text{Sum of quantities}}{\text{Average}}$
$\text{Sum of quantities} = \text{Average} \times \text{Number of quantities}$	

EXAMPLES

Example 1: What is the average of first 20 multiples of 7?

Solution: $\because$ First 20 multiples of 7 are 7, 14, 21, 28 ..... 133, 140

$\therefore$ The sum of first 20 multiples of 7

$$= 7 + 14 + 21 + ... 133 + 140 \quad = 7\,(1 + 2 + 3 + ... + 20)$$

$$= 7 \times \frac{20\,(20 + 1)}{2} = 70 \times 21 = 1470$$

Number of first 20 multiples of 7 = 20

$$\therefore \text{Average} = \frac{1470}{20} = 73.5.$$

Example 2: What is the averge of first five prime numbers greater than 20?

Solution: Since the first five prime numbers greater than 20 are 23, 29, 31, 37 and 41.

$\therefore$ Sum of these prime numbers = 23 + 29 + 31 + 37 + 41 = 161

And number of these prime numbers = 5

$$\therefore \text{Average} = \frac{161}{5} = 32.2.$$

Example 3: The ages of three boys are in the ratio of 7 : 6 : 5. If the age of the eldest of them is 28 years, determine their average age.

Solution: Sum of the three proportional numbers = 7 + 6 + 5 = 18

$$\therefore \text{Sum of the ages of the three boys} = \frac{28}{7} \times 18 = 72 \text{ years.}$$

$$\therefore \text{Average age of the boys} = \frac{72}{3} = 24 \text{ years.}$$

Example 4: The average age of 24 girls in a class is 14 years 7 months. Their average age decreases to 14 years 6 months when a new girl gets admission in the class. Determine the age of the new girl.

Solution: Average age of 24 girls = 14 years 7 months = $14\dfrac{7}{12}$ years.

$\therefore$ Sum of the ages of 24 girls = $24 \times 14\dfrac{7}{12} = 24 \times \dfrac{175}{12} = 350$ years.

After admission of a new girl, total number of girls in the class becomes 25.

And the average age of 25 girls = 14 years 6 months = $14\dfrac{1}{2}$ years.

$\therefore$ Sum of the ages of 25 girls = $25 \times 14\dfrac{1}{2} = 25 \times \dfrac{29}{2} = 362\dfrac{1}{2}$ years

$\therefore$ Age of the new girl = $362\dfrac{1}{2} - 350 = 12\dfrac{1}{2}$ or 12 years 6 months

Example 5: A cricket player's average run-rate of 16 innings increased by 3 runs when he made 85 runs in the 17th inning. Find out the average run rate of the player before 17th inning.

Solution: Let the average run rate of the player before 17th inning be x.

$\therefore$ Sum of runs till 16th inning = $16 \times x$

The player made 85 runs in 17th inning

$\therefore$ Sum of runs till 17th inning = $16x + 85$

And average run-rate of the player till 17th inning = $x + 3$

$\therefore$ Sum of runs till 17th inning = $17(x + 3) = 17x + 51$

$\therefore$ According to question, $17x + 51 = 16x + 85$ or, $x = 34$

$\therefore$ Average run-rate of the player before 17th inning was 34.

MULTIPLE CHOICE QUESTIONS

1. The average of first nine multiples of 3 is
   A. 12.0   B. 12.5   C. 15.0   D. 18.5

2. The average of 13 numbers is 68, the average of first 7 numbers is 63 and the average of last 7 numbers is 70. What is the 7th number?
   A. 43   B. 45   C. 47   D. 49

3. Nine men went to a hotel. Eight of them spent ₹ 3 for each over their meals and the ninth spent Rs. 2 more than the average expenditure of all the nine. What is the total money spent by them?
   A. ₹ 29.25   B. ₹ 29.50   C. ₹. 29   D. ₹ 30

4. Average age of 8 persons increased by 2 years, when two men whose ages are 20 and 24 years are replaced by two women. What is the average age of women?
   A. 30 years   B. 31 years   C. 28 years   D. 33 years

5. A batsman has a certain average of runs for 16 innings. In the 17th innings, he makes a score of 85 runs thereby increasing his average by 3. What is the average after the 17th inning?
   A. 33 runs   B. 34 runs   C. 37 runs   D. 36 runs

6. The average of 50 numbers is 38. If two numbers namely 45 and 55 are discarded, the average of the remaining numbers is
   A. 36.5   B. 37   C. 37.5   D. 37.52

7. The average of 6 observations is 12. A new seventh observation is included and the new average is decreased by 1. The seventh observation is
A. 1   B. 3   C. 5   D. 6

8. The average of marks obtained by 120 candidates was 35. If the average of marks of passed candidates was 39 and that of failed candidates was 15, the number of candidates who passed the examination is
A. 100   B. 110   C. 120   D. 150

9. The average of three numbers is 42. The first is twice the second and the second is twice the third. The difference between the largest and the smallest number is
A. 18   B. 36   C. 54   D. 72

10. Out of three numbers, the first is twice the second and is half of the third. If the average of the three numbers is 56, the three numbers in order are
A. 48, 96, 24   B. 48, 24, 96   C. 96, 24, 48   D. 96, 48, 24

11. The average age of 30 students in a class is 12 years. The average age of a group of 5 of the students is 10 years and that of another group of 5 of them is 14 years. The average age of the remaining students is
A. 8 years   B. 10 years   C. 12 years   D. 14 years

12. Out of four numbers, the average of first three is 15 and that of the last three is 16. If the last number is 19, the first is
A. 15   B. 16   C. 18   D. 19

13. The average age of 24 students in a class is 10. If the teacher's age is included, the average increases by one. The age of the teacher is
A. 25   B. 30   C. 35   D. 40

14. The average expenditure of a man for the first five months is ₹ 120 and for the next seven months it is ₹ 130. If he saves Rs. 290 in that year, his monthly average income is
A. ₹ 1000   B. ₹ 1800   C. ₹ 2000   D. ₹ 2500

15. The average weight of a class of 40 students is 40 kg. If the weight of the teacher be included, the average weight increases by 500 gms. The weight of the teacher is
A. 40.5 kg   B. 60 kg   C. 60.5 kg   D. 62 kg

16. The average weight of 8 persons is increased by 2.5 kg when one of them whose weight is 56 kg is replaced by a new man. The weight of the new man is
A. 66 kg   B. 75 kg   C. 76 kg   D. 86 kg

17. The average of four positive integers is 72.5. The highest integer is 117 and the lowest integer is 15. The difference between the remaining two integers is 12. Which integer is higher of these two remaining integers?
A. 85   B. 84   C. 73   D. 70

18. Out of the three given numbers, the first number is twice the second and thrice the third. If the average of three numbers is 121, what is the difference between the first and third number?
A. 144   B. 77   C. 99   D. 132

19. The average of 5 consecutive even numbers A, B, C, D and E is 34. What is the product of B and D?
A. 1152   B. 1368   C. 1224   D. 1088

20. The average of four consecutive odd numbers is 12. What is the lowest odd number?
A. 3   B. 5   C. 7   D. 9

ANSWERS

1	2	3	4	5	6	7	8	9	10
C	C	A	A	C	C	C	A	C	B
11	**12**	**13**	**14**	**15**	**16**	**17**	**18**	**19**	**20**
C	B	C	B	C	C	A	D	A	D

Explanatory Answers

1. Average $= \dfrac{3(1 + 2 + 3 + 4 + 5 + 6 + 7 + 8 + 9)}{9}$

$= \dfrac{135}{9} = 15$

2. Average of 13 numbers = 68

$\therefore$ Total of 13 numbers $= 13 \times 68 = 884$

Average of last 7 numbers = 70

$\therefore$ Total of last 7 numbers $= 7 \times 70 = 490$

$\therefore$ Average of first 6 numbers $= 884 - 490 = 394$

$\therefore$ Average of first 7 numbers = 63

$\therefore$ Total of first 7 numbers $= 63 \times 7 = 441$

$\therefore$ 7th number $= 441 - 394 = 47$

3. Let the average expenditure of all the nine = Rs. x

Now amount spent by eight $= ₹\,3 \times 8 = ₹\,24$

and total spent by the ninth $= ₹\,x + 2$

$\Rightarrow \dfrac{26 + x}{9} = x$

$\therefore$ Average amount spent by nine $= \dfrac{26 + x}{9}$

Total amount spent by nine $= 24 + x + 2 = 26 + x$

$\Rightarrow \qquad 9x = 26 + x$

or, $\qquad 8x = 26$

$\Rightarrow \qquad x = \dfrac{26}{8} = ₹\,3.25$

Hence total money spent $= ₹\,(3.25 \times 9)$

$= ₹\,29.25$

4. Total increase in the age of 8 persons

$= 2 \times 8 = 16$ years

Total age of two men being replaced

$= 20 + 24 = 44$ years

Total of the age of two women

$= 44 + 16 = 60$ years

$\Rightarrow$ The average age of women $= \dfrac{60}{2} = 30$ years.

5. Average increase in the score of 17 innings

$= 3$ runs

Total increase in the score of 17 innings

$= 3 \times 17 = 51$ runs

$\therefore$ His average of 16 innings $= 85 - 51$

$= 34$ runs

Hence, average after the 17th innings

$= 34 + 3 = 37$ runs

6. Total of 50 numbers $= 50 \times 38 = 1900$

Total of 48 numbers $= 1900 - (45 + 55)$

$= 1800$

$\therefore$ Average $= \dfrac{1800}{48} = 37.5$

7. Seventh observation $= (7 \times 11 - 6 \times 12) = 5$

8. Let the number of candidates who passed $= x$

$\Rightarrow 39 \times x + 15 \times (120 - x) = 120 \times 35$

$\Rightarrow \qquad 24x = 4200 - 1800$

$\therefore \qquad x = \dfrac{2400}{24} = 100$

9. Let the third number $= x$

Then, second number $= 2x$ and first number $= 4x$

$\therefore \dfrac{x + 2x + 4x}{3} = 42$

$\Rightarrow \dfrac{7x}{3} = 42 \Rightarrow x = \dfrac{42 \times 3}{7}$

$\Rightarrow \qquad x = 18$

So, (largest) $-$ (smallest) $= (4x - x) = 3x = 54$

10. Let second number $= x$

Then, first number $= 2x$

and third number $= 4x$

$\therefore \dfrac{x + 2x + 4x}{3} = 56$

$\Rightarrow \dfrac{7x}{3} = 56$

$\Rightarrow \qquad\qquad 7x = 56 \times 3$

$\Rightarrow \qquad\qquad x = 24$

So, the numbers are 48, 24 , 96

11. Let, the required average age be x

Then, $5 \times 10 + 5 \times 14 + 20 \times x = 30 \times 12$

$\Rightarrow \qquad\qquad 20x = 360 - 120$

$\Rightarrow \qquad\qquad 20x = 240$

$\Rightarrow \qquad\qquad x = 12$

12. Sum of four numbers $= (15 \times 3 + 19) = 64$

Sum of last three numbers $= (16 \times 3) = 48$

$\therefore \qquad$ First number $= (64 - 48) = 16$

13. Age of the teacher

$= (25 \times 11 - 24 \times 10)$ years $= 35$ years

14. Total income

$= (120 \times 5 + 130 \times 7 + 290) = ₹\ 1800$

15. Weight of the teacher

$= (41 \times 40.5 - 40 \times 40)$ kg $= 60.5$ kg

16. Total increase $\qquad = (8 \times 2.5)$ kg $= 20$ kg

Weight of new man $\ = (56 + 20)$kg $= 76$ kg

17. Let the remaining two positve integers be x and $x + 12$

Now, $117 + x + 12 + x + 15 = 4 \times 72.5$

$\Rightarrow 2x + 144 = 290$

$\Rightarrow 2x = 146 \qquad\qquad \therefore\ \ x = 73$

Hence, required number

$= x + 12 = 73 + 12 = 85$

18. Let the three numbers be $x,\ \dfrac{x}{2}$ and $\dfrac{x}{3}$ respectively,

Now, $\dfrac{1}{3}\left(x + \dfrac{x}{2} + \dfrac{x}{3}\right) = 121 \ \Rightarrow \dfrac{11x}{6} = 121 \times 3$

$\therefore \ \ x = \dfrac{121 \times 3 \times 6}{11} = 198$

Hence, required difference

$= x - \dfrac{x}{3} = \dfrac{2x}{3} = \dfrac{2}{3} \times 198 = 132$

19. Let 5 consecutive even numbers A, B, C, D and E be $x,\ x + 2,\ x + 4,\ x + 6$ and $x + 8$ respectively.

Now, $\dfrac{x + x + 2 + x + 4 + x + 6 + x + 8}{5} = 34$

$\Rightarrow 5x + 20 = 170$

$\Rightarrow 5x = 150 \qquad\qquad \therefore\ x = 30$

Then, $\ B = x + 2 = 30 + 2 = 32;$

$D = x + 6 = 30 + 6 = 36$

Hence, their product $= 32 \times 36 = 1152$

20. Let 4 consecutive odd numbers be $(x + 1)$, $(x + 3)$, $(x + 5)$ and $(x + 7)$.

Now, $\dfrac{x + 1 + x + 3 + x + 5 + x + 7}{4} = 12$

$\Rightarrow 4x + 16 = 48$

$\Rightarrow 4x = 32 \quad \therefore\ \ x = 8$

Hence, lowest odd number $= x + 1 = 8 + 1 = 9$

Square Roots and Cube Roots

The square root of a number is the number which when multiplied by itself produces the number in question. We use the radical sign '$\sqrt{}$' for the 'positive square root'.

Cube Roots

The Cube root of a number is the number, the third power of which gives the number in question. The Symbol used for cube root is '$\sqrt[3]{}$'. We can find the cube root of a number by prime factorization method only.

For example, $2 \times 2 \times 2 = 8$. $\therefore$ Cube root of 8 is 2.

Therefore cube root of $8 = \sqrt[3]{8} = \sqrt{2 \times 2 \times 2} = 2$

Similarly, cube root of $27 = \sqrt[3]{27} = \sqrt{3 \times 3 \times 3} = 3$

$$\text{cube root of } 64 = \sqrt[3]{64} = \sqrt{4 \times 4 \times 4} = 4$$

$$\text{cube root of } 216 = \sqrt[3]{216} = \sqrt{6 \times 6 \times 6} = 6$$

EXAMPLES

Example 1: Find the Square root of 2025.

Solution: Square root of $2025 = \sqrt{2025} = \sqrt{3 \times 3 \times 3 \times 3 \times 5 \times 5} = 3 \times 3 \times 5 = 45$

Example 2: Find the cube root of 2197.

Solution: $\qquad\qquad$ Cube root of $2197 = \sqrt[3]{2197} = \sqrt[3]{13 \times 13 \times 13} = 13$

Example 3: Find the value of $\sqrt{\dfrac{121}{289}}$

Solution: $\because \quad \sqrt{\dfrac{121}{289}} = \dfrac{\sqrt{121}}{\sqrt{289}} = \dfrac{\sqrt{11 \times 11}}{\sqrt{17 \times 17}} = \dfrac{11}{17}$

Example 4: Find the value of: $\sqrt{\sqrt[3]{64} + \sqrt[3]{125} + \sqrt[3]{343}}$

Solution: $\qquad\qquad\qquad \sqrt[3]{64} = \sqrt[3]{4 \times 4 \times 4} = 4$

$$\sqrt[3]{125} = \sqrt[3]{5 \times 5 \times 5} = 5$$

and $\qquad\qquad\qquad\qquad \sqrt[3]{343} = \sqrt[3]{7 \times 7 \times 7} = 7$

$\therefore \qquad\qquad \sqrt{\sqrt[3]{64} + \sqrt[3]{125} + \sqrt[3]{343}} = \sqrt{4 + 5 + 7} = \sqrt{16}$

$= \qquad\qquad\qquad\qquad \sqrt{2 \times 2 \times 2 \times 2} = 2 \times 2 = 4$

MULTIPLE CHOICE QUESTIONS

Directions: *Each of the questions given below is followed by four alternatives of which one is correct. The candidates are required to go through the question and the following alternatives carefully and select the correct answer.*

1. The square root of $5\dfrac{4}{9}$ is:

   A. $\dfrac{8}{3}$ 　　　　 B. $\dfrac{7}{3}$ 　　　　 C. $\dfrac{5}{3}$ 　　　　 D. $\dfrac{1}{2}$

2. What will be value of the square root of 15625?
   　A. 115 　　　　 B. 135 　　　　 C. 125 　　　　 D. 145

3. Square root of $\sqrt{1296}$ will be:
   　A. 6 　　　　 B. 36 　　　　 C. 16 　　　　 D. 26

4. Cube root of 10648 is:
   　A. 12 　　　　 B. 32 　　　　 C. 22 　　　　 D. 18

5. Square root of 176.252176 is:
   　A. 12.262 　　　　 B. 13.272 　　　　 C. 13.372 　　　　 D. 15.572

6. What will be the square root of 72 upto three decimal places?
   　A. 8.485 　　　　 B. 6.465 　　　　 C. 8.845 　　　　 D. 8.465

7. Square root of $7+\sqrt{7}$ upto three decimal places will be:
   　A. 3.105 　　　　 B. 3.203 　　　　 C. 3.125 　　　　 D. 3.015

8. What will be the value of $\sqrt{676} + \sqrt{784} - \sqrt{289}$?
   　A. 38 　　　　 B. 42 　　　　 C. 37 　　　　 D. 36

9. If $\dfrac{x}{7} = \dfrac{28}{x}$, what will be the value of x?
   　A. 12 　　　　 B. 21 　　　　 C. 18 　　　　 D. 14

10. If $\sqrt{1+\dfrac{x}{144}} = \dfrac{13}{12}$, what will be the value of x?

    　A. 25 　　　　 B. 24 　　　　 C. 36 　　　　 D. 28

11. If $\sqrt{18225} = 135$, what will be the value of $\sqrt{18225} + \sqrt{182.25} + \sqrt{1.8225}$?
    　A. 129.75 　　　　 B. 149.85 　　　　 C. 157.85 　　　　 D. 149.65

12. The value of $\sqrt{95+\sqrt{13+\sqrt{144}}}$ is:
    　A. 12 　　　　 B. 11 　　　　 C. 10 　　　　 D. 19

13. If 50% of ? = 20% of 10, which of the following should replace the sign (?)?
    　A. 16 　　　　 B. 12 　　　　 C. 13 　　　　 D. 16

14. If $\dfrac{1}{\sqrt{144}} = \dfrac{x}{7}$ then the value of x will be:

    A. $\dfrac{1}{3}$ 　　　　 B. $\dfrac{1}{18}$ 　　　　 C. $\dfrac{1}{9}$ 　　　　 D. $\dfrac{1}{27}$

15. If $\sqrt{4} + \sqrt{16} + \sqrt{25} = \sqrt{?}$, which of the following will replace the sign of interrogation (?)?

    A. 100   B. 81   C. 256   D. 121

ANSWERS

1	2	3	4	5	6	7	8	9	10
B	C	A	C	B	A	A	C	D	A

11	12	13	14	15
B	C	A	C	D

Explanatory Answers

1. Square root of $5\dfrac{4}{9}$ = Squre root of $\dfrac{49}{9}$

$$= \sqrt{\dfrac{49}{9}} = \dfrac{\sqrt{7 \times 7}}{\sqrt{3 \times 3}} = \dfrac{7}{3}$$

2.

```
          125
      ┌──────────
   1  │ 1 56 25
      │ 1
      ├──────────
  22  │   56
      │   44
      ├──────────
 245  │  1225
      │  1225
      ├──────────
      │    ×
```

∴ Square root of 15625 = 125.

3. Square root of $\sqrt{1296} = \sqrt{\sqrt{1296}}$

$$= \sqrt{\sqrt{6 \times 6 \times 6 \times 6}} = \sqrt{6 \times 6} = 6$$

4. Cube root of $10648 = \sqrt[3]{10648}$

$$= \sqrt[3]{2 \times 2 \times 2 \times 11 \times 11 \times 11}$$

$$= 2 \times 11 = 22.$$

5.

```
            13,272
        ┌────────────────
    1   │ 1 76. 25 21 76
        │ 1
        ├────────────────
   23   │   76
        │   69
        ├────────────────
  262   │   725
        │   524
        ├────────────────
 2647   │  19121
        │  18529
        ├────────────────
 26542  │  59276
        │  53084
        ├────────────────
        │   6192
```

∴ Square root of 176.252176 = 13.272.

6. ∵ 72 = 72.000000

Square root of 72.000000 upto three decimal places =

```
               8.485
       ┌────────────────
    8  │ 72.00 00 00
       │ 64
       ├────────────────
  164  │   800
       │   656
       ├────────────────
 1688  │  14400
       │  13504
       ├────────────────
 16565 │  89600
       │  82825
       ├────────────────
       │   6775
```

= 8.485.

7. ∵ $\sqrt{7} = \sqrt{7.000000}$

```
             2.645
       ┌────────────────
    2  │ 7.00 00 00
       │ 4
       ├────────────────
   46  │  300
       │  276
       ├────────────────
  524  │ 2400
       │ 2096
       ├────────────────
 5285  │ 30400
       │ 26425
       ├────────────────
       │  3975
```

∴ Square root of 7 upto three decimal places

$$= \sqrt{7} = 2.645.$$

According to question, $7 + \sqrt{7} = 7 + 2.645$

$$= 9.645$$

```
             3.105
       ┌────────────────
    3  │ 9.64 50 00
       │ 9
       ├────────────────
   61  │  64
       │  61
       ├────────────────
 6205  │ 35000
       │ 31025
       ├────────────────
       │  3975
```

∴ $\sqrt{9.645} = 6205$

$\therefore \quad \sqrt{7+\sqrt{7}} = \sqrt{9.645} = 3.105.$

8.
$$\sqrt{676} = \sqrt{26 \times 26} = 26,$$
$$\sqrt{784} = \sqrt{28 \times 28} = 28$$

and
$$\sqrt{289} = \sqrt{17 \times 17} = 17$$

$\therefore \sqrt{676} + \sqrt{784} - \sqrt{289} = 26 + 28 - 17 = 37.$

9. $\dfrac{x}{7} = \dfrac{28}{x}$

or $x^2 = 7 \times 28$ or $x^2 = 7 \times 7 \times 2 \times 2$

or $x = \sqrt{7 \times 7 \times 2 \times 2}$ or $x = 7 \times 2 = 14.$

10. $\sqrt{1 + \dfrac{x}{144}} = \dfrac{13}{12}$ or $1 + \dfrac{x}{144} = \left(\dfrac{13}{12}\right)^2$

or, $\dfrac{144 + x}{144} = \dfrac{169}{144}$ or $144 + x = 169$

or $x = 169 - 144$ or $x = 25.$

11. $\sqrt{18225} = 135$ (given)

$\therefore \sqrt{182.25} = 13.5$ and $\sqrt{1.8225} = 1.35$

$\therefore \sqrt{18225} + \sqrt{182.25} + \sqrt{1.8225}$
$$= 135 + 13.5 + 1.35 = 149.85.$$

12. $\sqrt{95 + \sqrt{13 + \sqrt{144}}} = \sqrt{95 + \sqrt{13 + 12}} = \sqrt{95 + \sqrt{25}}$

$= \sqrt{95 + 5} = \sqrt{100} = \sqrt{10 \times 10} = 10.$

13. 50% of $\sqrt{?} = 20\%$ of 10

$\therefore \dfrac{1}{2} \times \sqrt{?} = \dfrac{20}{100} \times 10 = 2$

$\therefore \sqrt{?} = 2 \times 2 = 4$

or $? = 4^2 = 16.$

14. $\dfrac{1}{\sqrt{441}} = \dfrac{\sqrt{x}}{7}$ or $\dfrac{1}{21} = \dfrac{\sqrt{x}}{7}$

or $\sqrt{x} = \dfrac{7}{21} = \dfrac{1}{3}$ or $x = \left(\dfrac{1}{3}\right)^2 = \dfrac{1}{9}.$

$\therefore \qquad$ Value of x is $\dfrac{1}{9}$

15. $\because \sqrt{4} = 2,\ \sqrt{16} = 4$ and $\sqrt{25} = 5$

$\therefore \sqrt{4} + \sqrt{16} + \sqrt{25} = \sqrt{?}$ (given)

or $2 + 4 + 5 = \sqrt{?}$ or $\sqrt{?} = 11$

or $? = (11)^2 = 121$

$\therefore$ Sign of interrogation should be replaced by 121.

Ratio and Proportion

RATIO

In ratio we compare two quantities of the same kind and consider what multiple, part or parts one is of the other. In comparing 8 with 4, observe that it is 2 times 4. This comparison can be represented as $8 \div 4$ or $\dfrac{8}{4}$.

Hence, *ratio is that relation between two numbers which is expressed by the fraction, the numerator is which is the measure of the first quantity and denominator is the measure of the second quantity.*

If the terms of a ratio be multiplied or divided by the same quantity the value of the ratio remains unaltered.

Thus, 3 : 4 is the same as 9 : 12 and 9 : 12 is the same as 3 : 4.

PROPORTION

The equality of two ratio is called proportion. Consider the two ratios:

Ist ratio	2nd ratio
5 : 15	7 : 21

Since, 5 is one-third of 15 and 7 is one-third of 21, the two ratios are equal. The equality of two ratios is called proportion and the numbers 5, 15, and 7, 21 are said to be in **proportion.**

The proportion may be written as 5 : 15 : : 7 : 21 (5 is to 15 as 7 is to 21)

$$\Rightarrow \quad 5 : 15 = 7 : 21$$

$$\Rightarrow \quad \frac{5}{15} = \frac{7}{21}$$

The numbers 5, 15, 7 and 21 are called the terms. 5 is the first term, 15 the second, 7 the third, and 21 the fourth.

The first and fourth terms, *i.e.*, 5 and 21 are called extremes (end terms), and the second and the third terms, *i.e.*, 15 and 7 are called the **means** (middle terms), 21 is called the fourth proportional.

MULTIPLE CHOICE QUESTIONS

1. If $x : y : : 5 : 2$, then $8x + 9y : 8x + 2y$ is equal to:
   A. 22 : 29   B. 29 : 22   C. 31 : 29   D. 21 : 29

2. If 76 is divided into the ratios of 7, 5, 3 and 4, then the smallest part will be:
   A. 14   B. 18   C. 32   D. 12

3. The sum of two numbers is 70 and their difference is 16. Ratio of these two numbers is:
   A. 43 : 27   B. 37 : 64   C. 43 : 16   D. 25 : 64

4. Two numbers are in the ratio of 12 and 19. If the sum of these two numbers is 217, the value of smaller number is:
   A. 81   B. 64   C. 70   D. 84

5. If the sum of ₹ 760 is divided by among A, B, C in such a manner that if A gets ₹ 2, B gets ₹ 3 and C gets ₹ 4.5, then the share of C exceeds that of A by:
   A. ₹ 200   B. ₹ 180   C. ₹ 215   D. ₹ 205

6. The ratio of ages of Gulshan and Pankaj is 10 : 9. If Gulshan's age after 6 years be 26 years, then the present age of Pankaj is:

  A. 18 years   B. 10 years   C. 17 years   D. 20 years

7. If a man covers a distance in 7 hrs and a tonga covers the same distance in $4\dfrac{1}{3}$ hrs, then what is the ratio of speed of man and tonga?

  A. 7 : 15   B. 6 : 13   C. 13 : 21   D. 13 : 20

8. One year ago the ratio of Tarun and Varun's ages was 4 : 5. If one year after the ratio of their ages is 5 : 6, then find the present age of Tarun.

  A. 7 years   B. 9 years   C. 11 years   D. 6 years

9. What is the value of x if 17 : 25 = x : 150 ?

  A. 108   B. 102   C. 96   D. 97

10. In what ratio two types of tea costing ₹ 15 per kg and ₹ 20 per kg are mixed so that cost price of the mixture is ₹ 16.50 per kg?

  A. 5 : 6   B. 7 : 3   C. 6 : 7   D. 3 : 7

11. The ratio of ages of Meena and Neetu is 4 : 3. The sum of their ages is 28 years. After 8 years their ratio of ages will be:

  A. 2 : 3   B. 5 : 3   C. 6 : 5   D. 3 : 5

12. Two numbers are in the ratio of 2 : 3. If 8 is added to each of them, they become in the ratio of 3 : 4. The numbers are:

  A. 8, 16   B. 16, 24   C. 16, 30   D. 24, 30

13. Two numbers are in the ratio of 3 : 4. If the sum of their squares is 625, find the numbers.

  A. 15, 20   B. 10, 15   C. 18, 24   D. 30, 40

14. The number that must be added to each of the numbers 8, 21, 13 and 31 to make the ratio of first two numbers equal to the ratio of last two numbers is:

  A. $\dfrac{26}{3}$ B. $\dfrac{11}{3}$ C. 5   D. $\dfrac{16}{3}$

15. If income of A, B and C in the ratio of 9 : 3 : 7 and income of C exceeds the income of B by ₹ 1200, then the income of A is:

  A. ₹ 2800   B. ₹ 3100   C. ₹ 2700   D. ₹ 3200

16. The ratio of sides of two squares is 3 : 4. What is the ratio of their perimeters?

  A. 3 : 4   B. 2 : 5   C. 4 : 5   D. 3 : 7

17. If $\dfrac{x}{y} = \dfrac{3}{4}$, then what is the value of $(2x + 3y) : (3y - 2x)$?

  A. 3 : 1   B. 3 : 2   C. 1 : 2   D. 2 : 3

18. A sum is divided between A, B and C in the ratio 1 : 4 : 7. If difference in shares of A and B is ₹ 2400, then what is the share of C?

  A. ₹ 5800   B. ₹ 5600   C. ₹ 7750   D. ₹ 8750

19. The ratio of ages of Om Dutt, Ajay and Sanjay is 9 : 4 : 7. If the difference in ages of Ajay and Sanjay is 9 years, then what is the difference in the ages of Om Dutt and Ajay?

  A. 18 years   B. 21 years   C. 15 years   D. 11 years

20. The three angles are in the ratio of 1 : 2 : 3. What is the value of greatest angle?

  A. 105°   B. 120°   C. 80°   D. 90°

ANSWERS

1	2	3	4	5	6	7	8	9	10
B	D	A	D	A	A	C	B	B	B

11	12	13	14	15	16	17	18	19	20
C	B	A	C	C	A	A	B	C	D

Explanatory Answers

1. $\because x : y :: 5 : 2$

$\Rightarrow \dfrac{x}{y} = \dfrac{5}{2}$

$\Rightarrow 2x = 5y$ or $8x = 20y$

[multiply by 4 both sides]

Now $8x + 9y = 20y + 9y$

[Adding $9y$ both sides]

$\therefore \quad 8x + 9y = 29y$

and $8x + 2y = 20y + 2y = 22y$

Hence, $8x + 9y : 8x + 2y = 29y : 22y = 29 : 22$.

2. We have to divide 76 in the ratio of $7 : 5 : 3 : 4$

Here, Sum of proportionals $= 7 + 5 + 3 + 4 = 19$

$\therefore$ Smallest share $= \dfrac{3}{19} \times 76 = 12$.

3. Let numbers are x and y

$x + y = 70$ ...(i)

and $x - y = 16$ ...(ii)

Solving (i) and (ii), we get $x = 43$, $y = 27$

$\therefore$ Required ratio $= 43 : 27$

4. Let numbers are $12x$ and $19x$

According to the question,

$12x + 19x = 217$

$\Rightarrow \quad 31x = 217$

$\therefore \quad x = \dfrac{217}{31} = 7$

numbers are $12 \times 7 = 84$ and $19 \times 7 = 133$

Hence, the value of smaller number is 84.

5. Ratio of the shares of A, B, and C

$= 2 : 3 : 4.5 = 20 : 30 : 45 = 4 : 6 : 9$

Sum of proportionals $= 4 + 6 + 9 = 19$

Difference between proportion of C and A

$= 9 - 4 = 5$

$\therefore$ Share of C exceeds the share of A by

$\dfrac{5}{19} \times 760 = ₹\ 200$.

6. Let present ages of Gulshan and Pankaj be $10x$ and $9x$.

According to the question,

After 6 years Gulshan's age $= 26$ years

$\therefore \quad 10x + 6 = 26 \Rightarrow 10x = 20$

$\Rightarrow \qquad x = 2$

Hence, Pankaj's present age $= 9 \times 2 = 18$ years.

7. Let distance $= x$ km

Man's speed $= \dfrac{\text{Distance}}{\text{Time}}$

$= \dfrac{x}{7}$ km/hr

Tonga's speed $= \dfrac{x}{\dfrac{13}{3}} = \dfrac{3x}{13}$ km/hr

$\therefore$ Required ratio $= \dfrac{x}{7} : \dfrac{3x}{13} = \dfrac{\dfrac{x}{7}}{\dfrac{3x}{13}}$

$= \dfrac{x}{7} \times \dfrac{13}{3x} = \dfrac{13}{21} = 13 : 21$.

8. Let present ages of Tarun and Varun be x years and y years respectively.

In First case, $\dfrac{x-1}{y-1} = \dfrac{4}{5}$ ...(i)

In Second case, $\dfrac{x+1}{y+1} = \dfrac{5}{6}$ ...(ii)

From (i) and (ii),

$5x - 4y - 1 = 0$ ...(iii)

$6x - 5y + 1 = 0$ ...(iv)

Multiply (iii) by 5 and (iv) by 4, we get,

$25x - 20y - 5 = 0$

$24x - 20y + 4 = 0$

$\underline{\quad - \qquad + \qquad - \qquad}$

$x \qquad\quad - 9 = 0 \Rightarrow x = 9$

Hence, Tarun's present age $= 9$ years.

9. $\because \dfrac{17}{25} = \dfrac{x}{150} \Rightarrow 25x = 17 \times 150$

$\Rightarrow x = \dfrac{17 \times 150}{25} = 17 \times 6 = 102$

Hence, the value of $x = 102$.

10. $\because$ Cost of the mixture

$= ₹\ 16.50$ per kg

Tea costing ₹ 15 per kg is cheaper from the mixture = ₹ 1.50 per kg

Tea costing ₹ 20 per kg is dearer from the mixture = ₹ 3.50 per kg.

To equal the cost of cheaper and dearer tea, we must multiply them by 3.50 and 1.50 respectively, *i.e.*, in the ratio of 7 : 3

Hence Required ratio = $\dfrac{3.50}{1.50} = \dfrac{35}{15} = 7 : 3$

11. Let present ages of Meena and Neetu be $4x$ years and $3x$ years respectively.

$4x + 3x = 28 \Rightarrow 7x = 28 \Rightarrow x = 4$

$\therefore$ Meena's age = $4 \times 4 = 16$ years

Neetu's age = $3 \times 4 = 12$ years.

After 8 years, Meena's age = $16 + 8 = 24$ years

After 8 years, Neetu's age = $12 + 8 = 20$ years

Required ratio = $\dfrac{24}{20} = \dfrac{6}{5} = 6 : 5$.

12. Let numbers are $2x$ and $3x$ respectively.

According to the question,

$\dfrac{2x+8}{3x+8} = \dfrac{3}{4}$

$\Rightarrow \quad 9x + 24 = 8x + 32$

$\Rightarrow \qquad x = 32 - 24 = 8$

$2x = 2 \times 8 = 16$

$3x = 3 \times 8 = 24$

Hence, numbers are 16 and 24.

13. Let numbers are $3x$ and $4x$ respectively.

According to the question,

$(3x)^2 + (4x)^2 = 625$

$\Rightarrow 9x^2 + 16x^2 = 625$

$\Rightarrow \qquad 25x^2 = 625$

$\Rightarrow \qquad x^2 = \dfrac{625}{25} = 25$

$\Rightarrow \qquad x = 5$

Hence, numbers are 15 and 20

$\begin{bmatrix} \because 3x = 3 \times 5 = 15 \\ 4x = 4 \times 5 = 20 \end{bmatrix}$

14. Let x be added to each of them

According to the question,

$\dfrac{x+8}{21+x} = \dfrac{x+13}{31+x}$

$\Rightarrow (x + 8)(31 + x) = (x + 13)(21 + x)$

$\Rightarrow 31x + x^2 + 248 + 8x = 21x + x^2 + 273 + 13x$

$\Rightarrow 39x - 34x = 273 - 248$

$\Rightarrow \qquad 5x = 25 \Rightarrow x = 5$

Hence, 5 should be added to each of the given numbers.

15. Let income of A, B, C are $9x$, $3x$ and $7x$ respectively.

According to the question,

$7x - 3x = 1200 \Rightarrow 4x = 1200$

$\Rightarrow \qquad x = 300$

Hence, income of A = $9x$

$= 9 \times 300 = ₹\ 2700$

16. Let sides of the squares be $3x$ and $4x$ respectively.

Perimeter of first square = $4 \times 3x = 12x$

Perimeter of 2nd square = $4x \times 4 = 16x$

Required ratio = $\dfrac{12x}{16x} = \dfrac{3}{4} = 3 : 4$.

17. $\dfrac{x}{y} = \dfrac{3}{4} \Rightarrow 4x = 3y$

Now, $2x + 3y = 2x + 4x = 6x$

and $3y - 2x = 4x - 2x = 2x$ $\qquad [\because 4x = 3y]$

$\therefore (2x + 3y) : (3y - 2x) = 6x : 2x = 3 : 1$.

18. Difference in ratio of A and B = $4 - 1 = 3$

$\therefore$ Share of C = $\dfrac{7}{3} \times 2400 = ₹\ 5600$.

19. Let the ages of Om Dutt, Ajay and Sanjay are $9x$, $4x$ and $7x$ respectively.

According to the question,

$7x - 4x = 9$

$\Rightarrow \qquad 3x = 9 \Rightarrow x = 3$

$\therefore$ Age of Om Dutt = $9 \times 3 = 27$ years

Age of Ajay = $4 \times 3 = 12$ years

Difference in their ages = $27 - 12 = 15$ years

20. $x + 2x + 3x = 180°$

$\Rightarrow \qquad 6x = 180°$

$\Rightarrow \qquad x = 30°$

Hence, the value of greatest angle = $3 \times 30 = 90°$

Simplification

Simplification is a mathematical operation by which a complex expression of numbers or fractions is converted into a simpler or less difficult form. It is erroneous to solve this type of questions on random basis and a very appropriate method is to apply BODMAS Rule for arriving at the solution of such problems. Each of the letters of the word 'BODMAS' when explained serially, has following implications:

1.	B	→	Bracket	[{ (⁻) }]
2.	O	→	of	of
3.	D	→	Division	÷
4.	M	→	Multiplication	×
5.	A	→	Addition	+
6.	S	→	Subtraction	−

Therefore, for simplification, we should remove the brackets first. Thereafter operation for 'of', then for 'division', after that the operation for 'multiplication' and thereafter for 'addition' and at last operation for 'subtraction' should be carried out.

EXAMPLES

Example 1: Find the value of 6 of $30 \div 5 \times 2 - 4$

Solution : According to BODMAS rule, mathematical operation for 'of' has to be carried out first, thereafter mathematical operations for 'division', multiplication, addition and subtraction have to carried out in subsequent steps.

6 of $30 \div 5 \times 2 - 4 = 180 \div 5 \times 2 - 4 = 36 \times 2 - 4 = 72 - 4 = 68$

Example 2: Simplify : $7680 \div 256 \div 64 \div 6$

Solution: $\quad 7680 \div 256 \div 64 \div 6 = \dfrac{7680}{256} \div 64 \div 8 = 30 \div 64 \div 8$

$$= \dfrac{30}{64} \div 8 = \dfrac{15}{32} \div 8 = \dfrac{15}{32 \times 8} = \dfrac{15}{256}$$

Example 3: Simplify: $\dfrac{24 + 24 \times 12 - 8}{160 + 18 \times 12 - 72}$

Solution: $\quad \dfrac{24 + 24 \times 12 - 8}{160 + 18 \times 12 - 72} = \dfrac{24 + 288 - 8}{160 + 216 - 72} = \dfrac{312 - 8}{376 - 72} = \dfrac{304}{304} = 1$

$$= 12 - 1 = 11$$

Example 4: Simplify: $3720 \div 30 - 2 \times (36 + 48 \div 24)$

Solution: $3720 \div 30 - 2 \times (36 + 48 \div 24)$

$$= 3720 \div 30 - 2 \times \left(36 + \frac{48}{24}\right) = 3720 \div 30 - 2 \times (36 + 2)$$

$$= 3720 \div 30 - 2 \times 38 = \frac{3720}{30} - 2 \times 38$$

$$= 124 - 2 \times 38 = 124 - 76 = 48$$

Example 5: Simplify: $3 \div \left[(8 - 5) \div \left\{ (4 - 2) \div \left(2 + \frac{8}{13} \right) \right\} \right]$

Solution: $3 \div \left[(8 - 5) \div \left\{ (4 - 2) \div \left(2 + \frac{8}{13} \right) \right\} \right] = 3 \div \left[(8 - 5) \div \left\{ 2 \div \frac{34}{13} \right\} \right]$

$$= 3 \div \left[3 \div \frac{2 \times 13}{34} \right] = 3 \div \left[\frac{3 \times 34}{26} \right] = \frac{3 \times 26}{3 \times 34} = \frac{13}{17}$$

MULTIPLE CHOICE QUESTIONS

1. $\sqrt{5^2 + 41 \times 5 - 17^2 - 75} = ?$

    A. 69   B. 61   C. 71   D. 79

2. $15 - 10 + 5 \times 2 \div 5 = ?$

    A. 70   B. 4   C. 5   D. None of these

3. $10 \times 10 \times 10 \div (20 \div 10 \times 10 - 10) + 6 = ?$

    A. 108   B. 111   C. 106   D. 114

4. $\frac{25}{3} - \frac{4}{7}$ of $\frac{7}{5} + \frac{11}{3} \div \frac{2}{3} - 4 = ?$

    A. $8\frac{1}{15}$ B. $9\frac{1}{30}$ C. $7\frac{1}{30}$ D. $9\frac{1}{5}$

5. $\dfrac{9 \div 2 \times 27 \div 9}{18 \div 7.5 \times 5 \div 4} = ?$

    A. 4.5   B. 5.7   C. 2.5   D. 6.8

6. 37% of $150 - 0.05\%$ of $1000 = ?$

    A. 50   B. 55   C. 55.5   D. 55.55

7. $\dfrac{2.70 \times 2.70 + 4.30 \times 4.30 + 8.60 \times 2.70}{2.70 + 4.30} = ?$

    A. 6.8   B. 7   C. 7.6   D. 8.5

8. $60 \times [35 - \{25 - (18 - \overline{9-3}) \div 11\}] = ?$

A. $566\dfrac{5}{7}$ B. $665\dfrac{5}{11}$ C. $665\dfrac{8}{11}$ D. $765\dfrac{5}{11}$

9. 14% of 255 + ? % of 405 = 124.8

A. 22   B. 24   C. 18   D. 15

10. (43% of 2750) – (38% of 2990) = ?

A. 49.3   B. 44.7   C. 43.6   D. 46.3

11. 1150 ÷ 50 ÷ 23 + 15 = ?

A. 16   B. 20   C. 22   D. 18

12. $\dfrac{140 - 44 \times 9 \div 3}{\dfrac{1}{2} \text{ of } 18 \div 9 + 2} = ?$

A. $2\dfrac{2}{3}$ B. $3\dfrac{1}{3}$ C. $4\dfrac{2}{3}$ D. $6\dfrac{4}{5}$

13. (5967 – 2437 – 1910) ÷ ? = 27

A. 60   B. 50   C. 65   D. 45

14. 28 × 104 ÷ (18 + 6) + 3 = ?

A. $124\dfrac{1}{3}$ B. $104\dfrac{1}{3}$ C. $125\dfrac{1}{3}$ D. 128

15. $\dfrac{(0.08)^3 + (0.011)^3}{(0.08)^2 - 0.08 \times 0.011 + (0.011)^2} = ?$

A. 0.087   B. 0.091   C. 0.077   D. 0.067

16. $1 + \dfrac{1}{1 + \dfrac{1}{1 + \dfrac{1}{3}}} = ?$

A. $1\dfrac{4}{7}$ B. $2\dfrac{4}{7}$ C. $3\dfrac{4}{7}$ D. $4\dfrac{4}{7}$

17. $\sqrt[3]{12167} \times \sqrt{?} = 621$

A. 841   B. 27   C. 625   D. None of these

18. 0.99 × 14 ÷ 11 ÷ 0.7 = ?

A. 2.9   B. 1.6   C. 1.8   D. 2.8

19. $22 \div \left[(28 - 13) \div \left\{ (32 - 8) \div \left(5 + \dfrac{1}{3} \right) \right\} \right] = ?$

A. 7.9   B. 6.8   C. 6.6   D. 5.7

20. $3 - \left[9 + \left\{ 14 - (6 - \overline{3 - 21}) \right\} \right] = ?$

A. 0   B. 4   C. 18   D. 6

ANSWERS

1	2	3	4	5	6	7	8	9	10
A	D	C	B	A	B	B	B	A	D

11	12	13	14	15	16	17	18	19	20
A	A	A	A	B	A	D	C	C	B

Explanatory Answers

1. $\sqrt{25 \times 41 \times 5 - 17 \times 17 - 75}$

$= \sqrt{5125 - 289 - 75} = \sqrt{4761} = 69$

2. $15 - 10 + 5 \times 2 \div 5$

$= 15 - 10 + 5 \times \dfrac{2}{5} = 17 - 10 = 7$

3. $10 \times 10 \times 10 \div (20 \div 10 \times 10 - 10) + 6$

$= 10 \times 10 \times 10 \div \left(\dfrac{20}{10} \times 10 - 10 \right) + 6$

$= 10 \times 10 \times 10 \div (20 - 10) + 6$

$= 10 \times 10 \times 10 \div 10 + 6$

$= 10 \times 10 \times 1 + 6 = 100 + 6 = 106.$

4. $\dfrac{25}{3} - \dfrac{4}{7}$ of $\dfrac{7}{5} + \dfrac{11}{3} \div \dfrac{2}{3} - 4$

$= \dfrac{25}{3} - \dfrac{4}{5} + \dfrac{11}{3} \div \dfrac{2}{3} - 4$

$= \dfrac{25}{3} - \dfrac{4}{5} + \dfrac{11}{2} - 4 = \dfrac{83}{6} - \dfrac{24}{5}$

$= \dfrac{415 - 144}{30} = \dfrac{271}{30} = 9\dfrac{1}{30}.$

5. $\dfrac{9 \div 2 \times 27 \div 9}{18 \div 7.5 \times 5 \div 4} = \dfrac{\dfrac{9}{2} \times \dfrac{27}{9}}{\dfrac{18}{7.5} \times \dfrac{5}{4}} = \dfrac{\dfrac{27}{2}}{\dfrac{90}{30}}$

$= \dfrac{27}{2} \times \dfrac{30}{90} = \dfrac{9}{2} = 4.5.$

6. 37% of $150 - 0.05\%$ of 1000

$= \dfrac{37}{100}$ of $150 - \dfrac{0.05}{100}$ of 1000

$= \dfrac{111}{2} - \dfrac{5}{10000} \times 1000 = 55.5 - .5 = 55.$

7. $\dfrac{\begin{array}{c} 2.70 \times 2.70 + 4.30 \times 4.30 \\ + 8.60 \times 2.70 \end{array}}{2.70 + 4.30}$

Let $2.70 = a$ and $4.30 = b$

$\dfrac{a^2 + b^2 + 2ab}{a + b} = \dfrac{(a+b)^2}{a+b} = a + b$

$= 2.70 + 4.30 = 7.$

8. $60 \times [35 - \{25 - (18 - \overline{9 - 3}) \div 11\}]$

$= 60 \times [35 - \{25 - (18 - 6) \div 11\}]$

$= 60 \times [35 - \{25 - 12 \div 11\}]$

$= 60 \times \left[35 - \left\{ 25 - \dfrac{12}{11} \right\} \right]$

$= 60 \times \left[35 - \dfrac{263}{11} \right]$

$= 60 \times \dfrac{122}{11} = 665\dfrac{5}{11}.$

9. 14% of $255 + x\%$ of $405 = 124.8$

$\Rightarrow 35.7 + 405 \times \dfrac{x}{100} = 124.8$

$\Rightarrow \dfrac{405 \times x}{100} = 124.8 - 35.7 = 89.1$

$\Rightarrow x = \dfrac{89.1 \times 100}{405} = \dfrac{891 \times 10}{405}$

$= \dfrac{891 \times 2}{81} = 11 \times 2 = 22.$

10. $(43\%$ of $2750) - (38\%$ of $2990)$

$= 0.43 \times 2750 - 0.38 \times 2990$

$= \dfrac{43}{100} \times 2750 - \dfrac{38}{100} \times 2990$

$$= \frac{43 \times 275}{10} - \frac{38 \times 299}{10}$$

$$= \frac{11825}{10} - \frac{11362}{10} = \frac{463}{10} = 46.3.$$

11. $1150 \div 50 \div 23 + 15$

$$= \frac{1150}{50} \div 23 + 15 = 23 \div 23 + 15 = 1 + 15 = 16.$$

12. $\dfrac{140 - 44 \times 9 \div 3}{\dfrac{1}{2} \text{ of } 18 \div 9 + 2} = \dfrac{140 - 44 \times 3}{9 \div 9 + 2}$

$$= \frac{140 - 132}{1 + 2} = \frac{8}{3} = 2\frac{2}{3}.$$

13. $(5967 - 2437 - 1910) \div x = 27$

$$\frac{1620}{x} = 27 \implies x = \frac{1620}{27} = 60.$$

14. $28 \times 104 \div (18 + 6) + 3$

$$= 28 \times 104 \div 24 + 3$$

$$= 28 \times \frac{104}{24} + 3 = 28 \times \frac{13}{3} + 3$$

$$= \frac{364}{3} + 3 = \frac{373}{3} = 124\frac{1}{3}.$$

15. $\dfrac{(0.08)^3 + (0.011)^3}{(0.08)^2 - 0.08 \times 0.011 + (0.011)^2}$

Let $0.08 = a$ and $0.011 = b$

$$\therefore \quad \frac{a^3 + b^3}{a^2 - ab + b^2}$$

$$= \frac{(a + b)(a^2 - ab + b^2)}{(a^2 - ab + b^2)}$$

$$= a + b = 0.08 + 0.011 = 0.091.$$

16. This type of questions is solved starting from the bottom.

$$1 + \cfrac{1}{1 + \cfrac{1}{1 + \cfrac{1}{3}}} = 1 + \cfrac{1}{1 + \cfrac{1}{\frac{3 + 1}{3}}}$$

$$= 1 + \cfrac{1}{1 + \cfrac{3}{4}} = 1 + \cfrac{1}{\frac{4 + 3}{4}}$$

$$= 1 + \frac{4}{7} = \frac{7 + 4}{7} = \frac{11}{7} = 1\frac{4}{7}.$$

17. $\because \sqrt[3]{12167} \times \sqrt{x} = 621$

$$\Rightarrow 23 \times \sqrt{x} = 621 \quad \Rightarrow \sqrt{x} = \frac{621}{23} = 27$$

$$\Rightarrow \left(\sqrt{x}\right)^2 = (27)^2 \qquad \therefore \quad x = 729$$

18. $0.99 \times 14 \div 11 \div 0.7 = 0.99 \times \dfrac{14}{11} \div 0.7$

$$= \frac{99}{100} \times \frac{14}{11} \times \frac{10}{7} = \frac{18}{10} = 1.8$$

19. $22 \div \left[(28 - 13) \div \left\{ (32 - 8) \div \left(5 + \frac{1}{3} \right) \right\} \right]$

$$= 22 \div \left[15 \div \left\{ 24 \div \frac{16}{3} \right\} \right]$$

$$= 22 \div \left[15 \div \left\{ 24 \times \frac{3}{16} \right\} \right]$$

$$= 22 \div \left[15 \div \frac{9}{2} \right] = 22 \div \left[15 \times \frac{2}{9} \right]$$

$$= 22 \div \frac{10}{3} = 22 \times \frac{3}{10} = \frac{66}{10} = 6.6.$$

20. $3 - \left[9 + \left\{ 14 - (6 - \overline{3 - 21}) \right\} \right]$

$$= 3 - \left[9 + \left\{ 14 - (6 + 18) \right\} \right]$$

$$= 3 - [9 + \{14 - 24\}] = 3 - [9 - 10]$$

$$= 3 + 1 = 4.$$

Percentage

Percentage indicates a proportional part of the given quantity or number. It signifies an allowance of so much for every hundred. In other words it gives an indication of rate per hundred.

For example 5 percent indicates 5 for every 100. It is written as $\dfrac{5}{100}$. Therefore the fraction, the denominator of which is 100, is called a percent and numerator of the fraction is called the rate percent. For convenience, the symbol '%' is used for percent.

Note: *(a) 100% means 1* $\left(\because 100\% = \dfrac{100}{100} = 1 \right)$

   (b) In the questions of percentage, unless some separate details are given, the whole thing is considered as 100%.

   (c) There is no unit or dimension of percentage.

$\boxed{\textbf{EXAMPLES}}$

Example 1: Find $6\dfrac{1}{4}\%$ of ₹ 1600

   Solution: $6\dfrac{1}{4}\%$ of ₹ 1600 $= \dfrac{25}{4 \times 100} \times 1600 = ₹\ 100.$

Example 2: What fraction is equivalent to $8\dfrac{1}{3}\%$?

   Solution: $8\dfrac{1}{3}\% = \dfrac{25}{3} \times \dfrac{1}{100} = \dfrac{1}{12}$

Example 3: What percentage is equivalent to $\dfrac{2}{25}$?

   Solution: $\dfrac{2}{25} \times 100 = 8\%$

Example 4: Find how much per cent is 40 of 100.

   Solution: $\dfrac{40}{100} \times 100 = 40\%$

Example 5: The population of a town has increased from 20000 to 24000. Find the increase per cent.
   Solution: Increase in population $= 24000 - 20000 = 4000$

   $\therefore$ Percentage increase $= \dfrac{4000}{20000} \times 100 = 20\%$

MULTIPLE CHOICE QUESTIONS

1. If x is 90% of y, then what per cent of x is y?
   A. 90   B. 190   C. 101.1   D. 111.1

2. A number exceeds 20% of itself by 40. The number is :
   A. 50   B. 60   C. 80   D. 320

3. 5% income of A is equal to 15% income of B and 10% income of B is equal to 20% income of C. If income of C is ₹ 2000, then total income of A, B and C is :
   A. ₹ 6000   B. ₹ 18000   C. ₹ 20000   D. ₹ 14000

4. A student who secures 20% marks in an examination fails by 30 marks. Another student who secures 32% gets 42 marks more than those required to pass. The percentage of marks required to pass is:
   A. 20   B. 25   C. 28   D. 30

5. In a college election, a candidate secured 62% of the votes and is elected by a majority of 144 votes. The total number of votes polled is :
   A. 600   B. 800   C. 925   D. 1200

6. What will be 80% of a number whose 200% is 90?
   A. 144   B. 72   C. 36   D. None of these

7. The price of cooking oil has increased by 25%. The percentage of reduction that a family should effect in the use of cooking oil so as not to increase the expenditure on this account is :
   A. 25%   B. 30%   C. 20%   D. 15%

8. The population of a town increases by 5% annually. If its population in 2008 was 138915, what it was in 2005?
   A. 110000   B. 100000   C. 120000   D. 90000

9. A's income is 10% more than B's. How much per cent is B's income is less than A's?
   A. 10%   B. 7%   C. $9\frac{1}{11}\%$ D. $6\frac{1}{2}\%$

10. A mixture of 40 litres of milk and water contains 10% water. How much water must be added to make water 20% in the new mixture?
    A. 10 litres   B. 7 litres   C. 5 litres   D. 3 litres

11. If the price of a television set is increased by 25%, then by what percentage should the new price be reduced to bring the price back to original level?
    A. 15%   B. 20%   C. 25%   D. 30%

12. A candidate needs 35% marks to pass. If he gets 96 marks and fails by 16 marks, then the maximum marks are :
    A. 250   B. 320   C. 300   D. 425

13. In an election one of the two candidates gets 40% votes and loses by 100 votes. Total number of votes is :
    A. 500   B. 400   C. 600   D. 1000

14. There are 1225 employees in an organisation, out of which 40% got transferred to different places. How many such employees got transferred?
    A. 490   B. 540   C. 630   D. 710

15. 56% of a number is 1064. What is 38% of the number?
    A. 666   B. 722   C. 856   D. 912

ANSWERS

1	2	3	4	5	6	7	8	9	10
D	A	B	B	A	C	C	C	C	C

11	12	13	14	15
B	B	A	A	B

Explanatory Answers

1. $x = 90\%$ of $y \Rightarrow x = \dfrac{90}{100}y$

Required percentage $= \dfrac{y}{9y/10} = \dfrac{10}{9} \times 100$

$= 111.1\%$

2. $x - 20\%$ of $x = 40$

$\Rightarrow x - \dfrac{x}{5} = 40 \Rightarrow \dfrac{4x}{5} = 40 \Rightarrow x = \dfrac{40 \times 5}{4} = 50$

3. 5% A $= 15\%$ B, and 10% B $= 20\%$ C

Then, A $= 3$B and B $= 2$C

$\therefore$ B $= 2$C $= 2 \times 2000 = ₹\,4000$

And A $= 3$B $= 3 \times 4000 = ₹\,12000$

$\therefore$ A $+$ B $+$ C $= 12000 + 4000 + 2000 = ₹\,18000$

4. 20% of $x + 30 = 32\%$ of $x - 42$

$\Rightarrow 12\%$ of $x = 72 \Rightarrow x = \dfrac{72 \times 100}{12} = 600$

Pass Mark $= 20\%$ of $600 + 30 = 150$

Pass percentage $= \left(\dfrac{150}{600} \times 100\right)\% = 25\%$

5. $(62\%$ of $x - 38\%$ of $x) = 144$

$\Rightarrow 24\%$ of $x = 144 \Rightarrow x = \dfrac{144 \times 100}{24} = 600$

6. 200% of $x = 90$

$\Rightarrow \qquad x = \dfrac{90 \times 100}{200} = 45$

$\therefore \quad 80\%$ of $x = \left(\dfrac{80}{100} \times 45\right) = 36$

7. Required reduction

$= \left[\dfrac{r}{(100 + r)} \times 100\right] = \left(\dfrac{25}{125} \times 100\right)\% = 20\%$

8. $x \times \left(1 + \dfrac{5}{100}\right)^{3} = 138915$

$\Rightarrow x \times \dfrac{21}{20} \times \dfrac{21}{20} \times \dfrac{21}{20} = 138915$

$\Rightarrow \quad x = \dfrac{138915 \times 20 \times 20 \times 20}{21 \times 21 \times 21} = 120000$

9. Required percentage

$= \left[\dfrac{10}{(100 + 10)} \times 100\right]\% = 9\dfrac{1}{11}\%$

10. Water $= 10/100 \times 40 = 4$ litres

Let x litres of water be added,

Then, $x + 4 = \dfrac{20}{100}(40 + x)$

$\Rightarrow 5x + 20 = 40 + x$

$\Rightarrow 4x = 20 \qquad \therefore \; x = 5$ litres

11. Required reduction $= \dfrac{25}{100 + 25} \times 100 = 20\%$

12. 35% of $x = 96 + 16 = 112$

$\Rightarrow \dfrac{35}{100} \times x = 112 \Rightarrow x = \dfrac{112 \times 100}{35} = 320$

13. Out of 100, difference in votes $= (60 - 40) = 20$

20% of $x = 100$

$\therefore x = \dfrac{100 \times 100}{20} = 500$

14. The number of employess got transferred

$= \dfrac{40}{100} \times 1225 = 490$

15. Let the number be x; then

$\dfrac{56}{100} \times x = 1064 \qquad \therefore \; x = \dfrac{1064 \times 100}{56} = 1900$

Now, 38% of $1900 = \dfrac{38}{100} \times 1900 = 722$

Profit & Loss

A consumer who goes to the market and buys certain goods. The buyer is called a customer and the shopkeeper who sells the goods to him is called a retailer. The retailer purchases goods in turn in bulk from a wholesaler who keeps a large stock of good and in this case, the retailer becomes the customer.

1. Cost price (C.P.) : Cost price is that price at which a particular article is bought. Profit and loss both are marked at cost price.

2. Selling Price (S.P.) : Selling price is that price at which a particular article is sold.

3. Overheads : The expenses incurred on transportation, maintenance, packaging, advertisements and the like are included as *Overhead*. These overheads and the profit when added to the cost price determine the selling price.

4. Profit or Gain : Whenever a person sells an article at price greater than the cost price he is said to have made a profit or gain.

$$\text{Profit or Gain} = \text{S.P.} - \text{C.P.}$$

5. Loss : If S.P. is less than the C.P. there is loss.

$$\text{Loss} = \text{C.P} - \text{S.P}$$

Some Basic Formulae :

(i) $\text{Gain \%} = \dfrac{\text{Gain} \times 100}{\text{C.P.}}$

(ii) $\text{Loss \%} = \dfrac{\text{Loss} \times 100}{\text{C.P.}}$

From these we can write direct expressions for S.P. and C.P.

(iii) $\text{S.P.} = \left(\dfrac{100 + \text{Gain\%}}{100}\right) \times \text{C.P.}$ in case of gain or profit

(iv) $\text{S.P.} = \left(\dfrac{100 - \text{Loss\%}}{100}\right) \times \text{C.P.}$ in case of loss

These can be rewritten as

$\text{C.P.} = \dfrac{100}{100 + \text{Gain\%}} \times \text{S.P.}$ in case of profit $\qquad$ $\text{C.P.} = \dfrac{100}{100 - \text{Loss\%}} \times \text{S.P.}$ in case of loss

(v) If the C.P. of x goods = S.P. of y goods, then

(a) $\text{Gain \%} = \dfrac{x - y}{y} \times 100$ $\qquad\qquad$ [In case of $x > y$]

(b) $\text{Loss \%} = \dfrac{y - x}{y} \times 100$ $\qquad\qquad$ [In case of $y > x$]

EXAMPLES

Example 1: A radio dealer marks a radio with a price which is 20% more than the cost price and allows a discount of 10% on it. Find the gain per cent.

Solution: Let   C.P. = ₹ 100 and Marked price = ₹ 120

        Since,   S.P. = 90% of ₹ 120 = ₹ 108   ($\because$ Discount = 10%)

        $\therefore$ Gain% = (108 − 100)% = 8%

Example 2: A tradesman marks his goods at such a price that after allowing a discount of 15%, he earns a profit of 20%. Find the marked price of an article which costs him ₹ 850.

Solution: $\therefore$ S.P. = $\left(\dfrac{120}{100} \times 850\right)$ = ₹ 1020

Now, 85% = 1020 $\therefore$ 100% = $\dfrac{1020}{85} \times 100$ = ₹ 1200

Hence, the marked price = ₹ 1200

Example 3: By selling an article for ₹ 247.50 we get a profit of $12\dfrac{1}{2}$%. Find the cost of the article.

Solution: $\therefore$ C.P. = $\left[\dfrac{100}{100 + \dfrac{25}{2}} \times 247.50\right]$ = $\left(\dfrac{100 \times 2}{225} \times 247.50\right)$ = ₹ 220

MULTIPLE CHOICE QUESTIONS

1. Ashok bought 25 kg of rice at the rate of ₹ 6 per kg and 35 kg of rice at the rate of ₹ 7 per kg. He mixed the two and sold the mixture at the rate of ₹ 6.75 per kg. What was his gain or loss in the transaction?
   A. ₹ 16 gain   B. ₹ 16 loss   C. ₹ 10 gain   D. None of these

2. A horse and a cow were sold for ₹ 12000 each. The horse was sold at a loss of 20% and the cow at a gain of 20%. The entire transaction resulted in
   A. no loss no gain   B. loss of ₹ 1000
   C. gain of ₹ 1000   D. loss of ₹ 2000

3. A dealer marks his goods 20% above cost price. He then allows some discount on it and makes a profit of 8%. The rate of discount is :
   A. 12%   B. 10%   C. 6%   D. 4%

4. A trader lists his articles 20% above C.P. and allows a discount of 10% on cash payment. His gain per cent is :
   A. 10%   B. 8%   C. 6%   D. 4%

5. Kabir buys an article with 25% discount on its marked price. He makes a profit of 10% by selling it at ₹ 660. The marked price is :
   A. ₹ 600   B. ₹ 700   C. ₹ 800   D. ₹ 885

6. The marked price of a radio is 20% more than its cost price. If a discount of 10% is given on the marked price, the gain percentage is:
   A. 8   B. 10   C. 12   D. 15

7. A fan is listed at ₹ 1400 and the discount offered is 10%. What additional discount must be given to bring the net selling price to ₹. 1200?

A. $4\dfrac{16}{21}\%$
B. 5%
C. 6%
D. $16\dfrac{2}{3}\%$

8. Saurabh bought a radio for ₹ 800 and spent ₹ 400 on it. He sold it for ₹ 1500. What is his gain per cent?

A. 25%
B. 35%
C. 52%
D. 55%

9. A shopkeeper buys two varieties of rice. One variety costs him ₹ 27 per kg and other ₹ 30 per kg. He mixed them in the ratio of 5 : 3 and sells the blended variety at the rate of ₹ 30 per kg. What is his gain per cent?

A. 5%
B. $6\dfrac{2}{3}\%$
C. 7%
D. 8%

10. A dishonest dealer sells his goods at the cost price and still earns a profit of 60% by underweight. What weight does he use for a kg?

A. 625 gms
B. 750 gms
C. 800 gms
D. 850 gms

11. A man sells two horses for ₹ 990 each. On one he gains 10% and the other he loses 10%. What is his total percentage of gain or loss in the transaction?

A. 1% gain
B. 1% loss
C. 2% gain
D. 2% loss

12. If a shirt coasting ₹ 385 is sold at a loss of 5% of the cost price, what is the selling price of the shirt?

A. ₹ 364
B. ₹ 364.74
C. ₹ 365
D. ₹ 365.75

13. If the cost price of 24 articles is equal to selling price of 21 articles, find the percentage gain or loss.

A. 12.5% gain
B. 12.5% loss
C. $14\dfrac{2}{7}\%$ gain
D. $14\dfrac{2}{7}\%$ loss

14. On selling an article for ₹ 270 there is a gain of 12.5%. What is its cost price?

A. ₹ 210
B. ₹ 220
C. ₹ 240
D. ₹ 250

15. A table clock is sold at a profit of 10%. Had it been sold for ₹ 40 less, there would have been a loss of 10%. What is the cost price?

A. ₹ 150
B. ₹ 175
C. ₹ 200
D. ₹ 324

ANSWERS

1	2	3	4	5	6	7	8	9	10
C	B	B	B	C	A	A	A	B	A

11	12	13	14	15
B	D	C	C	C

Explanatory Answers

1. C.P. of 60 kg mixture
$$= ₹\ (25 \times 6 + 35 \times 7) = ₹\ 395$$
S.P. of 60 kg mixtire $= ₹\ (60 \times 6.75)$
$$= ₹\ 405$$
∴ Gain $= ₹\ (405 - 395) = ₹\ 10$

2. Loss % $= \left(\dfrac{20}{10}\right)^2 = (2)^2 = 4\%$

Total S.P. $= ₹\ 24000$

and Total C.P. $= ₹\left(\dfrac{100}{96} \times 24000\right)$
$$= ₹\ 25000$$
∴ Loss $= ₹\ (25000 - 24000)$
$$= ₹\ 1000$$

3. Let C.P. be ₹ 100; then Marked price

$$= ₹ 120 \text{ and S.P.}$$
$$= ₹ 108$$

$$\therefore \quad \text{Discount} = \left(\frac{12}{120} \times 100\right)\% = 10\%$$

4. Let C.P. be ₹ 100
Then, marked price = ₹ 120

$$\text{S.P.} = ₹ \left(\frac{90}{100} \times 120\right) = ₹108$$

$$\therefore \quad \text{Gain }\% = \left(\frac{8}{100} \times 100\right)\% = 8\%$$

5. $\text{C.P.} = \dfrac{100}{110} \times 660 = ₹\,600$

$$\text{Hence, M.P.} = \frac{100}{75} \times 600 = ₹\,800$$

6. Let C.P. be ₹ 100; then marked price = ₹ 120

$$\text{Since, S.P.} = \frac{90}{100} \times 120 = ₹\,108$$

$$\therefore \quad \text{Profit} = 108 - 100 = ₹\,8, \text{ Hence, gain} = 8\%$$

7. Let second discount = $x\%$; then

$$\frac{90}{100} \times \frac{(100-x)}{100} \times 1400 = 1200$$

$$\Rightarrow (100 - x) = \frac{2000}{21}$$

$$\therefore \, x = 100 - \frac{2000}{21} = \frac{100}{21} = 4\frac{16}{21}\%$$

8. Net C.P. = $800 + 400 = ₹\,1200$
Gain = $1500 - 1200 = ₹\,300$

$$\text{Hence, Gain}\% = \frac{300}{1200} \times 100 = 25\%$$

9. C.P. of 1 kg blended variety

$$= \frac{5 \times 27 + 3 \times 30}{8} = ₹\,\frac{225}{8}$$

$$\text{Gain} = 30 - \frac{225}{8} = ₹\,\frac{15}{8}$$

$$\text{Hence, gain }\% = \frac{15/8}{225/8} \times 100 = \frac{20}{3} = 6\frac{2}{3}\%$$

10. Required weight $= \dfrac{100}{160} \times 1000 = 625$ gms.

11. Here, loss $\% = \left(\dfrac{10}{10}\right)^2 = 1\%$

12. S.P. $= \dfrac{95}{100} \times 385 = \dfrac{1463}{4} = ₹\,365.75$

13. Gain$\% = \dfrac{24-21}{21} \times 100 = \dfrac{100}{7} = 14\frac{2}{7}\%$

14. C.P. $= \dfrac{100}{112.5} \times 270 = ₹\,240$

15. Here, $20\% = 40$

$$\therefore \, 100\% = \frac{40}{20} \times 100 = 200$$

Hence, C.P. = ₹ 200

Simple and Compound Interest

SIMPLE INTEREST

Interest is the money paid for the use of money borrowed, *i.e.*, extra money paid for using other's money is called *interest*.

The sum borrowed is called the principal. The sum of interest and principal is called the *Amount*.

If the interest on a certain sum borrowed for a certain period is reckoned uniformly, then it is called simple interest, denoted by S.I.

Thus, if   A = Amount, P = Principal,
I = Interest, T = Time (in year),
R = Rate per cent per annum, then

(a) $I = \dfrac{P \times R \times T}{100}$ (b) $P = \dfrac{100 \times I}{R \times T}$

(c) $T = \dfrac{100 \times I}{P \times R}$ (d) $R = \dfrac{100 \times I}{P \times T}$

(e) $P = \dfrac{100\,A}{100 + RT}$ (f) $A = P + I.$

COMPOUND INTEREST

In business transaction if interest as it becomes due is not paid to the lender but is added on to the principal, the money is said to be lent at *compound interest* and the total sum owed after a given time is called the amount at compound interest for that time.

After a certain period, the difference between the amount and the original principal is called the compound Interest (C.I.).

Some Important Formulae :

Let   Principal = P
Time = n years
Rate = $r\%$ p.a.

then, the amount,

(a) when interest is compounded annually:

then,   Amount $= P\left(1 + \dfrac{r}{100}\right)^n$

(b) when interest is compounded half yearly:

then,   Amount $= P\left(1 + \dfrac{r/2}{100}\right)^{2n}$

(c) when interest is compounded quarterly :

then,   Amount $= P\left(1 + \dfrac{r/4}{100}\right)^{4n}$

(d) when time is fraction of a year, say $4\dfrac{1}{3}$ years,

then,   Amount $= P\left(1 + \dfrac{r}{100}\right)^4 \times \left(1 + \dfrac{\frac{1}{3}r}{100}\right)$

(e) when rates are $r_1\%$, $r_2\%$ and $r_3\%$ for Ist, IInd and IIIrd year respectively;
then,

$$\text{Amount} = P\left(1 + \frac{r_1}{100}\right)\left(1 + \frac{r_2}{100}\right)\left(1 + \frac{r_3}{100}\right)$$

EXAMPLES

Example 1: A man gets a simple interest of ₹ 1,000 on a certain principal at the rate of 5 p.c.p.a. in 4 years. What compound interest will the man get on twice the principal in two years at the same rate?

Solution: ∵ Principal $= \dfrac{1000 \times 100}{4 \times 5} = ₹\ 5000$

$$\therefore \text{ Required C.I. } = 1000\left[\left(1+\frac{5}{100}\right)^2 - 1\right] = 1000\left[\frac{441-400}{400}\right] = 1000 \times \frac{41}{400} = ₹\ 1025.$$

Example 2: The simple interest accrued on an amount of ₹ 25,000 at the end of four years is ₹ 8,000. What would be the compound interest accrued on the same amount at the same rate in the same period?

Solution: Rate $= \dfrac{8000 \times 100}{25000 \times 4}\% = 8\%$

$$\therefore \quad \text{C.I. } = 25000\left[\left(1+\frac{8}{100}\right)^4 - 1\right]$$

$$= 25000\left[\frac{\substack{27 \times 27 \times 27 \times 27 \\ -25 \times 25 \times 25 \times 25}}{25 \times 25 \times 25 \times 25}\right] = 25000\left[\frac{531441 - 390625}{390625}\right] = ₹\ 9012.224$$

Example 3: The difference between the amount of compound interest and simple interest accrued on an amount of ₹ 26,000 at the end of 3 years is ₹ 2994.134. What is the rate of interest p.c.p.a.?

Solution: $\because \quad 2994.134 = \dfrac{26000r^2}{(100)^2}\left(\dfrac{r}{100}+3\right) = \dfrac{26r^2}{10}\left(\dfrac{r+300}{100}\right)$

$$\Rightarrow \quad 2994134 = 26r^3 + 7800r^2 \quad \Rightarrow 115159 = r^3 + 300r^2 \qquad \therefore r = 19$$

Example 4: What would be the compound interest accrued on an amount of ₹ 45,000 at the end of two years at the rate of 15 p.c.p.a.?

Solution: C.I. $= 4540\left[\left(1+\dfrac{15}{100}\right)^2 - 1\right] = 4540\left[\dfrac{23}{20} \times \dfrac{23}{20} - 1\right] = 45400 \times \dfrac{129}{400} = \dfrac{29283}{2} = ₹\ 14641.5$

MULTIPLE CHOICE QUESTIONS

1. The simple interest on ₹ 500 for 6 years at 5% p.a. is:
   A. ₹ 250
   B. ₹ 150
   C. ₹ 140
   D. ₹ 120

2. If the simple interest on a certain sum of money at 6% per annum for 3 years is ₹ 90, the sum will be:
   A. ₹ 500
   B. ₹ 450
   C. ₹ 525
   D. ₹ 560

3. A sum of money doubles itself in 20 years. In how many years will it treble itself at the same rate of simple interest?
   A. 30 years
   B. 50 years
   C. 40 years
   D. 45 years

4. If the simple interest on ₹ 500 for 4 years is ₹ 40, the rate of interest is:
   A. $3\dfrac{1}{2}\%$
   B. 2%
   C. $2\dfrac{1}{2}\%$
   D. 3%

5. A man will get ₹ 87 as simple interest on ₹ 725 at 4% per annum in:
   A. 3 years
   B. $3\dfrac{1}{2}$ years
   C. 4 years
   D. 5 years

6. A invested ₹ 5000 at a certain rate of simple interest and ₹ 4000 at 1% higher rate of interest. If the interest in both cases is same, the former rate of interest is:
A. 3% B. 4% C. 6% D. 5%

7. A man lends ₹ 500 for 4 years and ₹ 600 for 3 years at a certain rate of simple interest. If he gets total ₹ 190 as interest in both cases, the rate percent per annum is:
A. 8% B. 5% C. 10% D. 4%

8. Which of the following sum of money will amount to ₹ 1050 in 5 years at 8% per annum simple interest?
A. ₹ 750 B. ₹ 825 C. ₹ 775 D. ₹ 730

9. A certain sum of money lent out on simple interest amount to ₹ 1760 in 2 years and to ₹ 2000 in 5 years. Find the sum:
A. ₹ 1650 B. ₹ 1500 C. ₹ 1580 D. ₹ 1600

10. After what time will the sum of ₹ 2000 become ₹ 2240 at 4% per annum simple interest?
A. 3 years B. 2 years C. 5 years D. 4 years

11. What will be the compound interest on ₹ 8000 for 3 years at 5% p.a.?
A. ₹ 1361 B. ₹ 1261 C. ₹ 1260 D. ₹ 1250

12. Find the amount of ₹ 4000 borrowed for 2 years at $2\frac{1}{2}$ % per annum compound interest.
A. ₹ 4202.50 B. ₹ 4102.50 C. ₹ 5202.50 D. ₹ 4000.50

13. After how many years will ₹ 3375 become ₹ 4096 at $6\frac{2}{3}$% per annum compound interest?
A. 4 years B. 2 years C. $2\frac{1}{2}$ years D. 3 years

14. A certain sum of money placed at compound interest amounts to ₹ 110 in 1 year and ₹ 121 in 2 years. The rate of interest per annum is:
A. 5% B. 10% C. 8% D. 4%

15. The difference between compound and simple interest on a certain sum of money for 2 years at 5% per annum is ₹ 21. Find the sum.
A. ₹ 7200 B. ₹ 8400 C. ₹ 9200 D. ₹ 8500

16. The difference between simple interest and the compound interest on a certain sum of money for 2 years at 10% is ₹ 8. The sum is:
A. ₹ 1600 B. ₹ 800 C. ₹ 1200 D. ₹ 640

17. ₹ 800 at 5% per annum compound interest amount to ₹ 882 in:
A. 4 years B. 3 years C. 2 years D. 1 year

18. A sum amounts to ₹ 1352 in 2 years at 4% compound interest. The sum is:
A. ₹ 1300 B. ₹ 1200 C. ₹ 1250 D. ₹ 1260

19. At what rate percent compound interest will ₹ 625 amount to ₹ 900 in 2 years?
A. 20% B. 15% C. 30% D. 25%

20. The compound interest on a certain sum of money for 2 years at 10% per annum is ₹ 420. The simple interest on the same sum at the same rate and same time will be:
A. ₹ 350 B. ₹ 375 C. ₹ 380 D. ₹ 400

ANSWERS

1	2	3	4	5	6	7	8	9	10
B	A	C	B	A	B	B	A	D	A

11	12	13	14	15	16	17	18	19	20
B	A	D	B	B	B	C	C	A	D

Explanatory Answers

1. S.I. $= \dfrac{p \times r \times t}{100} = \dfrac{500 \times 5 \times 6}{100} = ₹\ 150.$

2. P $= \dfrac{SI \times 100}{r \times t} = \dfrac{90 \times 100}{6 \times 3} = ₹\ 500.$

3. In the first case,

$$P = ₹\ x, \quad A = ₹\ 2x$$
$$t = 20 \text{ years}$$
$$SI = A - P = 2x - x = ₹\ x$$
$$r = \dfrac{SI \times 100}{p \times t} = \dfrac{x \times 100}{x \times 20} = 5\%$$

In the second case,

$$P = ₹\ x, \quad A = ₹\ 3x$$
$$\text{rate} = 5\%$$
$$SI = A - P = 3x - x = 2x$$
$$\therefore \quad t = \dfrac{SI \times 100}{p \times r} = \dfrac{2x \times 100}{x \times 5} = 40 \text{ years}$$

Therefore, the sum will treble itself in 40 years.

4. Rate $= \dfrac{SI \times 100}{p \times t} = \dfrac{40 \times 100}{500 \times 4} = 2\%.$

5. Time $= \dfrac{SI \times 100}{p \times r} = \dfrac{87 \times 100}{725 \times 4} = 3 \text{ years}.$

6. In the first case,

$$SI = \dfrac{5000 \times x \times t}{100}$$

In the 2nd case,

$$SI = \dfrac{4000 \times (x+1) \times t}{100}$$

According to the question,

$$\dfrac{5000 \times x \times t}{100} = \dfrac{4000 \times (x+1) \times t}{100}$$

$$\Rightarrow \quad 5000x = 4000x + 4000$$
$$\Rightarrow \quad 1000x = 4000$$
$$\Rightarrow \quad x = \dfrac{4000}{1000} = 4$$

$\therefore$ Former rate of SI $= 4\%.$

7. SI $= \dfrac{500 \times 4 \times x}{100} = ₹\ 20x$

Again $\quad$ SI $= \dfrac{600 \times 3 \times x}{100} = ₹\ 18x$

According to the question,

$$20x + 18x = 190$$
$$\Rightarrow \quad 38x = 190$$
$$\Rightarrow \quad x = \dfrac{190}{38} = 5$$

Hence rate percent in both cases $= 5\%$

8. Let P $= ₹\ 100$

$$SI = \dfrac{P \times r \times t}{100} = \dfrac{100 \times 8 \times 5}{100} = ₹\ 40$$
$$A = P + SI = 100 + 40 = ₹\ 140$$

when amount 140 then P $= 100$

when amount 1050 then P $= \dfrac{100}{140} \times 1050$

$\therefore \quad$ P $= ₹\ 750$

9. Amount after 5 years $= ₹\ 2000$

Amount after 2 years $= ₹\ 1760$

Interest for 3 years $= 2000 - 1760 = ₹\ 240$

Interest for 1 year $= \dfrac{240}{3} = ₹\ 80$

Interest for 2 years $= 80 \times 2 = ₹\ 160$

Principal sum = Amount after 2 years – Interest for 2 years

$$= 1760 - 160 = ₹\ 1600.$$

10. SI = A − P = 2240 − 2000 = ₹ 240

$$t = \frac{SI \times 100}{p \times r} = \frac{240 \times 100}{2000 \times 4}$$

$$= 3 \text{ years.}$$

11. $A = P\left(1 + \frac{r}{100}\right)^{t}$

$$= 8000\left(1 + \frac{5}{100}\right)^{3} = 8000\left(1 + \frac{1}{20}\right)^{3}$$

$$= 8000\left(\frac{21}{20} \times \frac{21}{20} \times \frac{21}{20}\right) = 9261$$

∴ C.I. = A − P = 9261 − 8000 = ₹ 1261.

12. $A = P\left(1 + \frac{r}{100}\right)^{t}$

$$= 4000\left(1 + \frac{5}{2 \times 100}\right)^{2}$$

$$= 4000\left(1 + \frac{1}{40}\right)^{2}$$

$$= 4000 \times \frac{41}{40} \times \frac{41}{40}$$

$$= \frac{8405}{2} = ₹ 4202.50.$$

13. $A = P\left(1 + \frac{r}{100}\right)^{t}$

$$4096 = 3375\left(1 + \frac{20}{3 \times 100}\right)^{t}$$

$$= 3375\left(1 + \frac{1}{15}\right)^{t}$$

$$\Rightarrow \frac{4096}{3375} = \left(\frac{16}{15}\right)^{t}$$

$$\Rightarrow \left(\frac{16}{15}\right)^{3} = \left(\frac{16}{15}\right)^{t}$$

$$\Rightarrow \quad t = 3 \text{ years.}$$

14. $x = ₹ 110, \ y = ₹ 121$

$$\therefore \text{ Rate of interest } = \left(\frac{y - x}{x} \times 100\right)\%$$

$$= \left(\frac{121 - 110}{110}\right) \times 100$$

$$= \frac{11}{110} \times 100 = 10\%$$

15. Let P = ₹ 100

$$S.I. = \frac{P \times r \times t}{100}$$

$$= \frac{100 \times 5 \times 2}{100} = ₹ 10$$

$$A = P\left(1 + \frac{r}{100}\right)^{t}$$

$$= 100\left(1 + \frac{5}{100}\right)^{2}$$

$$= 100 \times \frac{21}{20} \times \frac{21}{20} = \frac{441}{4}$$

$$C.I. = A - P = \frac{441}{4} - 100$$

$$= \frac{441 - 400}{4} = \frac{41}{4}$$

$$CI - SI = \frac{41}{4} - 10 = \frac{41 - 40}{4} = \frac{1}{4}$$

When difference $\frac{1}{4}$ then P = ₹ 100

When difference 21 then P

$$= \frac{100}{\frac{1}{4}} \times 21$$

$$\Rightarrow \quad P = 100 \times 4 \times 21 = ₹ 8400.$$

16. Let P = ₹ 100

$$SI = \frac{100 \times 10 \times 2}{100} = ₹ 20$$

$$CI = \left[P\left(1 + \frac{r}{100}\right)^{t} - P\right]$$

$$= \left[100\left(1 + \frac{10}{100}\right)^{2} - 100\right]$$

$$= 100 \times \frac{11}{10} \times \frac{11}{10} - 100$$

$$= 121 - 100 = 21$$

CI − SI = 21 − 20 = 1

When difference ₹ 1 then P = ₹ 100

When difference ₹ 8 then P

$$= 100 \times 8 = ₹ 800$$

Hence, P = ₹ 800.

17. $\quad A = P\left(1 + \dfrac{r}{100}\right)^{t}$

$\Rightarrow 882 = 800\left(1 + \dfrac{5}{100}\right)^{t}$

$\Rightarrow \dfrac{882}{800} = \left(\dfrac{21}{20}\right)^{t} \Rightarrow \dfrac{441}{400} = \left(\dfrac{21}{20}\right)^{t}$

$\left(\dfrac{21}{20}\right)^{2} = \left(\dfrac{21}{20}\right)^{t} \Rightarrow t = 2$ years.

18. Let the sum be P. Then,

$$1352 = P\left(1 + \dfrac{4}{100}\right)^{2}$$

$$\Rightarrow 1352 = \dfrac{26}{25} \times \dfrac{26}{25} P$$

$$\Rightarrow P = \dfrac{1352 \times 25 \times 25}{26 \times 26}$$

$$= ₹\ 1250.$$

19. $A = P\left(1 + \dfrac{r}{100}\right)^{t}$

$$\Rightarrow 900 = 625\left(1 + \dfrac{r}{100}\right)^{2}$$

$$\Rightarrow \dfrac{900}{625} = \left(\dfrac{100+r}{100}\right)^{2}$$

$\Rightarrow \left(\dfrac{30}{25}\right)^{2} = \left(\dfrac{100+r}{100}\right)^{2}$

$\Rightarrow \dfrac{30}{25} = \dfrac{100+r}{100}$

$\Rightarrow \dfrac{6}{5} = \dfrac{100+r}{100}$

$\Rightarrow 5r + 500 = 600$

$\Rightarrow \qquad 5r = 100$

$\therefore \qquad r = 20\%.$

20. Let principal be P. Then,

$$CI = \left[P\left(1 + \dfrac{r}{100}\right)^{t} - P\right]$$

$$\Rightarrow 420 = \left[P\left(1 + \dfrac{10}{100}\right)^{2} - P\right]$$

$$\Rightarrow 420 = \dfrac{121P}{100} - P$$

$$\Rightarrow 420 = \dfrac{121P - 100P}{100} = \dfrac{21P}{100}$$

$$\Rightarrow 21P = 420 \times 100$$

$$\Rightarrow P = \dfrac{420 \times 100}{21} = ₹\ 2000$$

$$S.I. = \dfrac{P \times r \times t}{100}$$

$$= \dfrac{2000 \times 10 \times 2}{100} = ₹\ 400.$$

Speed, Time and Distance

IMPORTANT FORMULAE

1. Speed = Distance ÷ Time
2. Distance = Time × Speed
3. Time = Distance ÷ Speed
4. x km/hr = $\left(x \times \dfrac{5}{18}\right)$ m/sec
5. x m/sec = $\left(x \times \dfrac{18}{5}\right)$ km/hr.
6. If the speed of a body is changed in the ratio $m : n$, then the ratio of the time taken changes in the ratio $n : m$.
7. When a man covers a certain distance with a speed of x km/h and another equal distance at the rate of y km/h, then for the whole journey, the average speed is given by

   $$\text{Average speed} = \frac{2xy}{x+y} \text{ km/h.}$$

8. The time taken by a train in passing a signal post or a telegraph pole or a man standing near a railway line = $\dfrac{\text{Length of the train}}{\text{Speed of the train}}$

9. The time taken by a train of length x passing a railway bridge or a platform or a tunnel or a train of length y at rest = $\dfrac{x+y}{\text{Speed}}$

10. (a) Time taken by faster train of length x and speed u to pass the slower train of length y and speed v in the same direction
    $$= \frac{x+y}{u-v}$$
    (b) Time taken by the trains in passing each other while moving in opposite direction
    $$= \frac{x+y}{u+v}$$

11. (a) Time taken by the train of length x and speed u to cross a man moving with speed v in same direction = $\dfrac{x}{u-v}$
    (b) Time taken by the train to cross a man moving in the opposite direction = $\dfrac{x}{u+v}$

12. If two trains start at the same time from two points A and B towards each other and after crossing, they take a and b hours in reaching B and A respectively. Then,

    A's speed : B's speed = $\left(\sqrt{b} : \sqrt{a}\right)$

EXAMPLES

Example 1: Distance between two railway stations A and B is 1536 kms. A train covers a journey between A to B at the uniform speed of 60 km/hr and returns from B to A at the uniform speed of 40 km/hr. What is the average speed of the train during the whole journey?

Solution: Average speed of train = $\dfrac{2 \times 40 \times 60}{40 + 60} = \dfrac{2 \times 40 \times 60}{100} = 48$ km/hr.

Example 2: A car covers the first 39 km of its journey in 45 minutes and covers the remaining 25 km in 35 minutes. What is the average speed of the car?

Solution: Total time = $\dfrac{45}{60}+\dfrac{35}{60}$ = $\dfrac{4}{3}$ hrs. and total distance = 39 + 25 = 64 km

$\therefore$ Average speed = $\dfrac{64\times3}{4}$ = 48 km/hr.

Example 3: A train covered a distance of 1235 km in 19 hours. Also, the average speed of a car is four-fifth the average speed of the train/ How much distance will the car cover in 22 hours?

Solution: Speed of the train = $\dfrac{1235}{19}$ = 65 km/hr

$\therefore$ Speed of the car = $65\times\dfrac{4}{5}$ = 52 km/hr

$\therefore$ Reqd. distance = 52 × 22 = 1144 km.

Example 4: A 320 metre long train moving with an average speed of 120 km/hr crosses a platform in 24 seconds. A man crosses the same platform in 4 minutes. What is the speed of man in metre/second?

Solution: Let the length of the platform be x metre. Then,

$\because$ Speed of the train = 120 km/hr = $120\times\dfrac{5}{18}$ = $\dfrac{100}{3}$ m/sec.

From question,

$\because$ 320m + x = $\dfrac{100}{3}\times24$ $\therefore$ x = 800 – 320 = 480 metre.

$\therefore$ Reqd. speed of man = $\dfrac{480\ m}{4\times60\ sec}$ = 2 m/sec.

Example 5: A 260 metre long train crosses a platform thrice its length in 80 seconds. What is the speed of the train in km/hour?

Solution: Speed of the train = $\dfrac{(260+780)}{80}\times\dfrac{18}{5}$ km/hr. = 46.8 km/hr.

MULTIPLE CHOICE QUESTIONS

1. A train crosses a pole in 10 seconds. If the length of the train is 150 m, then what is the speed of the train?
   A. 54 km/hr　　　　B. 60 km/hr　　　　C. 72 km/hr　　　　D. 45 km/hr

2. A train 160 m long crosses a platform of 160 m length in 16 seconds. What is the speed of the train?
   A. 68 km/hr　　　　B. 70 km/hr　　　　C. 72 km/hr　　　　D. 62 km/hr

3. Two trains are running towards each other at the speed of 40 km/hr and 30 km/hr respectively on parallel lines. If the distance between two trains is 105 km, then after how much time they will meet each other?
   A. $1\dfrac{1}{3}$ hr　　　　B. $1\dfrac{1}{2}$ hr　　　　C. 2 hr　　　　D. $1\dfrac{1}{4}$ hr

4. A train whose length is 120 m, crosses a bridge in 12 seconds at a speed of 60 km/hr. What is the length of the bridge?

   A. 75 m   B. 80 m   C. 85 m   D. 90 m

5. A boat in the direction of flow covers a distance of 60 km in 4 hours. If speed of the boat is double the speed of flow then how much distance it covers in 2 hours opposite the flow?

   A. 10 km   B. 8 km   C. 11 km   D. 15 km

6. A train running at a speed of 54 km/hr passes a man standing on the platform is 9 seconds. Length of the train in metre is:

   A. 140 m   B. 135 m   C. 145 m   D. 120 m

7. A train 110 m long is moving at a speed of 130 km/hr. How long will it take to pass a platform 165 m long?

   A. $8\dfrac{9}{13}$ seconds   B. $7\dfrac{9}{13}$ seconds   C. $7\dfrac{8}{13}$ seconds   D. $7\dfrac{8}{11}$ seconds

8. A car moving at 48 km/hr completes a journey in 10 hours. By how much the speed of this car should be increased so as to do this journey in 8 hours?

   A. 8 km/hr   B. 12 km/hr   C. 10 km/hr   D. 15 km/hr

9. Starting from a point at a speed of 4 km/hr a man reaches at a certain place and returns back to the point from where he had started journey on bicycle at the speed of 16 km/hr. His average speed during the entire journey will be:

   A. 6.4 km/hr   B. 8.4 km/hr   C. 5.4 km/hr   D. 10 km/hr

10. A motorist covers a certain distance at an average speed of 48 km/hr in 45 minutes. What speed in km/hr he must maintain to cover the same distance in 30 minutes?

   A. 66 km/hr   B. 79 km/hr   C. 80 km/hr   D. 72 km/hr

11. A train 180 m long is running at a speed of 42 km/hr. In what time it crosses a man going at a speed of 6 km/hr in the same direction?

   A. 11 seconds   B. 21 seconds   C. 23 seconds   D. 18 seconds

12. A man travels a distance of 6 km at a speed of 4 km/hr and a distance of 4 km at a speed of 3 km/hr. What is his average speed in total journey?

   A. $3\dfrac{9}{17}$ km/hr   B. $4\dfrac{9}{17}$ km/hr   C. $2\dfrac{1}{17}$ km/hr   D. $3\dfrac{1}{17}$ km/hr

13. A man travels a distance at a speed of 8 km/hr and returns at a speed of 6 km/hr. If he takes $3\dfrac{1}{2}$ hr time in total journey, then how much distance he covered?

   A. 25 km   B. 28 km   C. 24 km   D. 30 km

14. The circumference of a motor wheel is $4\dfrac{2}{7}$ m. The wheel completes 7 rounds in 4 seconds. What is the speed (in km/hr) of the motor?

   A. 22   B. 27   C. 30   D. 31

15. A certain distance is covered at a certain speed. If half the distance is covered in double time, then what is the ratio of two speeds?

   A. 4 : 1   B. 4 : 3   C. 3 : 1   D. 1 : 4

16. A and B start walking at the same time on a circular path with circumference 35 metre. If they walk in the same direction at 4 km/hr and 5 km/hr respectively, after what time will they meet together?

   A. 35 hrs   B. 27 hrs   C. 24 hrs   D. 40 hrs

17. While walking at $\dfrac{3}{5}$ of his usual speed Sonu reaches at his destination late by 30 minutes. His usual time consumed in reaching to his destination is:

A. 32 min B. 40 min C. 45 min D. 42 min

18. Two trains 150 m long and 100 m long are running in opposite directions on parallel lines at 50 km/hr and 70 km/hr respectively. How long does it take to pass each other?

A. $7\dfrac{1}{2}$ seconds B. $8\dfrac{1}{3}$ seconds C. $7\dfrac{3}{4}$ seconds D. $8\dfrac{3}{4}$ seconds

19. The speed of a boat in still water is 8 km/hr. If it can travel 12 km upstream at the same time as it can travel 120 km downstream, the rate of flow of stream in km/hr is:

A. 4 km/hr B. 2 km/hr C. 4.5 km/hr D. 5.5 km/hr

20. Kanchan walks from her home at 4 km/hr and reaches her school 5 minutes late. If she walks at 5 km/hr, she reaches the school $2\dfrac{1}{2}$ minutes earlier. How far is the school from her home?

A. 3.5 km B. 2.5 km C. 2.75 km D. 3.2 km

ANSWERS

1	2	3	4	5	6	7	8	9	10
A	C	B	B	A	B	C	B	A	D

11	12	13	14	15	16	17	18	19	20
D	A	C	B	A	A	C	A	B	B

Explanatory Answers

1. $\because$ The train crosses the pole. So in given time it covers the distance equal to its length.

$\therefore$ Speed of the train $= \dfrac{\text{Distance}}{\text{Time}}$

$= \dfrac{150}{10} = 15$ m/s $= 15 \times \dfrac{18}{5}$ km/hr

$= 3 \times 18 = 54$ km/hr

2. $\because$ The train crosses the platform

$\therefore$ Distance covered by the train

$=$ length of the train + length of the platform

$= 160 + 160 = 320$ m,

time $= 16$ seconds

Speed of the train $= \dfrac{\text{Distance}}{\text{Time}}$

$= \dfrac{320}{16} = 20$ m/s

$= 20 \times \dfrac{18}{5} = 72$ km/hr.

3. Two trains are moving towards each other

$\therefore$ Relative speed $= 40 + 30$

$= 70$ km/hr

Distance $= 105$ km

Time $= \dfrac{\text{Distance}}{\text{Speed}} = \dfrac{105}{70} = \dfrac{3}{2}$ hrs $= 1\dfrac{1}{2}$ hrs.

$\therefore$ Trains meet each other after $1\dfrac{1}{2}$ hrs.

4. Let the length of the bridge $= x$ metres

Distance covered by train

$=$ length of the train + length of the bridge $= (120 + x)$m

Time $= 12$ seconds

Speed $= \dfrac{\text{Distance}}{\text{Time}} = \dfrac{(120 + x)}{12}$ m/s

$= \dfrac{(120 + x)}{12} \times \dfrac{18}{5}$ km/hr

(1809) Math–7-II

But speed of the train = 60 km/hr (given)

$$\therefore \quad \frac{120+x}{12} \times \frac{18}{5} = 60$$

$$(120 + x) = \frac{12 \times 5 \times 60}{18} = 200$$

$$\Rightarrow \quad x = 200 - 120 = 80$$

$\therefore$ Length of the bridge = 80 m.

5. In the direction of flow:

Speed of the boat = $\dfrac{60}{4}$ = 15 km/hr

$\therefore$ Speed of the boat in still water
+ Speed of flow = 15 km/hr
According to the problem,
Speed of the boat in still water
   = 2 × speed of flow

$\therefore$ 3 × speed of the flow = 15 km/hr

$\therefore$ Speed of flow = $\dfrac{15}{3}$ = 5 km/hr

Speed of the boat in still water
   = 15 − 5 = 10 km/hr
Against the flow:
Distance covered by boat in 2 hrs
   = (Speed of boat in still water
       − speed of flow) × 2
= (10 − 5) × 2 = 5 × 2 = 10 km.

6. Here, the train has to cover a distance equal to its length.

Speed of the train = 54 km/hr

$$= 54 \times \frac{5}{18} \text{ m/s} = 15 \text{ m/s}$$

$\therefore$ Length of the train
   = Speed × time = 15 × 9 = 135 metres.

7. In this case the train will cover the distance equal to its own length plus length of the platform.

Distance covered by the train
   = 110 + 165 = 275 m

Speed of the train = 130 km/hr

$$= 130 \times \frac{5}{18} = \frac{325}{9} \text{ m/s}$$

Time taken to pass the platform

$$= \frac{275}{\dfrac{325}{9}} = \frac{275 \times 9}{325} = \frac{99}{13} = 7\frac{8}{13} \text{ Seconds.}$$

8. Distance covered by the car in 10 hrs at 48 km/hr = 48 × 10 = 480 km

Again, distance = 480 km,
   time = 8 hrs

$\therefore$ Speed of the car = $\dfrac{480}{8}$ = 60 km/hr

Hence, increase that should be effected in the speed of the car = 60 − 48 = 12 km/hr.

9. Distance covered by the man in the two cases are equal.

Here, a = 4 km/hr, b = 16 km/hr

Average speed during the entire journey

$$= \frac{2ab}{a+b} = \frac{2 \times 4 \times 16}{4 + 16}$$

$$= \frac{2 \times 4 \times 16}{20} = \frac{64}{10} = 6.4 \text{ km/hr.}$$

10. Distance covered by the motorist in 45 minutes at 48 km/hr

$$= 48 \times \frac{45}{60} = 12 \times 3 = 36 \text{ km}$$

Now, Distance = 36 km

$$\text{Time} = 30 \text{ min.} = \frac{1}{2} \text{ hrs}$$

$\therefore$ Speed of the motorist

$$= \frac{\text{Distance}}{\text{Time}} = \frac{36}{\dfrac{1}{2}} = 36 \times 2 = 72 \text{ km/hr.}$$

11. $\because$ Train and man are travelling in same direction
   $\therefore$ Resulting speed = 42 − 6 = 36 km/hr

$$= 36 \times \frac{5}{18} \text{ m/s} = 10 \text{ m/s}$$

Distance covered = 180 m

$$\therefore \text{ Time} = \frac{\text{Distance}}{\text{Speed}} = \frac{180}{10} = 18 \text{ seconds.}$$

12. Time required to cover a distance of 6 km at a speed of 4 km/hr

$$= \frac{6}{4} = \frac{3}{2} \text{ hrs}$$

Time required to cover a distance of 4 km at a speed of 3 km/hr

$$= \frac{4}{3} \text{ hrs}$$

Total time $= \dfrac{3}{2} + \dfrac{4}{3} = \dfrac{9+8}{6} = \dfrac{17}{6}$ hrs

Total distance $= 6 + 4 = 10$ km

$\therefore$ Average speed $= \dfrac{\text{Total distance}}{\text{Toral time}}$

$$= \dfrac{10}{\frac{17}{6}} = \dfrac{10 \times 6}{17}$$

$$= \dfrac{60}{17} = 3\dfrac{9}{17} \text{ km/hr.}$$

13. Let one side distance $= x$ km

Time required to cover a distance of x kilometer at a speed of 8 km/hr

$$= \dfrac{x}{8} \text{ hr}$$

Time required to cover a distance of x km at a speed of 6 km/hr

$$= \dfrac{x}{6} \text{ hr}$$

Total time $= 3\dfrac{1}{2}$ hr (given)

$\therefore \quad \dfrac{x}{8} + \dfrac{x}{6} = \dfrac{7}{2}$

$\Rightarrow \dfrac{3x+4x}{24} = \dfrac{7}{2} \Rightarrow \dfrac{7x}{24} = \dfrac{7}{2}$

$\Rightarrow x = 12$

$\therefore$ Total distance $= 12 + 12 = 24$ km.

14. Circumference of the wheel $= 4\dfrac{2}{7} \text{ m} = \dfrac{30}{7} \text{ m}$

Distance covered by the wheel in one round

$$= \dfrac{30}{7} \text{ m}$$

$\therefore$ Distance covered by the wheel in 7 rounds

$$= \dfrac{30 \times 7}{7} = 30 \text{ m}$$

According to problem, this distance is covered in 4 seconds

$\therefore$ Speed $= \dfrac{\text{Distance}}{\text{Time}} = \dfrac{30}{4} \text{ m/s}$

$$= \dfrac{30}{4} \times \dfrac{18}{5} = 27 \text{ km/hr}$$

$\therefore$ Speed of the motor $= 27$ km/hr.

15. Let distance $= x$ and speed $= V_1$

$\therefore$ time $(t) = \dfrac{x}{V_1} \Rightarrow V_1 = \dfrac{x}{t}$

According to the problem,

Distance $= \dfrac{x}{2}$ and time $= 2t$

$\therefore$ Speed $(V_2) = \dfrac{x/2}{2t} = \dfrac{x}{4t}$

$\therefore \quad \dfrac{V_1}{V_2} = \dfrac{x/t}{x/4t} = \dfrac{4}{1}$

$\Rightarrow V_1 : V_2 = 4 : 1$

16. The two persons walk in the same direction

$\therefore$ Their relative speed $= 5 - 4 = 1$ km/hr

Distance covered in 1 round on the circular path $= 35$ km

$\therefore$ They will meet after $\dfrac{35}{1} = 35$ hrs.

17. Let usual speed of Sonu is V km/hr and his destination is at a distance of x km.

$\therefore$ Usual time of arrival at the destination

$$= \dfrac{x}{V} \text{ hrs} \qquad ...(i)$$

Time taken in covering x km at $\dfrac{3}{5}$ V km/hr

$$= \dfrac{x}{3V/5} = \dfrac{5x}{3V} \text{ hrs}$$

$\therefore$ Usual time of arrival

$$= \left(\dfrac{5x}{3V} - \dfrac{30}{60}\right) \text{ hrs} \qquad ...(ii)$$

From equation (i) and (ii),

$\dfrac{x}{V} = \dfrac{5x}{3V} - \dfrac{1}{2} \Rightarrow \dfrac{5x}{3V} - \dfrac{x}{V} = \dfrac{1}{2}$

$\Rightarrow \dfrac{2x}{3V} = \dfrac{1}{2} \Rightarrow 4x = 3V$

$\Rightarrow \dfrac{x}{V} = \dfrac{3}{4} \text{ hrs}$

Therefore, it is clear that usual time of arrival at the destination $= \dfrac{3}{4}$ hrs

$$= \dfrac{3}{4} \times 60 = 3 \times 15 = 45 \text{ minutes.}$$

18. The two trains are running in opposite directions

∴ Relative speed = 50 + 70 = 120 km/hr

$$= 120 \times \frac{5}{18} \text{ m/s}$$

And distance covered by the train

= 150 + 100 = 250 m

∴ Time taken to pass each other

$$= \frac{250}{120 \times \dfrac{5}{18}} = \frac{250 \times 18}{120 \times 5}$$

$$= \frac{15}{2} = 7\frac{1}{2} \text{ seconds.}$$

19. Let the boat covers the distance in each of the two cases in t hrs.

In the first case:

Against the stream: Speed of the boat = $\dfrac{12}{t}$ km/hr

∴ Speed of the boat in still water

– speed of the current

$$= \frac{12}{t} \text{ km/hr} \qquad \qquad ...(i)$$

In the second case:

Down the stream: Speed of the boat = $\dfrac{20}{t}$ km/hr

Speed of the boat in still water

+ speed of the current

$$= \frac{20}{t} \text{ km/hr} \qquad \qquad ...(ii)$$

From (i) and (ii),

2 × speed of the boat in still water

$$= \frac{12}{t} + \frac{20}{t} = \frac{32}{t} \text{ km/hr}$$

But speed of the boat in still water

= 8 km/hr (given)

$$\therefore \quad 2 \times 8 = \frac{32}{t} \Rightarrow t = \frac{32}{16} = 2$$

From equation (i),

$$8 - \text{speed of the current} = \frac{12}{2} = 6$$

∴ Speed of the current = 8 – 6 = 2 km/hr.

20. Let the distance between her house to the school = x km

∴ Time spent in covering x km at the rate of 4 km/hr = $\dfrac{x}{4}$ hrs

But Kanchan reaches her school late 5 min.

∴ Usual time for reaching the school = $\dfrac{x}{4}$ hrs –

5 min. = $\left(\dfrac{x}{4} - \dfrac{1}{12} \right)$ hrs

And time spent in covering x km at 5 km/hr = $\dfrac{x}{5}$ hrs

But this time Kanchan reaches her school $2\dfrac{1}{2}$ minutes earlier.

Usual time of reaching the school

$$= \frac{x}{5} \text{ hrs} + 2\frac{1}{2} \text{ min}$$

$$= \left(\frac{x}{5} + \frac{1}{24} \right) \text{ hrs}$$

$$\frac{x}{4} - \frac{1}{12} = \frac{x}{5} + \frac{1}{24}$$

$$\Rightarrow \frac{x}{4} - \frac{x}{5} = \frac{1}{12} + \frac{1}{24}$$

$$\Rightarrow \frac{x}{20} = \frac{1}{8} \Rightarrow 8x = 20$$

$$\Rightarrow x = \frac{20}{8} = 2.5 \text{ km}$$

Therefore, her school is at a distance of 2.5 km from her home.

Time and Work

IMPORTANT FACTS:

1. If A can do a piece of work in n days, then work done by A in 1 day $= \dfrac{1}{n}$.

2. If work done by A in 1 day $= \dfrac{1}{n}$; then A can finish the whole work in n days.

3. If A is twice as good a workman as B then; Ratio of work done by A and B $= 2 : 1$
   Ratio of times taken by A and B to finish a work $= 1 : 2$.

EXAMPLES

Example 1: A can do a piece of work in 6 days. B can do the same work in 3 days. How long would both of them take to do the same work?

Solution: Here, A's 1 day's work $= \dfrac{1}{6}$ and also B's 1 day's work $= \dfrac{1}{3}$

Hence, (A + B)'s 1 day's work $= \dfrac{1}{6} + \dfrac{1}{3} = \dfrac{1}{2}$

So, (A + B)' could do the same work in 2 days.

Example 2: A and B can do a piece of work in 7 and 8 days respectively. If with the help of C they finish the work in 2 days, then how long would C alone take to finish this work?

Solution: Here, A's 1 day's work $= \dfrac{1}{7}$ and also B's 1 day's work $= \dfrac{1}{8}$

Now, (A + B + C)'s 1 day's work $= \dfrac{1}{2}$

Then, C's 1 day's work $= \dfrac{1}{2} - \left(\dfrac{1}{7} + \dfrac{1}{8}\right) = \dfrac{1}{2} - \dfrac{15}{56} = \dfrac{13}{56}$

Hence, C alone could do the same work $= \dfrac{56}{13} = 4\dfrac{4}{13}$ days

Example 3: A and B can complete a piece of work in 10 and 15 days respectively. If after working alone for 4 days, A leaves the work and goes home, then how long would B take to finish the remaining work?

Solution: A's 1 days' work = $\dfrac{1}{10}$; B's 1 day's work = $\dfrac{1}{4}$

Since, A's 4 day's work = $4 \times \dfrac{1}{10} = \dfrac{2}{5}$

Then, remaining work = $1 - \dfrac{2}{5} = \dfrac{3}{5}$

Required time = $\dfrac{3/5}{1/15} = \dfrac{3}{5} \times 15$ = 9 days

Hence, B could finish the remaining work in 9 days.

Example 4: A, B and C working together can complete a piece of work in 24 days. C alone can complete this work in 48 days. A works twice as fast as B. How long would A take to finish the work working alone?

Solution: Here, (A + B + C)'s 1 day's work = $\dfrac{1}{24}$; C's 1 day's work = $\dfrac{1}{48}$

Ratio of work done of A and B = 2 : 1
Hence, ratio of their time taken = 1 : 2
Let A and B can finish the work x and $2x$ days respectively.

Now, $\dfrac{1}{x} + \dfrac{1}{2x} + \dfrac{1}{48} = \dfrac{1}{24}$ $\qquad \Rightarrow \dfrac{3}{2x} = \dfrac{1}{48}$ $\qquad \therefore x = 72$ days

MULTIPLE CHOICE QUESTIONS

1. 12 boys can do a piece of work in 16 days. In how many days can 6 boys do the same work?
   A. 16 days
   B. 32 days
   C. 23 days
   D. 24 days

2. A can do a piece of work in 8 days while B can do the same work in 16 days. If they start working together, how long would they take to complete half portion of this work?
   A. $2\dfrac{2}{3}$ days
   B. $3\dfrac{5}{7}$ days
   C. $4\dfrac{1}{2}$ days
   D. $3\dfrac{1}{2}$ days

3. A can do a piece of work in 4 days. B is 50% more efficient than A. How long would B alone take to complete it.
   A. $3\dfrac{1}{3}$ days
   B. $5\dfrac{1}{4}$ days
   C. $2\dfrac{2}{3}$ days
   D. $1\dfrac{2}{3}$ days

4. A and B working together complete a work in 35 days. If A takes 60 days to complete it, how long would B alone take to complete it?
   A. 64 days
   B. 72 days
   C. 81 days
   D. 84 days

5. 10 men or 18 boys can do a piece of work in 15 days. In how many days would 25 men and 15 boys complete the same work working together?
   A. $5\dfrac{1}{2}$ days
   B. $4\dfrac{1}{2}$ days
   C. $6\dfrac{2}{3}$ days
   D. $2\dfrac{1}{3}$ days

6. A can do $\dfrac{1}{2}$ of a work in 9 days while B can do $\dfrac{1}{3}$ of the same work in 6 days. How long would take for A and B together to complete the work?
   A. 18 days
   B. 6 days
   C. 12 days
   D. 9 days

7. A, B and C can complete a work separately in 24, 36 and 48 days respectively. They started together but C left after 4 days of start and A left 3 days before the completion of work. In how many days will the work be completed?

A. 15 days   B. 18 days   C. 10 days   D. 12 days

8. 5 men and 2 boys together in 1 hour do 4 times work as 1 man and 1 boy do in an hour. Determine the ratio of the specified times of works of a man and a boy.

A. 4 : 1   B. 1 : 4   C. 3 : 4   D. 2 : 1

9. 75 boys finish a work in 24 days. How many men will complete twice the work in 20 days while 2 men do in a day same work as 3 boys do in a day?

A. 50   B. 120   C. 60   D. 24

10. Savita can do a piece of work in 20 days. Tripti is 25% more efficient than Savita. The number of days taken by Tripti to do the same piece of work is:

A. 15 days   B. 16 days   C. 18 days   D. 25 days

11. A, B and C together contracted to do a work for ₹ 450. If ratio of their work is 9 : 5 : 4 respectively, then find the share of A.

A. ₹ 220   B. ₹ 225   C. ₹ 325   D. ₹ 180

12. A can do a work in 16 days. If B's speed is double than A, then in how many days they together can do the work?

A. $5\dfrac{1}{3}$ days   B. $3\dfrac{1}{4}$ days   C. $4\dfrac{1}{3}$ days   D. $2\dfrac{1}{4}$ days

13. A and B together can do a work in 28 days. They finish the work with the help of C in 21 days. In how many days C alone can do the work?

A. 83 days   B. 84 days   C. 90 days   D. 45 days

14. Sapna and Sandhya can do a work in 12 days and 10 days respectively. If they work on alternative days and Sapna begins the work then in how many days the work will be completed?

A. 8 days   B. 11 days   C. 14 days   D. 5 days

15. A takes halftime than B to do a work. C takes time equal to A and B together. If three together can do the work in 7 days then in how many days A alone can do the work?

A. 21 days   B. 10 days   C. 8 days   D. 24 days

16. Working 7 hours daily 24 men can complete a piece of work in 27 days. In how many days would 14 men complete the same piece of work working 9 hours daily?

A. 32 days   B. 31 days   C. 36 days   D. 39 days

17. A, B and C undertake to do a piece of work for ₹ 529. If A and B working together do $\dfrac{19}{23}$ work and B and C working together do $\dfrac{8}{23}$ work, how should the money be divided among them?

A. ₹ 345, ₹ 102, ₹ 82   B. ₹ 345, ₹ 92, ₹ 92   C. ₹ 330, ₹ 107, ₹ 92   D. ₹ 330, ₹ 92, ₹ 107

18. Two men undertake to do a piece of work for ₹ 1400. First man alone can do this work in 7 days while the second man alone can do this work in 8 days. If they working together complete this work in 3 days with the help of a boy, how should money be divided?

A. ₹ 600, ₹ 500, ₹ 300   B. ₹ 600, ₹ 525, ₹ 275

C. ₹ 600, ₹ 550, ₹ 250   D. ₹ 500, ₹ 525, ₹ 375

19. 3 men and 5 women can do a piece of work in 8 days and 2 men and 7 boys can do the same work in 12 days. Find the number of boys if the work is done by 10 women.
A. 19 boys   B. 21 boys   C. 23 boys   D. 15 boys

20. A, B and C can complete a piece of work in 20, 12 and 18 days respectively. They start the work together but A drops out after 4 days and B drops out 2 days before the completion of work. The work is finished in :

A. $2\dfrac{22}{25}$ days   B. $6\dfrac{24}{29}$ days   C. $5\dfrac{24}{25}$ days   D. $6\dfrac{24}{25}$ days

ANSWERS

1	2	3	4	5	6	7	8	9	10
B	A	C	D	B	D	A	D	B	B

11	12	13	14	15	16	17	18	19	20
B	A	B	B	A	C	B	B	B	D

Explanatory Answers

1. 12 boys can do a piece of work in 16 days
1 boy can do this work in 16 × 12 days

6 boys can do this work in $\dfrac{16 \times 12}{6}$ days = 32 days.

2. Here, $x = 8$, $y = 16$
They both working together would complete $\dfrac{1}{2}$ work in

$= \dfrac{1}{2} \times \left(\dfrac{xy}{x+y}\right)$ days $= \dfrac{1}{2} \times \left(\dfrac{8 \times 16}{8 + 16}\right) = \dfrac{1}{2}\left(\dfrac{128}{24}\right)$

$= \dfrac{8}{3}$ days $= 2\dfrac{2}{3}$ days.

3. A does the work in 4 days

∴ B will do this work in $4 \times \dfrac{100}{150}$ days

$= \dfrac{8}{3}$ days $= 2\dfrac{2}{3}$ days.

4. Let B alone would take y days to complete this work.
Here $x = 60$
According to the question,
A and B working together complete this work in 35 days

$\Rightarrow \dfrac{xy}{x+y} = 35$

$\Rightarrow \dfrac{60 \times y}{60 + y} = 35$

$\Rightarrow 60y = 35 \times 60 + 35y \quad \Rightarrow 25y = 35 \times 60$

$\Rightarrow y = \dfrac{35 \times 60}{25} = 7 \times 12 = 84$

Therefore, B alone would complete this work in 84 days.

5. According to question,
Work done by 10 men = work done by 18 boys
Work done by 25 men = work done by 45 boys
∴ Work done by (25 men + 15 boys) = Work done by 45 + 15 = 60 boys
∵ 18 boys complete a work in 15 days
1 boy complete this work in 15 × 18 days

60 boys complete this work in $\dfrac{15 \times 18}{60} = \dfrac{9}{2}$

days $= 4\dfrac{1}{2}$ days

Therefore, 25 men and 15 boys working together would complete the work in $4\dfrac{1}{2}$ days.

6. A's 9 day's work $= \dfrac{1}{2}$

A's 1 day work $= \dfrac{1}{2 \times 9} = \dfrac{1}{18}$

(1809) Math–8

B's 6 day's work $= \dfrac{1}{3}$

B's 1 day work $= \dfrac{1}{3 \times 6} = \dfrac{1}{18}$

(A + B)'s 1 day work $= \dfrac{1}{18} + \dfrac{1}{18} = \dfrac{2}{18} = \dfrac{1}{9}$

∴ A and B both together will complete the work in 9 days.

7. Let the work be completed in x days.
Therefore, A worked for $(x - 3)$ days
       B worked for x days
and   C worked for 4 days

A's 1 day work $= \dfrac{1}{24}$

B's 1 day work $= \dfrac{1}{36}$

C's 1 day work $= \dfrac{1}{48}$

$(x - 3) \times \dfrac{1}{24} + x \times \dfrac{1}{36} + 4 \times \dfrac{1}{48} = 1$

$\Rightarrow \dfrac{x-3}{24} + \dfrac{x}{36} + \dfrac{1}{12} = 1$

$\Rightarrow \dfrac{3x - 9 + 2x + 6}{72} = 1$

$\Rightarrow 5x - 3 = 72$

$\Rightarrow 5x = 75 \Rightarrow x = 15$

Hence the work was completed in 15 days.

8. Work of (5 men + 2 boys)
    $= 4$ (work of 1 man + 1 boy)
    Work of 4 men + 4 boys
$\Rightarrow$ Work of (5 men – 4 men)
       $=$ Work of (4 boys – 2 boys)
$\Rightarrow$ Work of 1 man = work of 2 boys
∴ Required ratio $= 2 : 1$

9. Work of 3 boys = Work of 2 men

Work of 1 boy = Work of $\dfrac{2}{3}$ man

∴ Work of 75 boys = work of $\dfrac{2}{3} \times 75 = 50$ men

∵ 1 work is completed in 24 days by 50 men
∴ 1 work is completed in 1 day by 50×24 men
∴ 2 work are completed in 20 days by

$\dfrac{50 \times 24 \times 2}{20} = 120$ men

10. Ratio of times taken by Savita and Tripti
    $= 125 : 100 = 5 : 4$
Suppose Tripti takes x days to do the work

$5 : 4 : : 20 : x \Rightarrow \dfrac{5}{4} = \dfrac{20}{x}$

$\Rightarrow x = \dfrac{4 \times 20}{5} = 16$ days

Hence, Tripti takes 16 days to complete the work.

11. Sum of the ratios $= 9 + 5 + 4 = 18$

A's share $= \dfrac{9}{18} \times 450 = ₹\ 225.$

12. A can do a work in 16 days
B can do same work in 8 days

A's one day work $= \dfrac{1}{16}$ B's one day work $= \dfrac{1}{8}$

(A + B)'s one day work $= \dfrac{1}{16} + \dfrac{1}{8} = \dfrac{1+2}{16} = \dfrac{3}{16}$

(A + B)'s do $\dfrac{3}{16}$ work in 1 day

(A + B)'s do one work in $\dfrac{16}{3} = 5\dfrac{1}{3}$ days.

13. (A + B)'s 1 day work $= \dfrac{1}{28}$

(A + B + C)'s 1 day work $= \dfrac{1}{21}$

∴ C's 1 day work $= \dfrac{1}{21} - \dfrac{1}{28} = \dfrac{4-3}{84} = \dfrac{1}{84}$

∴ C can do the work in 84 days.

14. Sapna's 1 day work $= \dfrac{1}{12}$

Sandhya's 1 day work $= \dfrac{1}{10}$

(Sapna + Sandhya)'s 1 day work

$= \dfrac{1}{12} + \dfrac{1}{10} = \dfrac{5+6}{60} = \dfrac{11}{60}$

∵ They work on alternative days

∴ (Sapna + Sandhya)'s 5 – 5 day's work

$= \dfrac{11}{60} \times 5 = \dfrac{11}{12}$

∴ Remaining work $= 1 - \dfrac{11}{12} = \dfrac{1}{12}$

Now Sapna's turn comes

Sapna does $\dfrac{1}{12}$ work in 1 day

∴ Work will be completed in $5 + 5 + 1 = 11$ days

15. Let A alone complete the work in x days

$\therefore$ B can complete the work in $2x$ days

A's 1 day work $= \dfrac{1}{x}$

B's 1 day work $= \dfrac{1}{2x}$

C's 1 day work $= \dfrac{1}{x} + \dfrac{1}{2x} = \dfrac{3}{2x}$

$(A + B + C)$'s 1 day work

$= \dfrac{1}{x} + \dfrac{1}{2x} + \dfrac{3}{2x} = \dfrac{6}{2x} = \dfrac{3}{x}$

According to problem,

$(A + B + C)$'s 1 day work $= \dfrac{1}{7}$

$\therefore \dfrac{3}{x} = \dfrac{1}{7} \Rightarrow x = 21$

Hence A alone can do the work in 21 days.

16. Working 7 hours a day 24 men can do a work in 27 days

Working 1 hour a day 1 man can do same work in $27 \times 7 \times 24$ days

Working 9 hours a day 14 men will complete

the same work in $\dfrac{27 \times 7 \times 24}{9 \times 14} = 36$ days.

17. Work done by $(A + B) = \dfrac{19}{23}$

Work done by $(B + C) = \dfrac{8}{23}$

Work done by $(A + B) + (B + C)$

$= \dfrac{19}{23} + \dfrac{8}{23} = \dfrac{27}{23}$

$\Rightarrow A + 2B + C = \dfrac{27}{23}$

But work done by $(A + B + C) = 1$ work

Work done by $B = \dfrac{27}{23} - 1 = \dfrac{4}{23}$

Work done by $A = \dfrac{19}{23} - \dfrac{4}{23} = \dfrac{15}{23}$

Work done by $C = \dfrac{8}{23} - \dfrac{4}{23} = \dfrac{4}{23}$

$\therefore$ Share of B $= \dfrac{4}{23} \times 529 = ₹\ 92$

Share of A $= \dfrac{15}{23} \times 529 = ₹\ 345$

Share of C $= \dfrac{4}{23} \times ₹\ 529 = ₹\ 92$

$\therefore$ A, B and C should get ₹ 345, ₹ 92, ₹ 92 respectively.

18. Wages of the first man for 3 days
= Work done by him in 3 days $\times$ ₹ 1400

$= \dfrac{3}{7} \times 1400 = ₹\ 600$

Wages of the second man for 3 days
= Work done by him in 3 days $\times$ ₹ 1400

$= \dfrac{3}{8} \times 1400 = ₹\ 525$

$\therefore$ Wages of the boy for 3 days
$= ₹\ 1400 - ₹\ (600 + 525)$
$= ₹\ (1400 - 1125) = ₹\ 275$

Hence their shares will be ₹ 600, ₹ 525 and ₹ 275 respectively.

19. Work done by (3 men + 5 women) in 1 day $= \dfrac{1}{8}$

or Work done by (24 men + 40 women) in 1 day $= 1$

Work done by (2 men + 7 boys) in 1 day $= \dfrac{1}{12}$

or Work done by (24 men + 84 boys) in 1 day $= 1$

24 men + 40 women = 24 men + 84 boys

$\Rightarrow$ 40 women = 84 boys, 10 women = 21 boys

$\therefore$ 10 women will work equal to the work done by 21 boys.

20. Suppose work is finished in x days

A works for 4 days, B works for $(x - 2)$ days and C works for x days

$\because$ work done by A in 4 days + work done by B in $(x - 2)$ days + work done by C in x days = 1 work

$\therefore \dfrac{4}{20} + \dfrac{x-2}{12} + \dfrac{x}{18} = 1$

$\Rightarrow \dfrac{36 + 15x - 30 + 10x}{180} = 1$

$\Rightarrow 25x + 6 = 180 \quad \Rightarrow 25x = 174$

$\Rightarrow x = \dfrac{174}{25} = 6\dfrac{24}{25}$ days

Hence, work is finished in $6\dfrac{24}{25}$ days.

Area and Perimeter

Triangle

1. Perimeter = 3 × side (Equilateral triangle)

2. Area = $\dfrac{1}{2} \times$ base × height, or

   Area = $\sqrt{s(s-a)(s-b)(s-c)}$

   where a, b, c, are the lengths of the sides of triangle and $s = \dfrac{a+b+c}{2}$

Right Angled Triangle : It is one whose one of the angles is right angle, *i.e.*, 90°.

1. (Hypotenuse)^2 = (Perpendicular)^2 + (Base)^2

2. Area = $\dfrac{1}{2} \times$ Base × Perpendicular

Equilateral Triangle : All three sides are equal in length and all three angles are equal to 60°.

1. Area = $\dfrac{\sqrt{3}}{4} \times (\text{Side})^2$

2. Area = $\dfrac{(\text{Height})^2}{\sqrt{3}}$

3. Height = $\dfrac{\sqrt{3}}{2} \times$ side

4. Perimeter = 3 × side

Isosceles Triangle : Two sides are equal in lengths.

1. Area = $\dfrac{b}{4}\sqrt{4a^2 - b^2}$

   where a = lengths of equal sides
   b = length of unequal side

2. In an isosceles right triangle,

   (a) Hypotenuse = $\sqrt{2} \times$ congruent side (a)

   (b) Area = $\dfrac{1}{2} \times a^2$

   (c) Perimeter = $\sqrt{2} \times a\left(\sqrt{2}+1\right)$

Rectangle :

1. Area = length(l) × breadth (b)

2. Perimeter = 2(l + b)

3. Diagonal = $\sqrt{l^2 + b^2}$

Square :

1. Area = (Side)^2

2. Perimeter = 4 × side

3. Diagonal = side $\times \sqrt{2}$

Parallelogram: Area = Base × Height.

Trapezium : Area = $\dfrac{1}{2} \times$ Height × (Sum of parallel sides). Here, height is the distance between the two parallel sides.

Rhombus :

1. Area = $\dfrac{1}{2} \times$ Product of diagonals

2. Side = $\sqrt{\left(\dfrac{d_1}{2}\right)^2 + \left(\dfrac{d_2}{2}\right)^2}$, where d_1 and d_2 are diagonals

3. Perimeter = 4 × side

Quadrilateral : Area = $\dfrac{1}{2} \times$ One diagonal × (Sum of perpendicular to it from the opposite vertices)

$$= \dfrac{1}{2} \times d \times (a+b)$$

Circle :

1. Diameter = 2 × Radius

2. Area = $\pi r^2 = \dfrac{\pi}{4} d^2$;

   where d = diameter = $\sqrt{\dfrac{4A}{\pi}}$

3. Circumference $= 2\pi r = \pi d$

4. Radius $= \dfrac{\text{Circumference}}{2\pi} = \dfrac{\sqrt{\text{Area}}}{\pi}$

5. Length of an Arc $= \dfrac{\theta}{360°} \times 2\pi r$

6. Area of sector $= \dfrac{\theta}{360°} \times \pi r^2 = \dfrac{1}{2} \times \text{Arc} \times r$

Polygon :

1. Interior angle + Exterior angle $= 180°$

2. Each interior angle $= \left(\dfrac{2n-4}{n}\right) \times 90°$

where n = number of sides

3. Sum of Exterior angles $= 360°$

4. Perimeter = Number of sides × Length of side.

5. For an equilateral triangle of side 'a'

(a) radius of inscribed circle $= \dfrac{a}{2\sqrt{3}}$

and side of the triangle $= 2\sqrt{3}r$,

(b) radius of circumcircle $= \dfrac{a}{\sqrt{3}}$

6. Area of regular polygon $= \dfrac{1}{2}(\text{No. of sides})$

(Radius of the inscribed circle)

7. Area of regular hexagon $= \dfrac{3\sqrt{3}}{2}(\text{side})^2$

$= 2.598 \ (\text{side})^2$

8. Area of a regular octagon $= 2\left(\sqrt{2}+1\right)(\text{side})^2$

$= 4.828 \ (\text{side})^2$

9. Area of quadrilateral, A

$= \sqrt{s(s-a)(s-b)(s-c)(s-d)}$

where, $s = \dfrac{a+b+c+d}{2}$

EXAMPLES

Example 1: The total area of a circle and a square is equal to 5450 sq. cm. The diameter of the circle is 70 cms. What is the sum of the circumference of the circle and the perimeter of the square?

Solution: Let side of the square $= x$ cm

Also $\pi \times 35 \times 35 + x^2 = 5450$

$\Rightarrow \dfrac{22}{7} \times 35 \times 35 + x^2 = 5450 \qquad \Rightarrow x^2 = 5450 - 3850 = 1600$

$\therefore x = 40$ cm $\qquad \therefore$ Required sum $= \pi \times d + 4x = \left(\dfrac{22}{7} \times 70 \times 4 \times 40\right) = 380$ cm.

Example 2: Perimeter of a circle is equal to the prmimeter of a square whose area is 484 cm². What is the radius of the circle?

Solution: Side of a square $= \sqrt{\text{Area}} = \sqrt{484} = 22$ cm.

Perimeter of square $= 4 \times \text{side} = 4 \times 22 = 88$ cm. $\qquad \therefore 2\pi r = 88$

$\Rightarrow 2 \times \dfrac{22}{7} \times r = 88 \qquad \Rightarrow r = \dfrac{88 \times 7}{2 \times 22} = 14$ cm.

Example 3: The perimeter of a square is equal to twice the perimeter of a rectangle of length 8 cm and breadth 7 cm. What is the circumference of a semicircle whose diameter is equal to the side of the square? (Rounded off to the two decimal place)

Solution: $\because$ Perimeter of the square

$= 2 \times \text{Perimeter of rectangle} = 2(8 + 7) \times 2 = 60$ cm

One side of the square $= 15$ cm $\qquad$ Radius of the semicircle (R) $= \dfrac{15}{2}$ cm

$\therefore$ Perimeter of the semicircle $= \pi R + 2R = \dfrac{22}{7} \times \dfrac{15}{2} + 15 = 23.57 + 15 = 38.57$ cm

MULTIPLE CHOICE QUESTIONS

1. The width of a rectangular hall is $\frac{3}{4}$ of its length. If the area of the hall is 300 m², then the difference between its length and width is:
   A. 3 m B. 4 m C. 5 m D. 15 m

2. A room 8 m × 6 m is to be carpeted by a carpet 2 m wide. The length of carpet required is :
   A. 12 m B. 36 m C. 24 m D. 48 m

3. The dimensions of the floor of a rectangular hall are 4 m × 3 m. The floor of the hall is to be tiled fully with 8 cm × 6 cm rectangular tiles without breaking tiles to smaller sizes. The number of tiles required is:
   A. 4800 B. 2600 C. 2500 D. 2400

4. The length and breadth of a playground are 36 m and 21 m respectively. Flagstaffs are required to be fixed on all along the boundary at a distance 3 m apart. The number of flagstaffs will be :
   A. 37 B. 38 C. 39 D. 40

5. A rectangular carpet has an area of 120 m² and a perimeter of 46 m. The length of its diagonal is:
   A. 15 m B. 16 m C. 17 m D. 20 m

6. A rectangle is having 15 cm as its length and 150 cm² as its area. Its area is increased to $1\frac{1}{3}$ times the original area by increasing only its length. Its new perimeter is:
   A. 50 cm B. 60 cm C. 70 cm D. 80 cm

7. A man walked 20 m to cross a rectangular field diagonally. If the length of the field is 16 m, the breadth of the field is:
   A. 4 m B. 16 m
   C. 12 m D. Can not be determined

8. If only the length of a rectangular plot is reduced to $\frac{2}{3}$rd of its original length, the ratio of original area to reduced area is:
   A. 2 : 3 B. 3 : 2 C. 1 : 2 D. None of these

9. The length and breadth of a square are increased by 40% and 30% respectively. The area of resulting rectangle exceeds the area of the square by :
   A. 42% B. 62% C. 82% D. None of these

10. The area of a rectangle is thrice that of a square. Length of the rectangle is 40 cm and breadth of rectangle is $\frac{3}{2}$ times that of the side of the square.
    The side of the square in cms is:
    A. 60 B. 20 C. 30 D. 15

11. If the perimeter of a rhombus is 4a and lengths of the diagonals are x and y, then its area is:
    A. $a(x + y)$ B. $x^2 + y^2$ C. xy D. $\frac{1}{2}xy$

12. In a rhombus whose area is 144 cm². One of its diagonals is twice as long as the other. The lengths of its diagonals are :
    A. 24 cm, 48 cm B. 12 cm, 24 cm
    C. $6\sqrt{2}$ cm, $12\sqrt{2}$ cm D. 6 cm, 12 cm

13. If each of the dimensions of a rectangle is increased by 100%, its area is increased by

    A. 100%   B. 200%   C. 300%   D. 400%

14. The legs of a right triangle are in the ratio of 1 : 2 and its area is 36. The hypotenuse of the triangle is:

    A. 3   B. $\sqrt{5}$ C. $\sqrt{3}$ D. $6\sqrt{5}$

15. Each side of an equilateral triangle is increased by 1.5%. The percentage increase in its area is:

    A. 1.5%   B. 3%   C. 4.5%   D. 5.7%

ANSWERS

1	2	3	4	5	6	7	8	9	10
C	C	C	B	C	B	C	B	C	B

11	12	13	14	15
D	B	C	D	A

Explanatory Answers

1. Let length of rectangular hall $= x$ m.

$\therefore$ breadth of rectangular hall $= \dfrac{3}{4} x$ m

Area of rectangular hall

$$= l \times b = x \times \frac{3x}{4} = \frac{3x^2}{4} \text{ m}^2$$

But area of rectangular hall $= 300$ m^2

$\therefore \quad \dfrac{3x^2}{4} = 300$

$\Rightarrow x^2 = \dfrac{4 \times 300}{3} = 400$

$\Rightarrow x = 20$

$\therefore$ length $= 20$ m and breadth

$= \dfrac{3}{4} \times 20 = 15$ m

Difference $= 20 - 15 = 5$ m.

2. Area of room $= 8 \times 6 = 48$ m^2

Length of carpet $= \dfrac{\text{Area}}{\text{breadth}} = \dfrac{48}{2} = 24$ m.

3. Length of hall $= 4$ m $= 4 \times 100 = 400$ cm

breadth of hall $= 3$ m $= 3 \times 100 = 300$ cm

Area of the floor $= l \times b = 400 \times 300$ cm^2

Area of the tile $= 8 \times 6 = 48$ cm^2

Number to tiles $= \dfrac{400 \times 300}{48} = 2500.$

4.

```
D ________________ C
|                |
|                | 21 m
A |______________| B
        36 m
```

length of play ground $= 36$ m

breadth of play ground $= 21$ m

perimeter of playground $= 2(l + b)$

$= 2(36 + 21) = 2 \times 57 = 114$ m

Number of flagstaffs $= \dfrac{114}{3} = 38.$

5. Perimeter of rectangle $= 2(l + b)$

According to the question,

$\qquad 2(l + b) = 46$

$\therefore \qquad l + b = 23 \qquad \qquad ...(i)$

Area of rectangle $= l \times b$

$\qquad l \times b = 120 \qquad \qquad ...(ii)$

Now $(l - b)^2 = (l + b)^2 - 4\,lb$

$\qquad\qquad [\because (a - b)^2 = (a + b)^2 - 4ab]$

$\qquad = (23)^2 - 4 \times 120$

$\qquad = 529 - 480 = 49$

$\therefore \qquad l - b = 7 \qquad \qquad ...(iii)$

Solving (iii) and (i) we get

$\qquad l = 15 \text{ and } b = 8$

$\therefore$ Diagonal of rectangle

$= \sqrt{l^2 + b^2} = \sqrt{(15)^2 + (8)^2}$

$= \sqrt{225 + 64} = \sqrt{289} = 17$ m.

6. Area of rectangle = 150 cm^2
length of rectangle = 15 cm

$\therefore$ breadth of rectangle = $\dfrac{150}{15}$ = 10 cm

New area = $\left(150 \times \dfrac{4}{3}\right)$ = 200 cm^2

$\therefore$ New length = $\dfrac{\text{New area}}{\text{Original breadth}}$

$\dfrac{200}{10}$ = 20 cm

New perimeter = 2(20 + 10) = 60 cm.

7.

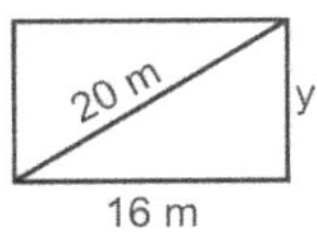

Breadth of rectangle

$= \sqrt{(20)^2 - (16)^2}$

$= \sqrt{400 - 256}$

$= \sqrt{144}$ = 12 m.

8. Let length = x and breadth = y

New length = $\dfrac{2}{3}x$ and breadth = y

$\therefore \dfrac{\text{Original area}}{\text{Reduced area}} = \dfrac{xy}{\dfrac{2}{3}xy} = \dfrac{3}{2}$ = 3 : 2.

9. Let original side = x
Area = x^2

New area = $\left(\dfrac{140}{100}x \times \dfrac{130}{100}x\right) = \dfrac{91}{50}x^2$

Change in area = $\left(\dfrac{91}{50}x^2 - x^2\right)$

$= \dfrac{91x^2 - 50x^2}{50} = \dfrac{41x^2}{50}$

Increase percent = $\dfrac{41x^2}{50} \times \dfrac{1}{x^2} \times 100$ = 82%.

10. Length of rectangle = 40 cm
Let side of square = x cm

Breadth of rectangle = $\dfrac{3}{2}x$ cm

$40 \times \dfrac{3}{2}x$ = 3 x^2

$\Rightarrow x = 20$

Hence, side of square = 20 cm.

11. Area of rhombus = $\dfrac{1}{2} \times d_1 \times d_2 = \dfrac{1}{2}xy$.

12. Let diagonals of rhombus are x cm and $2x$ cm

Area of rhombus = $\dfrac{1}{2} \times d_1 \times d_2$

$\Rightarrow \dfrac{1}{2} \times x \times 2x = 144$

$\Rightarrow x^2 = 144$

$\Rightarrow x = 12$

$\therefore$ Diagonals are 12 cm and 24 cm.

13. Let length = x and breadth = y
then, Area = xy
New length = $2x$
and new breadth = $2y$
Area = $2x \times 2y = 4xy$

$\therefore$ Increase percent = $\dfrac{3xy}{xy} \times 100 = 300\%$.

14. $\dfrac{1}{2} \times x \times 2x = 36 \Rightarrow x^2 = 36$

$\Rightarrow x = 6$

$\therefore$ Hypotenuse = $\sqrt{6^2 + 12^2}$

$= \sqrt{36 + 144}$

$= \sqrt{180}$

$= 6\sqrt{5}$.

15. Let original length of each side = a

Then, area = $\dfrac{\sqrt{3}}{4}a^2 = A$

New area = $\dfrac{\sqrt{3}}{4}\left[\left(\dfrac{101.5}{100}a\right)^2\right]$

$= \dfrac{\sqrt{3}}{4}\left(\dfrac{20.3}{20}\right)a^2 = \left(\dfrac{20.3}{20}\right)A$

Increase in area

$= \left(\dfrac{0.3}{20}A \times \dfrac{1}{A} \times 100\right) = 1.5\%$.

Mental Ability

In series, the letters/numbers follow a definite order. The given series of letters/numbers can be in natural order or in reverse order or combination of both. The letters/numbers may be skipped or repeated or consecutive. The given series may be single or may even comprise of two different series merged at alternate positions. While attempting questions on letter series one should note the pattern of alphabet series.

Alphabets in natural series are :

A B C D E F G H I J K L M N O P Q R S T U V W X Y Z

1st   5th   10th   15th   20th   25th

Alphabets in reverse series are :

Z Y X W V U T S R Q P O N M L K J I H G F E D C B A

1st   5th   10th   15th   20th   25th

Note : On reaching Z, the series restarts from A and on reaching A, it restarts from Z.

EXERCISE

Directions : *In each of the following series determine the order of the letters. Then from the given options select the one which will complete the given series.*

1. B Y C X D W E ?
A. S		B. T
C. U		D. V

2. B A F E J I P O ? U
A. V		B. T
C. S		D. Q

3. B A D C ? H G J I
A. E F		B. F E
C. F G		D. D F

4. ADG, XVT, BEH, WUS, ?
A. VTR		B. CFI
C. DFJ		D. STU

5. GMSY, IOUA, KQWC, ?
A. MSYE		B. NSYE
C. MTYE		D. MSYF

6. ADG, GJM, ?, SVY
A. MPS		B. MQR
C. MQS		D. SPM

7. XYZ, UVW, ?, OPQ
A. RST		B. STU
C. QRS		D. TUV

8. JOBS, KMEO, LKHK, ?, NGNC
A. MJLH		B. LIKG
C. MIKG		D. MNGM

9. AZ, GT, MN, ?, YB
A. KF		B. TS
C. RX		D. SH

10. BMY, DNW, FOU, ?
A. HPT		B. HPS
C. HQS		D. GPS

Directions : *Which letter(s) in each of the following series is wrong or is misfit in the series?*

11. A E H O U
A. U		B. O
C. H		D. E

12. C H M S W B
A. C		B. S
C. B		D. W

13. X S N I C Y
A. Y		B. C
C. S		D. I

14. Z A W B X C
A. D		B. C
C. X		D. W

15. M L O N Q P R
A. R	B. O
C. Q	D. L

Directions : *Which of the following groups of letters will complete the given series?*

16. ab---b-bbaa-
A. babba	B. abaab
C. abbab	D. baaab

17. aa-ab--aaa-a
A. baaa	B. abab
C. aaab	D. aabb

18. -baa-aab-a-a
A. baab	B. abab
C. aaba	D. aabb

19. -a cca-ccca-accccc-aaa
A. ccaa	B. acca
C. caac	D. caaa

20. c-bbb--abbbb-abbb-
A. abccb	B. bacbb
C. aabcb	D. abacb

Directions : *In the following questions, select the number(s) from the given options for completing the given series.*

21. 7776, 1296, 216, 36, 6, ?
A. 6	B. 0
C. 3	D. 1

22. 29282, 2662, 242, 22, ?
A. 1	B. 2
C. 0	D. 11

23. 1, 2, 2, 4, 16, ?, 65536
A. 276	B. 64
C. 256	D. 198

24. 3, 5, 9, 15, 23, ?, 45
A. 37	B. 35
C. 31	D. 33

25. 7, 21, 35, 49, 63, ?
A. 70	B. 77
C. 81	D. 108

26. 10, 14, 23, 39, 64, ?, 149
A. 78	B. 128
C. 103	D. 100

27. 6, 24, 29, 116, 121, ?, 489
A. 468	B. 484
C. 243	D. 363

28. 5, 50, 45, 450, 445, ?, 4445
A. 4450	B. 4600
C. 4550	D. 4500

29. 6.25, 9, 12.25, 16, 20.25, 25, 30.25?
A. 36	B. 32
C. 28.25	D. 40.25

30. 243, 5, 81, 15, 27, 45, 9, ?
A. 5	B. 15
C. 135	D. 27

Directions : *In the given series find the number which is wrong.*

31. 5, 25, 120, 625, 3125, 15625
A. 15625	B. 625
C. 120	D. 5

32. 4, 8, 11, 22, 18, 36, 24, 50
A. 8	B. 22
C. 36	D. 24

33. 2, 4, 12, 24, 72, 142, 432
A. 432	B. 12
C. 142	D. 72

34. 2, 3, 4, 4, 6, 8, 9, 12, 16
A. 3	B. 9
C. 6	D. 12

35. 97, 91, 86, 83, 79, 77, 76, 76
A. 86	B. 76
C. 91	D. 83

EXPLANATORY ANSWERS

1. D. : There are two alternate series.

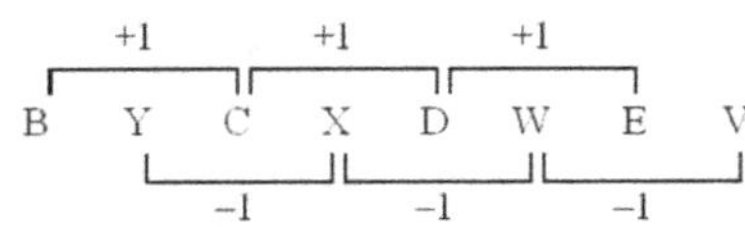

Series I : BCDE (natural order)

Series II : YXWV (reverse order)

2. A. : Each vowel (AEIOU) is preceded by the letter that comes next to it in the natural alphabetical series.

3. B. : The letters in natural series are divided into sections of two letters each. The letters in each section are written backward.

<u>BA</u> <u>DC</u> <u>FE</u> <u>HG</u> <u>JI</u>

4. B. : There are two alternate series.

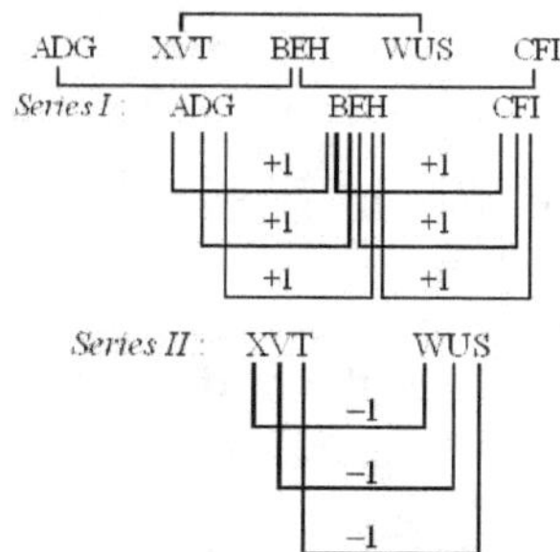

5. A. : The series is formed by moving each letter two steps forward from one group to the next.

(The series restarts from A on reaching Z)

6. A. : In each group of three letters the alphabet is in the succession of +3. The next group begins with the last alphabet of the previous group.

A D G   G J M   M P S   S V Y
+3 +3   +3 +3   +3 +3   +3 +3

7. A. : The alphabet from one group to the next are in recession of −3, *i.e.,*

XYZ   UVW   RST   OPQ
     −3   −3   −3
     −3   −3   −3
     −3   −3   −3

8. C. : The alphabets in each group follow the pattern +1, −2, +3 and −4 respectively from one group to the next group.

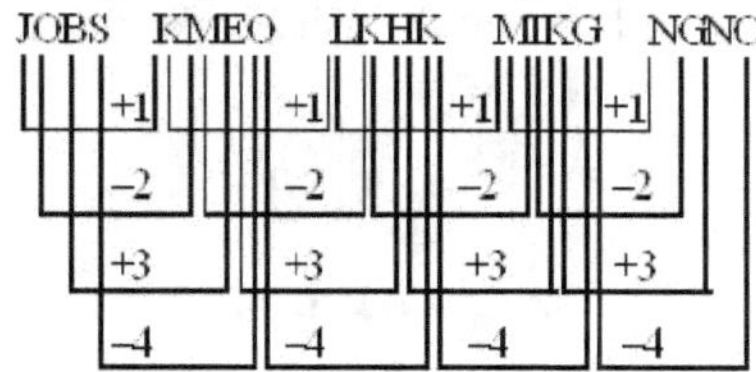

9. D. : The letters in one group correspond to the letters in the next group in the manner +6, −6 respectively, *i.e.,*

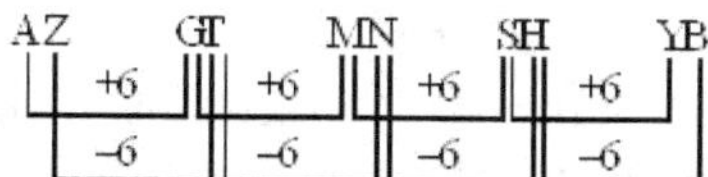

10. B. : The letters in one group correspond to the letters in the next group in the manner +2, +1, −2 respectively, *i.e.,*

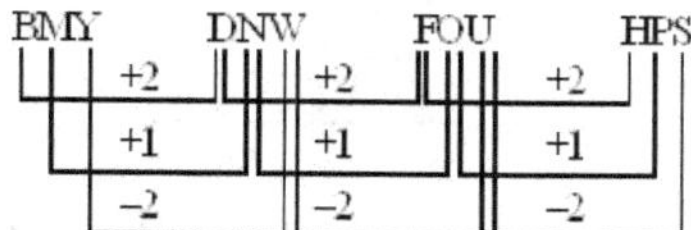

11. C. : The series is made with vowels only. AEIOU. I should be in place of H.

12. B. : The letters in the series are moved five steps forward.

C   H   M   R   W   B
  +5 +5 +5 +5 +5

R should be in place of S

(The series restarts from A on reaching Z)

13. B. : The pattern in the series is −5, *i.e.,*

X   S   N   I   D   Y
  −5 −5 −5 −5 −5

D should be in place of C.

14. D. : There are two alternate series

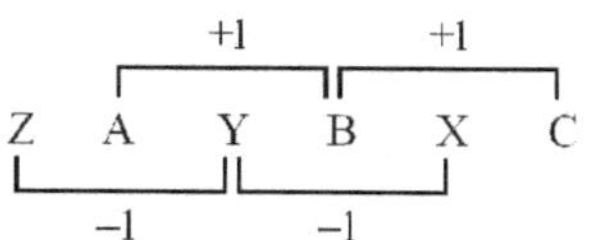

Series I : ZYX (reverse series)

Series II : ABC (natural series)

Y should be in place of W.

15. A. : Two consecutive letters are written backwards.

<u>ML</u>   <u>ON</u>   <u>QP</u>   <u>SR</u>

S should be in place of R.

16. D. : The series is abbaab, abbaab.

17. C. : The series is aaaaba, aaaaba.

18. B. : The series is aba, aba, aba, aba.

19. D. : The series is c,a,cc,aa, ccc, aaa, cccc, aaaa.

20. A. : The series is cabbbb, cabbbb, cabbbb.

21. D. : The numbers in this sequence are divided by 6 each time.

22. B. : The numbers in the series are divided by 11 at each step.

23. C. : The number in the series is product of all the numbers preceding it.

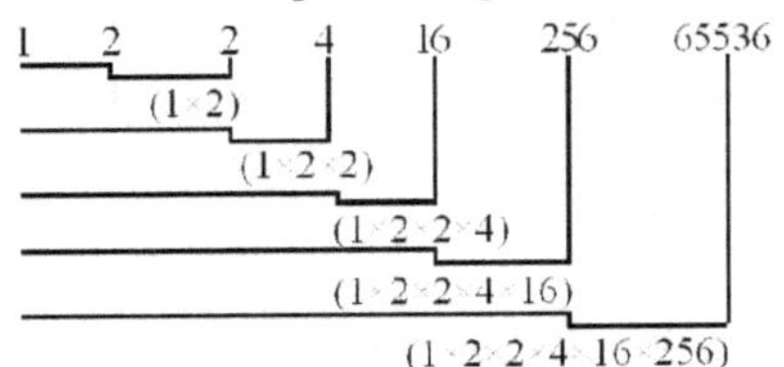

24. D. : The difference between consecutive numbers increases by 2 at each step.

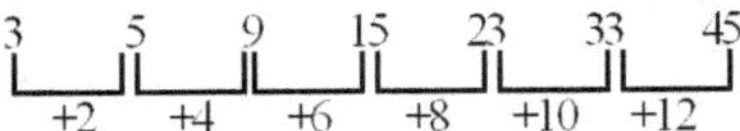

25. B. : The series is multiplication of 7 by odd numbers starting from 3.

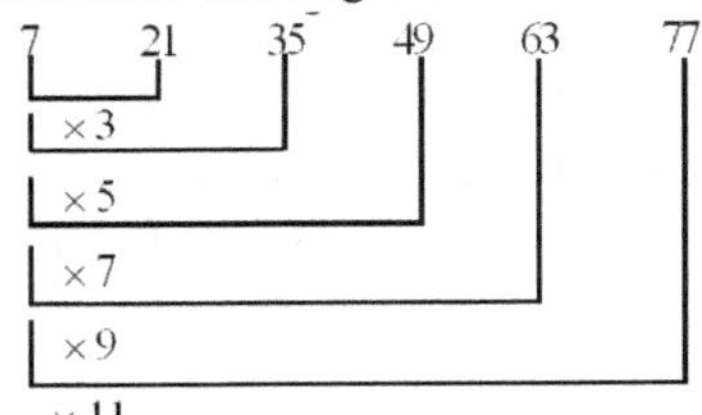

26. D. : The number plus the square of numbers in natural order starting from 2 gives the next number in the series.

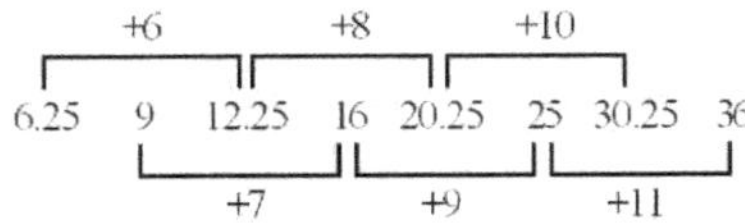

27. B. : The sequence in the series is ×4, +5, which is repeated.

28. A. : The sequence in the series is ×10, −5, which is repeated.

29. A. : There are two alternate series :

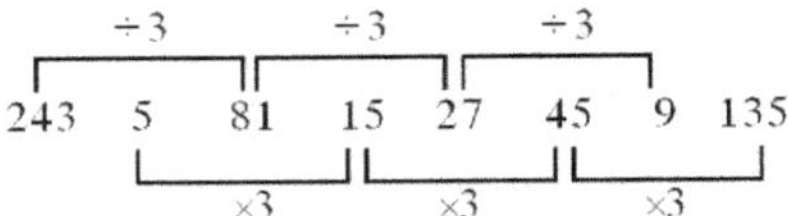

Series I : 6.25, 12.25, 20.25, 30.25 (sequence is +6, +8, +10)

Series II : 9, 16, 25, 36 (sequence is +7, +9, +11)

30. C. : There are two alternate series :

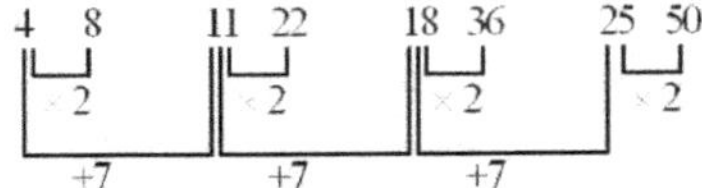

Series I : 243, 81, 27, 9 (division by 3)

Series II : 5, 15, 45, 135 (multiplication by 3)

31. C. : The numbers in the series are multiplied by 5 to get the next number.

∴ 125 should be in place of 120.

32. D. : Two numbers form a pair. The first number increases by 7 for the next pair and the second number is the double of first number.

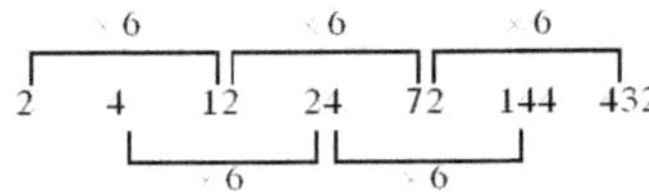

∴ 25 should be in place of 24.

33. C. : There are two alternate series and in each series, the numbers are multiplied by 6 to get the next number.

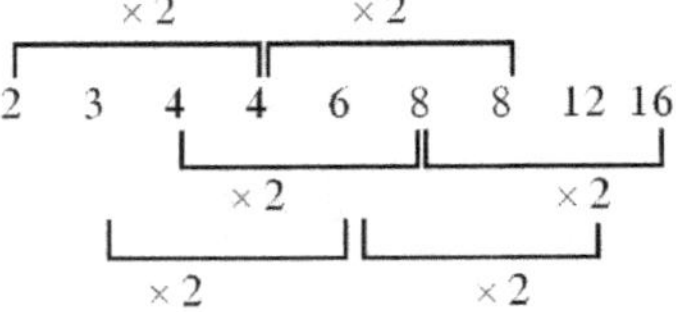

∴ 144 should be in place of 142.

34. B. : There are three alternate series and in each series, the numbers are multiplied by 2 to get the next number.

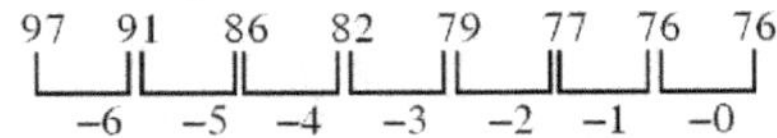

Series I : 2, 4, 8   *Series II* : 3, 6, 12

Series III : 4, 8, 16

∴ 8 should be in place of 9.

35. D. : The difference between the consecutive numbers in the series decreases by 1 at each step.

∴ 82 should be in place of 83.

❑ ❑ ❑

Analogy

In Analogy Tests, the relationship between two given words/letters/numbers is established and then applied to the other words/letters/numbers. The type of relationship may vary, so while attempting such questions the first step is to identify the type of relationship, which can be any one of the following.

EXERCISE

Directions : *In the questions given below one term is missing. Based on the relationship of the two given words find the missing term from the given options.*

1. HUNGER : FOOD : : THIRST : ?
   - A. Water
   - B. Drink
   - C. Tea
   - D. Coffee

2. HUNTER : GUN : : WRITER : ?
   - A. Book
   - B. Pen
   - C. Poem
   - D. Page

3. WOOL : SHEEP : : SILK : ?
   - A. Saree
   - B. String
   - C. Silkworm
   - D. Moth

4. FOOD : STOMACH : : FUEL : ?
   - A. Engine
   - B. Automobile
   - C. Rail
   - D. Aeroplane

5. WATER : SAND : : OCEAN : ?
   - A. Island
   - B. River
   - C. Desert
   - D. Waves

6. ADULT : BABY : : FLOWER : ?
   - A. Seed
   - B. Bud
   - C. Fruit
   - D. Butterfly

7. WRITER : READER : : PRODUCER : ?
   - A. Creator
   - B. Contractor
   - C. Creature
   - D. Consumer

8. ENTRANCE : EXIT : : LOYALTY : ?
   - A. Treachery
   - B. Patriotism
   - C. Fidelity
   - D. Reward

9. MOTHER : MATERNAL : : FATHER : ?
   - A. Eternal
   - B. Detrimental
   - C. Paternal
   - D. Formidable

10. PEARL : NECKLACE : : FLOWER : ?
    - A. Plant
    - B. Garden
    - C. Petal
    - D. Bouquet

11. BaBy : TaTa : : LiLy : ?
    - A. PooL
    - B. ROse
    - C. HaNd
    - D. DoWN

12. BCDA : STUR : : KLMJ : ?
    - A. VWXU
    - B. EFHG
    - C. SRTU
    - D. QSRP

13. AEI : LPT : : CGK : ?
    - A. OSV
    - B. RUY
    - C. TXC
    - D. FJN

14. RUX : TRP : : BEH : ?
    - A. SQN
    - B. QON
    - C. QOM
    - D. QNL

15. CART : ART : : FOUR : ?
    - A. RUN
    - B. TWO
    - C. QUE
    - D. OUR

16. FIK : JGO : : DFR : ?
    - A. BIO
    - B. HDV
    - C. GCU
    - D. FLP

17. LJH : KKI : : CIA : ?
    - A. BJB
    - B. DHB
    - C. BJC
    - D. BBJ

18. ACE : HIL : : MOQ : ?
    - A. SVW
    - B. TUX
    - C. RTW
    - D. WUS

19. BCDE : WVUT : : QRST : ?
    - A. EFHG
    - B. JIHG
    - C. POML
    - D. GEDC

20. PNLJ : IGEC : : USQO : ?
    - A. HJLN
    - B. LNJH
    - C. NLJH
    - D. JHNL

21. DIMO : DMIO : : JUVR : ?
    - A. JVRU
    - B. JRVU
    - C. JVUR
    - D. JUVR

Directions : *In the following questions, select the number from the given options which follows the same relationship as shared between the first two numbers.*

22. 1 : 11 : : 2 : ?
- A. 20
- B. 22
- C. 24
- D. 44

23. $\dfrac{1}{7} : \dfrac{1}{14}$: : $\dfrac{1}{9}$: ?
- A. $\dfrac{1}{88}$
- B. $\dfrac{1}{80}$
- C. $\dfrac{1}{81}$
- D. $\dfrac{1}{18}$

24. 0.16 : 0.0016 : : 1.02 : ?
- A. 10.20
- B. 0.102
- C. 0.0102
- D. 1.020

25. 663 : 884 : : 221 : ?
- A. 332
- B. 554
- C. 773
- D. 442

26. 16 : 0.16 : : ?
- A. 2 : 0.02
- B. 7 : 0.007
- C. 1.3 : 0.13
- D. 0.01 : 0.001

27. 3 : $\dfrac{1}{3}$: : ?
- A. 6 : 12
- B. 5 : 2/15
- C. 8 : 1/8
- D. 9 : 27

28. 65 : 13 : : 180 : ?
- A. 93
- B. 36
- C. 133
- D. 102

29. 125 : 27 : : 343 : ?
- A. 729
- B. 64
- C. 216
- D. 512

30. 357 : 73 : : ?
- A. 429 : 94
- B. 201 : 21
- C. 138 : 38
- D. 93 : 39

31. 731 : 902 : : 655 : ?
- A. 646
- B. 800
- C. 793
- D. 556

EXPLANATORY ANSWERS

1. A. : Hunger is satiated by food, thirst by water.

2. B. : Weapon of a hunter is a gun, weapon of a writer is a pen.

3. C. : Wool is obtained from sheep, silk is obtained from silkworm.

4. A. : Food is consumed in stomach, fuel is consumed in engine.

5. C. : The related words are near opposites.

6. B. : The youngone of an adult is a baby and that of a flower is a bud.

7. D. : A writer aims to please the readers by his writings, a producer aims to please the consumers by his products.

8. A. : The related words are opposites.

9. C. : Relations on the mother's side are maternal and on the father's side paternal.

10. D. : Many pearls make a necklace, many flowers make a bouquet.

11. C. : In each group the alternate letters are capitals.

12. A. : In each group the first three letters are consecutive and they follow the fourth letter.

A B C D : R S T U : : J K L M : U V W X

13. D. : In each group the letters jump three letters between them, *i.e.,* they are moving to the fourth letter.

A E I : L P T : : C G K : F J N
+4 +4   +4 +4   +4 +4   +4 +4

14. C. : The letters in first set are jumping two letters, *i.e.,* moving three steps forward and in the second they are jumping one letter, *i.e.* moving two steps backward.

R U X : T R P : : B E H : Q O M
+3 +3   −2 −2   +3 +3   −2 −2

15. D. : The first set of letters drop the first letter to get the second set.

C A R T : A R T : : F O U R : O U R

16. B. : The three letters in first set are moved +4, −2, and +4 steps respectively.

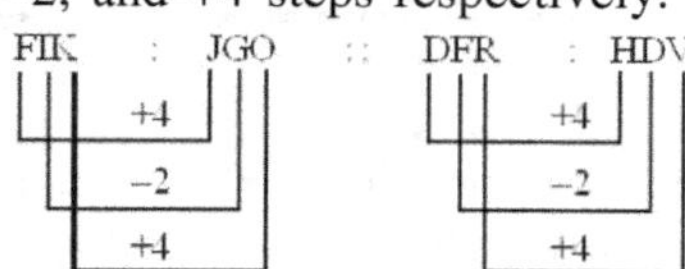

17. A. : The letters in the first set are moved −1, +1 and +1 steps respectively.

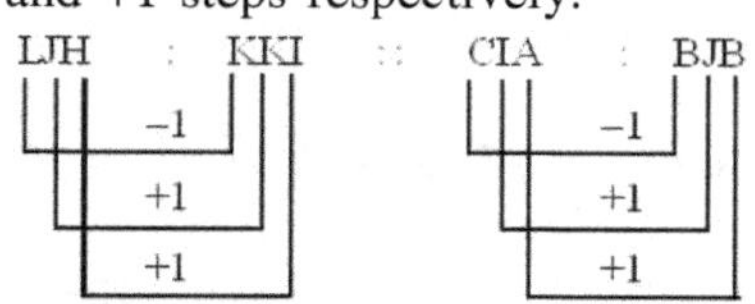

18. B. : The three letters are moved +7, +6 and +7 steps forward respectively.

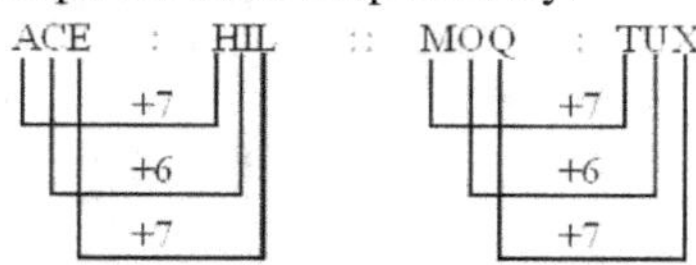

19. B. : The consecutive letters in the first set are in natural order and in the second set, they are in reverse order.

$$\text{BCDE} \xrightarrow{\quad} : \text{WVUT} \xleftarrow{\quad} :: \text{QRST} \xrightarrow{\quad} : \text{JIHG} \xleftarrow{\quad}$$

20. C. : The letters are moved seven steps backwards.

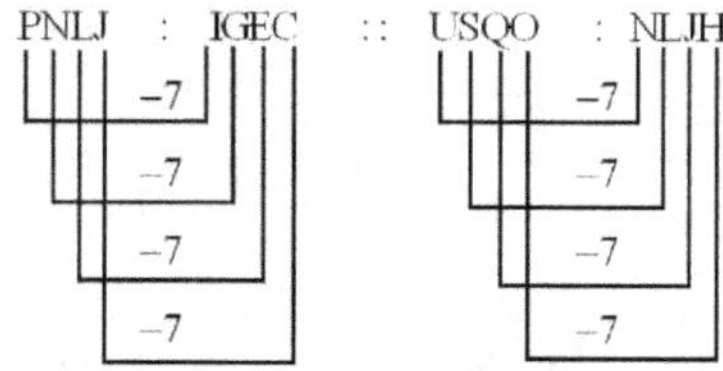

21. C. : Only the middle letters are reversed to obtain the second set of letters.

DIMO : DMIO :: JUVR : JVUR

22. B. : The first number is repeated to obtain the second number.

23. D. : The first fraction is multiplied by half to obtain the second fraction.

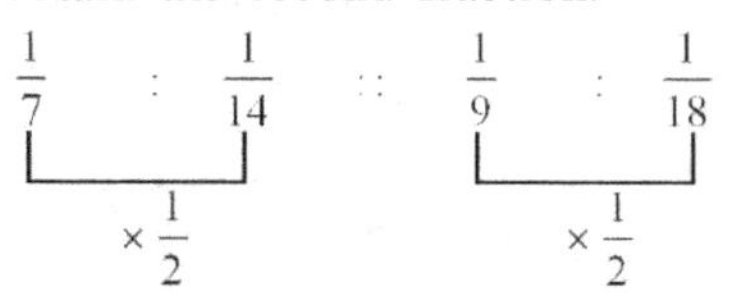

24. C. : The decimals are divided by 100.

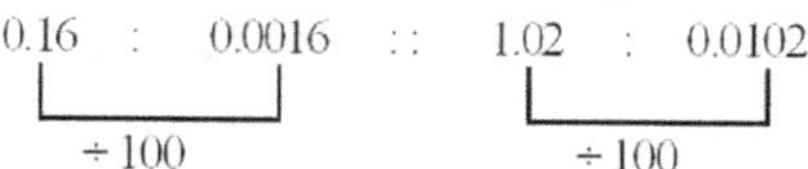

25. D. : The digits at tens and hundreds place is same but the digit at the units place is half the other identical digits.

66 <u>3</u> : 88 <u>4</u> : : 22 <u>1</u> : 44 <u>2</u>

26. A. : Of the two related numbers, the second number is the result of first number divided by 100.

27. C. : Of the two related numbers, the second number is the part fraction of the first number, *i.e.* 3 is related to one-third $\left(\dfrac{1}{3}\right)$.

Similarly, 8 will be related to one-eighth $\left(\dfrac{1}{8}\right)$.

28. B. : The first number is divided by 5 to get the second number.

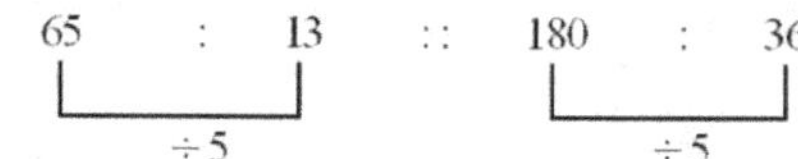

29. A. : The numbers are cubes of different odd numbers.

$$125 : 27 :: 343 : 729$$
$$\downarrow \qquad \downarrow \qquad \downarrow \qquad \downarrow$$
$$5^3 \qquad 3^3 \qquad 7^3 \qquad 9^3$$

30. A. : The central digit of the first number is left out and the corner digits written in reverse order to get the second number.

357 : 73 :: 429 : 94

31. A. : The sum of the digits of both the numbers is same.

$$731 : 902 \rightarrow 7 + 3 + 1$$
$$= 9 + 0 + 2 \ i.e. \ 11 = 11$$
$$655 : 646 \rightarrow 6 + 5 + 5$$
$$= 6 + 4 + 6 \ i.e. \ 16 = 16.$$

□ □ □

Odd One Out ▶▶

In this type of classification, four words/letters/numbers are given out of which three are almost same in matter or meaning and only one is different from the common three. One has to find out the one which is different from the rest.

EXERCISE

Directions : *In each of the following questions, three words are alike in some manner. Spot the odd one out.*

1. A. Green   B. Red
   C. Colour   D. Orange

2. A. Stable   B. Hole
   C. Canoe   D. Sty

3. A. Nose   B. Eyes
   C. Skin   D. Teeth

4. A. Venus   B. Moon
   C. Pluto   D. Mars

5. A. Happy   B. Gloomy
   C. Lively   D. Cheerful

Directions : *Three of the following four in each question are alike in a certain way and so form a group. Select the group of letters that does not belong to that group.*

6. A. ACE   B. LOR
   C. GIK   D. VXZ

7. A. TSR   B. LKJ
   C. PQO   D. HGF

8. A. EF LM   B. KJ SR
   C. XW HG   D. ED YX

9. A. JOPK   B. BOPC
   C. QOPR   D. TOPS

10. A. DfH   B. MoQ
    C. UwY   D. lnO

Directions : *In each of the following questions, there are four options. Three numbers, in these options, are alike in certain manner. Only one number does not fit in. Choose the one which is different from the rest.*

11. A. 1948   B. 2401
    C. 966   D. 1449

12. A. 182   B. 169
    C. 130   D. 158

13. A. 129   B. 130
    C. 131   D. 132

14. A. 3215   B. 9309
    C. 4721   D. 2850

15. A. 1776   B. 2364
    C. 1976   D. 3776

Directions : *In the following questions select the pair which is different from the other three.*

16. A. Chair - Furniture
    B. Shirt - Garment
    C. Necklace - Jewellery
    D. Bogie - Engine

17. A. Crayon - Paper   B. Pencil - Lead
    C. Pen - Ink   D. Brush - Paint

18. A. War - Peace   B. Real - Natural
    C. Premiere - First   D. Wrath - Anger

19. A. Finger - Thimble   B. Head - Cap
    C. Waist - Tiara   D. Foot - Shoe

20. A. Day - Night   B. Clever - Foolish
    C. Clear - Blurred   D. Arrive - Come

Directions : *In the following questions, which of the following pair of letters is different from the other three?*

21. A. FGH - HIJ   B. PQR - RST
    C. MNO - OPQ   D. CDE - DEF

22.	A. JuM - jUm	B. iLo - Ilo
	C. PSa - psA	D. ZeX - zEx

23.	A. NQT - JMP	B. CFI - RUX
	C. ADG - FGH	D. SVY - ORU

24.	A. DXD - XDX	B. KUK - UKU
	C. FHF - EHE	D. RSR - SRS

25.	A. AYT - BZU
	B. FNG - EMF
	C. RWO - QVN
	D. HJD - GIC

Directions : *Which of the following pair of numbers is different from the other three pairs?*

26.	A. 28, 4	B. 63, 7
	C. 56, 8	D. 35, 5

27.	A. 3, 11	B. 8, 16
	C. 5, 13	D. 14, 24

28.	A. 13, 156	B. 12, 144
	C. 15, 180	D. 16, 176

29.	A. 32, 13	B. 46, 20
	C. 51, 24	D. 72, 45

30.	A. 5, 25	B. 9, 81
	C. 4, 64	D. 6, 36

31.	A. 91, 10	B. 57, 12
	C. 69, 15	D. 72, 13

32.	A. 20, 10	B. 45, 27
	C. 15, 12	D. 30, 18

33.	A. 7, 3	B. 13, 9
	C. 11, 7	D. 17, 8

34.	A. 10, 20	B. 40, 50
	C. 30, 40	D. 50, 60

35.	A. 16, 26	B. 3, 4
	C. 26, 24	D. 27, 25

EXPLANATORY ANSWERS

1. C. : All others are types of colour.

2. C. : Canoe is a boat. Others are resting places of birds/animals.

3. D. : All others are sense organs.

4. B. : All others are planets.

5. B. : All others are expressions of joy.

6. B. : The sequence in each group is +2. Only option **B.** has sequence in +3, *i.e.,*

A B C D E
+2   +2

L M N O P Q R
+3   +3

G H I J K
+2 +2

V W X Y Z
+2   +2

7. C. : The sequence of alphabet in each group is in reverse order. Only option **C.** has sequence in disturbed order.

8. A. : Two consecutive alphabet in each group are in reverse sequence (–1), *i.e.,*

KJ SR: XW HG: ED YX
–1 –1   –1   –1   –1   –1

Only in option **A.** the sequence is in natural order (+1), *i.e.,*

E F
+1

L M
+1

9. D. : In each group, letters 'OP' are common. The two corner alphabet are in natural order (+1); *i.e.,*

JOPK :   BOPC :   QOPR
+1   +1   +1

Only in option **D.** they are in reverse order (–1); *i.e.,*

TOPS
–1

10. D. : In other groups, only the alphabet in the centre is of lower case. In this option letter 'L' on the left is also in lower case.

11. A. : Other numbers are divisible by 7.

12. D. : Other numbers are multiples of 13.

13. C. : 131 is a prime number.

14. B. : In other numbers, no digit is repeated.

15. B. : In other numbers, the last two digits are same.

16. D. : Bogie is a part of train which is a type of conveyance. Chair, Shirt and Necklace are types of furniture, garment and jewellery respectively.

17. A. : The medium used for writing with pencil is lead, with pen it is ink and with brush, it is paint. With crayon it should be wax.

18. A. : The pair of words are opposite. Other pairs are synonyms.

19. C. : Tiara is worn on the head.

20. D. : Other words are opposite to each other.

21. D. : In all other groups, the letters are in natural series and the last letter of first part is the first letter of the second part.

22. B. : In all other groups, only the vowel is in lower case in the first part and in second part the case is reversed.

23. C. : In all other groups, the letters jump two letters in between them.

24. C. : In all other groups, the single letter in first part is repeated in the second and vice versa.

25. A. : In all other groups, the letters in the first part are one step forward than the corresponding letters in the second part.

26. B. : In all other pairs 7 times the second number is the first number. In this option 9 times 7 is the first number.

27. D. : In all other groups, the difference between the two numbers is 8.

28. D. : In other groups 12 times, the first number is the second number.

In this option 11 times the first number is the second number.

29. A. : 13 is a prime number.

30. C. : In all other pairs, the second number is a perfect square of the first.

31. D. : In all other pairs, the second number is the sum of the digits of the first number.

32. A. : In all other pairs, the numbers are divisible by 3.

33. D. : In other groups, the difference between the numbers is 4.

34. A. : In this option, the second number is double the first number. In other groups the difference between the two numbers is 10.

35. A. : In other groups, the first digits of the two numbers are same (consider 3 and 4 as 03 and 04).

❑ ❑ ❑

Coding and Decoding ▶▶

Coding is a secretive language which is used to change the representation of the actual term/word/value. This coded language can be framed by *(i)* moving the letters one or more steps forward or backward; *(ii)* substituting numbers for letters and vice–versa; *(iii)* writing the letters of the given word in reverse order in part or in whole; and *(iv)* replacing the letters in their natural series by the same positioned letters in their reverse series.

There is variety in ways of coding. Coding language is not only for words and numbers but also for hiding a group of words, statements or even sentences. This form of coding pattern may appear to be confusing but after solving only a few questions it is very easy to understand. Questions based on this coding pattern require no moving of steps or straining efforts of calculations, but only quick tallying or comparing ability. The codes can be letters or numbers.

EXERCISE

Directions : *In the following questions select the right option which indicates the correct code for the word or letter given in the question.*

1. If MUSK is coded as 146816, then ZERO will be coded as :
   A. 113811   B. 122912
   C. 15915   D. 2651815

2. If BAD is coded as 7, HIS as 9, LOW will be coded as :
   A. 50   B. 8
   C. 23   D. 5

3. In a certain code LIBERATE is written as 56403170, TRIBAL will be written in the same code as :
   A. 734615   B. 736415
   C. 136475   D. 034615

4. In certain military code, SYSTEM is written as SYSMET, and NEARER as AENRER, what will be the code for FRACTION?
   A. CRAFNOIT   B. FRCAITNO
   C. CARFNOIT   D. FRACNOIT

5. If CRUDE is written as BSTED, then MOIST will be coded as :
   A. NNJRU
   B. LNHRS
   C. NPJTU
   D. LPHTS

6. In a certain code ALPACA is written as ACAPLA. How will ANIMAL be written in that code?
   A. LAMINA   B. ALAMIN
   C. LAMNIA   D. AAMLIN

7. In a certain code FINGER is written as DGLECP. What will be the code for KIDNEY?
   A. IGBLCW   B. IGCLBW
   C. IBCGLE   D. IGBKCV

8. In a certain code QUESTION is written as NXBVQLLQ. How will REPLY be coded?
   A. YHMOV   B. OBMVI
   C. VHSOB   D. OHMOV

9. If in a certain code SKEW is coded as PNCY, then what will JXQV will stand for?
   A. MUTS   B. MUST
   C. MTSU   D. STUM

10. In a certain code LONDON is written as MPOEPO. What will IVOHSZ mean in the same code?
    A. HUNGRY   B. HUNDRY
    C. GRUNHY   D. HONDUS

11. In a certain code language 8514 is a code for HEAD, 3945 for RIDE and 057 for BEG. What will be the code for GRADE?
    A. 71345   B. 73415
    C. 74135   D. 73145

12. If MOTHERLAND is coded as 9501623748, how will DREAM be coded?
A. 82697
B. 86297
C. 82769
D. 82679

13. If OATH is coded in a certain language as TEYL, then how will WORD be coded?
A. BWRH
B. HRWB
C. BSWH
D. CSXI

14. If FINANCE is coded as GKQESIL, then how will BANK be coded in the same manner?
A. CBOL
B. CDRP
C. CCQO
D. CCPN

15. PLANNING is coded in a certain language as UFFHSCSA. How will AUTHORITY be coded in the same language?
A. FOYBTLNND
B. FYOTBNNLT
C. FBOYTLNTN
D. FBOYTNLTN

Directions : *In the following questions study the coded patterns and then select the right option from the given alternatives.*

16. In a certain language, **A.** 'go ju mi' stands for 'plenty of money'; **B.** pao ju go nei vu' for 'money creates lots of problems'; **C.** 'kol vu nei' for 'problems create tension'; and **D.** 'sol tun ju haw' for 'still money is needed'. Which of the following words stand for 'money'?
A. nei
B. ju
C. haw
D. go

17. In a certain language, **A.** 'FOR' stands for 'old is gold'; **B.** 'ROT' stands for 'gold is pure'; **C.** 'ROM' stands for 'gold is costly'. How will 'pure old gold is costly' be written?
A. TFROM
B. FOTRM
C. FTORM
D. TOMRF

18. In a certain code '415' means 'milk is hot'; '18' means 'hot soup'; and '895' means 'soup is tasty'. What number will indicate the word 'tasty'?
A. 9
B. 8
C. 5
D. 4

19. In a certain code '643' means 'she is beautiful', '593' means 'he is handsome', and '567' means 'handsome meets beautiful'. What number will indicate the word 'meets'?

A. 5
B. 3
C. 7
D. 6

20. In a certain code language, A. 'dugo hui mul zo' stands for 'work is very hard'; B. 'hui dugo ba ki' for 'Bingo is very smart'; C. 'nano mul dugo' for 'cake is hard', and D. 'mul ki qu' for 'smart and hard'. Which of the following words stand for 'Bingo'?
A. jalu
B. dugo
C. ki
D. ba

Directions : *Read the given coded information and choose the correct answer from the given options.*

21. If 'water' is called 'blue', 'blue' is called 'red', 'red' is called 'white', 'white' is called 'sky', 'sky' is called 'rain', 'rain' is called 'green', 'green' is called 'air' and 'air' is called 'table', which of the following is the colour of milk?
A. white
B. rain
C. sky
D. green

22. If 'light' is called 'dark', 'dark' is called 'green', 'green' is called 'blue', 'blue' is called 'red', 'red' is called 'white' and 'white' is called 'yellow', what is the colour of blood?
A. red
B. dark
C. white
D. yellow

23. If 'sky' is called 'sea', 'sea' is called 'water', 'water' is called 'air', 'air' is called 'cloud' and 'cloud' is called 'river', then what do we drink when thirsty?
A. sky
B. air
C. water
D. sea

24. If 'yellow' means 'red', 'white' means 'green', 'red' means 'orange', 'blue' means 'white' and 'green' means 'blue', then the colour of sky is :
A. white
B. green
C. blue
D. yellow

25. If 'land' is called 'sky', 'sky' is called 'air', 'air' is called 'water', 'water' is called 'sand' and 'sand' is called 'solid', where do fishes swim?
A. air
B. sky
C. water
D. sand

EXPLANATORY ANSWERS

1. B. : The coded number signifies the position of the alphabet in its reverse order of the alphabetical series (ZYXW...)

M   U   S   K → MUSK
↓   ↓   ↓   ↓
14th 6th 8th 16th → 146816

Similarly,

Z   E   R   O → ZERO
↓   ↓   ↓   ↓
1st 22nd 9th 12th → 122912

2. D. : The coded number is the sum of number digits signifying the position of the alphabet in the natural order.

B   A   D
↓   ↓   ↓
2nd 1st 4th *i.e.,* 2 + 1 + 4 = 7

Similarly,

H   I   S
↓   ↓   ↓
8th 9th 19th *i.e.,* 8 + 9 + 19 = 36
further, 3 + 6 = 9

Also,

L   O   W
↓   ↓   ↓
12th 15th 23rd *i.e.,* 12 + 15 + 23 = 50
further, 5 + 0 = 0

3. B. : The letters of the word TRIBAL are picked from LIBERATE. So will be the coded numbers.

L I B E R A T E → given word
5 6 4 0 3 1 7 0 → codes

Similarly,

T R I B A L → word to be coded
7 3 6 4 1 5 → answer codes

4. C. : The word is divided into two equal parts and the letters of each part are written in reverse order.

SYS TEM SYS MET NEA RER AEN RER

Similarly,

FRAC TION   CARF NOIT

5. D. : The code is formed by moving the letters one step backwards and one step forward alternately.

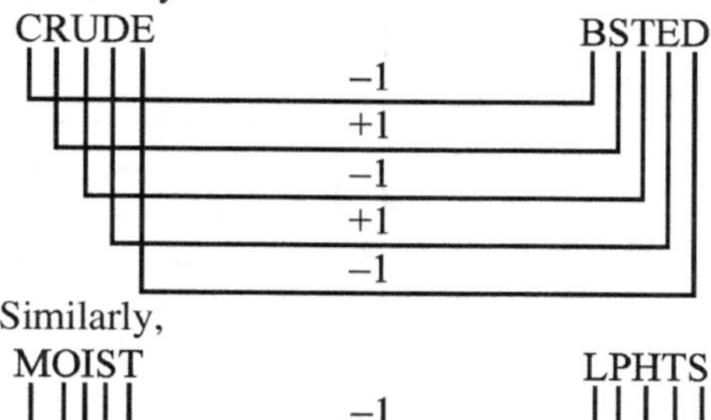

Similarly,

6. A. : The letters of the word are written backwards.

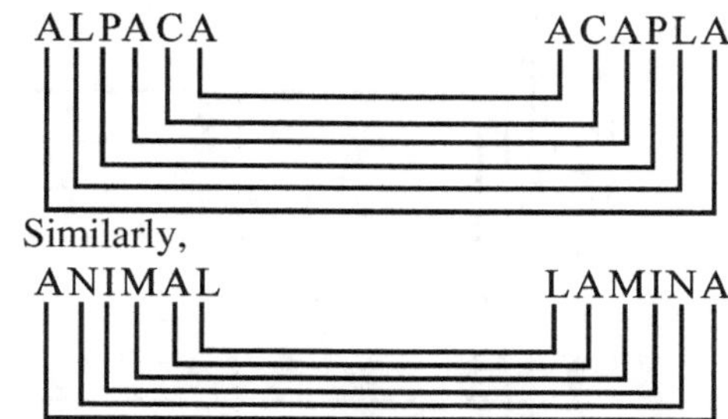

Similarly,

7. A. : The word is coded by moving the letters two steps backwards.

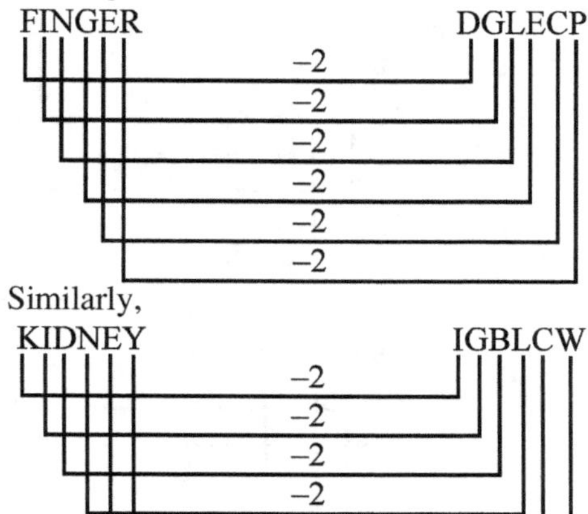

Similarly,

8. D. : The letters of the word are coded by moving three steps backward and three steps forward alternately.

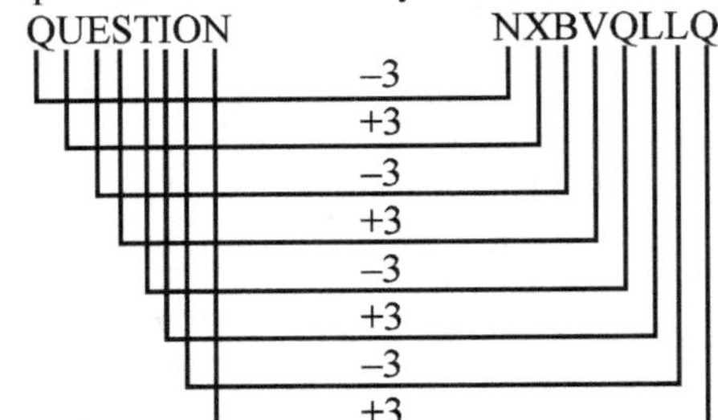

Similarly,

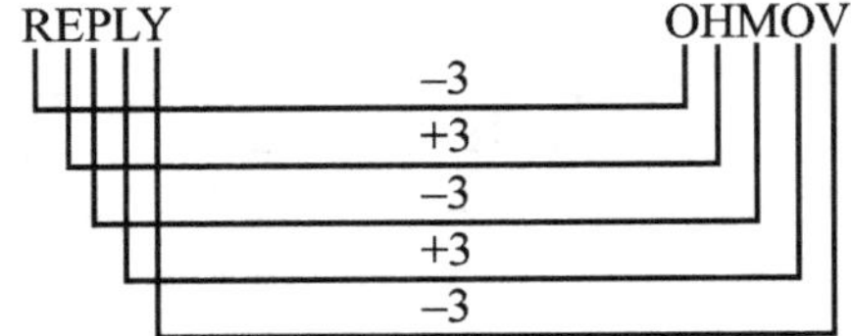

9. B. : The letters are decoded by moving the letters +3, −3, +2 and −2 steps respectively.

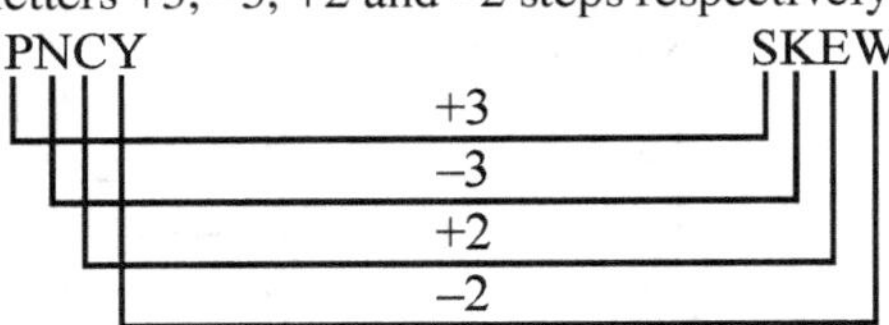

Similarly,

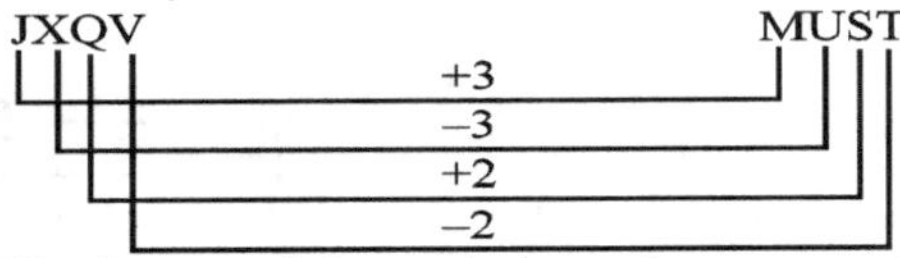

10. A. : The letters of the coded word are moved one step backward.

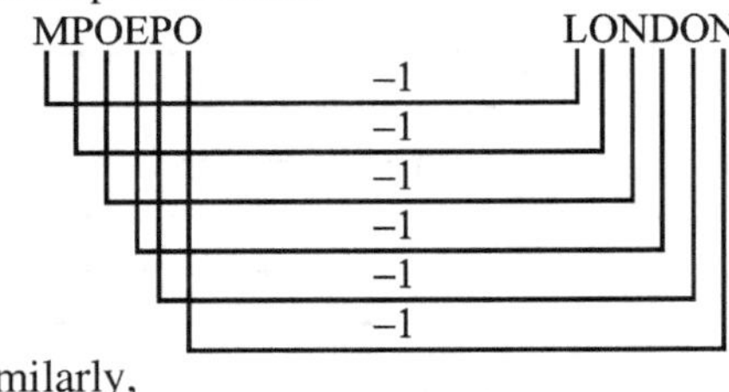

Similarly,

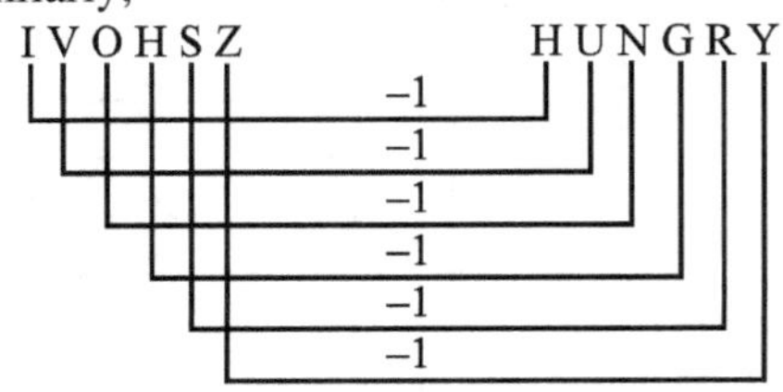

11. D. : The word GRADE is framed by letters in the given words. So, in order to find the code for GRADE select the respective number codes.

H E A D R I D E B E G → letters
8 5 1 4 3 9 4 5 0 5 7 → codes
So,
G R A D E   → letters
7 3 1 4 5   → answer codes

12. D. : The letters of the word are coded by numbers. So to find the code for DREAM select the respective numbers.

M O T H E R L A N D → letters
9 5 0 1 6 2 3 7 4 8 → codes
So, D R E A M → letters
     8 2 6 7 9 → answer codes

13. C. : The letters are coded by moving five and four steps forward alternately.

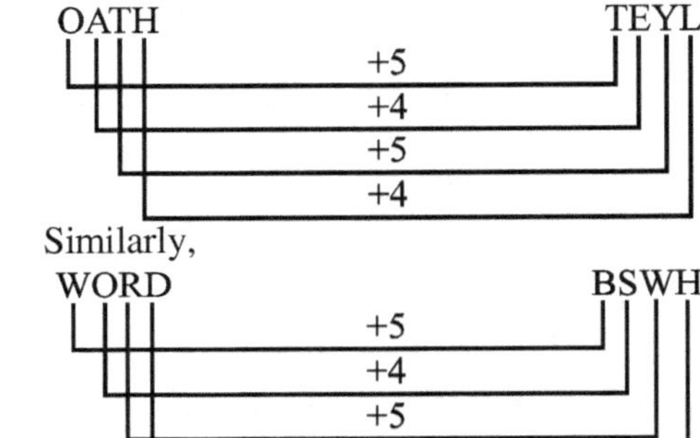

Similarly,

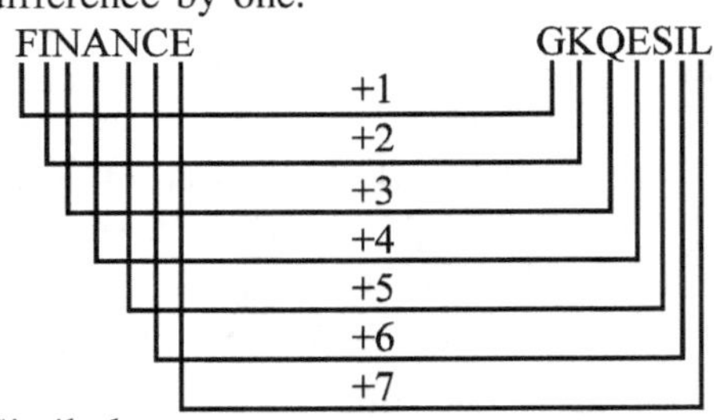

14. C. : The letters of the word are coded by moving one step ahead and increasing the difference by one.

FINANCE   GKQESIL

Similarly,

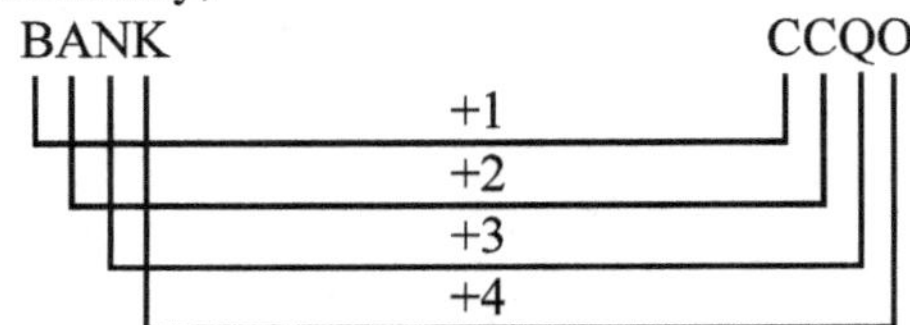

15. A. : The letters of the word are coded by moving five steps forward and six steps backward alternately.

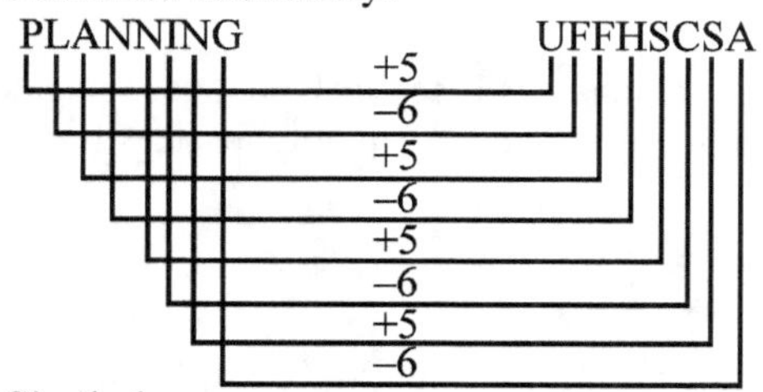

Similarly,

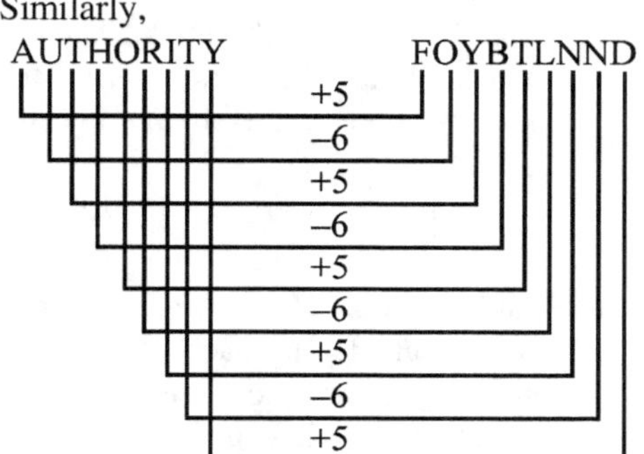

16. B. :

	Code	Sentence
1.	go *ju* mi	plenty of *money*
2.	pao *ju* go nei vu	*money* creates lots of problems
3.	kol vu nei	problems create tension
4.	sol tun *ju* haw	still *money* is needed

In 1st, 2nd and 4th codes and their sentences the word 'ju' is repeated and so is 'money'.

17. A. :

Code — Sentence

1. FOR — old is gold

2. ROT — gold is pure

3. ROM — gold is costly

Therefore,

F	stands	for	old
O	stands	for	is
R	stands	for	gold
T	stands	for	pure
M	stands	for	costly

So, 'pure old gold is costly' will be written as 'TFROM'.

18. A. :

	Code	Sentence
1.	415	milk is hot
2.	18	hot soup
3.	895	soup is *tasty*

From 3rd code and its sentence neither number '9' is repeated nor the word 'tasty'.

19. C. :

	Code	Sentence
1.	643	she is beautiful
2.	593	he is handsome
3.	567	handsome *meets* beautiful

From 3rd code and its sentence, neither number '7' nor the word 'meets' is repeated.

20. D. :

	Code	Sentence
1.	*dugo hui* mul zo	work *is very* hard
2.	*hui dugo* **ba** *ki*	**Bingo** *is very smart*
3.	nano mul *dugo*	cake *is hard*
4.	mul *ki* qu	*smart* and hard

From 2nd code and its sentence, neither 'ba' nor 'Bingo' is repeated.

(Words repeated are in italics)

21. C. : Colour of milk is 'white' and 'white' is called 'sky'.

22. C. : Colour of blood is 'red' and 'red' is called 'white'.

23. B. : We drink 'water' when we are thirsty and 'water' is called 'air'.

24. A. : Colour of sky is 'blue' and 'blue' means 'white'.

25. D. : Fishes swim in 'water' and 'water' is called 'sand'.

❑ ❑ ❑

Place Arrangement ▶▶

Place arrangement generally refers to the positioning of persons or objects in a manner indicated by set of information given. One has to understand the order of placement and then attempt questions following the given information.

EXERCISE

Directions : *In the following questions, understand the arrangement pattern and then select the right answer from the given options :*

1. Five boys are sitting in a row. Raghu is not adjacent to Shyam or Amit. Ajay is not adjacent to Shyam. Raghu is adjacent to Mayank. If Mayank is at the middle in the row, then Ajay is adjacent to whom out of the following?
   A. Amit
   B. Raghu
   C. Mayank
   D. Shyam

2. Mini is to the right of Rajni but to the left of Ananta. Saya is to the right of Mini but to the left of Jaya. Who is on the extreme left if all the girls are facing North?
   A. Jaya
   B. Mini
   C. Rajni
   D. Saya

3. O, P, Q, R, S and T are standing on a bench according to their height. P is taller than O but shorter than S. Only S is taller than T. R is shorter than P but taller than Q. Who is the shortest?
   A. O
   B. Q
   C. P
   D. Cannot be said

4. Five personalities are living in a multistoried building. Mr. Effortless lives in a flat above Mr. Active, Mr. Charge lives in a flat below Mr. Diligent, Mr. Active lives in a flat above Mr. Diligent and Mr. Behaved lives in a flat below Mr. Charge. Who lives in the topmost flat?
   A. Mr. Charge
   B. Mr. Diligent
   C. Mr. Effortless
   D. Mr. Behaved

5. Six friends are sitting in a circle and playing cards. Kenny is to the left of Danny. Michael is in-between Bob and John. Roger is in between Kenny and Bob. Who is sitting to the right of Michael?
   A. Danny
   B. John
   C. Kenny
   D. Bob

6. Four girls A, B, C and D are sitting in a circle. B and C are facing each other. Which of the following is definitely true?
   A. A is to the left of C
   B. D is to the left of C
   C. A and D are facing each other
   D. A is not between B and C

7. Brijesh, Jayesh, Amar and Praveer are playing a game of cards. Amar is to the right of Jayesh who is to the right of Brijesh. Who is to the right of Amar?
   A. Brijesh
   B. Praveer
   C. Brijesh or Praveer
   D. Jayesh

8. In a pile of 10 books there are 3 of History, 3 of Hindi, 2 of Maths, and 2 of English. Taking from above there is an English book between a History and Maths book, a History book between a Maths and an English book, a Hindi book between an English and a Maths book, a Maths book between two Hindi books, and two Hindi books between a Maths and a History book. Book of which subject is at the sixth position from the top?
   A. English
   B. Hindi
   C. History
   D. Maths

18

9. Five persons A, B, C, D and E are sitting in a row facing you such that D is on the left of C and B is on the right of E. A is on the right of C and B is on the left of D. If E occupies a corner position, then who is sitting in the centre?

A.	A	B.	B
C.	C	D.	D

10. Six friends A, B, C, D, E and F are standing in a circle. B is between F and C; A is between E and D; F is to the left of D. Who is between A and F?

A.	C	B.	B
C.	D	D.	E

11. Among five friends, A is heavier than B; C is lighter than D; B is lighter than D but heavier than E. Who among them is the heaviest?

A.	B	B.	C
C.	A	D.	Can't say

12. Pune is bigger than Jhansi, Sitapur is bigger than Chittor. Raigarh is not as big as Jhansi, but is bigger than Sitapur. Chittor is not as big as Sitapur. Which is the smallest?

A.	Jhansi	B.	Pune
C.	Chittor	D.	Sitapur

13. Ajay works more than Ram. Alok works as much as Raju. Pankaj works less than Alok. Ram works more than Alok. Who works the most of all?

A.	Ajay	B.	Ram
C.	Alok	D.	Raju

14. Among five friends P, Q, R, S and T, who is the youngest? To arrive at the answer which of the following information given in the statements (A) and (B) is sufficient?
(A) R is younger than P and T.
(B) S is younger than Q.
A. Only A alone is sufficient
B. Either A or B is sufficient
C. Both A and B together are needed
D. Both A and B together are not sufficient

15. A is elder to B while C and D are elder to E who lies between A and B. If C be elder to B, which one of the following statements is necessarily true?
A. E is elder to B
B. A is elder to C
C. C is elder to D
D. D is elder to C

EXPLANATORY ANSWERS

1. B. : The order of sitting is :
Amit, Shyam, Mayank, Ajay, Raghu
or
Ajay, Raghu, Mayank, Amit, Shyam

2. C. : The order in which the girls are positioned is :
Rajni, Mini, Ananta, Saya, Jaya
or
Saya, Jaya, Ananta
or
Saya, Ananta, Jaya

3. D. : In descending order of height, the standing positions are :

S		S
T		T
P	*or*	P
R		R
O		Q
Q		O

Either O or Q is the shortest. The information given is not enough to clarify the answer.

4. C. : The personalities living in flats in multi-storied building are in order given below :

Mr. Effortless
Mr. Active
Mr. Diligent
Mr. Charge
Mr. Behaved

5. D. : The order in which the friends are sitting is :

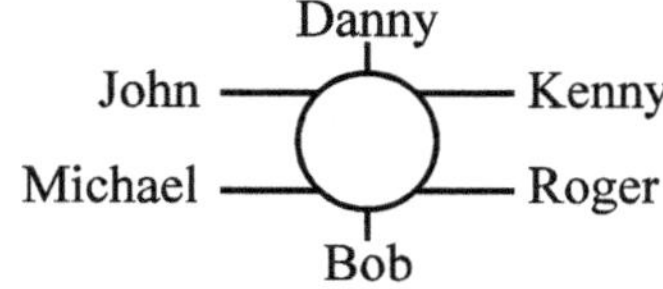

6. C. : The sitting positions are :

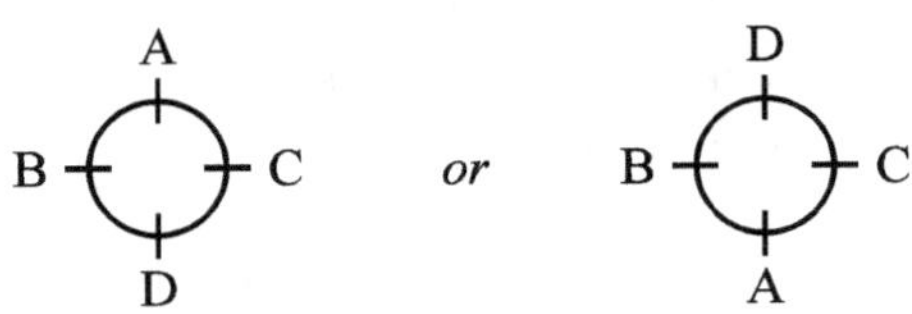

7. B. : The order from left to right is :
Brijesh, Jayesh, Amar, Praveer

8. B. : The pile of books is in the order :

1st —	History
	English
	Maths
	History
	English
6th —	Hindi
	Maths
	Hindi
	Hindi
10th —	History

9. D. : Sitting order while facing us is :
A, C, D, B, E

10. C. : The pattern of standing is :

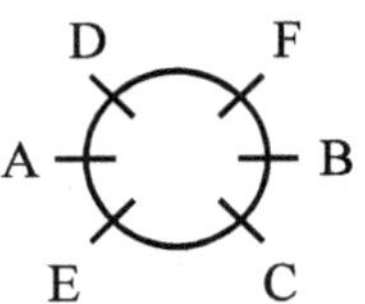

11. D. : The five friends in descending order of weight are : A/D, B/C, E or A/D, B, C/E. Either A or D is the heaviest.

12. C. : The order of cities in descending order of size is : Pune, Jhansi, Raigarh, Sitapur, Chittor.

13. A. : On the basis of doing work, the descending order will be : Ajay, Ram, Alok/Raju, Pankaj.

14. D. : Statements are not inter-related.

15. A. : The order in descending seniority will be : A/C/D, E, B.

❑ ❑ ❑

Direction Sense ▶▶

In these type of tests, the directions in questions needs to be perceived. Such questions are based on the direction chart.

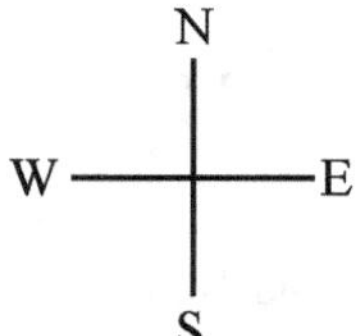

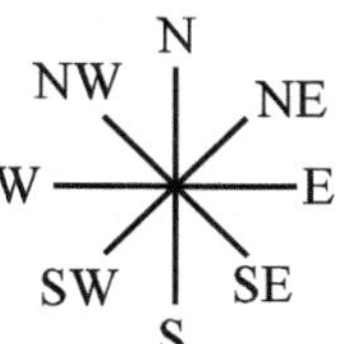

N = North S = South E = East W = West

The sense of the different directions are guided by the left and right turns or angular turns.

EXERCISE

Directions : *In the following questions, select the right answer from the given options to depict the correct direction/distance.*

1. Kittu walks towards East and then towards South. After walking some distance he turns towards West and then turns to his left. In which direction is he walking now?
   A. North
   B. South
   C. East
   D. West

2. A person is driving towards West. What sequence of directions should he follow so that he is driving towards South?
   A. left, right, right
   B. right, right, left
   C. left, left, left
   D. right, right, right

3. Richa drives 8 km to the South, turns left and drives 5 km. Again, she turns left and drives 8 km. How far is she from her starting point?
   A. 3 km
   B. 5 km
   C. 8 km
   D. 13 km

4. Dingi runs 40 km towards North then turns right and runs 50 km. He turns right and runs 30 km, and once again turns right and runs 50 km. How far is he from his starting point?
   A. 90 km
   B. 50 km
   C. 10 km
   D. 5 km

5. If North is called North-West, North-West is called West, West is called South-West and so on. What will South-East be called?
   A. East
   B. West
   C. North-East
   D. South-East

6. A man travels 100 km towards South. From there he turns right and travels 100 km and again turns right to travel 50 km. Which direction is he in from his starting point?
   A. North
   B. North-East
   C. East
   D. South-West

7. A train runs 120 km in West direction, 30 km in South direction and then 80 km in east direction before reaching the station. In which direction is the station from the train's starting point?
   A. South-West
   B. North-West
   C. South-East
   D. South

8. Facing the West direction, Priya jogs for 20 m, turns left and goes further 40 m. She turns left again and jogs for 20 m. Then she turns right to go 20 m to reach the park. How far is the park from her starting point and in which direction?
   A. 20 m South
   B. 40 m West
   C. 60 m South
   D. 100 m East

9. If all the directions are rotated, *i.e.,* if North is changed to West and East to North and so on, then what will come in place of North-West?
A. South-West
B. North-East
C. East-North
D. East-West

10. A and B start together from one point. They walk 10 km towards North. A turns left and covers 5 km whereas B turns right and covers 3 km. A turns left again and covers 15 km whereas B turns right and covers his 15 km. How far is A from B?
A. 18 km
B. 10 km
C. 5 km
D. 8 km

11. Tarun is walking towards East. What direction he should not follow if he should walk towards North?
A. right, right, left, right, right
B. right, right, left, left, left
C. right, right, right
D. right, left, right, left

12. Sony and Moni start walking from a point. Sony walks in West direction and Moni in South direction. After covering 20 km, Soni turns left and walks 15 km. Moni walks 10 km, turns left and walks 5 km. Soni, then turns left again and walks 25 km, whereas Moni turns right and walks 5 km. How far are Sony and Moni from each other?
A. 5 km

B. They are back at the starting point
C. They are at same place at the finishing point
D. Data is insufficient

13. I was walking in South-East direction. After a while I turned 90° to the right and walked ahead. Later I turned 45° to the right. In which direction am I walking now?
A. North
B. North-East
C. South-West
D. East

14. Two friends Jack and Bunny start a race, and together they run for 50 mts. Jack turns right and runs 60 mts while Bunny turns left and runs 40 mts. Then Jack turns left and runs 50 mts while Bunny turns right and runs 50 mts. How far are the two friends now from each other?
A. 60 mts
B. 100 mts
C. 20 mts
D. 150 mts

15. A policeman left his police post and proceeded south 4 km, after hearing a loud sound from point A. On reaching the place he heard another sound and proceeded 4 km to his left to the point B, only to find that the sound was coming from left of B. From B he proceeded left to reach that place 4 km away. In which direction he has to go to reach his police post?
A. North
B. South
C. East
D. West

EXPLANATORY ANSWERS

1. B. : 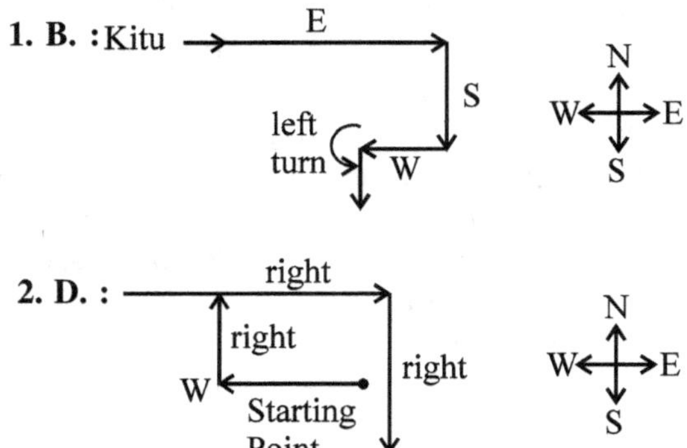

2. D. :

3. B. : 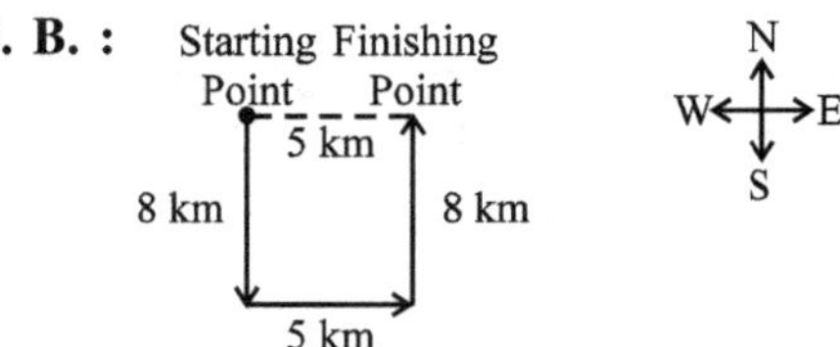

4. C. : 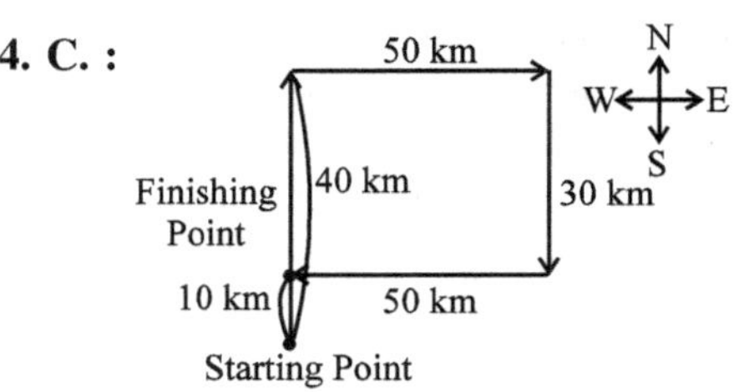

5. A. :

Original Directions

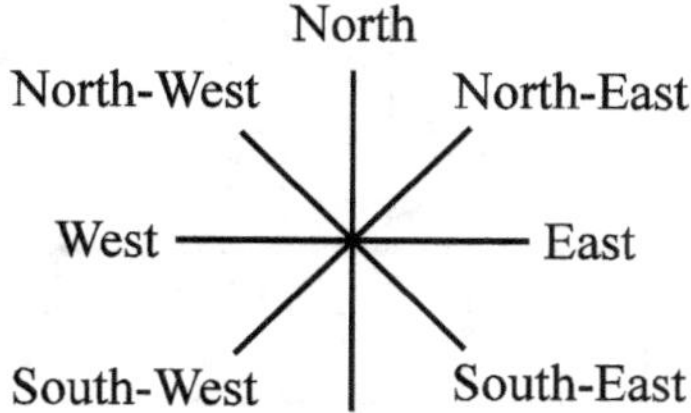

Changed Directions

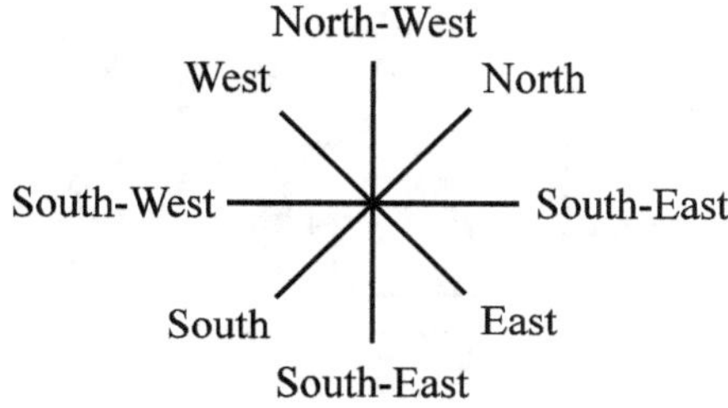

6. D. :

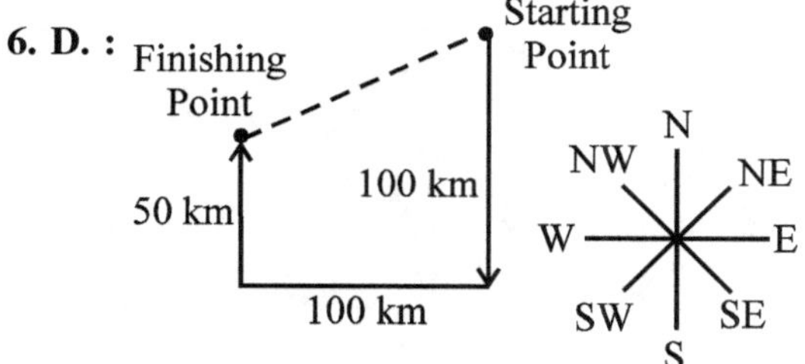

7. A. :

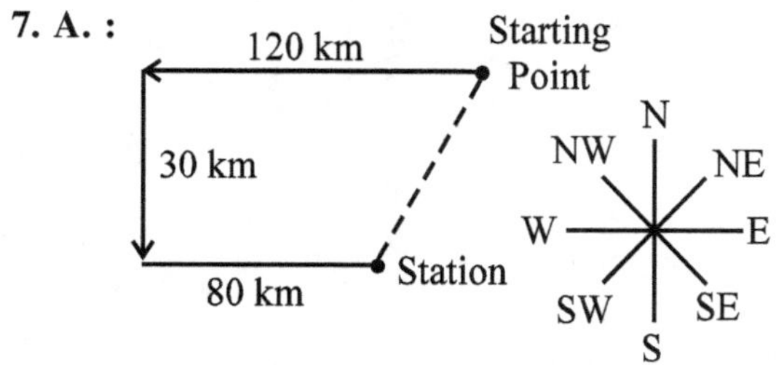

8. C. : (40 + 20) = 60 metres South

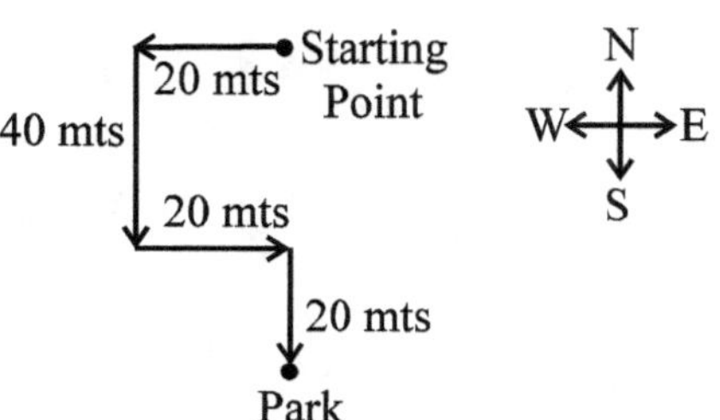

9. A. : Original Directions

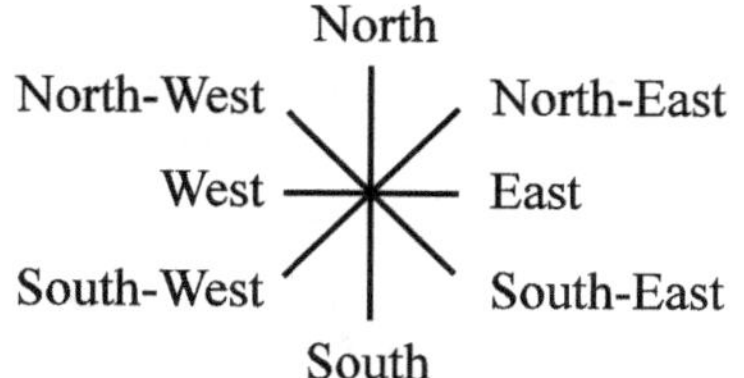

Changed Directions

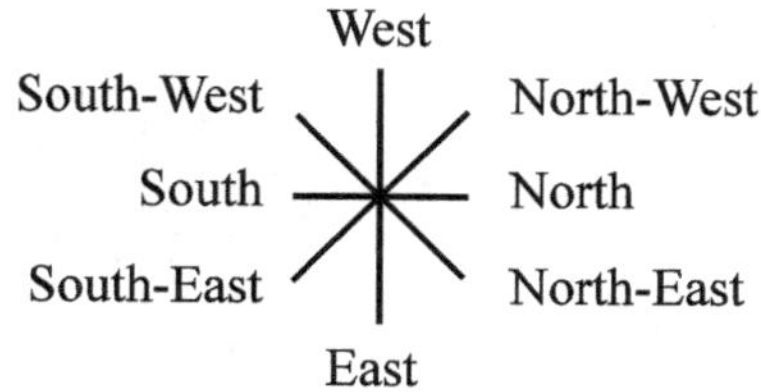

10. D. :

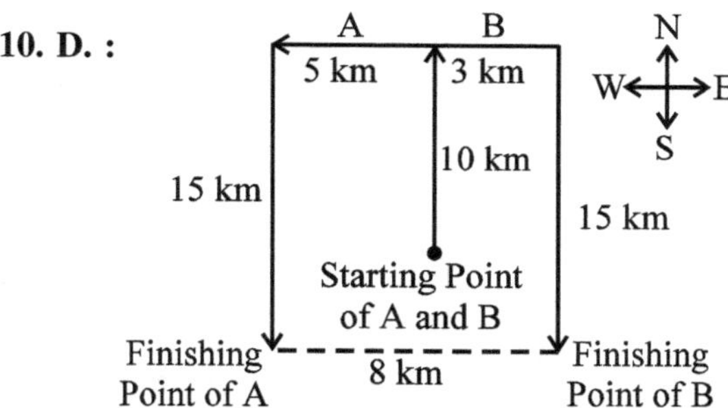

11. D. : Option A

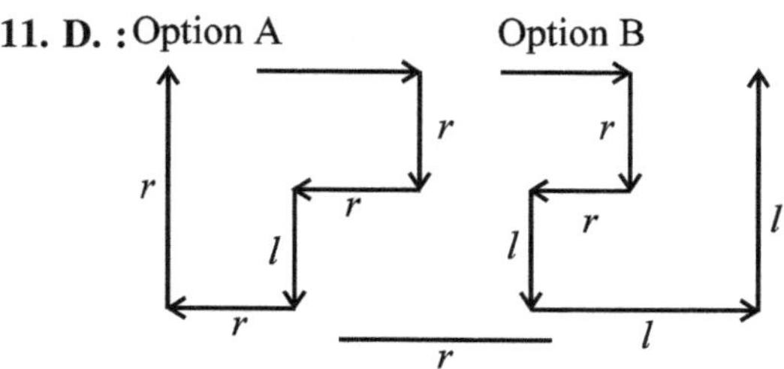

Option C   Option D

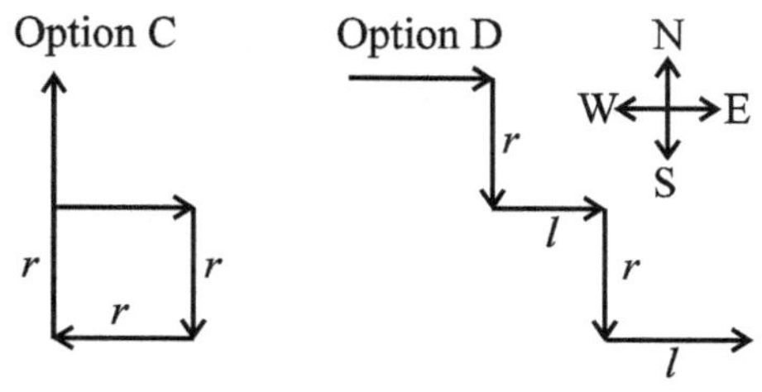

12. C. :

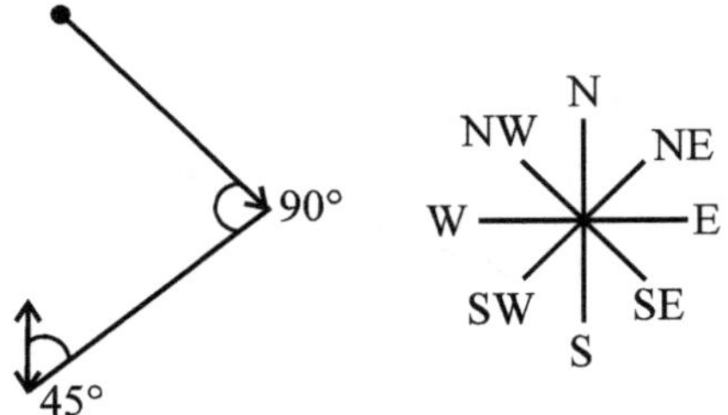

13. A. : The direction of the movement is :

14. B. : The track of both the friends is :

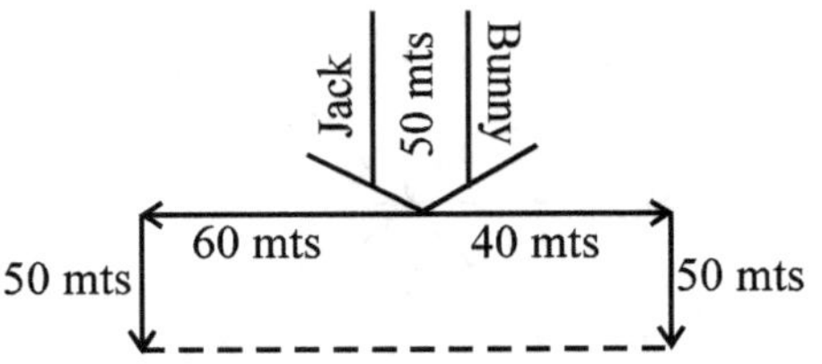

The two friends are 60 + 40 = 100 mts apart

15. D. :

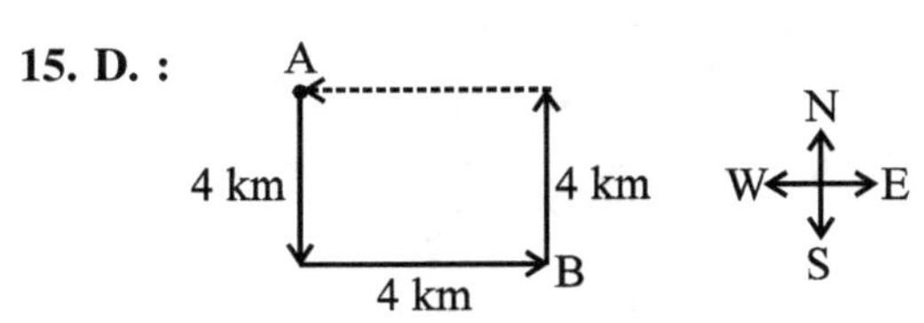

❑ ❑ ❑

Blood Relationships ▶▶

While attempting questions on blood relations, one should be clear of all the relation patterns that can exist between any two individuals. These type of questions are given mainly to test one's relationship ability.

Very well-known relations are :

Mother	Grandmother	Father	Grandfather
Son	Grandson	Daughter	Granddaughter
Brother	Brother-in-law	Sister	Sister-in-law
Niece	Father-in-law	Nephew	Mother-in-law
Uncle	Son-in-law	Aunt	Daughter-in-law
Husband	Cousin	Wife	

The patterns of some relationships which help in solving questions in these tests are :

Father's *or* Mother's Father	—	Grandfather (Paternal *or* Maternal)
Father's *or* Mother's Mother	—	Grandmother (Paternal *or* Maternal)
Father's *or* Mother's Son	—	Brother
Father's *or* Mother's Daughter	—	Sister
Father's Brother	—	Paternal Uncle
Father's Sister	—	Paternal Aunt
Mother's Brother	—	Maternal Uncle
Mother's Sister	—	Maternal Aunt
Uncle *or* Aunt's Son *or* Daughter	—	Cousin
Son's Wife	—	Daughter-in-law
Daughter's Husband	—	Son-in-law
Husband's *or* Wife's Brother	—	Brother-in-law
Husband's *or* Wife's Sister	—	Sister-in-law
Brother's Wife	—	Sister-in-law
Sister's Husband	—	Brother-in-law
Brother's Son	—	Nephew
Brother's Daughter	—	Niece

EXERCISE

Directions : *In each of the following questions keenly study the relationship mentioned between the persons, and then from the given options select the right relationship as the answer.*

1. A lady said, "The person standing there is my grandfather's only son's daughter". How is the lady related to the standing person?
A. Sister
B. Mother
C. Aunt
D. Cousin

2. Ajay is the brother of Vijay. Mili is the sister of Ajay. Sanjay is the brother of Rahul and Mehul is the daughter of Vijay. Who is Sanjay's Uncle?
A. Rahul
B. Ajay
C. Mehul
D. Data inadequate

3. A man introduced the boy coming with him as "He is son of the father of my wife's daughter". What relation did the boy bear to the man?
A. Son-in-law
B. Son
C. Brother
D. Father

4. If Amit's father is Billoo's father's only son and Billoo has neither a brother nor a daughter, what is the relationship between Amit and Billoo?
   A. Uncle — Nephew
   B. Father — Daughter
   C. Father — Son
   D. Cousins

5. Pointing to a woman in the photograph a man said, "She is the daughter of my grand-mother's only son. How is the woman related to the man?
   A. Mother   B. Daughter
   C. Sister-in-law   D. Sister

6. Pointing to a photograph, a woman said, "She is the only daughter of my mother's father." How is the woman related to the person in the photograph?
   A. Mother
   B. Grandmother
   C. Daughter
   D. Cannot be determined

7. Ram is the brother of Shyam and Mahesh is the father of Ram. Jagat is the brother of Priya and Priya is daughter of Shyam. Who is the uncle of Jagat ?
   A. Shyam   B. Mahesh
   C. Ram   D. Data insufficient

8. Introducing a man, a woman said, "His wife is the only daughter of my father". How is the man related to the woman?
   A. Husband   B. Father
   C. Father-in-law   D. Brother

9. If Maya is the only daughter of Richa's grandmother's brother, how is Maya's daughter related to Richa?
   A. Niece   B. Cousin
   C. Aunt   D. Mother

10. Pointing to a woman, a man said, "Her husband's mother is the wife of my father's only son". How is the man related to the woman?
   A. Son   B. Brother-in-law
   C. Uncle   D. Father-in-law

EXPLANATORY ANSWERS

1. A. : Grand father

Lady's grandfather's son is lady's father and father's daughter will only be lady's sister.

2. D. : 1. Mili ——→ Ajay ——→ Vijay
   (sister)   (brother) ↓
                Mehul
   2. Sanjay ——→ Rahul   (daughter)
      (brother)

There are two sets of relationship. Information given is incomplete and no relation can be established between the two sets.

3. B. : The relationship chart based on problem is:

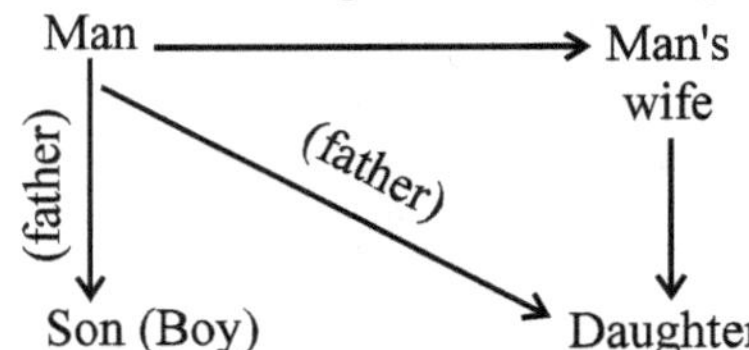

'Father of the man's wife's daughter' is the man himself and the boy in question is the man's son.

4. C. : The relationship chart based on problem is :

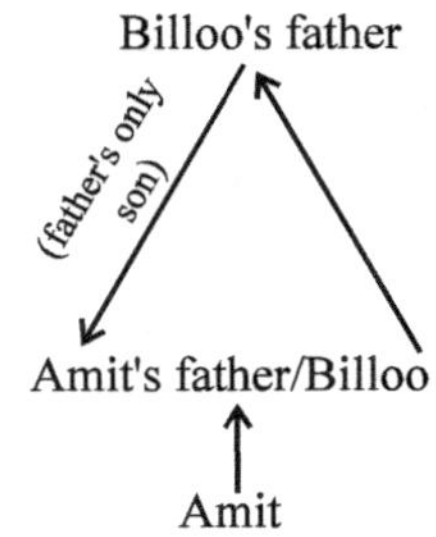

Amit's father is Billoo's father's only son means Billoo is the only son in question also, he is the father of Amit. It must be noted that Billoo has no brother which means he is single and also, when he has no daughter, Amit is his only son.

5. D. :

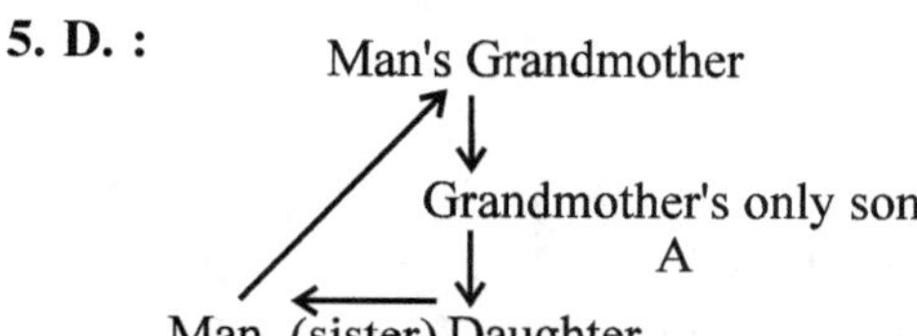

'My grandmother's only son' is the father of the man, and 'daughter of my grand-mother's only son' is the sister of the man.

6. C. :

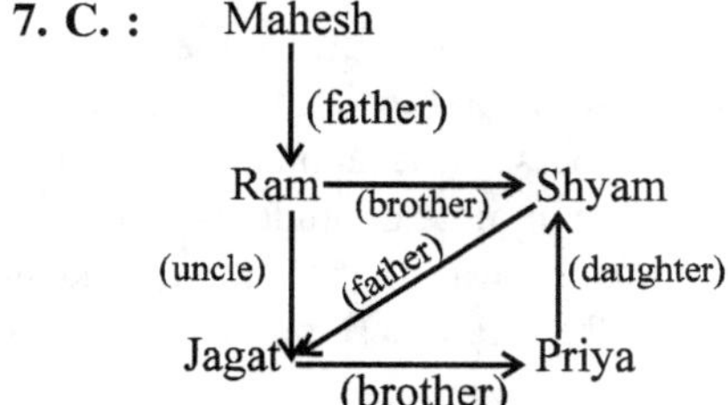

'Only daughter of my mother's father' is the person in the photograph and she is also the mother of the woman. So, the woman is the daughter of the person in the photo-graph.

7. C. :

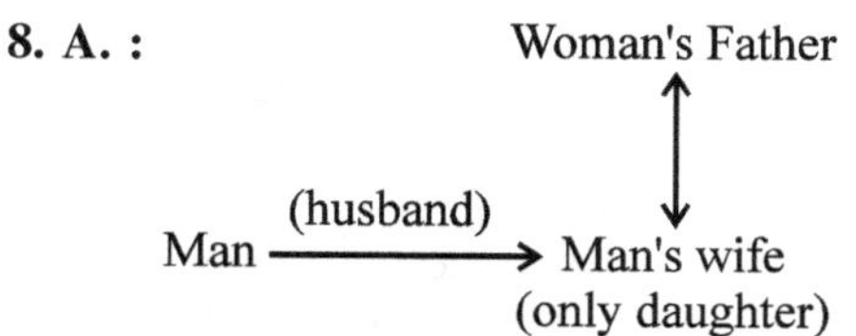

Jagat is brother of Priya and Priya is daughter of Shyam. So Shyam is also the father of Jagat. Ram is the brother of Shyam. So, Jagat's father's brother Ram is the uncle of Jagat.

8. A. :

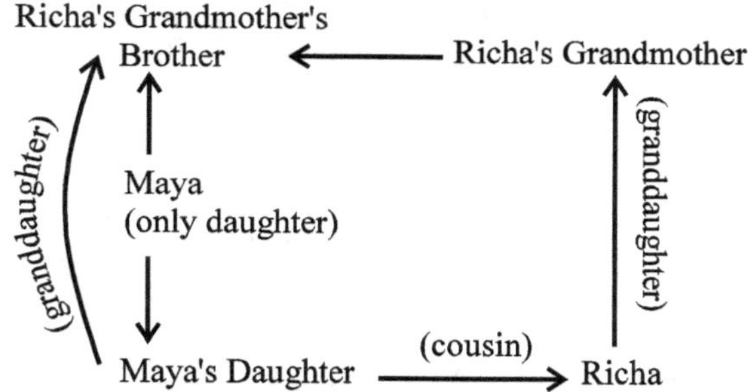

'Only daughter of my father' is the woman herself and the man is her husband.

9. B. :

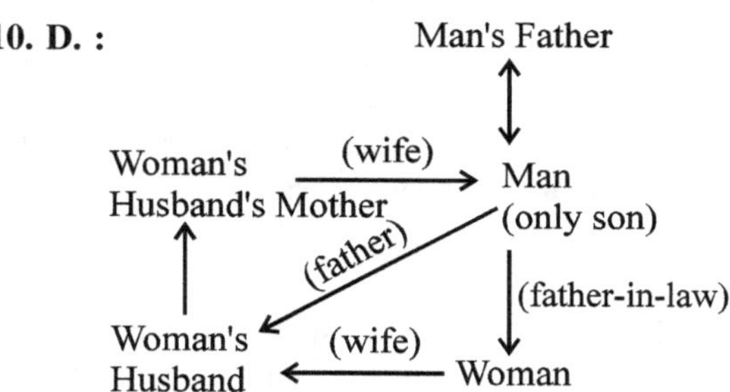

Both Maya's Daughter and Richa are granddaughters of a brother and a sister respectively. So Maya's daughter is the cousin of Richa.

10. D. :

'My father's only son' is the man himself. 'Her husband's mother' is the wife of the man and so the man is the father of the woman's husband. As the woman is the wife of man's son, the man is the father-in-law of the woman.

Rows and Ranks ▶▶

These type of problems need easy calculations to find out the number of objects in a row, lane or queue or to find a person's rank in a class of certain number of students; or to find the total number of students.

EXERCISE

1. In a row of trees, one tree is fifth from either end of the row. How many trees are in the row?
   A. 11
   B. 8
   C. 10
   D. 9

2. Jaya ranks 5th in a class of 53. What is her rank from the bottom in the class?
   A. 49th
   B. 48th
   C. 47th
   D. 50th

3. Mohan ranks twenty-first in a class of sixty-five students. What will be his (Mohan's) rank if the lowest candidate is assigned rank 1?
   A. 44th
   B. 45th
   C. 46th
   D. Data inadequate

4. If Rahul finds that he is 12th from the right in a line of boys and 4th from the left, how many boys should be added to the line such that there are 28 boys in the line?
   A. 12
   B. 14
   C. 20
   D. 13

5. In a row of boys, Rajan is tenth from the right and Suraj is tenth from the left. When Rajan and Suraj interchange their positions, Suraj will be twenty-seventh from the left. Which of the following will be Rajan's position from the right?
   A. Tenth
   B. Twenty-sixth
   C. Twenty-ninth
   D. None of these

6. Mahesh and Suresh are ranked 11th and 12th respectively from the top in a class of 41 students. What will be their respective ranks from the bottom?
   A. 32nd and 33rd
   B. 29th and 30th
   C. 30th and 31st
   D. 31st and 30th

7. Uma ranked 8th from the top and 37th from bottom in a class. How many students are there in the class?
   A. 47
   B. 46
   C. 45
   D. None of these

8. In a queue, Sadiq is 14th from the front and Joseph is 17th from the end, while Jane is in between Sadiq and Joseph. If Sadiq be ahead of Joseph and there be 48 persons in the queue, how many persons are there between Sadiq and Jane?
   A. 5
   B. 6
   C. 7
   D. 8

9. Rohan ranked eleventh from the top and twenty-seventh from the bottom among the students who passed the annual examination in a class. If the number of students who failed in the examination was 12, how many students appeared for the examination?
   A. 48
   B. 49
   C. 50
   D. Cannot be determined

10. Some boys are sitting in a row. P is sitting fourteenth from the left and Q is seventh from the right. If there are four boys between P and Q, how many boys are there in the row?
    A. 19
    B. 21
    C. 25
    D. 23

EXPLANATORY ANSWERS

1. (d):

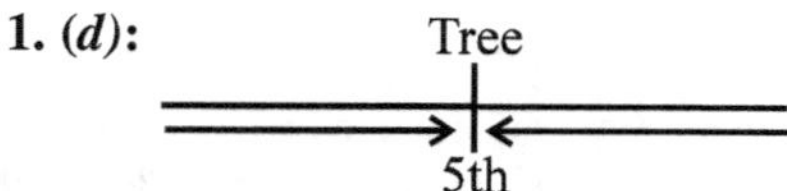

Total number of trees in the row are :

$(5 + 5) - 1 = 9$.

2. A. :

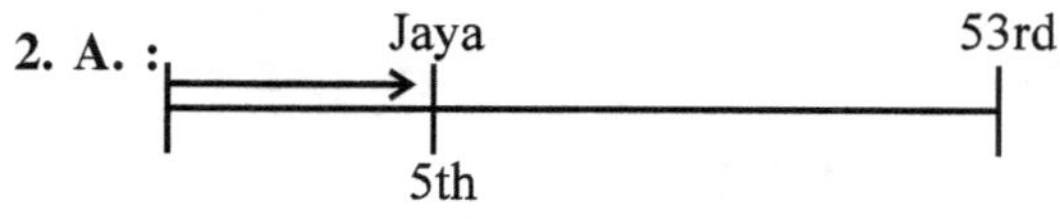

Jaya's rank from the bottom is :

$(53 - 5) + 1 = 49$th.

3. B. :

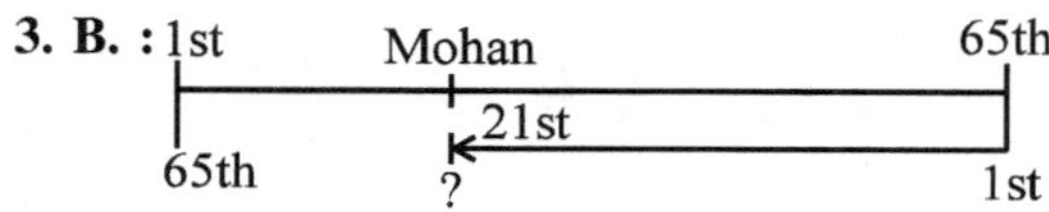

Note : Mohan's rank from the last or the question asked means the same.

Mohan's rank is $(65 - 21) + 1 = 45$th.

4. D. :

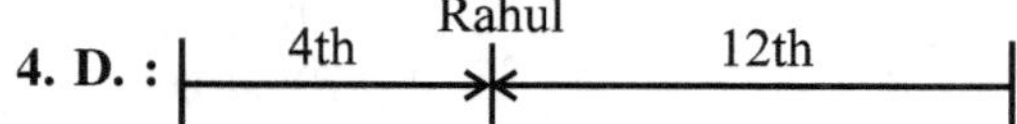

The number of boys in the line are :

$(4 + 12) - 1 = 15$

To make a line of 28 boys, $(28 - 15)$ *i.e.* 13 more boys are needed.

5. D. :

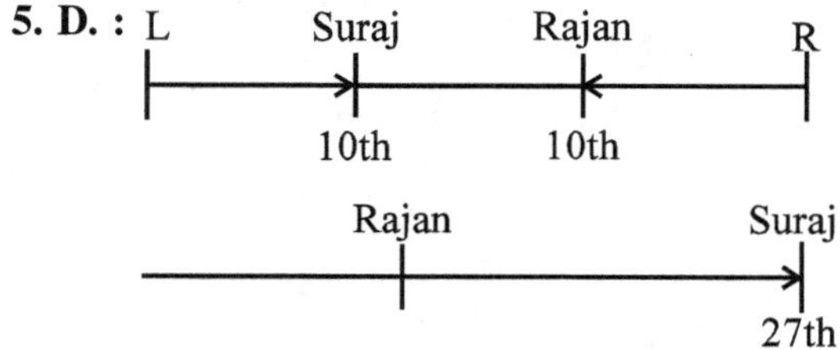

As the position of boys is equal from both ends, Rajan will also be 27th from the right after changing positions.

6. D. :

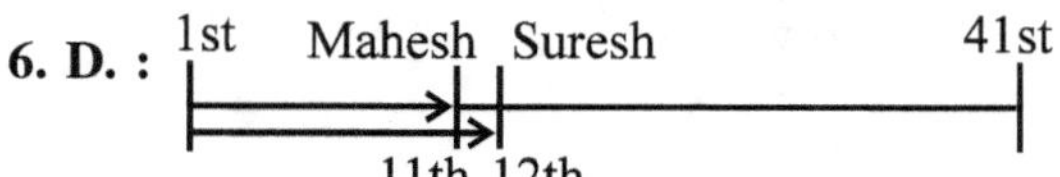

Mahesh's position from bottom is :

$(41 - 11) + 1 = 31$st

Suresh's position from bottom is :

$(41 - 12) + 1 = 30$th.

7. D. :

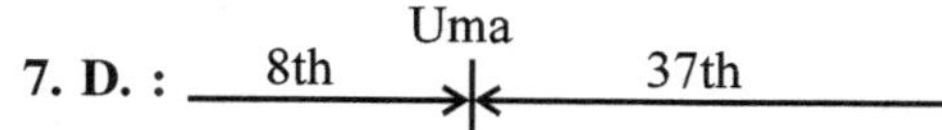

Total number of students in the class are :

$(8 + 37) - 1 = 44$.

8. D. :

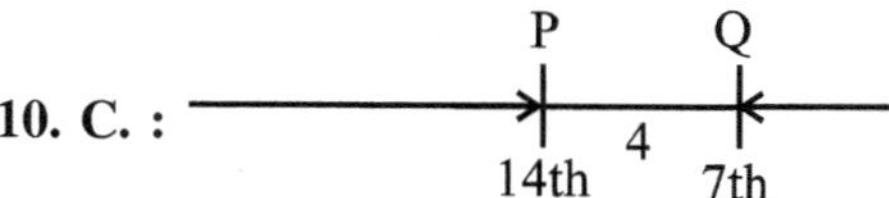

Sadiq's position from front : 14th

Joseph's position from last :

17th or $48 - 17 + 1 = 32$nd from front.

Middle postion between Sadiq & Joseph

$$= \frac{(32 - 14)}{2} + 14 = 23 \text{ rd.}$$

Hence, Jane position is 23rd from front

Person between Sadiq & Jane

$= 23 - 14 - 1 = 8$.

9. B. :

Number of students who passed the examination $(11 + 27) - 1 = 37$

Those who failed $= 12$

Total number of students who appeared in the examination $= 37 + 12 = 49$.

10. C. :

The number of boys in the row are :

$(14 + 4 + 7) = 25$.

❑ ❑ ❑

Permutations and Combinations ▶▶

In these type of questions, the only factor essential is alertness. In every question, a word is given. By using the letters of this given word the options are formed. The candidates are required to find from the given options the word *(i)* which cannot be formed by using the letters of the given word or *(ii)* which can be formed by using the letters of the given word.

EXERCISE

Directions : *Find out the one word among the options which cannot be formed by using the letters of the word as given in each question.*

1. ROTATION
- A. TORN
- B. NOTE
- C. TART
- D. RAIN

2. PHILOSOPHY
- A. SOIL
- B. SHIP
- C. SOLO
- D. SPIN

3. SLAVATION
- A. INJURY
- B. CADDY
- C. DICY
- D. ACRID

4. ACADEMY
- A. DEMY
- B. MACE
- C. DIRE
- D. MADE

5. INCOGNITO
- A. GOING
- B. INACTION
- C. IGNITION
- D. TONGO

6. JUDICIARY
- A. INJURY
- B. CADDY
- C. DICY
- D. ACRID

7. DOCTRINE
- A. CRUST
- B. DOCTOR
- C. TIRED
- D. CREED

8. EDUCATED
- A. DATE
- B. CUTE
- C. EAST
- D. DUCT

9. INSUFFICIENT
- A. ENTICE
- B. SCENT
- C. SUFFICE
- D. THENCE

10. DECEMBER
- A. REDEEM
- B. DECREE
- C. BRACED
- D. MEMBER

11. FUGITIVE
- A. EXIT
- B. FIVE
- C. GIVE
- D. GIFT

12. CATASTROPHE
- A. TASTE
- B. CHEAP
- C. POUCH
- D. STARE

13. TORRENTIAL
- A. TRAIL
- B. MENTAL
- C. LEARN
- D. RETAIL

14. INFRASTRUCTURE
- A. RAPTURE
- B. INSECURE
- C. CRAFTS
- D. STRUCTURE

15. RECOMMEND
- A. MEND
- B. ROME
- C. CANE
- D. OMEN

Directions : *Find out the one word among the options which can be formed by using the letters of the word as given in each question.*

16. INVESTIGATE
- A. INVERT
- B. GLIDE
- C. STING
- D. ACTED

17. MAJORITY
- A. MORE
- B. JURY
- C. READ
- D. TRAY

18. WATERMELON
- A. MAKER
- B. WRITE
- C. TOWER
- D. NOVEL

19. PREDICTION
- A. DESIRE
- B. CREDIT
- C. ACTION
- D. PICKED

20. BARGAIN
- A. GRAIN
- B. BARGE
- C. ANGRY
- D. TRING

21. THERMOSTAT
- A. MOTHER
- B. STAMEN
- C. THRUST
- D. HOIST

22. LEARNED
- A. DREAM
- B. CLEAR
- C. ELDER
- D. DRAPE

23. ADVENTURE
- A. AWARE
- B. EVENT
- C. TRUCE
- D. DRIED

24. THANKSGIVING
- A. AVENGE
- B. HAUNTS
- C. GRAINS
- D. SAVING

25. NOCTURNAL
- A. CRUST
- B. TRAIL
- C. CORAL
- D. OCEAN

ANSWERS

1	2	3	4	5	6	7	8	9	10
B	D	A	C	B	A	A	C	D	C
11	**12**	**13**	**14**	**15**	**16**	**17**	**18**	**19**	**20**
A	C	B	A	C	C	D	C	B	A
21	**22**	**23**	**24**	**25**					
A	C	B	D	C					

❑ ❑ ❑

Symbol Substitution 

Questions in these category are easy to attempt. Candidates must be quick in substituting symbols and calculations. The common pattern of questions asked are given below.

EXERCISE

1. If "+" means "–"; "–" means "×"; "×"means "÷" and "÷" means "+", then
$15 \times 5 \div 10 + 5 – 3 = ?$
   A. 9.5 B. 0
   C. – 2 D. 24

2. If "+" means "×"; "–" means "÷"; "÷"means "+" and "×" means "–", then what will be the value of $20 \div 40 – 4 \times 5 + 6 = ?$
   A. 60 B. 1.67
   C. 150 D. 0

3. If × stands for addition, < for subtraction, + stands for division, > for multiplication, – stands for equal to, ÷ for greater than, and = stands for less than, state which of the following is true?
   A. $5 \times 3 < 7 \div 8 + 4 \times 1$
   B. $3 \times 4 > 2 – 9 + 3 < 3$
   C. $5 > 2 + 2 = 10 < 4 \times 8$
   D. $3 \times 2 < 4 \div 16 > 2 + 4$

4. If → stands for subtract, ← stands for add, •↑↑ stands for multiply, ↓↓ stands for divide, ↔ for greater than, ⟷ stands for equal to, then which of the following alternatives is true?
   A. $4 \leftarrow 6 \uparrow\uparrow 2 \longleftrightarrow 3 \rightarrow 12 \leftarrow 12$
   B. $10 \downarrow\downarrow 5 \uparrow\uparrow 5 \longleftrightarrow 9 \rightarrow 3 \leftarrow 4$
   C. $15 \uparrow\uparrow 2 \rightarrow 5 \longleftrightarrow 12 \downarrow\downarrow 4 \leftarrow 3$
   D. $13 \downarrow\downarrow 13 \leftarrow 1 \leftrightarrow 20 \rightarrow 5 \uparrow\uparrow 2$

5. If Δ denotes =; + denotes >, – denotes <, □ denotes ≠, × denotes > and ÷ denotes < then
a + b – c denotes
   A. b Δ c □ a
   B. b □ a ÷ c
   C. a ÷ b × c
   D. b – a + c

6. If '✻' denotes 'x', 'Δ' denotes '÷', '□' denotes '–', '•' denotes '+', 'α' denotes '=' and 'β' denotes ≠, then which of the following euations is correct?
   A. 2 □ 10 ✻ 4 Δ 5 α 5 • 12 Δ 6
   B. 27 Δ 9 • 6 β 3 ✻ 6 □ 9
   C. 4 Δ 2 ✻ 0 α 7 Δ 1 ✻ 0
   D. 5 • 6 Δ 3 □ 2 α 8 Δ 4 ✻ 3

7. If ↓ stands for '÷', ↑ stands for 'x', → stands for '+' and ← stands for '–', then
$25 \downarrow 5 \rightarrow 3 \uparrow 6 \leftarrow 8 = ?$
   A. 9 B. 12
   C. 16 D. 15

8. If the + and × signs of the following equations are interchanged, which will be the correct equation?
   A. $7 \times 5 + 3 = 20$ B. $4 + 9 \times 1 = 42$
   C. $6 \times 5 + 8 = 46$ D. $2 + 11 \times 4 = 28$

9. If '+' stands for multiplication, 'x' stands for addition, '÷' stands for subtraction and '–' stands for division, then what will be the result of the following equation?
$7 \times 4 \div 10 \times 2 + 5 = ?$
   A. 7 B. 0
   C. 11 D. 15

10. If 'A' means '÷', 'B' means '+', 'C' means 'x' and 'D' means '–', then
12 C 4 A 24 D 10 B 1 = ?
   A. $11\dfrac{1}{3}$ B. 23
   C. – 7 D. $16\dfrac{4}{5}$

EXPLANATORY ANSWERS

1. C. : $15 \div 5 + 10 - 5 \times 3$

$3 + 10 - 15 = -2$

2. D. : $20 + 40 \div 4 - 5 \times 6$

$20 + 10 - 30 = 0$

3. C. : A. $5 + 3 - 7 > 8 \div 4 + 1$

         $1 > 3$

     B. $3 + 4 \times 2 = 9 \div 3 - 3$

         $11 = 0$

     C. $5 \times 2 \div 2 < 10 - 4 + 8$

         $5 < 14$

     D. $3 + 2 - 4 > 16 \times 2 \div 4$

         $1 > 8$

4. B. : A. $4 + 6 \times 2 = 3 - 12 + 12$

         $16 = 3$

     B. $10 \div 5 \times 5 = 9 - 3 + 4$

         $10 = 10$

     C. $15 \times 2 - 5 = 12 \div 4 + 3$

         $25 = 6$

     D. $13 \div 13 + 1 > 20 - 5 \times 2$

         $2 > 10$

5. D. : What is given is $a > b < c$

The equations are :

     A. $b = c \ne a$ which is wrong

     B. $b \ne a < c$ which is wrong

     C. $a < b > c$ which is wrong

     D. $b < a > c$ which is correct

Therefore, D. is the answer.

6. C. : The solved equations will be :

     A. $2 - 10 \times 4 \div 5 = 5 + 12 \div 6$

         $2 - 8 = 5 + 2$

         $-6 = 7$

         which is wrong

     B. $27 \div 9 + 6 \ne 3 \times 6 - 9$

         $3 + 6 \ne 18 - 9$

         $9 \ne 9$

         which is wrong

     C. $4 \div 2 \times 0 = 7 \div 1 \times 0$

         $2 \times 0 = 7 \times 0$

         $0 = 0$

         which is correct

     D. $5 + 6 \div 3 - 2 = 8 \div 4 \times 3$

         $5 = 6$

         which is wrong

7. D. : $25 \div 5 + 3 \times 6 - 8$

$5 + 18 - 8 = 15$

8. C. : After interchanging the signs the equations are :

     A. $7 + 5 \times 3 = 22$ which is wrong

     B. $4 \times 9 + 1 = 37$ which is wrong

     C. $6 + 5 \times 8 = 46$ which is correct

     D. $2 \times 11 + 4 = 26$ which is wrong

9. C. : $7 + 4 - 10 + 2 \times 5$

$7 + 4 - 10 + 10 = 11$

10. C. : $12 \times 4 \div 24 - 10 + 1$

$2 - 10 + 1 = -7$

❑ ❑ ❑

Missing Numbers ▶

Playing with numbers and mathematical skills are needed to attempt these type of tests. The candidates have to work out the right combination of arithmetical symbols to arrive at the answer options which will take the place of the interrogation sign in the given questions.

EXERCISE

Directions: *In each question given below which one number can be placed at the sign of interrogation?*

1. 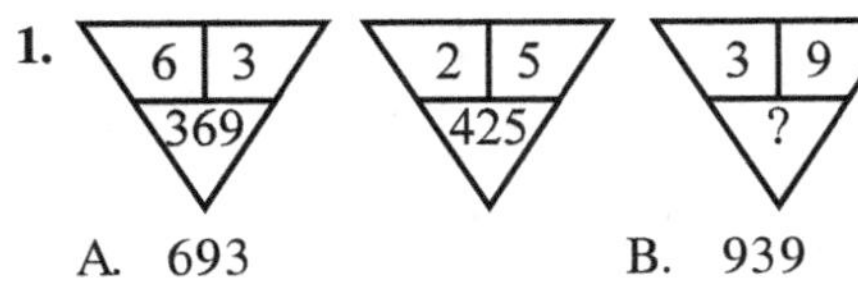

A. 693
C. 981
B. 939
D. 993

2. 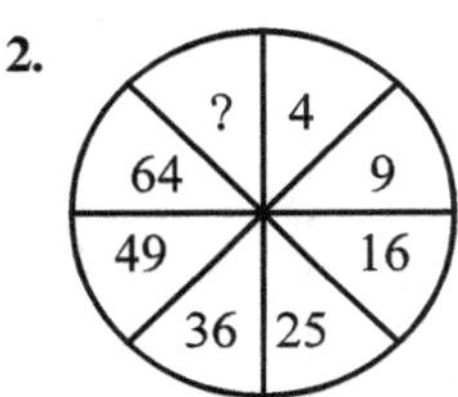

A. 68
C. 72
B. 100
D. 81

3. 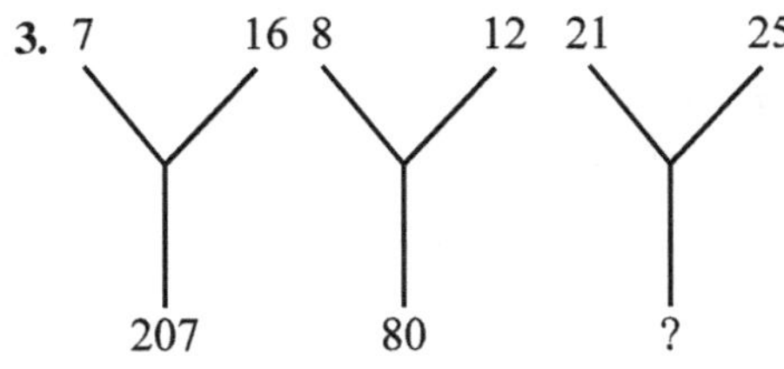

A. 425
C. 241
B. 184
D. 210

4. 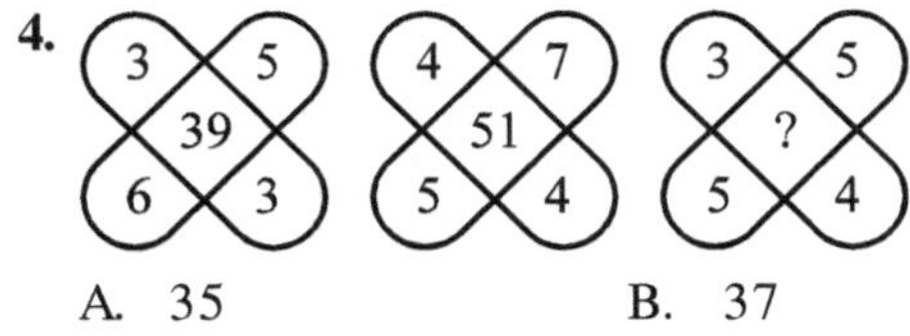

A. 35
C. 45
B. 37
D. 48

5. 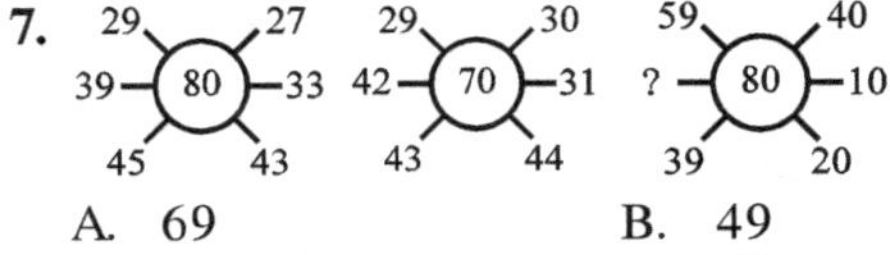

A. 4
C. 20
B. 8
D. 14

6.

14	9	4
12	7	2
10	5	0
16	11	?

A. 9
C. 3
B. 6
D. 7

7. 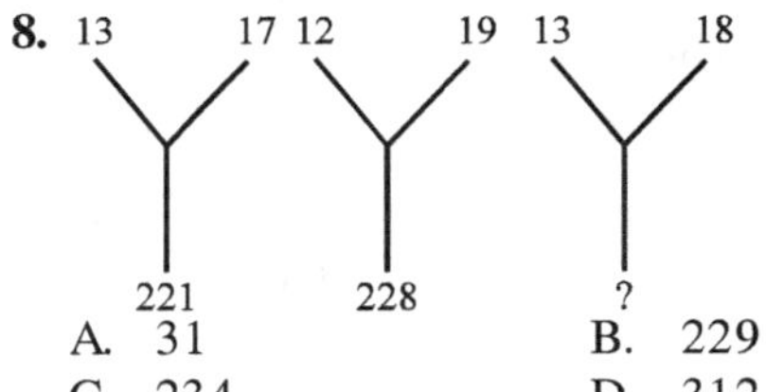

A. 69
C. 50
B. 49
D. 60

8. 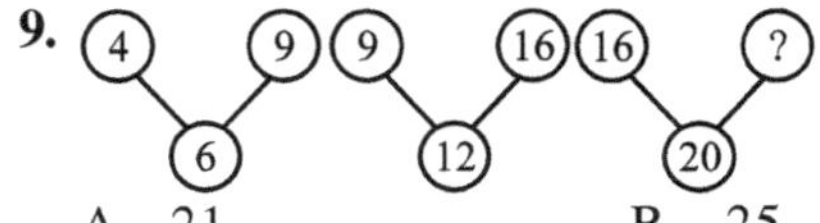

A. 31
C. 234
B. 229
D. 312

9. (4) (9)(9) (16)(16) (?) / (6) (12) (20)

A. 21
C. 50
B. 25
D. 60

10.

51	(11)	61
64	(30)	32
35	(?)	43

A. 25
C. 32
B. 27
D. 37

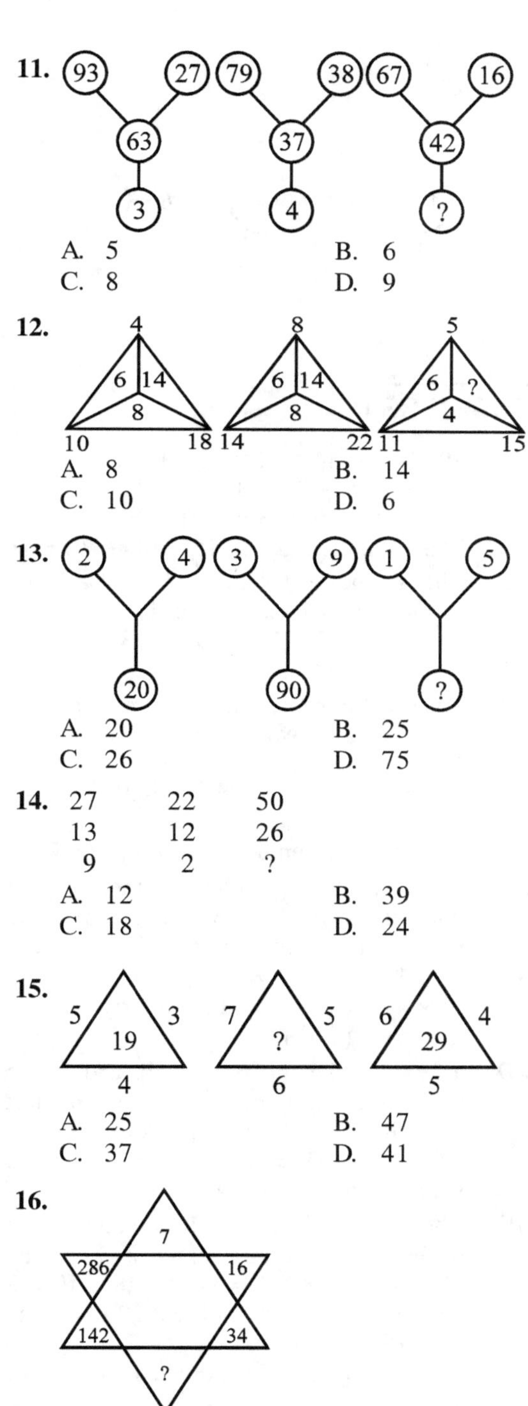

11.

A. 5   B. 6
C. 8   D. 9

12.

A. 8   B. 14
C. 10   D. 6

13.

A. 20   B. 25
C. 26   D. 75

14.

27	22	50
13	12	26
9	2	?

A. 12   B. 39
C. 18   D. 24

15.

A. 25   B. 47
C. 37   D. 41

16.

A. 70   B. 68
C. 56   D. 92

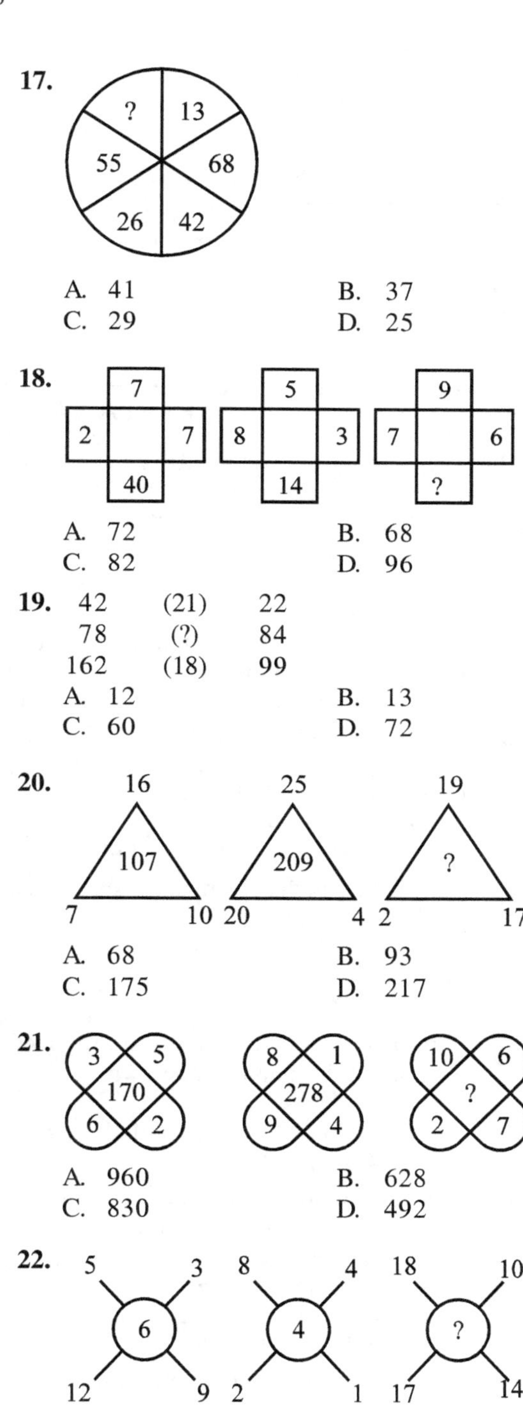

17.

A. 41   B. 37
C. 29   D. 25

18.

A. 72   B. 68
C. 82   D. 96

19.

42	(21)	22
78	(?)	84
162	(18)	99

A. 12   B. 13
C. 60   D. 72

20.

A. 68   B. 93
C. 175   D. 217

21.

A. 960   B. 628
C. 830   D. 492

22.

A. 18   B. 10
C. 36   D. 24

23.

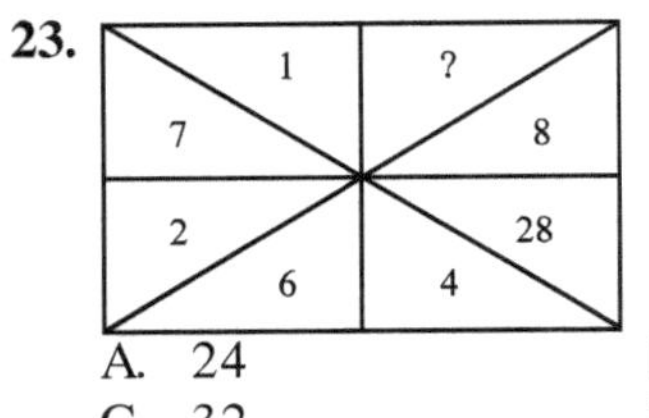

A. 24 B. 10
C. 32 D. 12

24.

6	(40)	4
3	(12)	3
7	(?)	2

A. 51 B. 36
C. 22 D. 4

25.

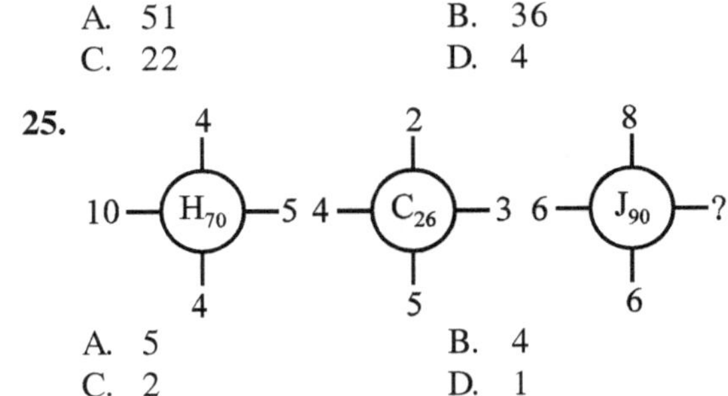

A. 5 B. 4
C. 2 D. 1

EXPLANATORY ANSWERS

1. C. : The squares of two numbers on the top placed side by side gives the number inside the bottom triangle, *i.e.*,
$$6^2 \text{ and } 3^2 = 369$$
$$2^2 \text{ and } 5^2 = 425, \text{ similarly}$$
$$3^2 \text{ and } 9^2 = 981.$$

2. D. : Starting from number 4 the numbers are the squares of numbers in natural order *i.e.*, $2^2 = 4$, $3^2 = 9$, $4^2 = 16 \ldots \ldots 9^2 = 81$.

3. B. : The number at the bottom is the difference of the squares of two numbers at the top, *i.e.*, $16^2 - 7^2 = 256 - 49 = 207$
$$12^2 - 8^2 = 144 - 64 = 80, \text{ similarly}$$
$$25^2 - 21^2 = 625 - 441 = 184.$$

4. B. : The number in the centre is the sum of the products of diagonal numbers, *i.e.*,
$$(3 \times 3) + (5 \times 6) = 39$$
$$(4 \times 4) + (7 \times 5) = 51, \text{ similarly}$$
$$(3 \times 4) + (5 \times 5) = 37.$$

5. D. : Sum of two numbers on the top divided by 2 gives the third number, *i.e.*,
$$(7 + 5) \div 2 = 6$$
$$(5 + 21) \div 2 = 13, \text{ similarly}$$
$$(24 + 4) \div 2 = 14.$$

6. B. : The numbers in 2nd and 3rd columns are 5 less than the nunbers in 1st and 2nd columns respectively, *i.e.*,
$$14 - 5 = 9 \text{ and } 9 - 5 = 4$$
$$12 - 5 = 7 \text{ and } 7 - 5 = 2, \ldots \text{ similarly}$$
$$16 - 5 = 11 \text{ and } 11 - 5 = 6.$$

7. A. : The sum of 3 numbers in each line in one figure is same, *i.e.*,
$$29 + 80 + 43 \text{ or } 39 + 80 + 33$$
$$\text{or } 45 + 80 + 27 = 152$$
$$29 + 70 + 44 \text{ or } 42 + 70 + 31$$
$$\text{or } 43 + 70 + 30 = 143, \text{ similarly}$$
$$59 + 80 + 20 \text{ or } 39 + 80 + 40 = 159.$$
The missing number is : $159 - (80 + 10) = 69$.

8. C. : The number at the bottom is the product of two numbers at the top, *i.e.*,
$$13 \times 17 = 221; 12 \times 19 = 228, \text{ similarly}$$
$$13 \times 18 = 234.$$

9. B. : Square of number at the bottom is equal to the product of two numbers at the top, *i.e.*,
$$6^2 = 4 \times 9, \textit{ i.e., } 36$$
$$12^2 = 9 \times 16, \textit{ i.e., } 144, \text{ similarly}$$
$$20^2 = 16 \times ?, \textit{ i.e., } 400.$$
The missing number is $400 \div 16 = 25$.

10. B. : The sum of the products of the digits of numbers in 1st and 3rd columns is the number in the 2nd column, *i.e.*,
$$(5 \times 1) + (6 \times 1) = 11$$
$$(6 \times 4) + (3 \times 2) = 30, \text{ similarly}$$
$$(3 \times 5) + (4 \times 3) = 27.$$

11. D. : The sum of numbers on right and centre subtracted from the number on the left gives the number at the bottom, *i.e.*,
$$93 - (27 + 63) = 3; 79 - (38 + 37) = 4,$$
similarly $67 - (16 + 42) = 9$.

12. C. : The number inside each triangle is the difference of the numbers at its base *i.e.*
$$10 - 4 = 6, 18 - 4 = 14 \text{ and } 18 - 10 = 8$$
$$14 - 8 = 6, 22 - 8 = 14 \text{ and } 22 - 14 = 8,$$
similarly
$$11 - 5 = 6, 15 - 5 = 10 \text{ and } 15 - 11 = 4.$$

13. C. : The sum of squares of two numbers at the top gives the third number below, *i.e.*,
$$2^2 + 4^2 = 20$$

$3^2 + 9^2 = 90$, similarly
$1^2 + 5^2 = 26$.

14. A. : The sum of numbers in 1st and 2nd column plus 1 is the number in the 3rd column, *i.e.,* $27 + 22 + 1 = 50$
$$13 + 12 + 1 = 26, \text{ similarly}$$
$$9 + 2 + 1 = 12.$$

15. D. : The product of numbers on either side of the triangle plus the number at the base is the number inside the triangle, *i.e.,*
$$(5 \times 3) + 4 = 19$$
$$(6 \times 4) + 5 = 29, \text{ similarly}$$
$$(7 \times 5) + 6 = 41.$$

16. A. : Clockwise starting from number 7, the next number is obtained by doubling the number and adding 2, *i.e.,*
$$(7 \times 2) + 2 = 16$$
$$(16 \times 2) + 2 = 34 \ldots, \text{ similarly}$$
$$(34 \times 2) + 2 = 70$$
$$(70 \times 2) + 2 = 142$$
$$(142 \times 2) + 2 = 286.$$

17. C. : The difference between the numbers in opposite sectors is 13, *i.e.,*
$26 - 13 = 13$; $68 - 55 = 13$, similarly
The missing number is $42 - 13 = 29$
$(42 + 13 = 55$ is not given as option).

18. B. : The number at the bottom is obtained by subtracting the sum of two numbers in the centre grid line from the square of the number at the top, *i.e.,*
$$7^2 - (2 + 7) = 40$$
$$5^2 - (8 + 3) = 14, \text{ similarly}$$
$$9^2 - (7 + 6) = 68.$$

19. B. : The number inside the brackets is obtained by multiplying the number on the left by 2 and then dividing the product by the sum of digits of number on the right, *i.e.,*
$$(42 \times 2) \div (2 + 2) = 21$$
$$(162 \times 2) \div (9 + 9) = 18, \text{ similarly}$$
$$(78 \times 2) \div (8 + 4) = 13.$$

20. A. : Subtracting the sum of squares of two numbers at the base from the square of number at the apex gives the number inside the triangle, *i.e.,*
$$16^2 - (7^2 + 10^2) = 107$$

$25^2 - (20^2 + 4^2) = 209$, similarly
$19^2 - (2^2 + 17^2) = 68$.

21. C. : The number in the centre is the product of all the 4 numbers minus 10, *i.e.,*
$$(3 \times 5 \times 2 \times 6) - 10 = 170$$
$$(8 \times 1 \times 4 \times 9) - 10 = 278, \text{ similarly}$$
$$(10 \times 6 \times 7 \times 2) - 10 = 830.$$

22. D. : The number inside the circle is the product of difference of two numbers above and difference of two numbers below, *i.e.,*
$$(5 - 3)(12 - 9) = 6$$
$$(8 - 4)(2 - 1) = 4, \text{ similarly}$$
$$(18 - 10)(17 - 14) = 24.$$

23. A. : Starting from number 1 anticlockwise the number in the diagonally opposite section is its multiplication by 4, *i.e.,*
$$1 \times 4 = 4, \; 7 \times 4 = 28,$$
$$2 \times 4 = 8,$$
similarly $\quad 6 \times 4 = 24$.

24. A. : Square of the number on the left plus the number on the right is the number within brackets, *i.e.,* $\quad 6^2 + 4 = 40$
$$3^2 + 3 = 12, \text{ similarly}$$
$$7^2 + 2 = 51.$$

25. B. : Letter H is 8th in order of alphabetical series. Taking the sum of numbers placed vertically outside the circle + 8; multiplying it by the number on the right; then subtracting from the product the number on the left, gives the number inside the circle, *i.e.,*
Step I $\quad\rightarrow\quad 4 + 8 + 4 = 16$
Step II $\quad\rightarrow\quad 16 \times 5 = 80$
Step III $\rightarrow\quad 80 - 10 = 70$
Letter C is 3rd in order, so
Step I $\quad\rightarrow\quad 2 + 3 + 5 = 10$
Step II $\quad\rightarrow\quad 10 \times 3 = 30$
Step III $\rightarrow\quad 30 - 4 = 26$
Similarly, J is 10th in order, so
Step I $\quad\rightarrow\quad 8 + 10 + 6 = 24$
Step II $\quad\rightarrow\quad 24 \times ?$
Step III $\rightarrow (24 \times ?) - 6 = 90$
Simplifying the above equation :
$$24 \times ? = 90 + 6, i.e., 96$$
$$? = 96 \div 24 = 4.$$

Alphabet problems are fun to attempt. They are based on alphabetical series in natural as well as reverse order.

Natural Order

A B C D E F G H I J K L M N O P Q R S T U V W X Y Z

Reverse Order

Z Y X W V U T S R Q P O N M L K J I H G F E D C B A

Note : The series starts from A on reaching Z and from Z on reaching A. Of these A E I O U are vowels and the rest are consonants.

EXERCISE

1. Which letter should be ninth letter to the left of ninth letter from the right if the first half of the alphabet is reversed?
   A. I   B. D
   C. F   D. E

2. Starting from the fifth letter from the left, if twelve letters are written in reverse order, then which letter will be the seventh to the left of the fourteenth letter from the right?
   A. N   B. H
   C. L   D. O

3. What letter will come in the centre of sixth letter from the right and thirteenth letter from the left?
   A. Q   B. R
   C. P   D. S

4. If in the word "DISTURBANCE", the first letter is interchanged with the last letter, the second letter is interchanged with the tenth letter and so on, which letter would come after the letter "T" in the newly formed word?
   A. I
   B. U
   C. N
   D. S

5. If it is possible to make a meaningful word with the third, the fifth, the seventh and the tenth letters of the word PROJECTION. If no such word can be made, give 'O' as the answer.

If more than one such word can be made, give 'M' as the answer.
   A. T   B. N
   C. O   D. M

6. A meaningful word is made if we take the first, fourth, fifth, seventh, tenth, eleventh and the twelfth letters of the word "FELICITA-TIONS". Which of the following will be the fifth letter of that word from the right end of that word?
   A. T   B. C
   C. N   D. I

7. On rearranging the jumbled spelling of the word SKARTINS, a language is obtained. What is the fifth letter from the right of the rearranged word?
   A. N   B. K
   C. R   D. S

8. If the 1st, 3rd, 5th, 7th, 10th and 13th letters of the word "ENTERTAINMENT" are used to make a meaningful word, then what two letters will come in the centre?
   A. A M   B. T T
   C. R E   D. N A

9. On rearranging the jumbled spelling of the word GRUBY a sport is obtained. What is the letter in the centre?
   A. R   B. B
   C. G   D. U

10. If the letters 'ERVSECI' can be rearranged to form a meaningful word what will be the fifth letter from the right?

A. R

B. V

C. E

D. None of these

11. From the word HASTEN how many independent meaningful English words can be made without changing the order of the letters and using each letter only once?

A. 1   B. 2

C. 3   D. 4

EXPLANATORY ANSWERS

1. D. : 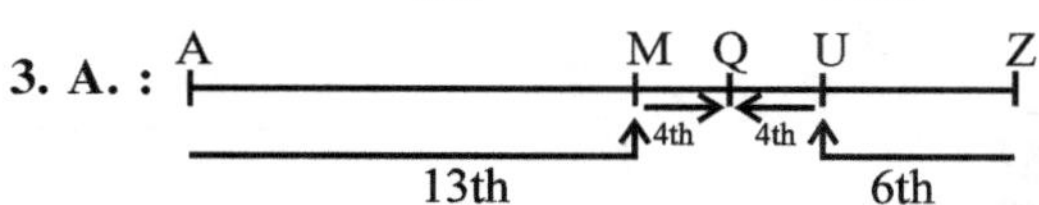
MLKJIGHFEDCBANOPQRSTUVWXYZ
          9th   9th

2. D. : ABCDPONMLKJIHGFEQRSTUVWXYZ
     7th   14th

3. A. :
A   M Q U   Z
           4th   4th
    13th   6th

13th letter from left is 'M' and 6th letter from right is 'U'. The letter in the centre of 'M' and 'U' is 'Q'.

4. D. : E C N A B R U T S I D

5. D. : P R O J E C T I O N

The 3rd, 5th, 7th and 10th letters are OETN.

The words formed are TONE and NOTE.

6. B. : F E L I C I T A T I O N S

The 1st, 4th, 5th, 7th, 10th, 11th and 12th lettes are FICTION.

The word is FICTION and 5th letter from right is 'C'.

7. D. : The word is SANSKRIT and 5th letter from right is 'S'.

8. B. : E N T E R T A I N M E N T

The 1st, 3rd, 5th 7th, 10th and 13th letters are ETRAMT.

The word formed is MATTER.

9. C. : The sport is RUGBY. The letter in the centre is 'G'.

10. A. : The word is SERVICE and fifth letter from right is 'R'.

11. B. : The words formed are : HAS, TEN.

❑ ❑ ❑

These are mathematical problem based on calculations of time by a clock or calendar and computations of speed or distances.

SOLVED EXAMPLE

1. If day-after-tomorrow is Sunday, what was day-before-yesterday?
   A. Wednesday   B. Thursday   C. Friday   D. Saturday
   E. None of the above
   Ans. A. :

Day-after-tomorrow	—	Sunday
Tomorrow	—	Saturday
Today	—	Friday
Yesterday	—	Thursday
Day-before-yesterday	—	Wednesday

EXERCISE

1. If the day before yesterday was Thursday, when will Sunday be?
   A. Tomorrow
   B. Day after tomorrow
   C. Today
   D. Two days after today
   E. None of these

2. If the seventh day of a month is three (3) days earlier than Friday, what day will it be on the nineteenth day of the month?
   A. Sunday   B. Monday
   C. Wednesday   D. Friday
   E. Tuesday

3. Radha remembers that her father's birthday is after 16th but before 21st of March, while her brother Mangesh remembers that his father's birthday is before 22nd but after 19th of March. On which date is the birthday of their father?
   A. 19th   B. 20th
   C. 21st   D. Cannot be determined
   E. None of these

4. A man is three (3) years older than his wife and four (4) times as old as his son. If the son attains an age of fifteen (15) years after three (3) years, what is the present age of the mother?
   A. 60 years   B. 51 years
   C. 48 years   D. 45 years
   E. 65 years

5. A clock is so placed that at 12 noon its minute hand points towards north-east. In which direction does its hour hand point at 1.30 P.M.?
   A. East   B. West
   C. North   D. South
   E. None of these

6. If in the above question clock is turned through an angle of 135° in an anticlockwise direction, in which direction will its minute hand point at 8.45 P.M.?
   A. East   B. West
   C. North   D. South
   E. None of these

7. Manoj left home for the bus stop 15 minutes earlier than the usual time. It takes 10 minutes to reach the stop. He reached the stop at 8.40 a.m. What time does he usually leave home for the bus stop?
   A. 8.30 a.m.   B. 8.55 a.m.
   C. 8.45 p.m.   D. Data inadequate
   E. None of these

8. Mamuni went to the movies nine days ago. She goes to the movies only on Thursday. What day of the week is today?
A. Sunday
B. Tuesday
C. Thursday
D. Saturday
E. Friday

9. If Thursday was the day after the day before yesterday five days ago, what is the least number of days ago when Sunday was three days before the day after tomorrow?

A. Two days ago
B. Three days ago
C. Four days ago
D. Five days ago
E. None of these

10. If the third day of a month is Monday, which of the following will be the fifth day from 21st of that month?
A. Tuesday
B. Monday
C. Wednesday
D. Thursday
E. None of these

EXPLANATORY ANSWERS

1. A. : Thursday — Day-before-yesterday

Friday — Yesterday

Saturday — Today

Sunday — Tomorrow

2. A. : 7th day is 3 days earlier than Friday so, 10th day is Friday, so also is 17th.

∴ 19th day will be 2nd day ahead of Friday, *i.e.*, Sunday.

3. B. : Father's birthday

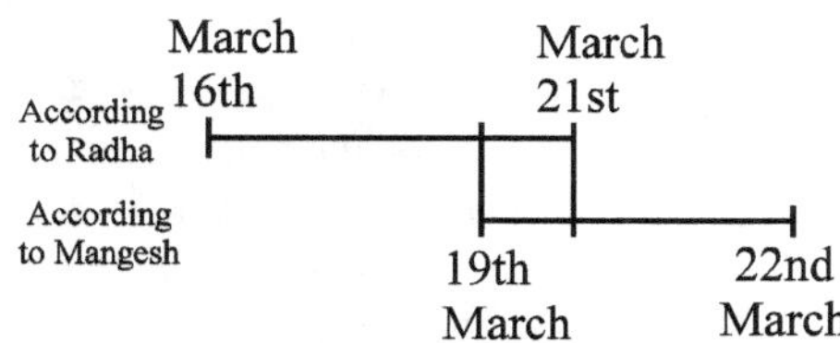

∴ Their father's birthday is on 20th March.

4. D. : Present age of son is 15-3 = 12 years. Age of the man is 4 times the age of son, *i.e.*,

12 × 4 = 48 years

Man is 3 years elder to his wife/son's mother.

So Age of the mother is 48 – 3 = 45 years

5. A. :

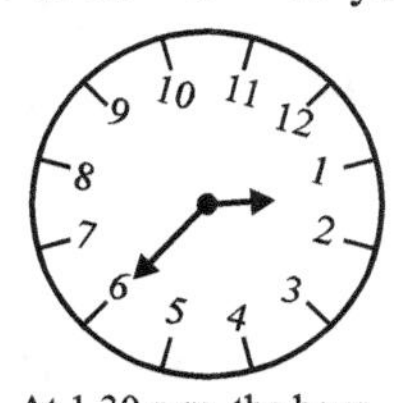

At 12 noon   At 1.30 p.m. the hour hand will point towards East.

6. D. :

After rotating the clock in earlier question, its minute hand will point towards South at 8:45 p.m.

7. E. : Manoj reached the bus stop at 8.40 a.m. He left his home at 8:40 – 10 minutes = 8:30 a.m. He left 15 minutes earlier than usual, so his actual time of leaving home is 8:30 am + 15 minutes = 8:45 a.m.

8. D. : Mamuni goes to the movies on Thursday, so nine days ago was Thursday.

∴ Two days ago was also Thursday. So, today is Saturday.

9. A. : Day after the day-before-yesterday five days ago is the 6th day which is Thursday. And so, the 3rd day will be Sunday. Three days before the day-after-tomorrow is Yesterday which is the 1st day of the five days. So, two days ago was Sunday.

10. C. : 3rd day of the month is Monday

5th day from 21st is 26th

26 – 3 = 23 days

23 days later, 23/7 leaves 2 days.

So, two days ahead of Monday will be Wednesday.

Syllogism ▶▶

In this reasoning pattern, the two premises are followed by two conclusions drawn from them. Five options *(a)*, *(b)*, *(c)*, **D.** and **E.** are given as answers. Based on the two statements the candidate has to select the right option as answer.

EXERCISE

Directions: *In each question below are given two statements followed by two conclusions numbered I and II. You have to take the two given statements to be true even if they seem to be at variance from commonly known facts and then decide which of the given conclusions logically follows from the two given statements, disregarding commonly known facts. Read both the statements and—*

Give answer A. if only conclusion I follows;

Give answer B. if only conclusion II follows;

Give answer C. if either I or II follows;

Give answer D. if neither I nor II follows and

Give answer E. if both I and II follows.

1. Statements   *I :* All tomatoes are red.
                II : All grapes are tomatoes.
    Conclusions *I :* All grapes are red.
                II : Some tomatoes are grapes.

2. Statements   *I :* All painters are smilling.
                II : Some authors are painters.
    Conclusions *I :* All smiling authors are painters.
                II : Some authors are smiling.

3. Statements   *I :* All peons in this office are efficient.
                II : Ramu is not efficient.
    Conclusions *I :* Ramu is not peon in this office.
                II : Ramu should be more efficient.

4. Statements   *I :* All weavers are hard working.
                II : No hard working men are foolish.
    Conclusions *I :* No weavers are foolish.
                II : Some foolish are weavers.

5. Statements   *I :* All fishes are cars.
                II : All cars are vegetables.
    Conclusions *I :* Some vegetables are cars.
                II : Some vegetables are fishes.

6. Statements   *I :* Some dogs are pups.
                II : All horses are pups.
    Conclusions *I :* Some dogs are horses.
                II : Some horses are dogs.

7. Statements   *I :* All beautiful women are mothers.
                II : All mothers are understanding.
    Conclusions *I :* All beautiful women are understanding.
                II : All mothers are beautiful women.

8. Statements   *I :* Some toys are tables.
                II : No table is black.
    Conclusions *I :* Some toys are black.
                II : Some toys are not black.

9. Statements   *I :* All rivers are mountains.
                II : Some rivers are deserts.
    Conclusions *I :* Some mountains are deserts.
                II : Some deserts are not mountains.

10. Statements   *I :* All men are horses.
                II : All horses are elephants.
    Conclusions *I :* All men are elephants.
                II : All elephants are men.

EXPLANATORY ANSWERS

1. E. : When all tomatoes are red and all grapes are tomatoes, then all grapes are also red. When all grapes are tomatoes, then some tomatoes must be grapes. Therefore, both conclusions I and II are correct.

2. B. : When all painters are smiling and some authors are painters, then some authors are smiling. Therefore, only conclusion II is correct.

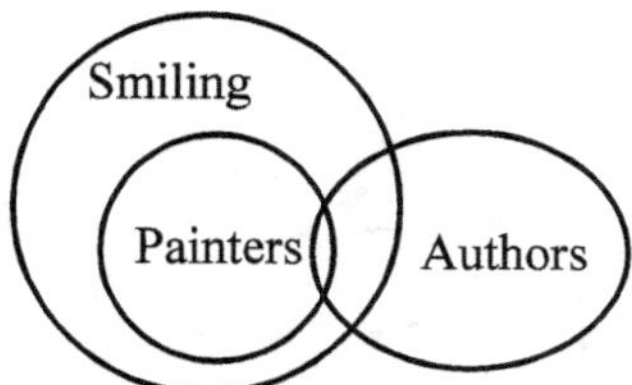

3. A. : When all the peons of the office are efficient, then Ramu cannot be a peon in this office. Therefore, only conclusion I is correct.

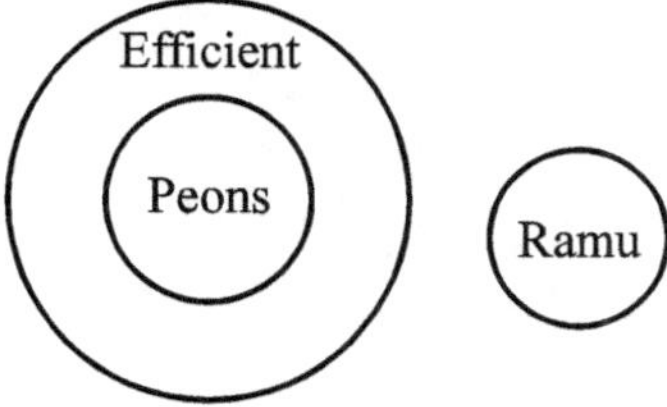

4. A. : When all weavers are hardworking and no hardworking men are foolish, then no weavers are foolish. Therefore, only conclusion I is correct.

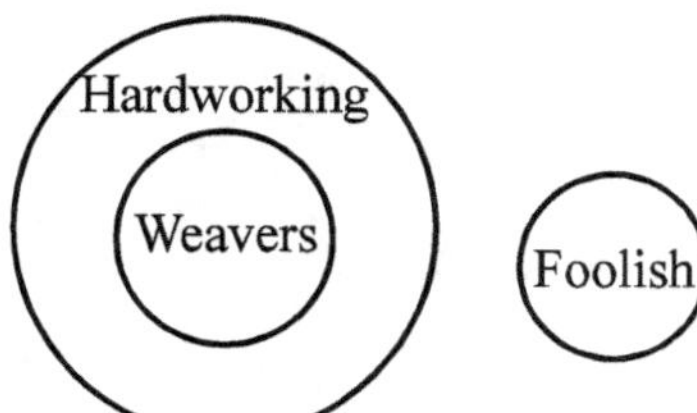

5. E. : When all fishes are cars and all cars are vegetables, then all fishes will naturally be vegetables. This means that some vegetables are fishes. And when all cars are vegetables, then some vegetables will be cars naturally. Therefore, both the conclusions I and II are correct.

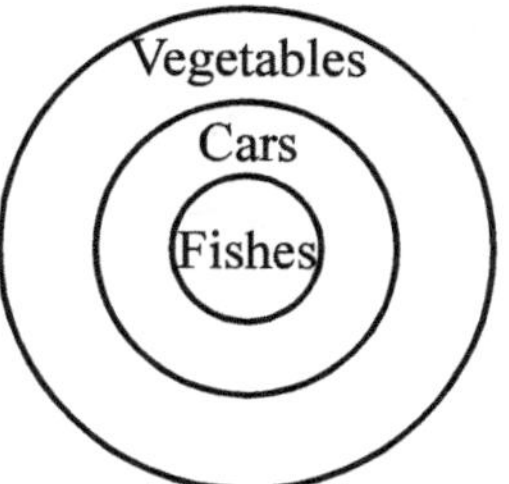

6. D. : No relationship can be established between the two statements. Therefore, neither conclusion I nor conclusion II is correct.

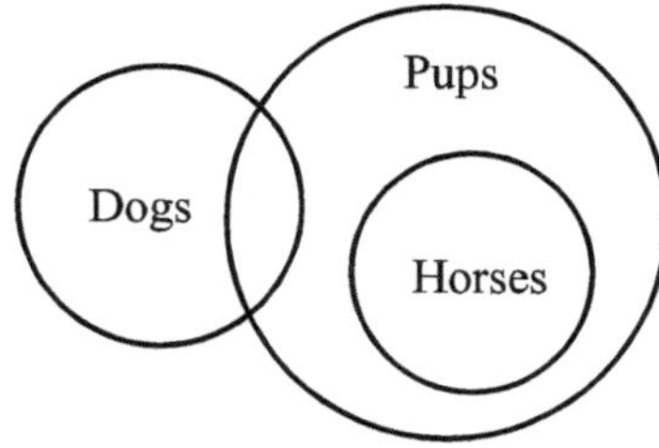

7. A. : When all beautiful women are mothers and all mothers are understanding, then naturally all beautiful women are understanding. All mothers need not be beautiful women. Therefore, only conclusion I is correct.

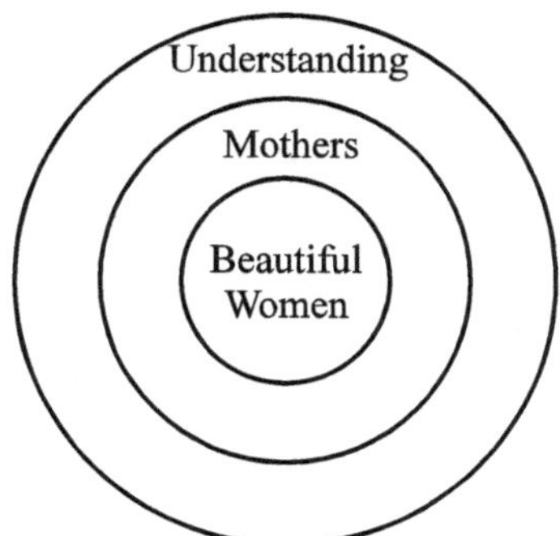

8. C. : When some toys are tables and no table is black, then it is indicated that some toys can be black, as all toys are not tables. On the other hand, some toys may not be black. Therefore, there is a possibility that some toys may or may not be black. As such, either conclusion I or conclusion II can be correct.

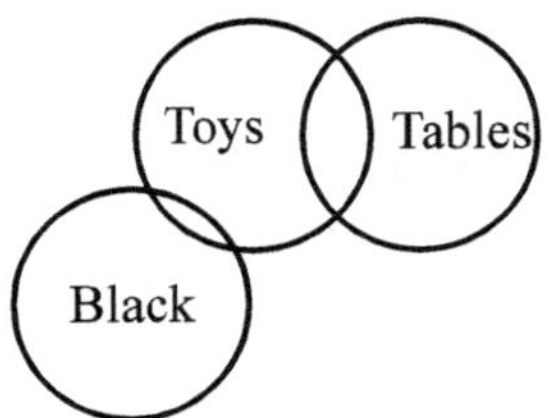

9. E. : When all rivers are mountains and some rivers are deserts, then some deserts cannot be mountains and also, some mountains need not be deserts. Therefore, both conclusion I and conclusion II are correct.

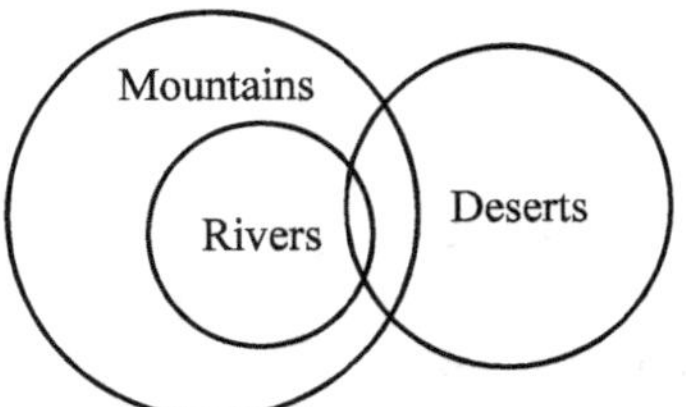

10. A. : When all men are horses and all horses are elephants then, naturally all men are elephants, but all elephants need not be men. Therefore, only conclusion I is correct.

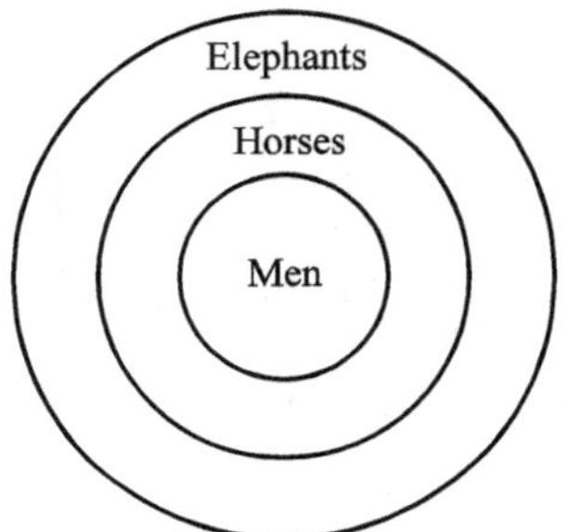

❑ ❑ ❑

Non-Verbal Series

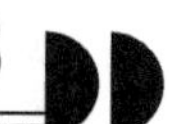

EXERCISE

Directions (Q. 1–10) : *In each of the following questions which one of the five answer figures given below should come after the problem figures if the sequence are continued?*

Problem Figures | **Answer Figures**

1\. 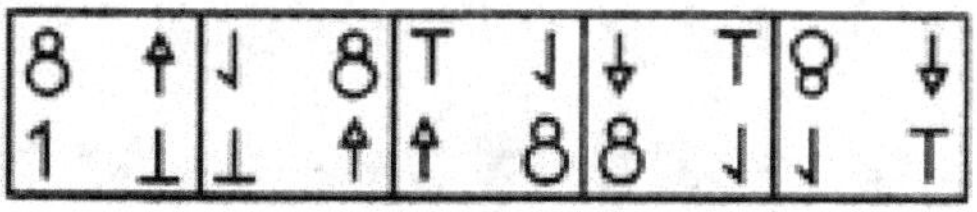 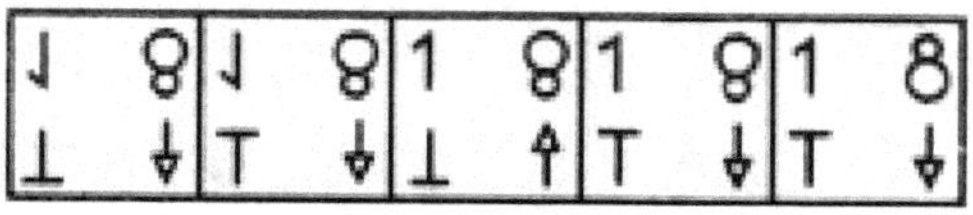

A. B. C. D. E.

2\. 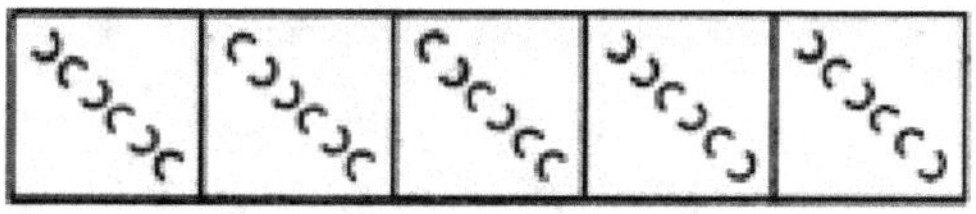 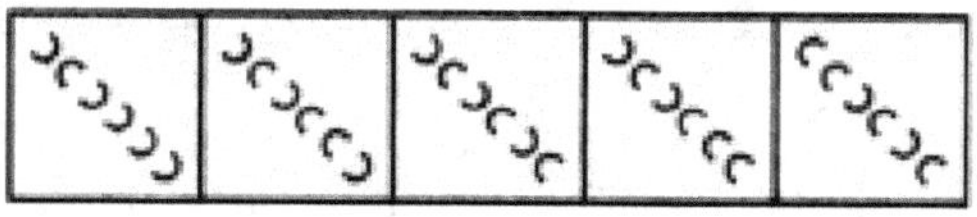

A. B. C. D. E.

3\. 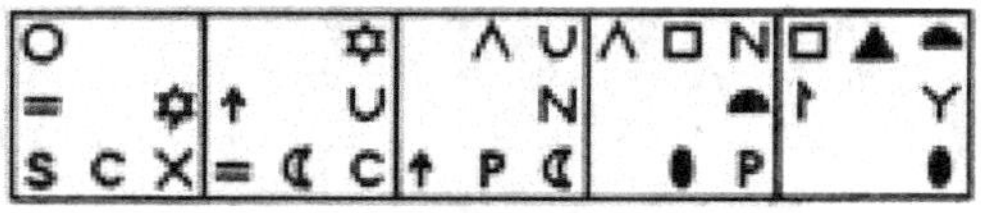 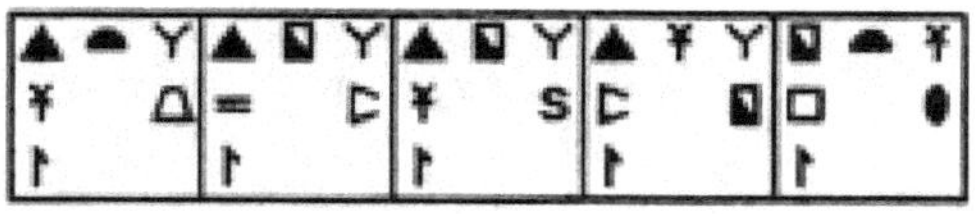

A. B. C. D. E.

4\. 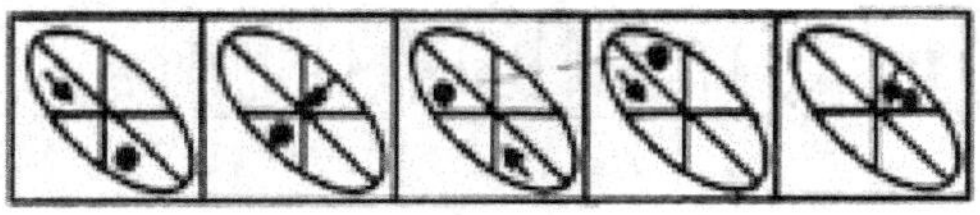 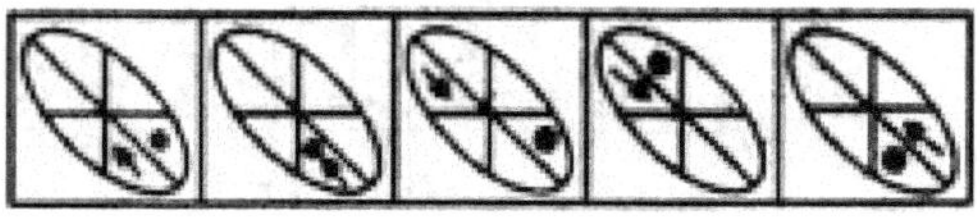

A. B. C. D. E.

5\. 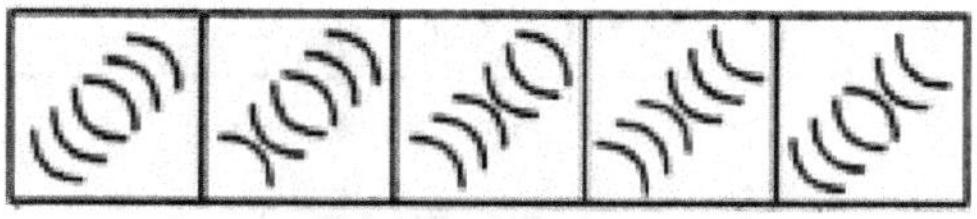 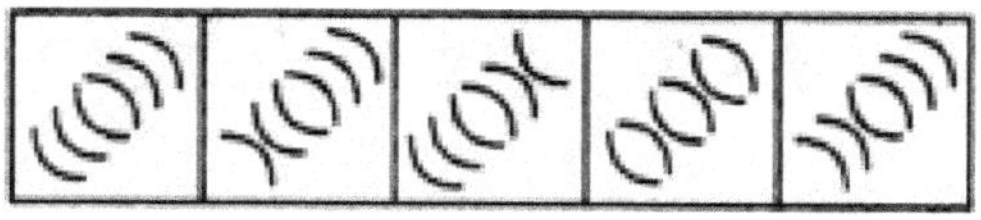

A. B. C. D. E.

6\. 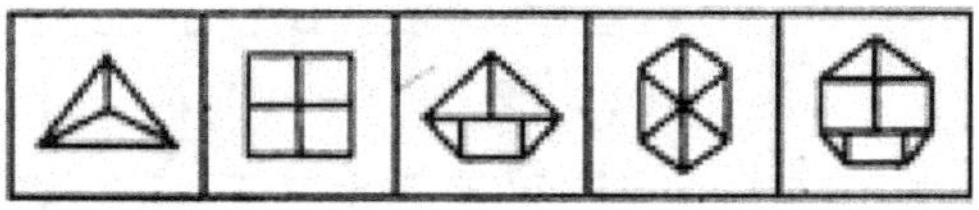 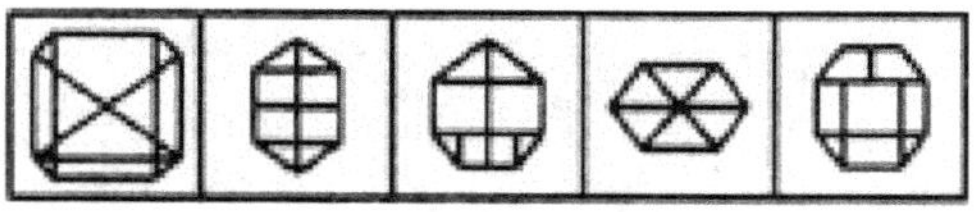

A. B. C. D. E.

7\. 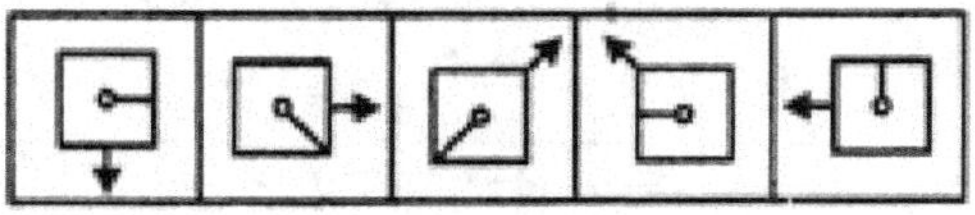 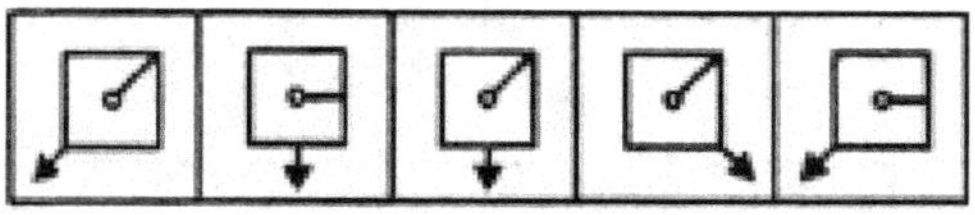

A. B. C. D. E.

Problem Figures

Answer Figures

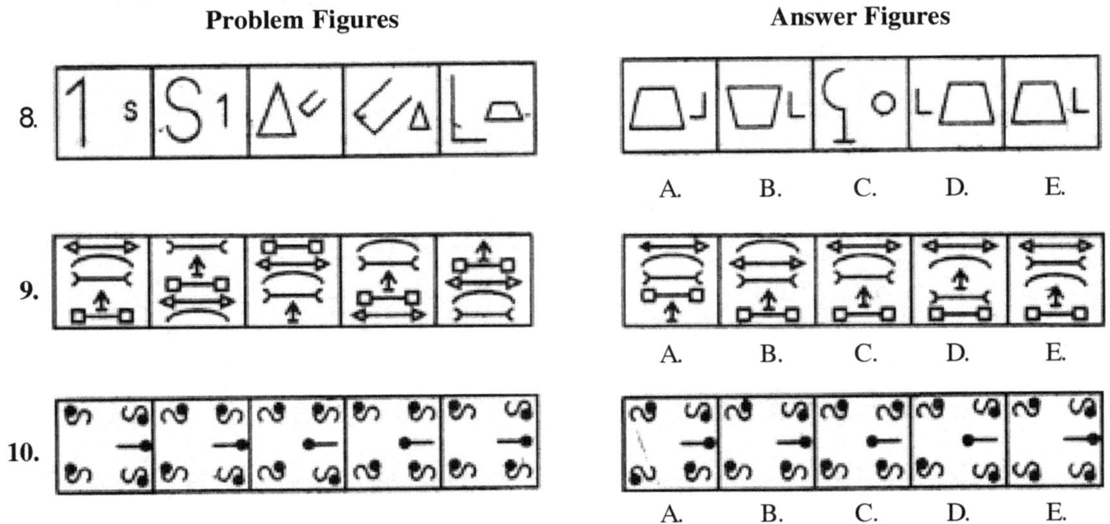

Directions (Q. 11-20) : *In each of these questions, a series begins with an unmarked figure on the extreme left in the row of figures. One and only one of the five lettered figures in the series does not fit into the series. The two unmarked figures, one on the extreme left and the other on the extreme right fit into the series. Take as many aspects into account as possible of the figures in the series and find out the one and only of the five marked figures which does not fit into the series. The letter of that figure is the answer.*

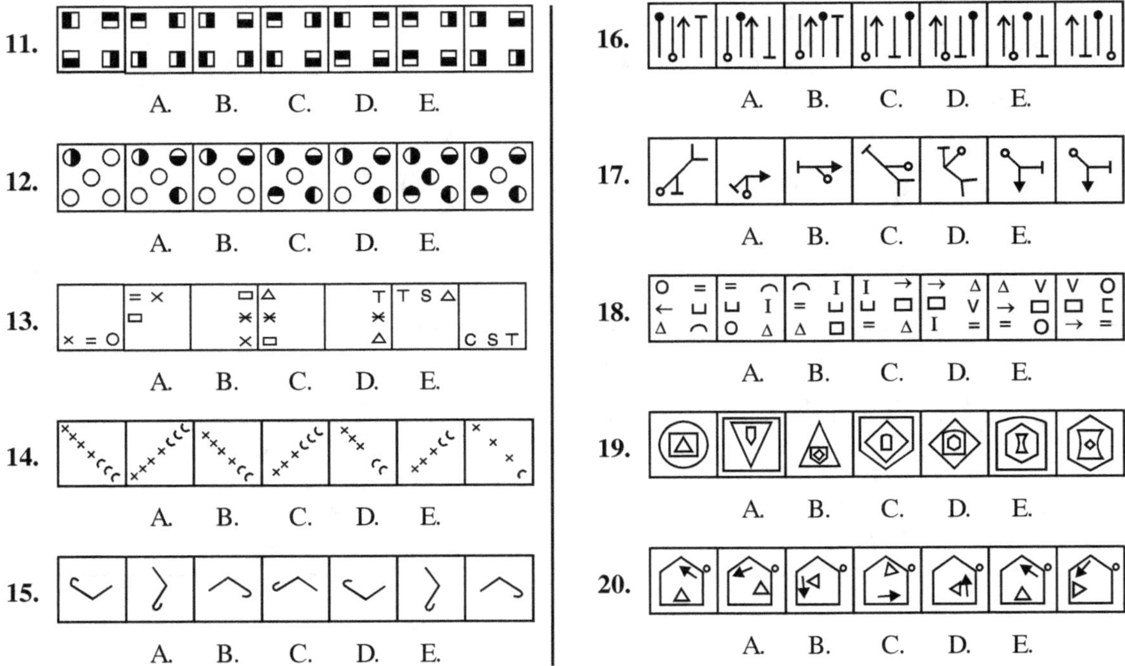

Directions (Q. 21–30) : *Each of the following questions consist of problem figures followed by answer figures. Select a figure from amongst the answer figures which will continue the same series or pattern as established by the problem figures.*

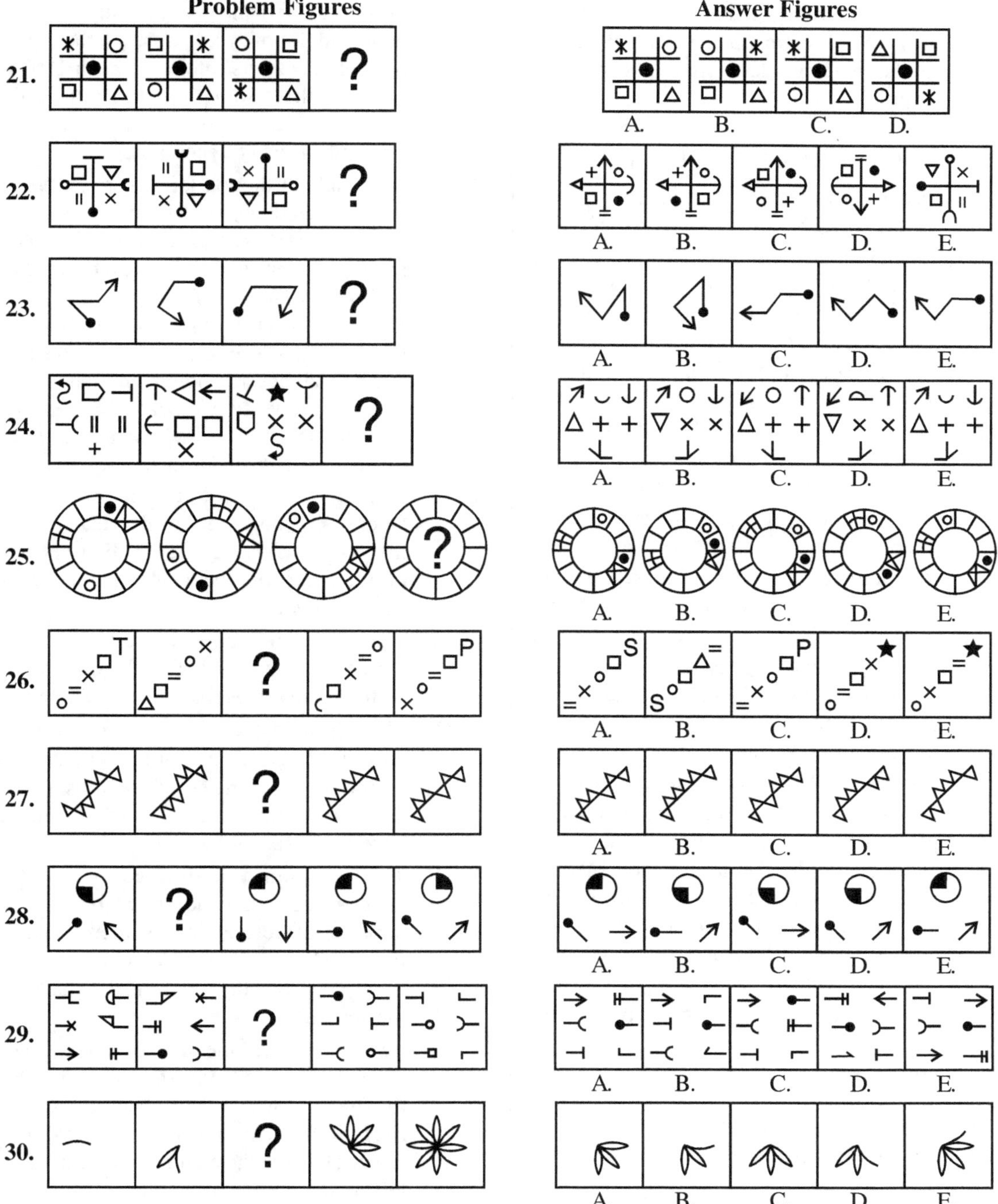

EXPLANATORY ANSWERS

1. D. : In each step, all the elements move to the adjacent corner (of the square boundary) in a CW direction and the element that reaches the upper-left corner gets vertically inverted.

2. C. : We can label the arcs as shown . The arcs get inverted in the sequence (1 & 2), (3, 4 & 5), (6 & 1), (2, 3 & 4), (5 & 6), ...

3. D. : All the elements move half-a-side of the square boundary in ACW direction in each step. Also, first, third and fifth elements are replaced by new elements in one step and second, fourth and sixth elements are replaced by new elements in the next step. The two steps are repeated alternately.

4. A. : In each step, the dot moves one space CW and the arrow moves two spaces CW.

5. C. : One arc and four arcs get inverted alternately.

6. E. : The number of parts increases by one along with the number of sides in the figure.

7. C. : The pin rotates 45°CW and 90°CW alternately and moves one space (each space is equal to half-a-side of the square) and two spaces CW alternately. The arrow rotates 90°ACW and 45°ACW alternately and moves two spaces and one space.

8. E. : In one step, the two elements interchange positions and the smaller element gets enlarged while the larger element gets reduced in size. In the next step, the smaller element is replaced by a new small element and the larger element is replaced by a new large element.

9. C. : In each step, the elements move in the order .

10. B. : The upper-left element gets laterally inverted in first, third, fifth. .... steps; the upper-right element gets rotated through 180° is first, fourth, seventh,.... steps; the lower-left element gets laterally inverted in second, fourth, sixth, ... steps; the lower-right element gets rotated through 180° in third, sixth,... steps and the pin at the middle-right position gets laterally inverted in every second step.

11. A. : The shade in the top left square is moved one step clockwise till figure B and then reversed, the process is repeated. The shade in the top right square is moved one step anticlockwise till figure D and then reversed. The shade in the bottom left square is moved one step clockwise in alternate figures and the shade in bottom right square is moved one step clockwise after two figures. In figure 'A' the rule is isolated by the shade in the bottom left square.

12. E. : In alternate figures a new circle is shaded clockwise. The pattern of the shade is also moved clockwise. In figure 'E' right half of the circle in the centre should have been shaded.

13. A. : The three elements are placed either horizontally or vertically. In option 'A' neither of the placements can be applied.

14. C. : The placement of elements is same in alternate figures. The number and type of elements is same in two subsequent figures. In this manner, figure 'C' should have four crosses and two C shapes.

15. C. : The element is moved one step anticlockwise and the arc at one end is turned outside and inside alternately. In figure 'C' the element should be on the right side with the arc turned outside on the top side.

16. E. : The left most element, line segment with the dot is moved one step towards right till figure C where it reaches the extreme right position. This process is repeated from figure D where the element on the extreme left, line segment with a circle, is moved.

In figure 'E' the placement of the elements does not follow the rule of the series.

17. E. : The 'T' line is rotated 45° clockwise and the line with the circle 45° anticlockwise. The 'Y' shape and the arrow are repeated twice after two figures. In option E, the 'T' shape and the line with the circle are rotated by 90°.

18. E. : First the elements in the four corners are moved one step anticlockwise, next the four elements from the top are moved one step anticlockwise and then the four elements from the bottom are moved one step anticlockwise. Of the remaining two elements, the one on the left is made new each time and then their places are interchanged. This process is repeated from figure D. In option 'E' open square should have been in place of circle to continue the series.

19. A. : At each step the outermost figure is removed and a new figure is placed right in the centre of other two figures. In option 'A' the triangle is turned upside down, which violates the rule of the series.

20. A. : The arrow is moved one step anticlockwise and the triangle one step clockwise. In figure 'A' the triangle should have been on the left side of the figure.

21. A. : The places of star, circle and square are moved one step clockwise at each step.

22. E. : The elements in the four quadrants are moved one step clockwise and the elements at the ends of the cross are moved one step anticlockwise in this series.

23. A. : In alternate figures, the line with the dot is turned 90° clockwise and the arrow 180° clockwise.

24. E. : In alternate figures, the element in the top left position is horizontally inverted and moved one and half steps anticlockwise, the top middle element is turned 90° clockwise and moved one step anticlockwise, the top right element is turned 135° clockwise and moved one step anticlockwise, the element at the bottom is replaced by a new element and moved to the top middle position, and the two identical elements are replaced by two new identical elements.

25. A. : The cross and the circle move one and two steps clockwise respectively (at each step), the plus moves 3, 4 and 5 steps clockwise, and the dot 6, 5 and 4 steps clockwise.

26. A. : At first step, the fifth or the bottom most element is moved to the second place from top, the second element moved to the fourth place, the fourth element is moved to the third place, the third element is moved to the first or the topmost place and the element on the top, which is made new, is moved to the last or the fifth place. At second step i.e., from second problem figure to third problem figure the above process is reversed. The bottom most element is the first and the top most element is the last or fifth. Hereafter, the process is repeated from the beginning. Option 'A' is the right answer.

27. C. : Starting from the bottom, one triangle is moved to the opposite side at each step in upward order. Option 'C' fits into the question marked space.

28. C. : The shade inside the circle is rotated clockwise in alternate figures; the line segment with a dot is rotated 135° clockwise in alternate figures and the arrow is rotated 135° anticlockwise in alternate figures. By this process answer figure 'C' completes the series.

29. A. : At each step the elements are moved diagonally upward and then laterally inverted, and the top two elements are made new and placed at the bottom line. By this process, option figure 'A' completes the series.

30. A. : The number of arcs making the petals of the flower are increased by one, one and half, two, two and half respectively at each step. Also, the flower is turned 45° anticlockwise. By this process, option 'A' is the right answer.

Non-Verbal Analogy ▶▶

EXERCISE

Directions (Q. 1-15): *The second figure in the first unit of the Problem Figures bears a certain relationship to the first figure. Similarly, one of the figures in the Answer Figures bears the same relationship to the first figures in the second unit of the Problem Figures. Locate the figure which would fit the questions marks.*

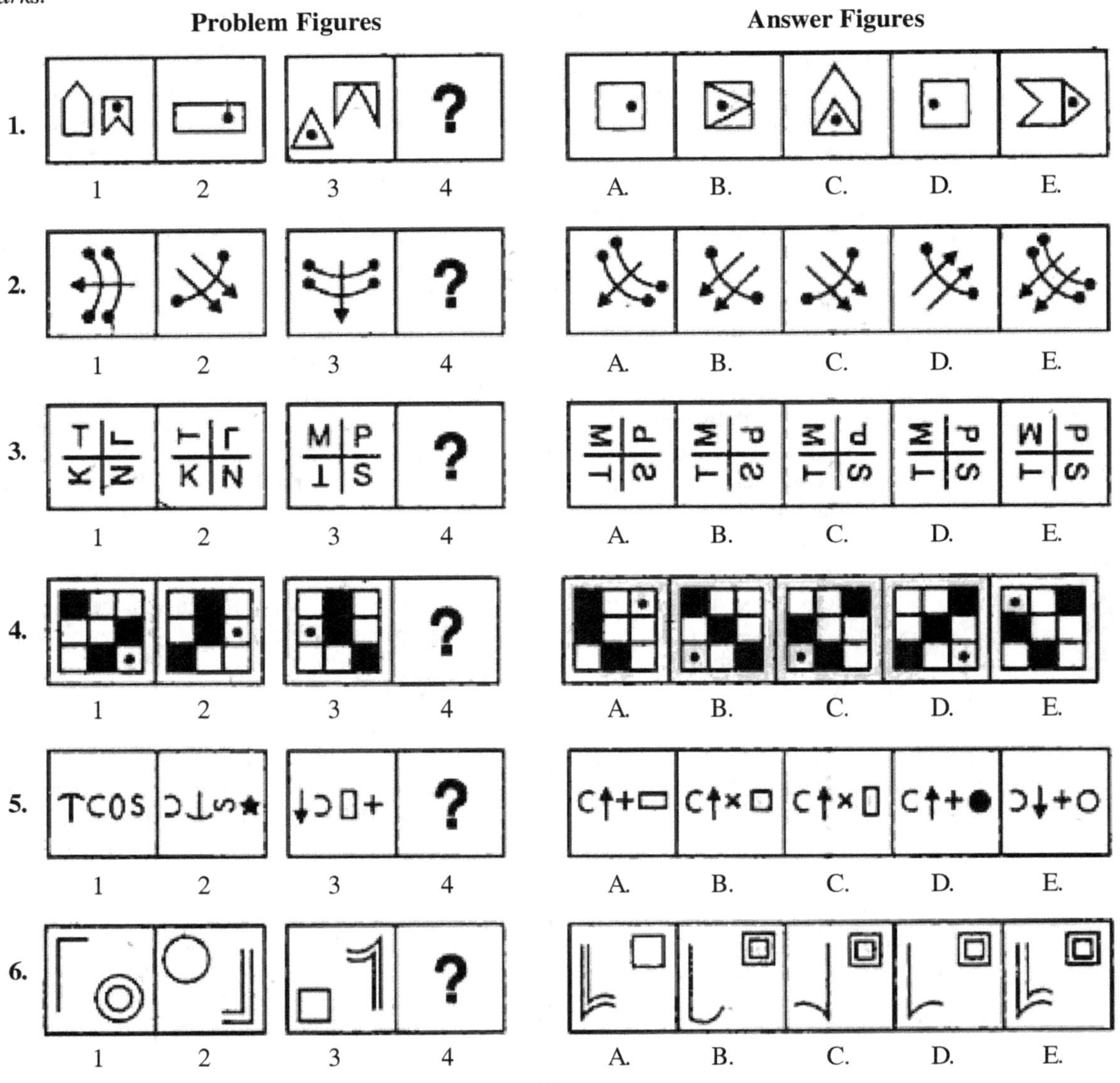

(1809) Mental Ablity (E)—7-II

Problem Figures   **Answer Figures**

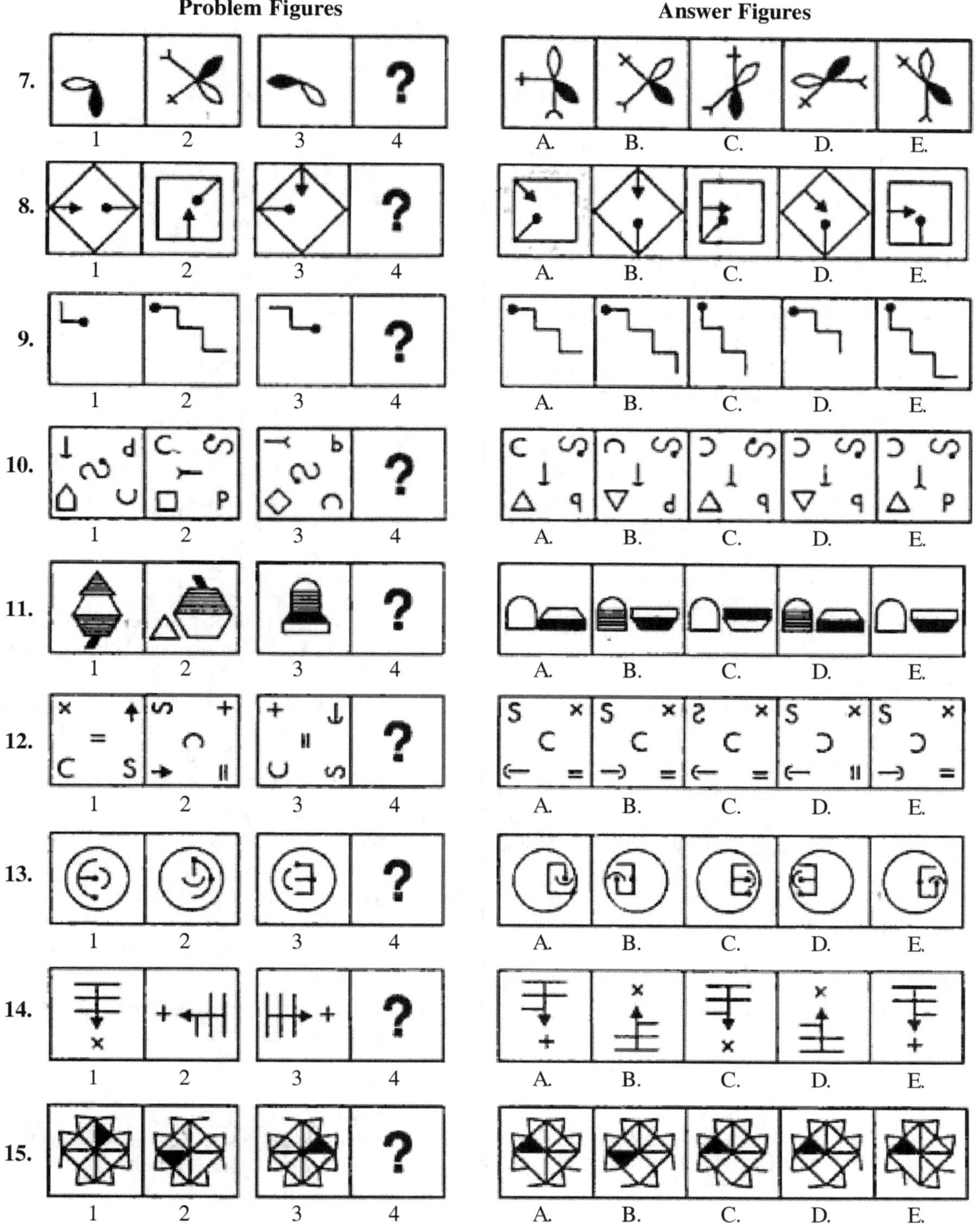

EXPLANATORY ANSWERS

1. B. : The R.H.S. figure is fitted into the L.H.S. figure and the resulting figure is rotated 90° CW.

2. B. : The figure rotates 45° ACW, the arrow changes to a curved line with dotted ends and the curved lines with dotted ends get converted to arrows.

3. D. : The top left symbol rotates 90° ACW while all other symbols rotate 90° CW.

4. E. : The black portion in top layer moves one step to the right; the black portions in the middle and the lower layers move one step to the left and the dot moves one step upwards.

5. D. : The first and second symbols from the left interchange positions and the other two symbols also interchange positions. The symbol that reaches the first position from the left gets laterally inverted; the symbol that reaches the second position gets inverted, the third symbol rotates 90° CW and the fourth symbol gets replaced by a new one.

6. D. : The single figure is replaced by a figure similar to the double figures and the double figures are replaced by figures similar to the single figure.

7. E. : The figure rotates 135° ACW; a 'T' appears diagonally opposite to the black leaf and a 'Y' appears diagonally opposite to the white leaf.

8. C. : The square rotates through 45°. The arrow moves 90° ACW and the pin moves 45° ACW.

9. B. : The figure rotates through 180° and three lines forming a zig-zag, get attached to its lower end.

10. D. : The symbols move in the order

The symbol that reaches the central position rotates 90° CW and its arc gets inverted; the 'P' shaped symbol rotates through 180°; the 'C' shaped symbol rotates 90° CW; the 'S' Shaped symbol gets laterally inverted and the fifth symbol gets replaced by a new one.

45°, the symbol that reaches the lower right corner rotates 90° ACW and a new symbol appears in middle-left position.

11. E. : The upper and the lower parts of the figure get separated. Shading is removed from the upper part and the lower part is inverted. The two parts are then placed side by side.

12. A. : The symbols move in the order

The symbol that reaches the top-left corner rotates 90° ACW; the symbol in the top-right corner rotates through 45°; the symbols in the lower-left corner and in the central positions rotates 90° CW and the symbol that reaches the lower-right corner rotates through 90°.

13. E. : The figure gets laterally inverted. The dot on the larger arc, the pin and the small arc rotate 90° ACW. Also, the pin gets inverted.

14. C. : The figure rotates 90° CW. One half of one of the lines on the arrow is lost. The figure in front of the arrowhead rotates through 45°.

15. D. : The missing line segment in the first figure is replaced in second. Then moving ACW, the third line segment is removed along the two next consecutive sides of the square. Shaded portion in the first figure moves three steps ACW. Similarly, the third figure gives figure (D).

Odd Man Out ▶▶

In this type of reasoning a statement is followed by inferences drawn from it. From these inferences only one definitely follows which is the hidden proposition of the sentence and it is the right answer to the question.

EXERCISE

Directions (Q. 1–10) : *In each question below five figures are given. Four are similar in a certain way and so form a group. The question is— which one of the figures **does not** belong to that group?*

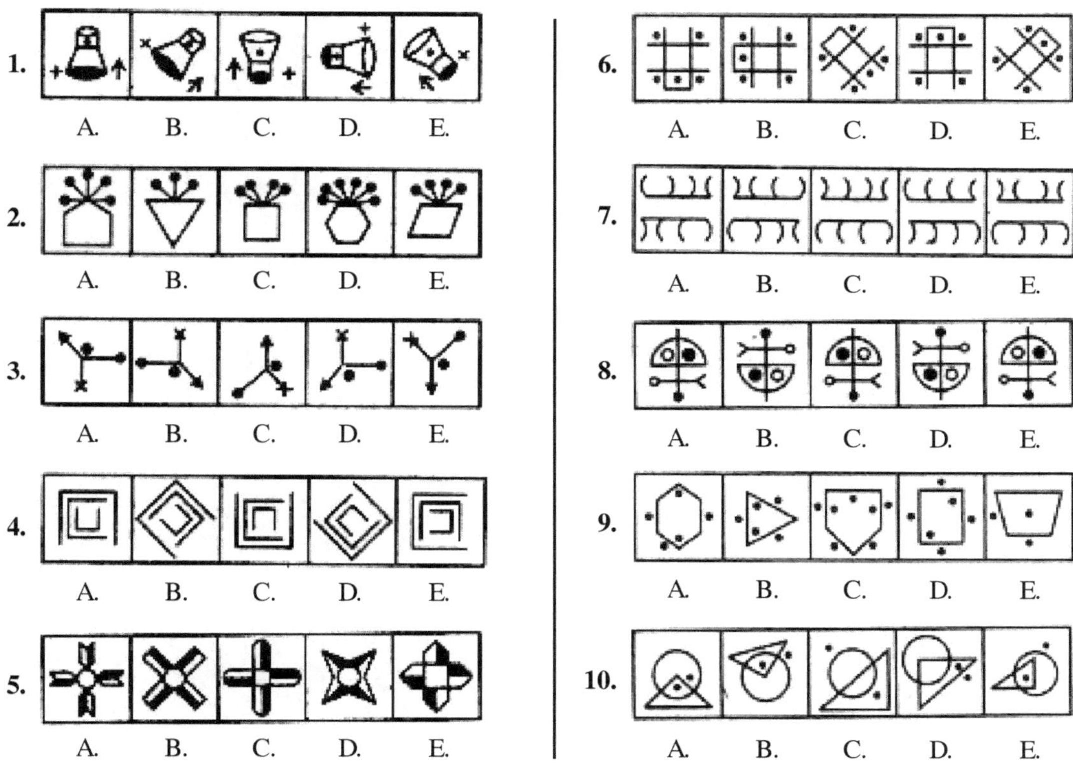

EXPLANATORY ANSWERS

1. D. : In all other figures, the arrow and the + sign lie towards the black end of the main figure.

2. A : The pins, equal in number of sides in the main figure are attached to the midpoint of a side of the main figure in case of figures (B), (C), (D) and (E). In figure (A), these pins are attached to a vertex of the main figure.

3. C : In all other figures, the dot appears in the angle formed between the arrow and the pin.

4. A : All other figures can be rotated into each other. (In each figure except figure (A), the middle element is obtained by rotating the outer element through 90° CW and the inner element is obtained by rotating the middle element through 90° CW).

5. C : All other figures have at least one line of symmetry.

6. C : All other figures can be rotated into each other.

7. E : In each one of the other four figures, four arcs are curved towards the left and four other arcs are curved towards the right.

8. C : All other figures can be rotated into each other.

9. D : In all other figures, the number of dots outside the main figure is one more than the number of dots inside the main figure.

10. A : In all other figures, one of the dots lies outside the triangle as well as the circle.

❑ ❑ ❑

Spatial Visualization 

In such questions, cut-out pieces are given alongwith the whole figure, that is the figure out of which the figures have been cut. By looking at the cut-out figures one has to find out the figure which may be constituted by putting the pieces together, i.e., one has to find out the figure of which the pieces have been cut. One has to be very imaginative and has to use space perception in finding out the solution. The whole process is mental and requires special skill in visualising different spatial patterns. It is not easy to develop this skill overnight but it can certainly be cultivated by practice and the method of trial and error.

SOLVED EXAMPLE

1. Which one figure can be made out of given paper cut-outs?

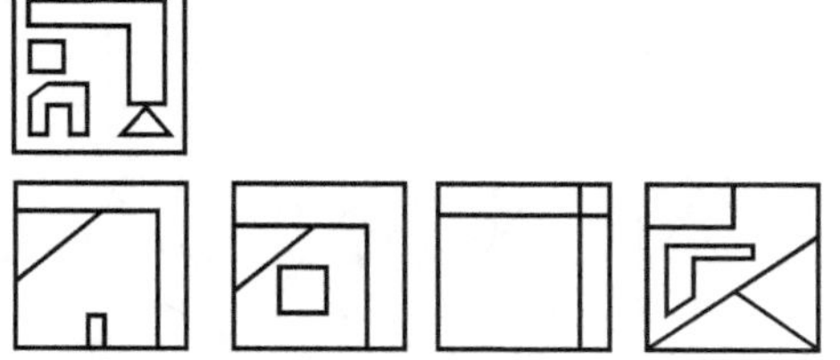

Answer A : The cut-outs when arranged will form figure A in this manner.

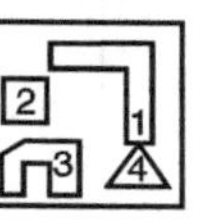

when arranged will be 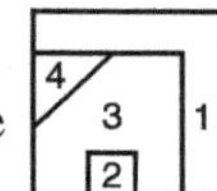

EXERCISE

Directions (Qs. 1-10) : *Which one figure can be made out of given paper cut-outs?*

1.

2.

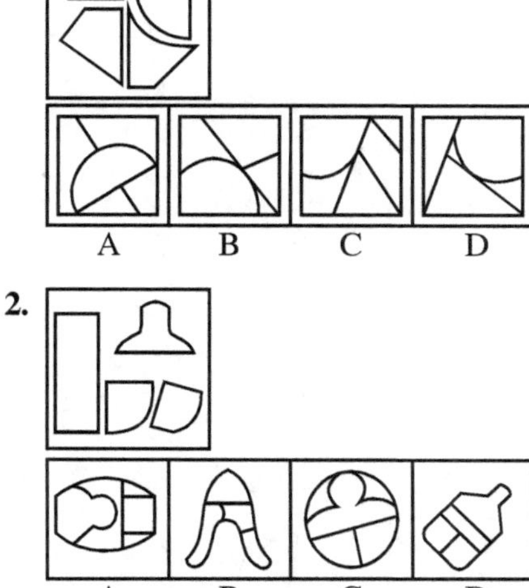

3.

4.

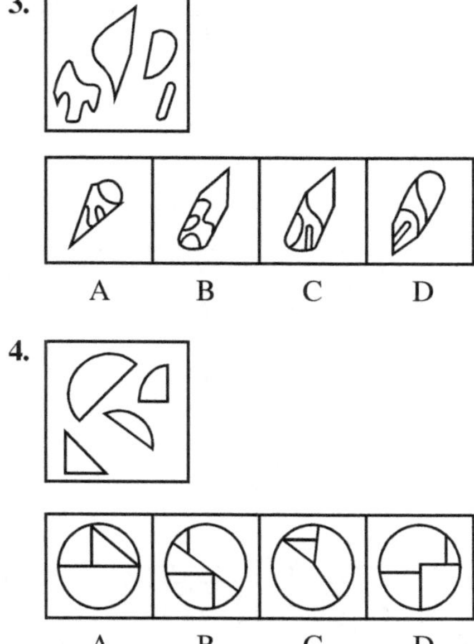

55

5.

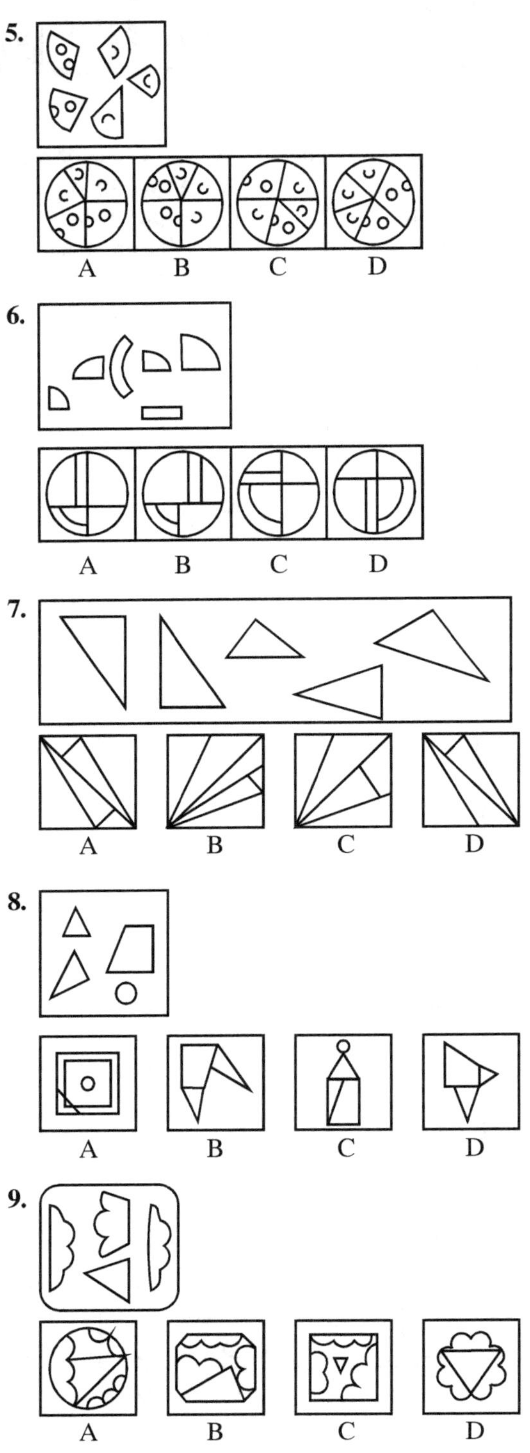

6.

7.

8.

9.

10.

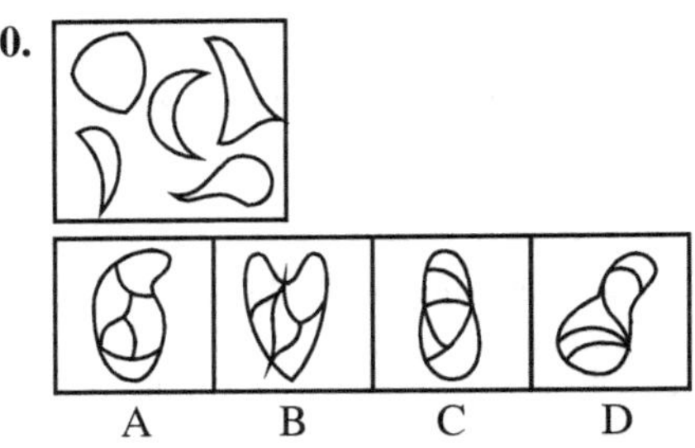

Direction (Qs. 11-15) : *In each of the following questions an irregular piece of paper has been cut into two pieces. One piece has been shown on the left while the other piece has been given as one of the four alternatives against it. Find the correct alternative:-*

11.

12.

13.

14.

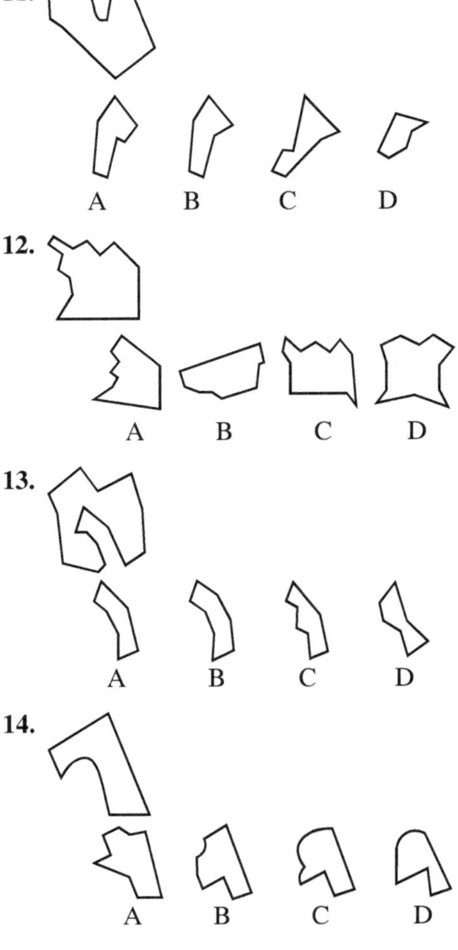

15.

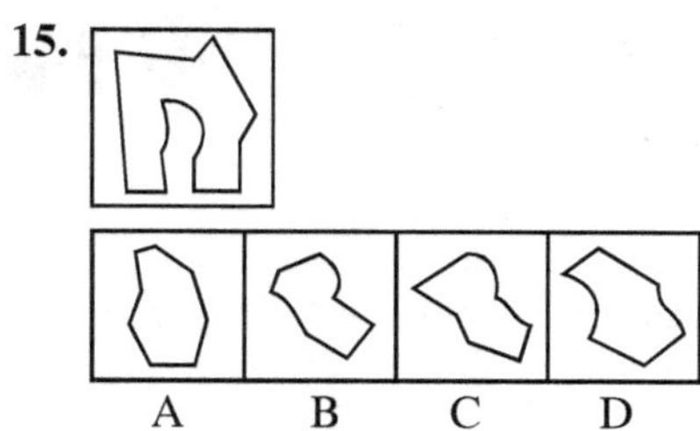

Directions (Qs. 16-20) : *In each of the following questions five diagrams marked A to E are given. Three of these when put together form an equilateral triangle and have been given as one of the four alternatives under the question. Find the correct alternative in each case.*

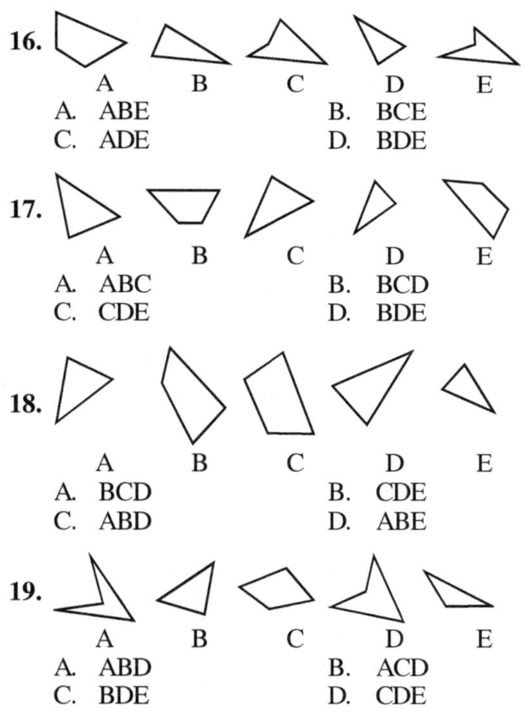

16.

A. ABE   B. BCE
C. ADE   D. BDE

17.

A. ABC   B. BCD
C. CDE   D. BDE

18.

A. BCD   B. CDE
C. ABD   D. ABE

19.

A. ABD   B. ACD
C. BDE   D. CDE

20.

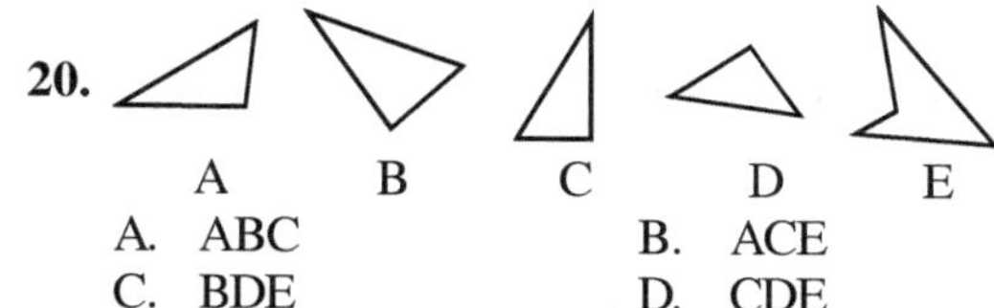

A. ABC   B. ACE
C. BDE   D. CDE

Directions (Qs. 21-24) : *In each of the following ques-tions five diagrams A, B, C, D and E have been given. Three of these diagrams make a complete square which have been given as one of the four alternatives under it. Find the correct alternative in each case.*

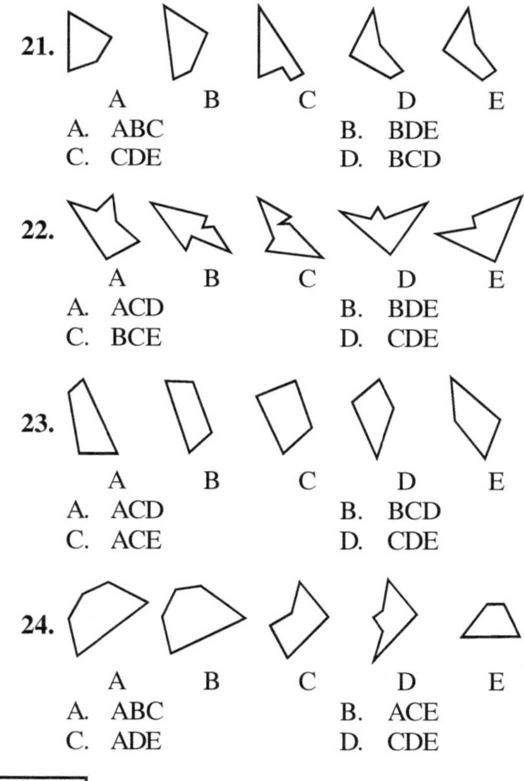

21.

A. ABC   B. BDE
C. CDE   D. BCD

22.

A. ACD   B. BDE
C. BCE   D. CDE

23.

A. ACD   B. BCD
C. ACE   D. CDE

24.

A. ABC   B. ACE
C. ADE   D. CDE

ANSWERS

1	2	3	4	5	6	7	8	9	10
B	D	C	A	B	A	D	C	D	D

11	12	13	14	15	16	17	18	19	20
B	C	A	D	C	C	D	D	B	B

21	22	23	24
D	B	C	C

❑ ❑ ❑

Paper Cutting & Folding

These type of questions are based on a piece of paper which is folded and cut or punched in a particular manner. One of the option figures either resembles the pattern that would be formed when the paper is unfolded or resembles the form in which the paper is folded and cut or punched.

SOLVED EXAMPLE

1. How would the following paper folded along the arrows and then punched look when unfolded?

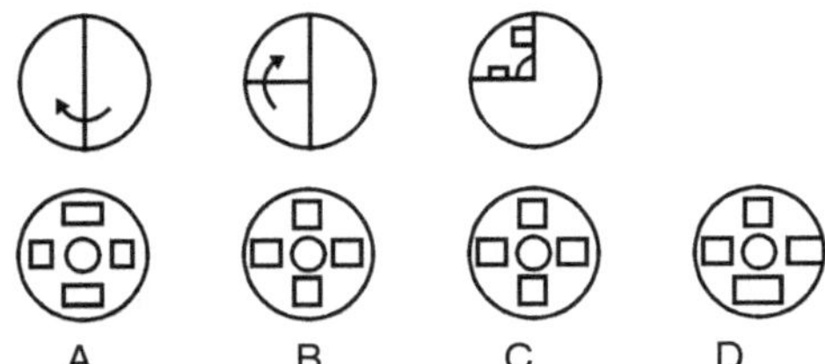

Answer A : When unfolded the steps will be :

EXERCISE

Directions : *In each one of the following problems, a square transparent sheet with a pattern is given. Figure out from amongst the four alternatives as to how the pattern would appear when the transparent sheet is folded at the dotted line.*

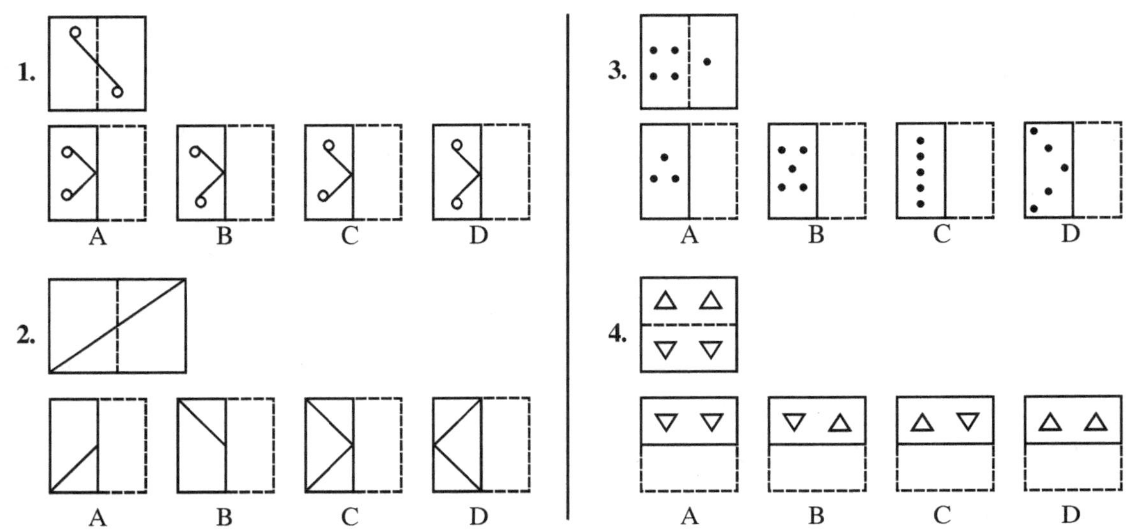

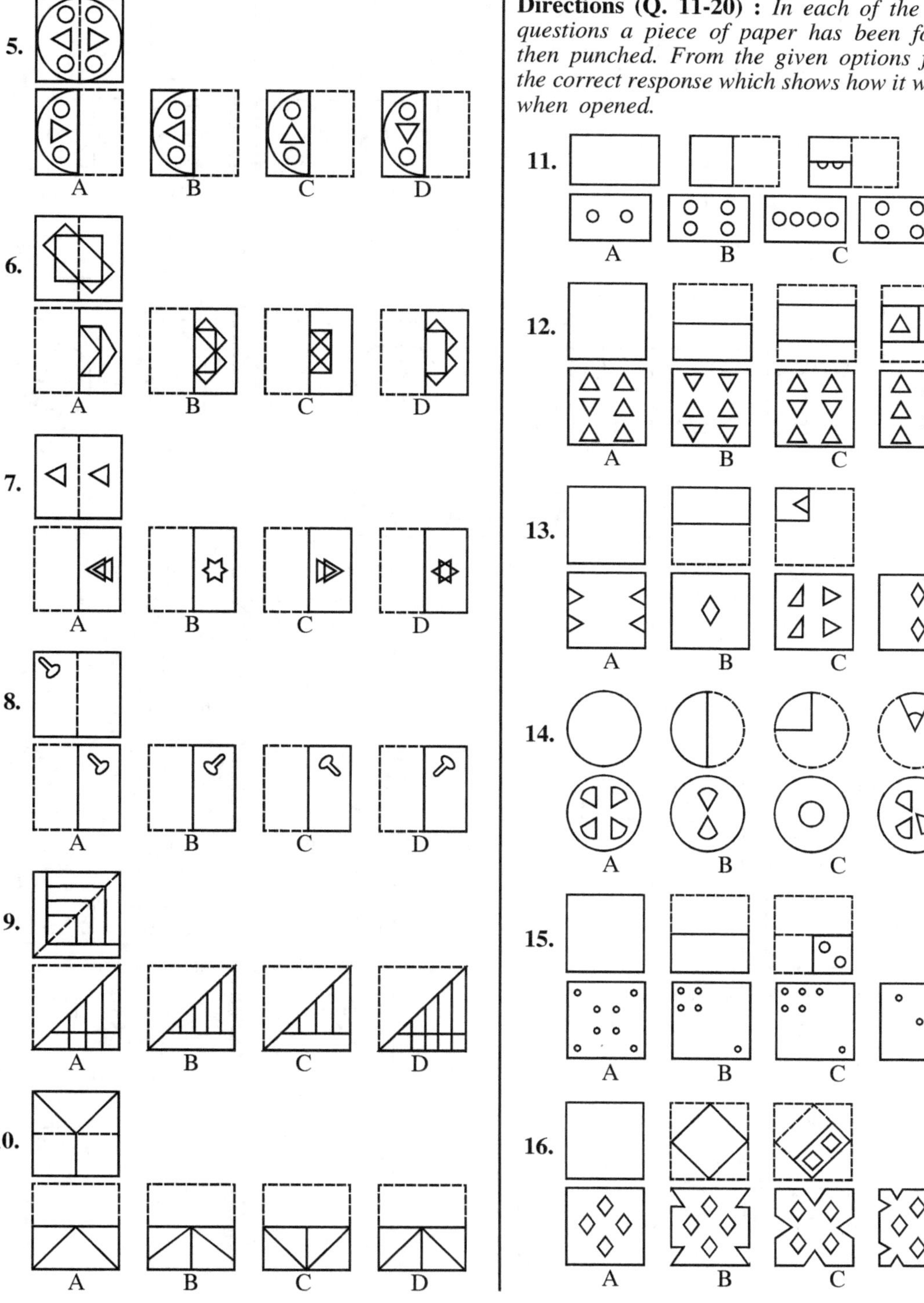

Directions (Q. 11-20) : In each of the following questions a piece of paper has been folded and then punched. From the given options figure out the correct response which shows how it will appear when opened.

17.

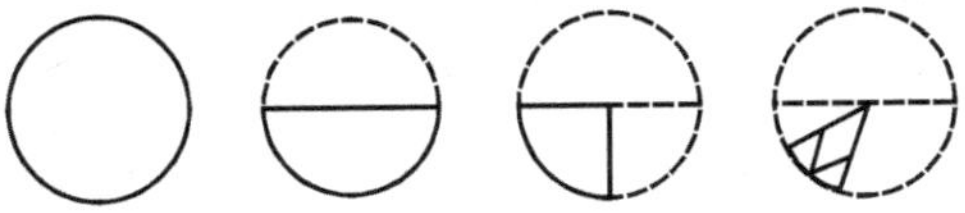

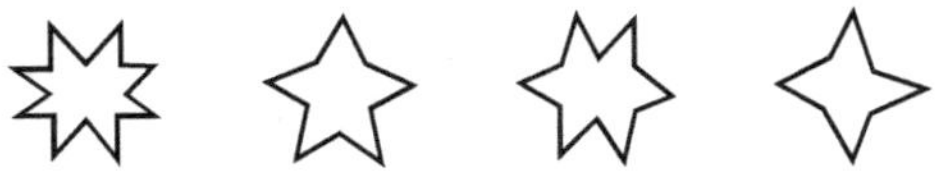

A B C D

18.

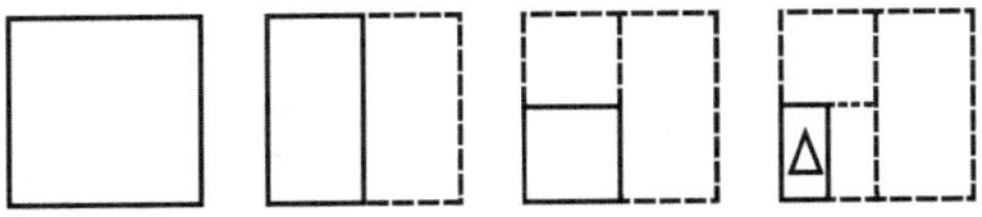

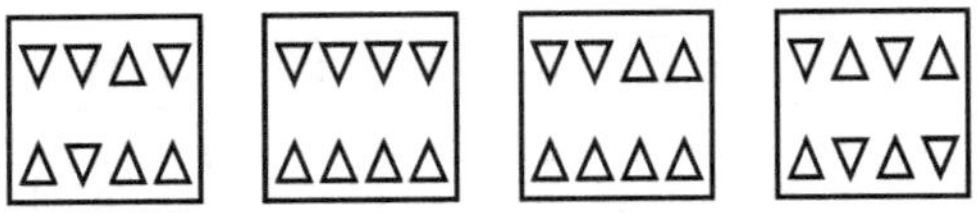

A B C D

19.

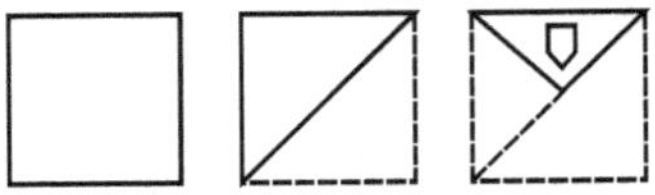

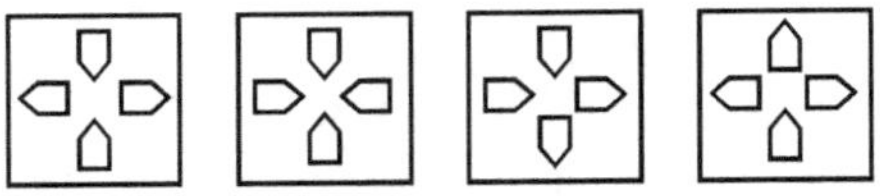

A B C D

20.

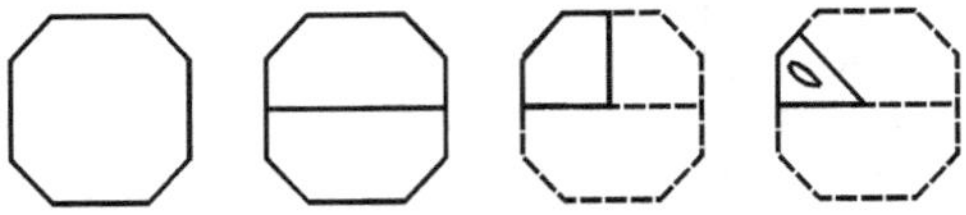

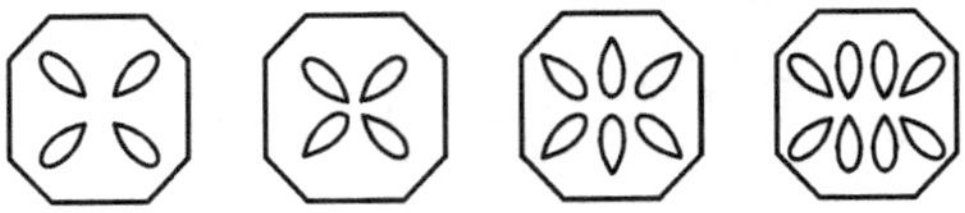

A B C D

EXPLANATORY ANSWERS

1. D **2. C** **3. B** **4. D** **5. B**
6. B **7. D** **8. B** **9. C** **10. D**

11. C : When unfolding, the steps will be :

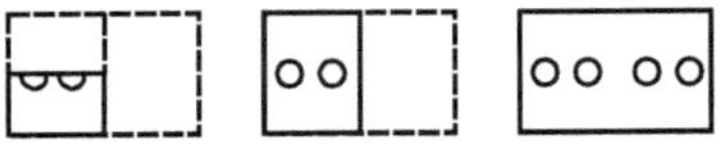

12. B : When unfolding, the steps will be :

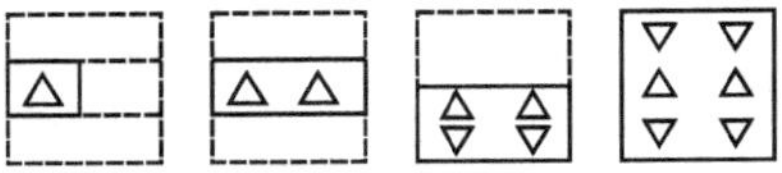

13. D : When unfolding, the steps will be :

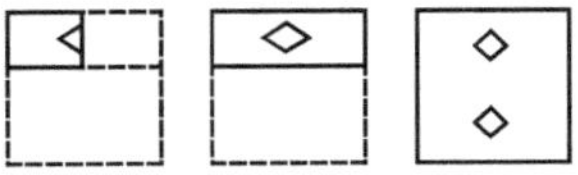

14. C : When unfolding, the steps will be :

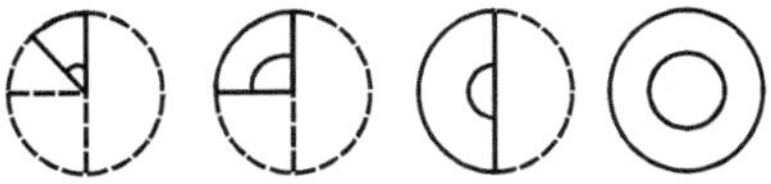

15. A : When unfolding, the steps will be :

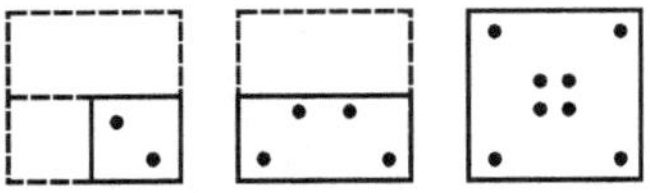

16. D : When unfolding, the steps will be :

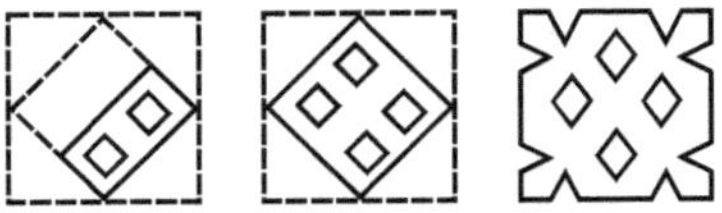

17. A : When unfolding, the steps will be :

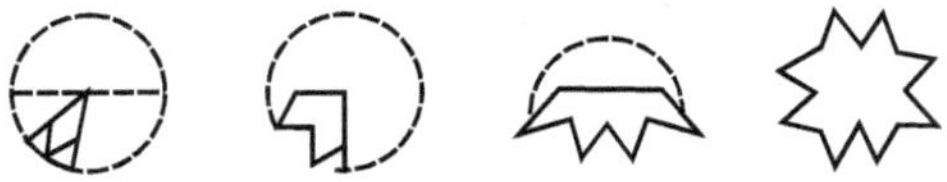

18. B : When unfolding, the steps will be :

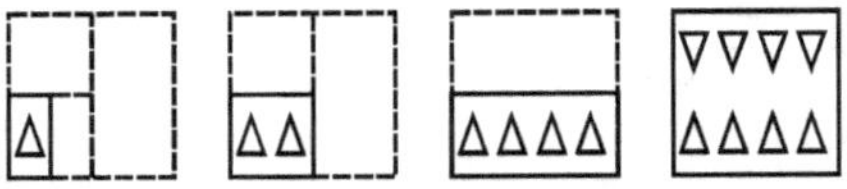

19. B : When unfolding, the steps will be :

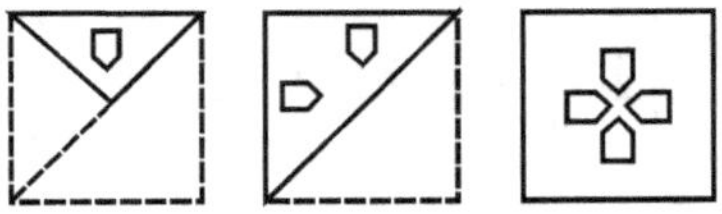

20. D : When unfolding, the steps will be :

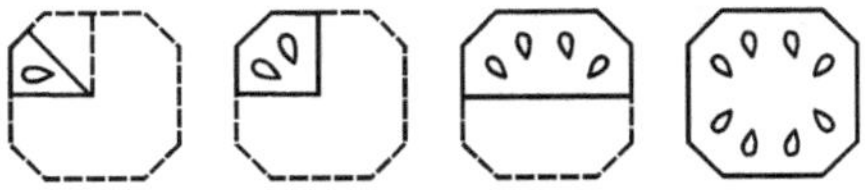

❑ ❑ ❑

Completing Incomplete Figures

In these type of questions an incomplete figure pattern is given followed by alternative figures of which one will complete the given figure pattern. These figure patterns are mainly based on symmetries.

SOLVED EXAMPLE

Which one of the alternative figures will complete the figure pattern?

1. Pattern 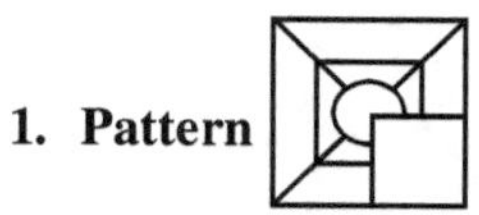

Alternative figures

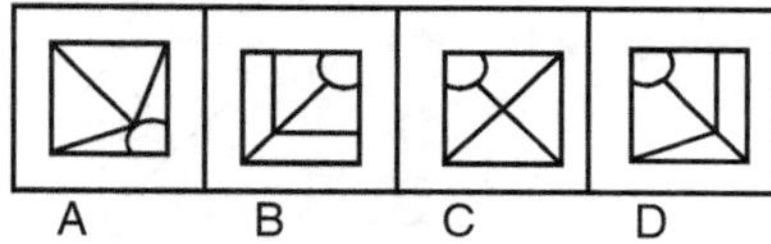

A   B   C   D

Answer B : Observe that this figure has a square, a circle in the centre and diagonal lines radiating from the circle. So, the complete figure will look like this :

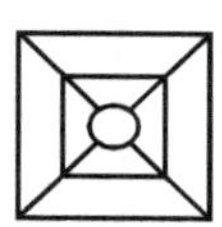

EXERCISE

Directions : *In each question, which one of the alter-native figures will complete the given figure pattern?*

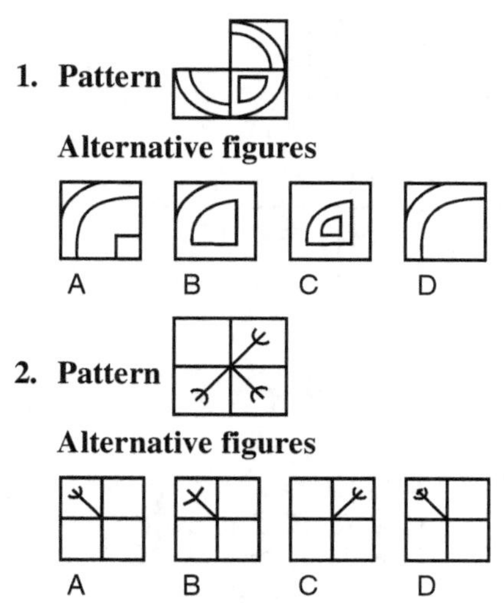

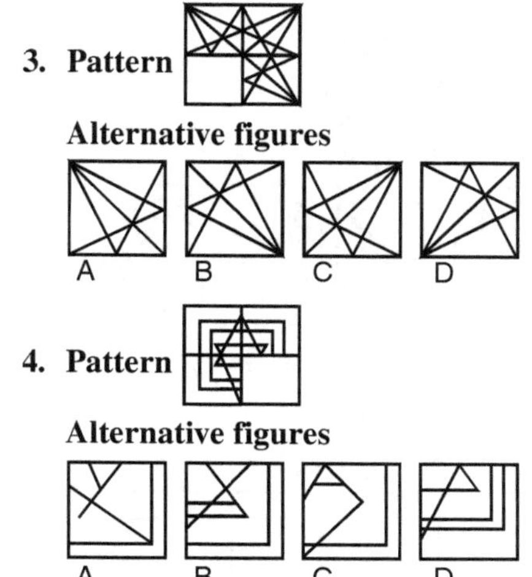

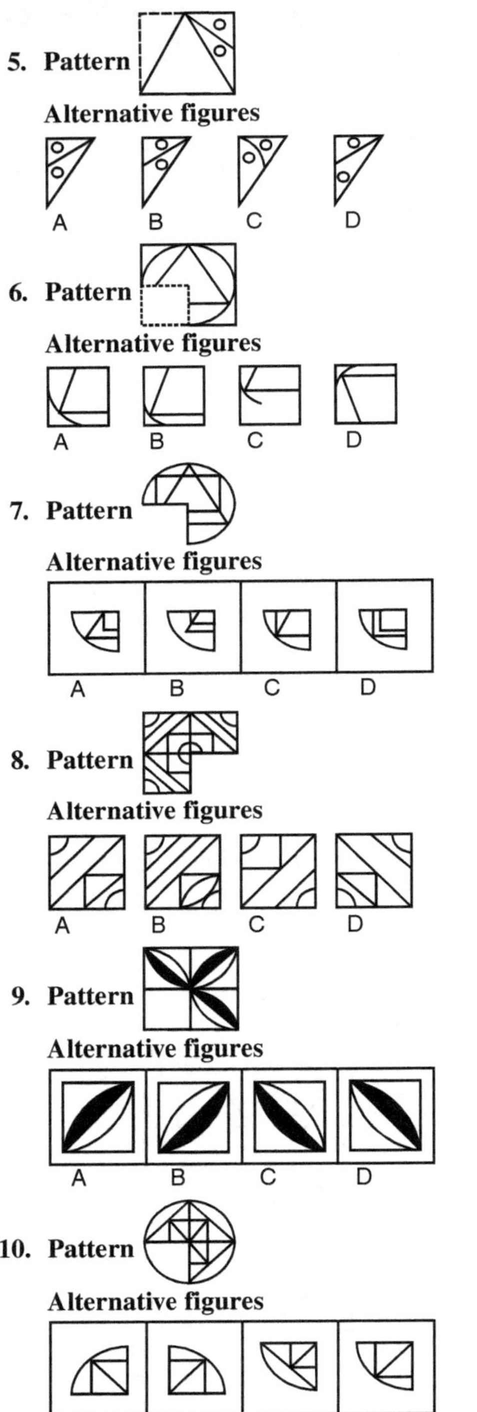

5. Pattern
Alternative figures
A   B   C   D

6. Pattern
Alternative figures
A   B   C   D

7. Pattern
Alternative figures
A   B   C   D

8. Pattern
Alternative figures
A   B   C   D

9. Pattern
Alternative figures
A   B   C   D

10. Pattern
Alternative figures
A   B   C   D

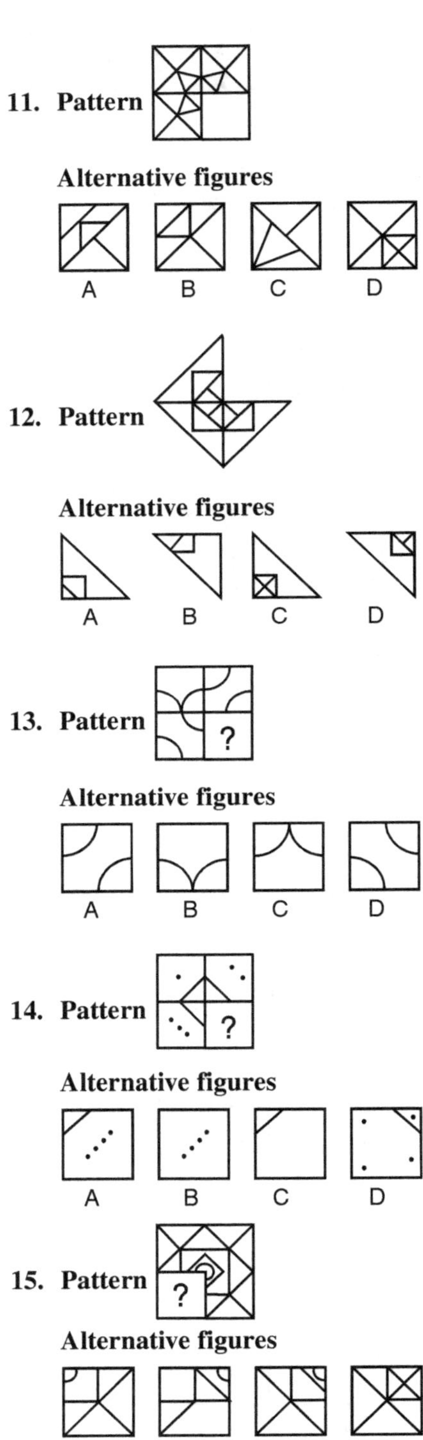

11. Pattern
Alternative figures
A   B   C   D

12. Pattern
Alternative figures
A   B   C   D

13. Pattern
Alternative figures
A   B   C   D

14. Pattern
Alternative figures
A   B   C   D

15. Pattern
Alternative figures
A   B   C   D

EXPLANATORY ANSWERS

All the completed figures will look like this:

1. B : 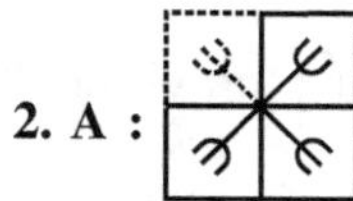

2. A : 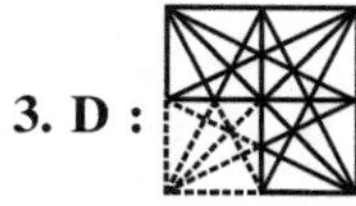

3. D : 

4. D : 

5. A : 

6. A : 

7. B : 

8. C :

9. B : 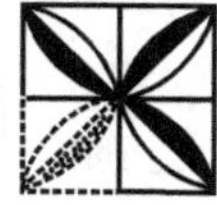

10. C : 

11. B : 

12. D : 

13. B : 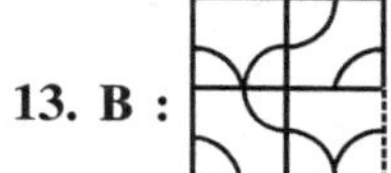

14. A : 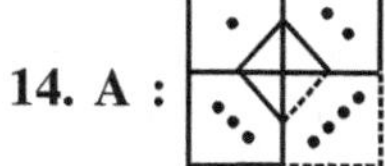

15. C : 

❑ ❑ ❑

Spotting Hidden Patterns 

In these type of questions a figure form is given followed by alternative figures. In one of these figure options the given form is embedded. Practice of visualisation comes handy in attempting such easy questions.

SOLVED EXAMPLES

1. Select the answer figure in which the question figure is hidden.

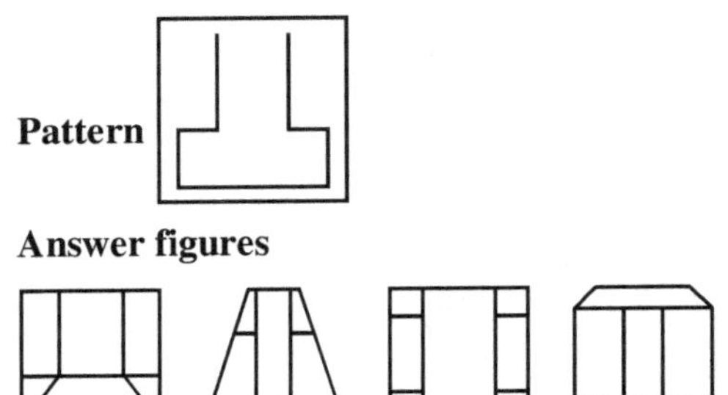

Pattern

Answer figures

A   B   C   D

Answer A : The question figure form is hidden in the option figure A as depicted below :

A quick look at all pattern the figures enables one to pick out the correct option.

In another type of problem a complete figure is given followed by four alternative figures. One of the given option figure pattern is embedded in the given figure.

EXERCISE

Directions (Qs. 1 to 10) : *In the questions given below a figure is given. From the given alternatives select the one in which the given figure is embedded.*

1. 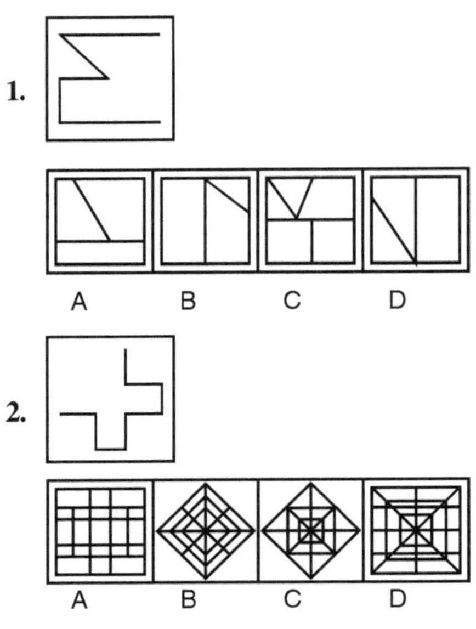

A   B   C   D

2.

A   B   C   D

3. 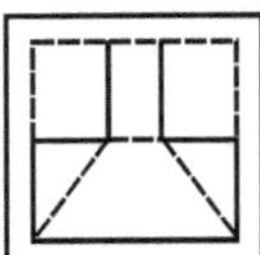

A   B   C   D

4. 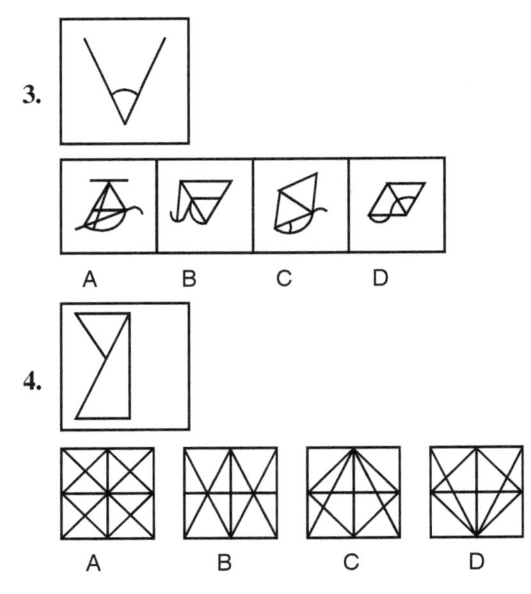

A   B   C   D

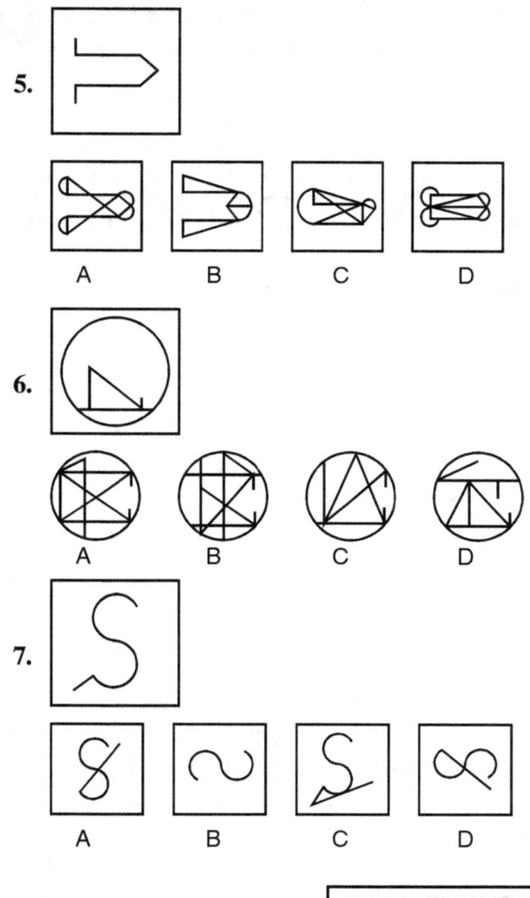

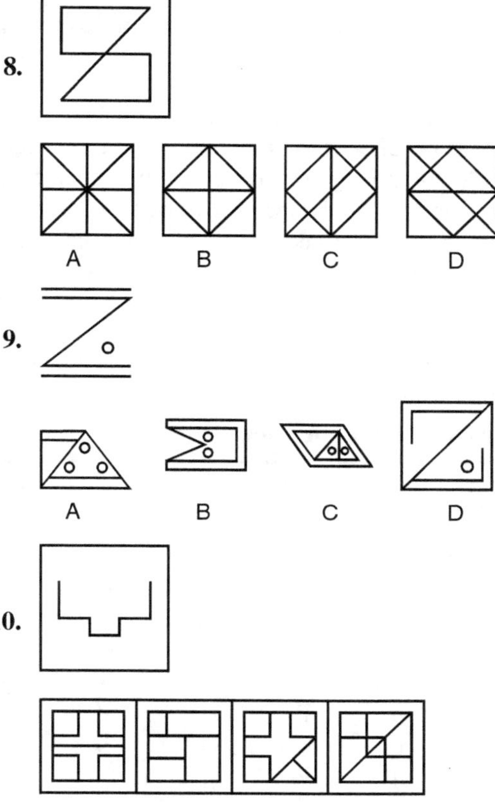

EXPLANATORY ANSWERS

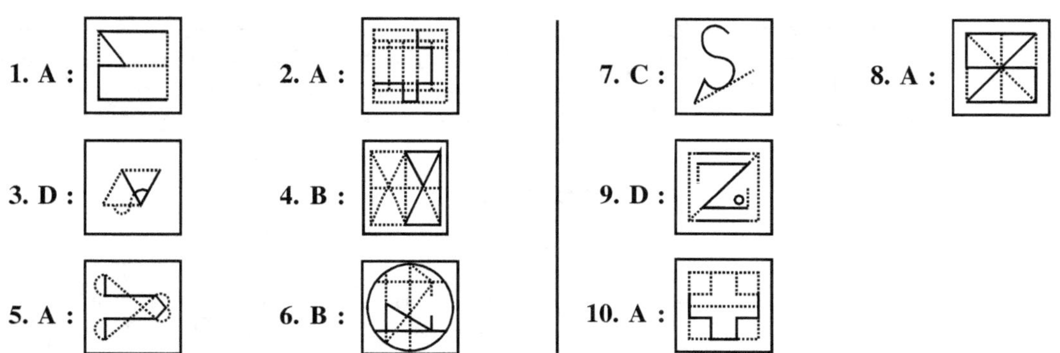

Images and Reflections ▶▶

These type of problems are based on the mirror images or reflections of number, letters and figures. While attempting such questions one must be able to visualise clearly the questioned reflections, be they on vertical plane or on horizontal plane. Study the chart and information given below. The visualisation of letters and numbers is easier than the visualisation of figures for the simple reason that the figures have many forms and all cannot be summed up.

Horizontal Mirror Images of Capital Letters

Letter	HMI	Letter	HMI	H letter	HMI
A	A	J	ſ	S	Ƨ
B	ꓭ	K	ꓘ	T	T
C	Ɔ	L	⅃	U	U
D	ꓷ	M	M	V	V
E	Ǝ	N	И	W	W
F	Ⅎ	O	O	X	X
G	ꓦ	P	�	Y	Y
H	H	Q	Ό	Z	Ƹ
I	I	R	Я		

Note : HMI of A, H, I, M, O, T, U, V, W, X and Y remain unchanged.

Exceptions in style need caution. Example : A will be A, or X will be X.

Vertical Mirror Images of Capital Letters

Letters :	A	B	C	D	E	F	G	H	I	J	K	L	M
VMI :	∀	B	C	D	E	Ⅎ	ꓨ	H	I	ſ	K	Ⅎ	W

Letters :	N	O	P	Q	R	S	T	U	V	W	X	Y	Z
VMI :	И	O	ꓞ	Ꝺ	Я	Ƨ	⊥	∩	ʌ	M	X	⅄	Z

Note : VMI of C, D, E, H, I, K, O and X remain unchanged.

Horizontal Mirror Images of Small Letters

Letter	HMI	Letter	HMI	Letter	HMI
a	ɐ	j	į	s	ƨ
b	d	k	ʞ	t	ɟ
c	ɔ	l	I	u	ɥ
d	b	m	m	v	v
e	ɘ	n	ɥ	w	w
f	ʇ	o	o	x	x
g	ᶾ	p	q	y	ʏ
h	ꓺ	q	p	z	ƨ
i	i	r	ɪ		

Note : HMI of o, v, w and x remain unchanged.

Vertical Mirror Images of Small Letters

Letter :	a	b	c	d	e	f	g	h	i	j	k	l	m
VMI :	ɒ	d	c	b	ɘ	ʇ	ᶾ	ʜ	i	ͺ	ʞ	l	ɯ

Letter :	n	o	p	q	r	s	t	u	v	w	x	y	z
VMI :	ɯ	o	b	d	ɹ	ƨ	ɟ	ɥ	ʌ	ʍ	x	ʎ	z

Note : VMI of c, o and x remain unchanged. Letter l has exceptions: if it is a straight vertical line – 1 then it remains unchanged.

EXERCISE

Directions (Qs. 1 to 6) : *In each question below which is the exact horizontal mirror image?*

1. DuST

   A. ꓔƨuꓷ   B. TƨuꓷD

   C. TƨuꓷD   D. ꓷuƨT

2. CHAIR

   A. CAHIЯ   B. ЯIAHƆ

   C. ЯIAHƆ   D. ЯIAHƆ

3. WHOM

   A. MOHW   B. WOHM

   C. MHOW   D. MOHW

4. PRICKLY
   A. ЬʁICKLY   B. YLKɔIʁԀ
   C. ЬʁICKLY   D. ЬʁICYLЬ

5. taxi
   A. tɐxı   B. ıɒxʇ
   C. ɿɒxı   D. ɿɒxı

6. pond
   A. boпq   B. bouq
   C. boпp   D. bouq

Directions (Qs. 7 to 15) : *In each question given below which one would be the mirror image of the given figure when the mirror is placed along the line shown in each figure.*

7. Problem Figure

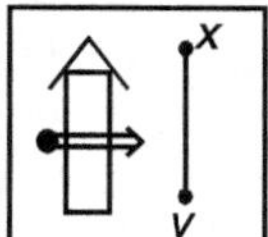

Answer Figures

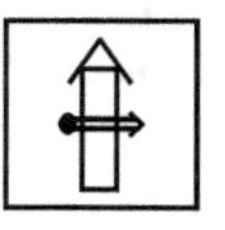  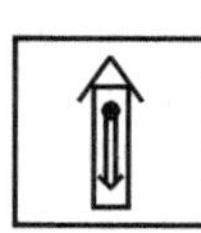 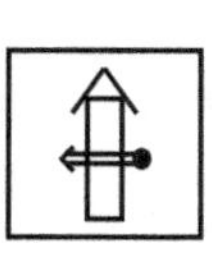

  A   B   C   D

8. Problem Figure

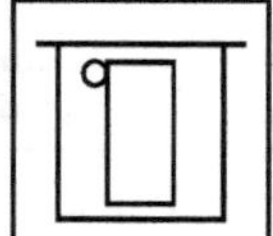

Answer Figures

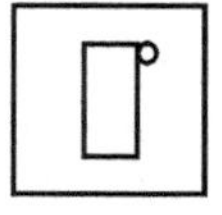 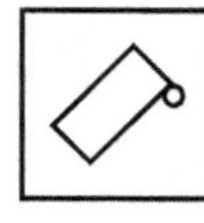 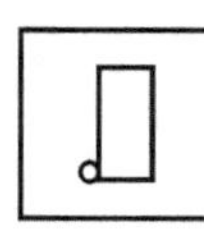 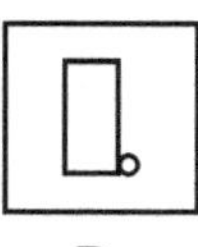

  A   B   C   D

9. Problem Figure

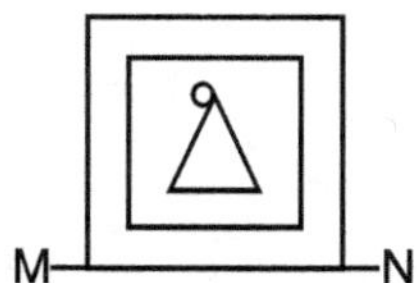

Answer Figures

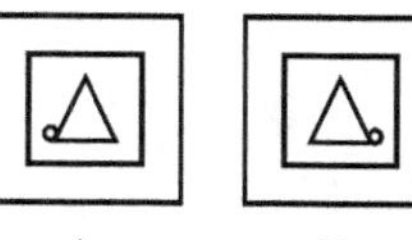

  A   B   C   D

10. Problem Figure

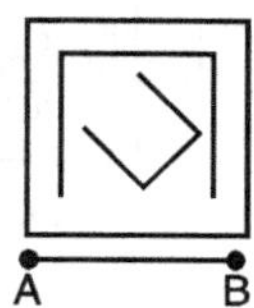

Answer Figures

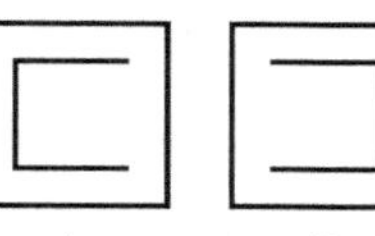

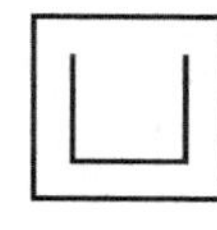 

  A   B   C   D

11. Problem Figure

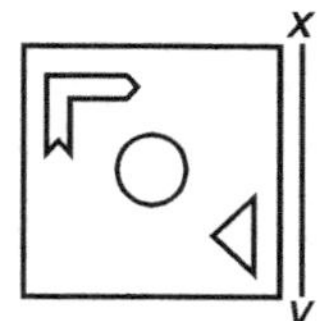

Answer Figures

 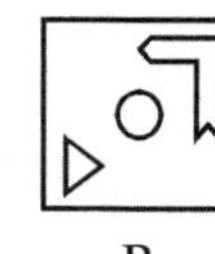 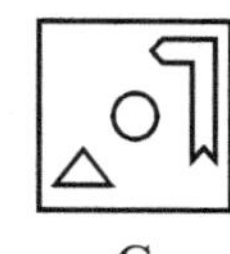 

  A   B   C   D

12. Problem Figure

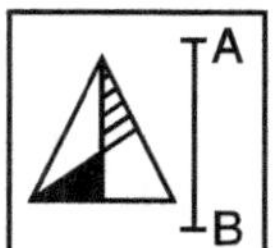

Answer Figures

  A   B   C   D

13. Problem Figure

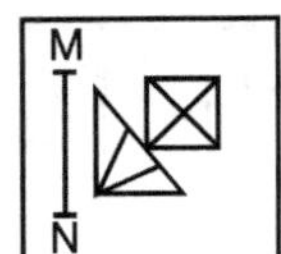

Answer Figures

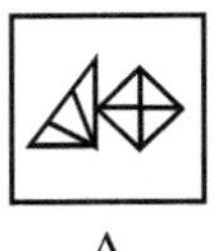  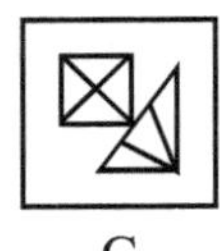 

   A   B   C   D

14. Problem Figure

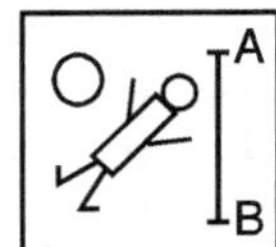

Answer Figures

 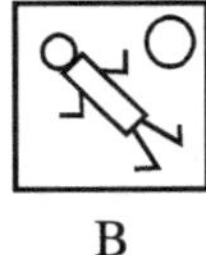  

   A   B   C   D

15. Problem Figure

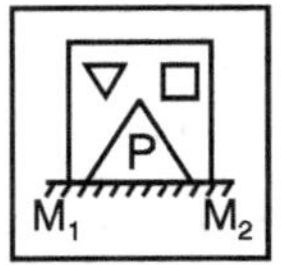

Answer Figures

   A   B   C   D

ANSWERS

1	2	3	4	5	6	7	8	9	10
C	B	A	C	A	B	D	C	C	D

11	12	13	14	15
B	B	C	D	A

❑ ❑ ❑

English Language Comprehension

Spelling Errors

The most common errors in English are of spellings of words. Even the most learned men are sometimes confused about the correct spellings of some words. One must keep and use a dictionary religiously. Never ignore and let pass a new word casually.

A number of question to test your knowledge of spellings are compiled here. Try to solve as many as you can.

Multiple Choice Questions

Directions: *Find the correctly spelt word out of the four options in each question.*

1. A. Accompalish   B. Ackmplesh
   C. Acomplush   D. Accomplish

2. A. Acommodation   B. Acomodation
   C. Accomodation   D. Accommodation

3. A. Astonished   B. Astronished
   C. Astoneshed   D. Asstonished

4. A. Benefeted   B. Benefitted
   C. Benifited   D. Benefited

5. A. Belligerent   B. Beligirent
   C. Belligarant   D. Belligerrent

6. A. Chancelery   B. Chancellery
   C. Chancellary   D. Chancelary

7. A. Discriminate   B. Discremineta
   C. Discrimenate   D. Discriminat

8. A. Damage   B. Dammage
   C. Damaige   D. Dammege

9. A. Efficiant   B. Effecient
   C. Efficient   D. Eficient

10. A. Extravagant   B. Extreragent
    C. Extreregant   D. Extravegent

11. A. Efflorascence   B. Eflorescene
    C. Effllorescence   D. Efflorescence

12. A. Equinimity   B. Equanimmity
    C. Equannimity   D. Equanimity

13. A. Farmament   B. Farmement
    C. Fermament   D. Fremament

14. A. Grieff   B. Grief
    C. Grieef   D. Grrief

15. A. Guarantee   B. Garuntee
    C. Guaruntee   D. Gaurantee

16. A. Hypocritical   B. Hypocretical
    C. Hypocriticel   D. Hypocirticel

17. A. Humurous   B. Humorous
    C. Humoreus   D. Humorrous

18. A. Itenerary   B. Itinarery
    C. Itinarary   D. Itinerary

19. A. Indipenseble   B. Indispansible
    C. Indispensable   D. Indipensable

20. A. Imprecticability   B. Impracticebility
    C. Impracticibility   D. Impracticability

21. A. Incradulous   B. Incredulous
    C. Incridulous   D. Incredalous

22. A. Juddicious   B. Judiceous
    C. Judicious   D. Judiceus

23. A. Kleptomonia   B. Kleptemonia
    C. Kleptomania   D. Klaptomania

24. A. Lackdaisical   B. Lackadaisical
    C. Lckadaisicle   D. Lackadisical

25. A. Licentious   B. Licontious
    C. Licenttious   D. Licientious

26. A. Meddicine   B. Medicine
    C. Medicene   D. Medicinne

27. A. Meritricious   B. Merefrecious
    C. Meretricious   D. Merritricious

28. A. Missunderstood   B. Miesunderstood
    C. Misunderstood   D. Misunderstod

29. A. Occurad   B. Occurred
    C. Ocurred   D. Occured

30. A. Osttentatious   B. Ostentetious
    C. Ostentatious   D. Ostenttatious

31. A. Obnosious   B. Obnoxeous
    C. Obnoxious   D. Obnoseous

32. A. Omenous   B. Ominous
    C. Ommineous   D. Omineous

33. A. Pecification   B. Pacification
    C. Pecifacation   D. Pecefication

34. A. Prograssive   B. Progressive
    C. Progresive   D. Prograsive

35. A. Pasiveness   B. Passiveness
    C. Passeveniss   D. Passivines

36. A. Polyendry   B. Poliendry
    C. Pollyendry   D. Polyandry

37. A. Puerille   B. Puerrile
    C. Puerile   D. Purrile

38. A. Pesanger   B. Passenger
    C. Pessenger   D. Pasanger

39. A. Querrelsome   B. Quarrelsame
    C. Quarrelsome   D. Querralsome

40. A. Rigourous   B. Rigerous
    C. Rigorous   D. Regerous

41. A. Survellance   B. Surveilance
    C. Surveillance   D. Survaillance

42. A. Schedule   B. Schdule
    C. Schedale   D. Schedeule

43. A. Sepalchrle   B. Sepalchral
    C. Sepulchrle   D. Sepulchral

44. A. Sympathetic   B. Smypathetic
    C. Sympothetic   D. Sympethetic

45. A. Sincerely   B. Sencerely
    C. Sincerelly   D. Sincerrely

46. A. Satellite   B. Sattellite
    C. Satelite   D. Sattelite

47. A. Teracherous   B. Treacherous
    C. Treacheraus   D. Treachereans

48. A. Uncivilized   B. Uncevilized
    C. Uncivillized   D. Uncevelized

49. A. Vainglorious   B. Vaniglorious
    C. Vaniglerious   D. Vaingloreus

50. A. Vulnarable   B. Valnerable
    C. Velnerable   D. Vulnerable

ANSWERS

1	2	3	4	5	6	7	8	9	10
D	D	A	B	A	C	A	A	C	A

11	12	13	14	15	16	17	18	19	20
D	D	C	B	A	A	B	D	C	D

21	22	23	24	25	26	27	28	29	30
B	C	C	B	A	B	C	C	B	C

31	32	33	34	35	36	37	38	39	40
C	B	B	B	B	D	C	B	C	C

41	42	43	44	45	46	47	48	49	50
C	A	D	A	A	A	B	A	A	D

Spotting Errors

The most common errors in English are of spellings, grammar and usage of words. By regular practice, the errors can be easily spotted and minimised.

Multiple Choice Questions

Directions: *In this section, each sentence has three parts, indicated by (A), (B) and (C). Read each sentence to find out whether there is an error. If you find an error in any one of the parts (A, B, C), indicate your response by marking the letter related to that part. If a sentence has no error, indicate this by marking '(D)' which stands for "No error". Errors may belong to grammar, usage or idiom. Ignore errors of punctuation, if any.*

1. (A) Beware of/(B) a fair-weather friend/(C) who is neither a friend in need nor a friend indeed/(D) No error.

2. (A) Copernicus proved/(B) that Earth/(C) moves round the Sun./(D) No error.

3. (A) Seldom we have been treated/(B) in such a rude manner/(C) by the police personnel./(D) No error.

4. (A) Some men are born great,/(B) some achieve greatness/(C) and some had greatness thrust on them./(D) No error.

5. (A) The property/(B) was divided/(C) among the two brothers./(D) No error.

6. (A) I am quite certain/(B) that the lady is not only greedy/(C) but miserly./(D) No error.

7. (A) The aircraft overloaded/(B) there was something wrong of the battery/(C) and the engine was making a queer noise/(D) No error.

8. (A) A thorough inquiry of the misappropriation of funds/(B) is now imperative/(C) to bring the guilty to book/(D) No error.

9. (A) The brilliant success in the examination/(B) as well as his record in sports/(C) deserves high praise/(D) No error.

10. (A) While travelling by a train/(B) on a cold winter night/(C) an argument rose between two passengers in our compartment/(D) No error.

11. (A) I cannot find/(B) where has he gone/(C) though I have tried may best/(D) No error.

12. (A) If I was/(B) the Prime Minister of India/(C) I would work wonders/(D) No error.

13. (A) Amit's severe bout of flu/(B) debilitated him so much/(C) that he was too tired to do for work for a week./(D) No error.

14. (A) This is the crux of the entire problem;/(B) everything centres on/(C) it being resolved./(D) No error.

15. (A) One of the major aims of the Air Force/(B) was the complete demolition of all means of transportation/(C) by the bombing of rail lines and terminals./(D) No error.

16. (A) His strong voice cut over/(B) the hum of conversation/(C) like a knife through butter./(D) No error.

17. (A) Even though they weren't expecting us/(B) they managed to knock up/(C) a marvellous meal./(D) No error.

18. (A) The celebrated singer was/(B) surrounded by the usual crowd/(C) of lackeys and hangers-ons./(D) No error.

19. (A) If it weren't/(B) for you,/(C) I wouldn't be alive today./(D) No error.

20. (A) He looked like a lion/(B) baulked from/(C) its prey./(D) No error.

21. (A) Widespread flooding/(B) is effecting/(C) large areas of the villages./(D) No error.

22. (A) She regards/(B) negotiating prices with customers/(C) as her special preserve./(D) No error.

23. (A) Often in political campaigns, a point is reached at which/(B) the candidates take out their gloves./(C) and start slugging with bare fists./(D) No error.

24. (A) If we really set to/(B) we can get the whole house/(C) cleaned in an afternoon./(D) No error.

25. (A) Pieces of rock plummeted/(B) down the mountainside/(C) in the ground below./(D) No error.

26. (A) Since the two parties each won/(B) the same number of seats,/(C) the minority party holds the balance of power./(D) No error.

27. (A) It's arrogant for you/(B) to assume you'll/(C) win every time./(D) No error.

28. (A) We've paid for our travel and accommod-ation,/(B) so we need only to take/(C) some pocket-money with us./(D) No error.

29. (A) There's no evidence to show/(B) that information technology secrets are more/(C) vulnerable in India than Britain or the US./(D) No error.

30. (A) It is shameful that hunting/(B) is still considered sport/(C) by some unscrupulous people in the civilized world./(D) No error.

31. (A) The Prime Minister's good looks won him/(B) the election but he has still to prove/(C) that he's not a just pretty face./(D) No error.

32. (A) The two books are the same/(B) except for the fact that this/(C) has an answer in the back./(D) No error.

33. (A) He estimated his income tax bill/(B) by extrapolation over figures/(C) submitted in previous years./(D) No error.

34. (A) The modern office block/(B) sticks out like a sore thumb/(C) among the old buildings in the area./(D) No error.

35. (A) I will try to put over/(B) some feelers to gauge/(C) people's reactions to our proposal./(D) No error.

36. (A) A major contribution of Mathura sculptors/(B) of that period were the creation and popularization/(C) of the Buddha's image in human form./(D) No error.

37. (A) Amit has been deceiving Mona/(B) for many years but she/(C) has not still tumbled to it./(D) No error.

38. (A) Mahavira was an advocate of nonviolence and vegetarianism,/(B) who revived and reorganized the Jain doctrine/(C) and established rules for their monastic order. (D) No error.

39. (A) Microwaves are the principle carriers/(B) of television, telephone and data transmissions/(C) between stations on earth and between the earth and satellites./(D) No error.

40. (A) An unit is an abstract idea,/(B) defined either by reference to/(C) a randomly chosen material standard or to a natural phenomenon./(D) No error.

41. (A) With the crisis deepening,/(B) the critics sense an opportunity/(C) about putting in place a more radical strategy./(D) No error.

42. (A) The salesman gave us/(B) a big spiel about why/(C) we should buy his product./(D) No error.

43. (A) I will need several weeks/(B) to invent the lie of the land before/(C) I can make any decision about the future of the business./(D) No error.

44. (A) You should be cautious/(B) and make a few discrete enquiries about/(C) the firm before you sign anything./(D) No error.

45. (A) Your husband doesn't/(B) believe that you are older/(C) than I./(D) No error.

46. (A) We are meeting today afternoon/(B) to discuss the matter/(C) and reach a compromise./(D) No error.

47. (A) Either Ram or/(B) you is responsible/(C) for this action./(D) No error.

48. (A) The student flatly denied/(B) that he had copied/(C) in the examination hall./(D) No error.

49. (A) By the time you arrive tomorrow/(B) I have finished/(C) my work./(D) No error.

50. (A) The speaker stressed repeatedly on/(B) the importance of improving/(C) the condition of the slums./(D) No error.

51. (A) The captain with the members of his team/(B) are returning/(C) after a fortnight./(D) No error.

52. (A) After returning from/(B) an all-India tour/(C) I had to describe about it/(D) No error.

53. (A) The teacher asked his students/(B) if they had gone through/(C) either of the three chapters included in the prescribed text./(D) No error.

54. (A) Although they are living in the country/(B) since they were married/(C) they are now moving to the town./(D) No error.

55. (A) Do you know/(B) how old were you/(C) when you came here?/(D) No error.

56. (A) The company has/(B) set off itself some stiff production/(C) goals for this year/(D) No error.

57. (A) The music was so loud/(B) that we had to bellow over each/(C) other to be heard./(D) No error.

58. (A) When this beautiful girl arrived, (A) all the men in the room/(C) gravitated over her./(D) No error.

59. (A) The children are/(B) really in their element/(C) playing on the beach./(D) No error.

60. (A) The refugees are/(B) badly off for blankets,/(C) and even worse for food./(D) No error.

61. (A) From their vintage-point on the cliff,/(B) the children could watch/(C) the ships coming and going./(D) No error.

62. (A) A cogent remark/(B) compels acceptance because/(C) of their sense and logic./(D) No error.

63. (A) Credit cards have/(B) brought about a revolution/(C) in people's spending habits./(D) No error.

64. (A) In financial matters/(B) it is important to/(C) get disinterested advice./(D) No error.

65. (A) Some women admit that/(B) their principle goal in life/(C) is to marry a wealthy man./(D) No error.

ANSWERS

1	2	3	4	5	6	7	8	9	10
D	B	A	C	C	C	B	A	D	C
11	12	13	14	15	16	17	18	19	20
B	A	C	C	B	A	A	C	C	C
21	22	23	24	25	26	27	28	29	30
C	A	A	A	C	A	A	B	D	B
31	32	33	34	35	36	37	38	39	40
C	C	C	D	A	B	C	C	A	A
41	42	43	44	45	46	47	48	49	50
C	D	D	D	C	A	B	D	B	A
51	52	53	54	55	56	57	58	59	60
B	C	C	B	D	B	B	C	B	D
61	62	63	64	65					
A	C	D	D	D					

Articles

Definite and Indefinite Articles

(*i*) 'A' and 'an' are Indefinite Articles.

(*ii*) 'The' is Definite Article.

(*iii*) 'A' and 'an' modify a noun in a general way.

(*iv*) 'The' particularises it. *e.g.,*

Mohan has **a pen.**

The pen which you gave me was expensive.

Vowel and Consonant Sounds

(*i*) 'A' is used before words starting with the sound of a consonant.

(*ii*) 'An' is used before a vowel sound (vowels a, e, i, o, u) *e.g.,*

a book, a cat, a useful thing, a European girl, a university,

but an FDR, an MA, an honest boy, an hour, an owl, an egg, an umbrella, etc.

Use of Articles 'A' and 'An'

A cat mews.   (*i.e.,* every cat)

The cat of my neighbour mews day and night.

(*i.e.,* a particular cat)

He gave me **an** egg.   (Here 'an' means 'one')

Use of Article 'The'

1. 'The' is used before names of rivers, mountains, seas, oceans:

   The Himalayas, the Ganga, the Yamuna, the Bay of Bengal, the Indian Ocean, the Nile, the English Channel, *etc.*

2. Names of newspapers and magazines:

   The Times of India, the Tribune, The Sun, *etc.*

3. Names of the famous and holy books:

   The Guru Granth Sahib, The Gita, The Ramayana, *etc.*

4. Names of creations of nature:

   the sun, the earth, the moon, the sky, *etc.*

5. While using Adjectives as Nouns:

   The poor should be helped by **the rich.**

6. Sometimes with the Comparative Degree:

   The more you think, **the more** you worry.

7. With the Superlative Degree:

   She is **the most intelligent** girl in our school.

8. Before the imaginary lines and directions:

   The Latitude, The Equator, the east, the west, etc.

9. Before the names of musical instruments:

   the violin, the piano, the flute, etc.

10. While using a Proper Noun as a Common Noun:

    Mohan is **the Sachin** of our team.

Omission of Article 'The'

1. Before some Nouns used to convey general sense, articles are not used but are used to particularise them:

   Man is mortal.

2. Before Proper Nouns:

   Rakesh is an intelligent boy.

3. With Abstract Noun:

   Childhood is the prime time of one's life.

   The childhood of Sohan was full of sorrow.

4. With Material Nouns:

   Milk is an essential food.

   The milk of the cow is sweet.

5. Usually no article is used before names of diseases:

Cancer is a fatal disease.

However, when we talk about a disease figuratively, we use an article before its name, *e.g.*

Corruption is a cancer.

6. Names of games and language:

I like football.

I can speak Punjabi, Hindi and English.

7. Gold is a precious metal.

NOTE: As you must have noted above, the definite article 'the' has been used where a noun is particularised.

Double Use of Article 'The'

Read the following sentences carefully to understand this :

1. The poet and novelist has been honoured.

   (The same person is the poet as well as novelist)

2. The poet and the novelist have been honoured.

   (The poet and the novelist are two different persons).

3. I have a black and white dog.

   (that is, one dog)

4. I have a black and a white dog.

   (that is, two dogs)

Multiple Choice Questions

Directions : *Fill in the blanks with suitable articles. Mark 'D' if no article required.*

1. Do you know .... boy in white?

   A. a   B. an

   C. the   D. No article

2. She is .... girl I am looking for.

   A. a   B. an

   C. the   D. No article

3. Have you read .... Mahabharat?

   A. a   B. an

   C. the   D. No article

4. ....rich are not always happy.

   A. A   B. An

   C. The   D. No article

5. Oranges are sold by .... dozen.

   A. a   B. an

   C. the   D. No article

6. Milk is sold by .... litre.

   A. a   B. an

   C. the   D. No article

7. .... Amazon is the longest river in the world.

   A. A   B. An

   C. The   D. No article

8. .... higher you climb, the colder it gets.

   A. A   B. An

   C. The   D. No article

9. She is .... untidy girl.

   A. a   B. an

   C. the   D. No article

10. I am .... M.A. is English.

   A. a   B. an

   C. the   D. No article

11. I have already spent .... few rupees I had.

   A. a   B. an

   C. the   D. No article

12. .... English are very hard-working.

   A. A   B. An

   C. The   D. No article

13. April is the fourth month of .... year.

   A. a   B. an

   C. the   D. No article

14. Rice is sold by .... kilogram

   A. a   B. an

   C. the   D. No article

15. She is .... best of the three girls.

   A. a   B. an

   C. the   D. No article

16. .... man in the car is a friend of mine.

   A. A   B. An

   C. The   D. No article

17. Brevity is .... soul of wit.
   A. a   B. an
   C. the   D. No article

18. .... thing of beauty is a joy for ever.
   A. A   B. An
   C. The   D. No article

19. .... little learning is a dangerous thing.
   A. A   B. An
   C. The   D. No article

20. .... best sauce for food is hunger.
   A. A   B. An
   C. The   D. No article

21. Birds of .... feather flock together.
   A. a   B. an
   C. the   D. No article

22. He makes .... living by begging.
   A. a   B. an
   C. the   D. No article

23. It is .... pity that he died so young.
   A. a   B. an
   C. the   D. No article

24. What .... nuisance it is?
   A. a   B. an
   C. the   D. No article

25. Delhi is .... London of India.
   A. a   B. an
   C. the   D. No article

26. Where is .... will, there is a way.
   A. a   B. an
   C. the   D. No article

27. Her father is .... physician and surgeon.
   A. a   B. an
   C. the   D. No article

28. This will benefit .... poor.
   A. a   B. an
   C. the   D. No article

29. ....bird in hand is better than two in a bush.
   A. A   B. An
   C. The   D. No article

30. As he is hard-working, he will win .... prize.
   A. a   B. an
   C. the   D. No article

31. .... water of this well is dirty.
   A. A   B. An
   C. The   D. No article

32. Only .... wearer knows where the shoe pinches.
   A. a   B. an
   C. the   D. No article

33. .... action will be taken against you.
   A. A   B. An
   C. The   D. No article

34. .... sun rises in the east.
   A. A   B. An
   C. The   D. No article

35. She was promoted to .... highest post.
   A. a   B. an
   C. the   D. No article

36. Did you see .... Taj Mahal?
   A. a   B. an
   C. the   D. No article

37. He is .... one-eyed man.
   A. a   B. an
   C. the   D. No article

38. This is .... useful book.
   A. a   B. an
   C. the   D. No article

39. Cloth is sold by .... metre.
   A. a   B. an
   C. the   D. No article

40. The sun sets in .... west.
   A. a   B. an
   C. the   D. No article

41. Amar bought......umbrella yesterday.
   A. a   B. an
   C. the   D. No article

42. Surinder is ...... honest boy.
   A. a   B. an
   C. the   D. No article

43. She wrote ...... book in French.
   A. a   B. an
   C. the   D. No article

44. ...... lion roars.
   A. A   B. An
   C. The   D. No article

45. ..... apple a day keeps the doctor away.
A. A
B. An
C. The
D. No article

46. John bought ...... car yesterday.
A. a
B. an
C. the
D. No article

47. His father is ..... engineer in the U.S.A.
A. a
B. an
C. the
D. No article

48. It is hard for ..... owl to fly during the day times.
A. a
B. an
C. the
D. No article

49. She had ..... rimmed hat.
A. a
B. an
C. the
D. No article

50. My uncle is ..... heart specialist.
A. a
B. an
C. the
D. No article

51. He looks as foolish as .... ass.
A. a
B. an
C. the
D. No article

52. Did you go to .... prison to visit him?
A. a
B. an
C. the
D. No article

53. I found .... one-rupee note in the market.
A. a
B. an
C. the
D. No article

54. It is a pleasure to meet such .... efficient man.
A. a
B. an
C. the
D. No article

55. The Sanyasi lived in a cave in .... Himalayas.
A. a
B. an
C. the
D. No article

56. There is .... union in our factory.
A. a
B. an
C. the
D. No article

57. He hit his wife on the head with .... umbrella.
A. a
B. an
C. the
D. No article

58. I caught him by .... collar.
A. a
B. an
C. the
D. No article

59. Child is .... father of man.
A. a
B. an
C. the
D. No article

60. He gazed at .... moon for two hours.
A. a
B. an
C. the
D. No article

ANSWERS

1	2	3	4	5	6	7	8	9	10
C	C	C	C	C	C	C	C	B	B

11	12	13	14	15	16	17	18	19	20
C	C	C	C	C	C	C	A	A	C

21	22	23	24	25	26	27	28	29	30
A	A	A	A	C	A	A	C	A	A

31	32	33	34	35	36	37	38	39	40
C	C	B	C	C	C	A	A	C	C

41	42	43	44	45	46	47	48	49	50
B	B	A	A	B	A	B	B	A	A

51	52	53	54	55	56	57	58	59	60
B	C	A	B	C	A	B	C	C	C

Prepositions

4

A Preposition is a word that comes before a Pronoun or a Noun and expresses the relationship between Noun or Pronoun and some part of the remaining sentence.

(*a*) He is busy **with** his work.
(*b*) The boy jumped **into** the river.
(*c*) The birds are chirping **in** the trees.

In these sentences the words **with**, **into** and **in** show the relationship between the verbs **busy, jumped** and **chirping** with the nouns **work, river** and **trees** respectively.

Position of the Preposition

A. A Preposition usually precedes its object.
  (*i*) He laughs **at** the poor.
  (*ii*) He is angry **with** you.
  (*iii*) She agrees **with** me.

B. In the case of Relative Pronouns it comes after the subject.
  (*i*) This is the boy whom I was looking **for**.
  (*ii*) That is the pen whose mention I was making **of**.

C. In the following cases, the Preposition comes after its object.
  (*i*) Where is the boy you were complaining **against**?
  (*ii*) What things are there you are looking **for**?
  (*iii*) Who is there, you are waiting **for**?

Omission of the Prepositon

In many cases when the sentences contain Nouns of Time or Place, the Prepositions **from, in** and **for** are often omitted.

(*i*) He walked many kilometres.
(*ii*) He came to see me last year.
(*iii*) As I could not find my puppy anywhere, I looked here and there.

Prepositions are small words that show the relationship between one word and another. Prepositions in the following sentences show the position of the paper in relation to the desk, the book, hand and the door.

The paper is **on** the desk.
The paper is **under** the book.
The paper is **in** his hand.
The paper is **by** the door.

Common Prepositions

about	at	by
in	onto	toward
above	before	concerning
inside	out	under
across	behind	despite
into	over	until
after	below	down
like	since	up
against	beneath	during
near	through	upon
along	beside	except
of	throughout	with
amid	between	for
off	till	within
among	beyond	from
on	to	without

Multiple Choice Questions

Directions: *Select the most appropriate preposition from the given alternatives to fill in the blanks and make the sentence meaningfully complete.*

1. Don't try to be an advocate ..... these criminals.
   A. for
   B. with
   C. across
   D. in
2. The audience admired him ..... his sweet voice.
   A. to
   B. on
   C. for
   D. at
3. I want to check your bag ..... fake currency notes.
   A. to
   B. for
   C. upon
   D. on
4. The dew drops clung .... the blades of grass.
   A. for
   B. on
   C. to
   D. in
5. The thief was chased ..... by the police.
   A. on
   B. after
   C. into
   D. at
6. Please carry this bag ..... my room.
   A. on
   B. for
   C. to
   D. in
7. A lorry bumped ..... a car.
   A. on
   B. over
   C. into
   D. to
8. They were begging ..... food.
   A. for
   B. on
   C. to
   D. after
9. She always boasts ..... her wealth.
   A. of
   B. for
   C. on
   D. after
10. She banged ..... the door violently.
    A. for
    B. to
    C. on
    D. down
11. I applied ..... the post of a clerk.
    A. for
    B. on
    C. in
    D. to
12. I applied ..... the Principal for the post of a teacher.
    A. to
    B. on
    C. with
    D. for
13. I begged ..... him not to divulge the secret.
    A. for
    B. of
    C. with
    D. to
14. You had better borrow a pen ..... Rakesh.
    A. over
    B. into
    C. from
    D. by

15. I baked a cake ..... the guests.
    A. to
    B. for
    C. on
    D. of
16. She is confident ..... (her) success.
    A. with
    B. on
    C. of
    D. for
17. The doctor will cure you ..... malaria.
    A. of
    B. with
    C. for
    D. from
18. This law is common ..... all.
    A. to
    B. upon
    C. over
    D. at
19. She was condemned ..... her bad hand writing.
    A. on
    B. for
    C. into
    D. of
20. In summer there will be a great demand ..... desert cooler.
    A. on
    B. with
    C. for
    D. of
21. We shall wait ..... you.
    A. on
    B. for
    C. towards
    D. after
22. Tom displayed his injury ..... all his friends.
    A. for
    B. upon
    C. to
    D. at
23. She distributed the sweets ..... the two brothers.
    A. among
    B. between
    C. for
    D. in
24. Please distribute these apples ..... all.
    A. among
    B. to
    C. for
    D. at
25. It rarely happened that he defended ..... an innocent person.
    A. against
    B. for
    C. upon
    D. at
26. The parents were disappointed ..... the performance of their son.
    A. on
    B. with
    C. at
    D. of
27. Common salt dissolves ..... water.
    A. for
    B. in
    C. with
    D. by
28. This medicare is free ..... sugar.
    A. on
    B. to
    C. from
    D. of

29. The manager granted leave ..... the clerk.
   A. to
   B. on
   C. into
   D. for

30. The air was heavy ..... aroma of perfumes.
   A. on
   B. with
   C. into
   D. from

31. She had a quick glance ..... the magazine.
   A. at
   B. from
   C. into
   D. to

32. The climate of Kashmir is favourable ..... me.
   A. with
   B. in
   C. to
   D. for

33. They hate you ..... your poverty.
   A. for
   B. on
   C. in
   D. of

34. He is eligible ..... this post.
   A. for
   B. to
   C. with
   D. at

35. The smoke was emerging ..... down the foot of the hill.
   A. on
   B. to
   C. from
   D. at

36. The criminal managed to escape ..... the prison.
   A. upon
   B. from
   C. with
   D. of

37. You should educate your friends ..... the benefits of living in villages.
   A. on
   B. towards
   C. upon
   D. in

38. She made a lot of efforts ..... win the match.
   A. for
   B. to
   C. upon
   D. at

39. The new inspector will enquire ..... the murder case.
   A. on
   B. for
   C. into
   D. at

40. The retired soldiers were exempted ..... all taxes.
   A. from
   B. to
   C. on
   D. of

41. She was adept ..... journalism.
   A. at
   B. on
   C. with
   D. in

42. She is afraid ..... snakes.
   A. on
   B. to
   C. of
   D. with

43. I agree ..... your proposal.
   A. for
   B. on
   C. to
   D. with

44. The children were amazed ..... so big a python.
   A. at
   B. on
   C. in
   D. with

45. She was anxious ..... the final match.
   A. about
   B. on
   C. with
   D. for

46. He apologized ..... his being late.
   A. towards
   B. for
   C. on
   D. as

47. The children were amused ..... his jokes.
   A. for
   B. to
   C. at
   D. on

48. She is angry ..... you.
   A. to
   B. with
   C. on
   D. for

49. She is angry ..... your teasing remark.
   A. at
   B. in
   C. for
   D. with

50. A big patch of land was allocated ..... the refugees.
   A. to
   B. for
   C. in
   D. upon

ANSWERS

1	2	3	4	5	6	7	8	9	10
A	C	B	C	B	C	C	A	A	C

11	12	13	14	15	16	17	18	19	20
A	A	B	C	B	C	A	A	B	C

21	22	23	24	25	26	27	28	29	30
B	C	B	A	A	C	B	C	A	B

31	32	33	34	35	36	37	38	39	40
A	C	A	A	C	B	A	B	C	A

41	42	43	44	45	46	47	48	49	50
A	C	C	A	A	B	C	B	A	A

Synonyms & Antonyms

There are thousands of words in English language. No one can remember their meanings easily but with regular practice one can memorise most of them. A number of words with their Synonyms and Antonyms are compiled here. Try to learn as many as you can and answer the questions thereafter.

Words	Synonyms	Antonyms
Abandon	Cease, Forsake	Continue
Abhor	Hate, Loathe, Detest	Like, Love
Abiding	Enduring, Durable	Fleeting
Able	Proficient, Competent	Incompetent, Unfit
Ability	Skill, Power	Disability, Inability
Abortive	Fruitless, Futile	Fruitful, Successful
Abolish	Destroy, Undo	Restore, Revive
Abridge	Shorten, Curtail	Lengthen, Expand
Absolve	Forgive, Pardon, Excuse	Condemn
Accelerate	Hasten	Retard
Accord	Agreement, Harmony	Discord, Disagreement
Accumulate	Collect, Store, Amass	Distribute, Scatter
Adamant	Hard, Inflexible	Flexible
Adversity	Misfortune, Distress	Prosperity
Adept	Expert, Skilful	Inexpert, Unskillful
Aggravate	Heighten, Intensify	Quell, Suppress
Base	Low, Mean, Ignoble	Noble, Exalted
Boisterous	Noisy, Stormy	Calm, Quiet
Brave	Courageous, Daring, Bold, Plucky	Cowardly, Dastardly, Timid
Brief	Short, Concise, Laconic	Lengthy, Diffuse
Bright	Vivid, Radiant	Dull, Dark
Brutal	Savage, Cruel	Humane, Kindly
Callous	Hard, Cruel, Indifferent	Soft, Tender, Concerned

Words	Synonyms	Antonyms
Cautious	Careful, Wary	Rash, Reckless, Foolhardy
Censure (*n*)	Blame, Condemnation	Praise
Censure (*vb*)	Blame, Condemn	Praise, Commend
Circumscribed	Restricted, Confined, Limited	Unconfined, Unrestricted
Civil	Polite, Courteous, Gracious, Urbane	Rude, Uncivil, Impolite, Ungracious
Coerce	Compel, Force	Volunteer
Compassionate	Pitiful, Sympathetic, Merciful	Unsympathetic, Merciless, Cruel
Compress	Condense, Abbreviate	Expand, Lengthen
Conspicuous	Noticeable, Manifest	Inconspicuous
Death	Decease, Demise	Existence, Life
Dearth	Scarcity, Lack, Want, Paucity, Shortage	Plenty, Abundance
Decay	Dissolution, Decline, Decomposition	Regeneration
Deference	Respect, Reverence	Disrespect, Irreverence
Deficient	Lacking, Inadequate	Complete, Sufficient
Desolate	Lonely, Deserted	Crowded, Occupied
Earthly	Terrestrial, Mundane	Celestial, Heavenly, Unearthly
Eligible	Qualified, Suitable	Ineligible, Unsuitable
Emancipate	Liberate, Free	Enslave
Excited	Impassioned, Stimulated	Composed, Cool, Impassive
Extraordinary	Uncommon, Remarkable, Marvellous	Commonplace, Ordinary
Extravagant	Lavish, Prodigal, Wastrel, Spendthrift	Thrifty, Economical, Frugal
Fabricate	Construct, Make	Destroy
Fabulous	Fictitious, Mythical	Actual, Real
False	Untrue, Mendacious	True, Genuine
Famous	Well-known, Renowned	Obscure, Unknown
Fantastic	Fanciful, Imaginative, Visionary	Practical, Down to earth
Fearful	Nervous, Anxious, Afraid, Scared	Fearless, Dauntless
Felicity	Happiness	Sorrow
Gaiety	Joyousness, Hilarity	Mourning, Dullness
Garrulous	Talkative, Loquacious	Taciturn, Silent, Reserved
Generous	Liberal, Magnanimous	Stingy, Miserly
Gigantic	Huge, Colossal	Minute, Small
Graphic	Vivid, Pictorial, Meaningful	Vague
Guest	Visitor	Host
Guile	Fraud, Trickery	Artlessness, Ingenuousness
Gratitude	Gratefulness	Ingratitude, Ungratefulness

Words	Synonyms	Antonyms
Gratuitous	Voluntary, Spontaneous,	Involuntary, Forced
Hamper	Hinder, Obstruct	Facilitate, Ease
Haughty	Arrogant, Proud	Humble, Modest
Hazardous	Dangerous, Perilous	Safe, Secure Protected
Headstrong	Obstinate, Stubborn	Weak-willed, Flexible
Hope	Belief, Conviction, Expectation	Despair, Hopelessness
Improvident	Prodigal, Carelessness	Provident, Economical
Incessant	Unceasing, Continuous	Discontinuous
Indolent	Slothful, Lethargic	Active, Energetic
Joy	Delight, Pleasure	Sadness, Gloom
Jolly	Jovial, Merry	Gloomy, Sad
Judicious	Discreet, Prudent	Indiscreet, Injudicious
Knowledge	Enlightenment, Learning	Ignorance, Stupidity
Laborious	Industrious, Assiduous	Slothful, Lazy
Laxity	Slackness, Looseness	Firmness
Lenient	Mild, Forbearing	Strict, Stern
Lethal	Deadly, Fatal, Mortal	Life-giving, Vital, Vivifying
Liberal	Generous, Tolerant	Intolerant, Illiberal
Liberty	Freedom, Independence	Slavery, Bondage
Magnanimous	Generous, Largehearted	Ungenerous, Stingy
Malady	Illness, Ailment	Health
Manifest	Noticeable, Obvious	Obscure, Puzzling
Negligent	Careless, Heedless	Careful
Notorious	Infamous, Disreputable	Reputable
Obedient	Submissive, Compliant, Docile	Disobedient, Recalcitrant, Wayward
Obsolete	Antiquated, Out-of-Date	Current, Modern
Opportune	Timely, Seasonable	Inopportune
Opulence	Wealth, Riches	Penury, Poverty
Onerous	Heavy, Burdensome	Light, Easy
Palatable	Tasty, Delicious	Unpalatable
Pathetic	Touching	Joyous, Cheery
Persuade	Urge, Induce	Dissuade
Praise (*vb*)	Applaud, Eulogise	Condemn
Praise (*n*)	Applause, Eulogy	Condemnation
Precarious	Risky, Uncertain	Safe, Certain
Pretence	Pretext, Excuse	Candour, Frankness
Propagate	Breed, Circulate	Terminate, Restrict
Quaint	Odd, Singular	Usual, Ordinary
Quell	Suppress, Subdue	Agitate, Arouse
Rare	Uncommon, Scarce	Common, Ordinary

Words	Synonyms	Antonyms
Refined	Polished, Elegant	Crude, Coarse
Remote	Distant	Near, Close
Renown	Fame, Reputation	Infamy, Notoriety
Rigid	Stiff, Unyielding	Flexible, Yielding
Remorseful	Regretful, Repentant	Unrepentant
Rebellion	Revolt, Mutiny, Insurgency	Loyalty
Scared	Holy, Consecrated	Profane, Unholy
Sane	Sensible, Sound	Insane
Scold	Chide, Rebuke	Praise
Serious	Grave, Earnest	Frivolous
Tame	Gentle, Mild, Domesticated	Savage, Wild
Teacher	Instructor, Educator	Student, Pupil
Tedious	Wearisome, Monotonous	Agreeable, Lively
Temporal	Worldly, Secular	Spiritual
Temperate	Moderate	Immoderate, Intemperate
Tortuous	Winding, Circuitous	Straight, Direct
Tough	Hard, Strong	Tender, Soft, Flexible
Ugly	Unsightly, Repulsive	Beautiful, Attractive
Useful	Advantageous, Serviceable	Useless
Vehemence	Passion, Force	Apathy, Indifference
Vindictive	Revengeful	Forgiving
Wholesome	Healthy	Unwholesome, Morbid
Wicked	Evil, Impious	Pious, Good
Wise	Sagacious, Erudite	Foolish, Stupid
Wrath	Anger, Fury, Rage	Love, Peace, Calm
Wreck	Ruin, Destroy	Create, Construct
Yield	Surrender, Submit	Resist, Revolt
Yielding	Submissive, Supple	Inflexible, Intractable
Yoke	Oppression, Bondage	Freedom
Zeal	Passion, Fervour	Apathy, Indifference
Zest	Relish, Enthusiasm	Distaste, Disrelish

Multiple Choice Questions

Directions (Qs. 1 to 25): *In the following questions choose the word which best expresses the MEANING of the given word.*

1. TEPID
   - A. Hot
   - B. Warm
   - C. Cold
   - D. Boiling

2. MAYHEM
   - A. Jubilation
   - B. Havoc
   - C. Excitement
   - D. Defeat

3. TIMID
   - A. Fast
   - B. Slow
   - C. Medium
   - D. Shy

4. CANTANKEROUS
A. Quarrelsome	B. Rash
C. Disrespectful	D. Noisy

5. PRECARIOUS
A. Cautious	B. Critical
C. Perilous	D. Brittle

6. TACITURNITY
A. Dumbness	B. Changeableness
C. Hesitation	D. Reserve

7. INEBRIATE
A. Dreamy	B. Stupefied
C. Unsteady	D. Drunken

8. HARBINGER
A. Massenger	B. Steward
C. Forerunner	D. Pilot

9. INTIMIDATE
A. To hint	B. Frighten
C. Bluff	D. Harass

10. IRONIC
A. Inflexible
B. Bitter
C. Good-natured
D. Disguisedly sarcastic

11. STRINGENT
A. Tense	B. Stringy
C. Strict	D. Causing to shrink

12. ECSTATIC
A. Animated	B. Bewildered
C. Enraptured	D. Willful

13. COMMENSURATE
A. Measurable	B. Proportionate
C. Beginning	D. Appropriate

14. DESTITUTION
A. Humility	B. Moderation
C. Poverty	D. Beggary

15. ASCEND
A. Leap	B. Grow
C. Deviate	D. Mount

16. UNCOUTH
A. Ungraceful	B. Rough
C. Slovenly	D. Dirty

17. LYNCH
A. Hang	B. Madden
C. Killed	D. Shoot

18. LAUD
A. Lord	B. Eulogy
C. Praise	D. Extolled

19. CORRESPONDENCE
A. Agreements	B. Contracts
C. Documents	D. Letters

20. VENUE
A. Place	B. Agenda
C. Time	D. Duration

21. STERILE
A. Barren	B. Arid
C. Childless	D. Dry

22. SYNOPSIS
A. Index	B. Mixture
C. Summary	D. Puzzle

23. GERMANE
A. Responsible	B. Logical
C. Possible	D. Relevant

24. PONDER
A. Think	B. Evaluate
C. Anticipate	D. Increase

25. CANNY
A. Obstinate	B. Handsome
C. Clever	D. Stout

Directions (Qs. 26 to 50): *In the following questions choose the word which is the exact OPPOSITE of the given words.*

26. STRINGENT
A. General	B. Vehement
C. Lenient	D. Magnanimous

27. FLIMSY
A. Frail	B. Filthy
C. Firm	D. Flippant

28. BUSY
A. Occupied	B. Engrossed
C. Relaxed	D. Engaged

29. ADAPTABLE
A. Adoptable	B. Flexible
C. Yielding	D. Rigid

30. LOVE
A. Villainy	B. Hatred
C. Compulsion	D. Force

31. BALANCE
- A. Disbalance
- B. Misbalance
- C. Debalance
- D. Imbalance

32. RELINQUISH
- A. Abdicate
- B. Renounce
- C. Possess
- D. Deny

33. MOUNTAIN
- A. Plain
- B. Plateau
- C. Precipice
- D. Valley

34. FICKLE
- A. Courageous
- B. Sincere
- C. Steadfast
- D. Humble

35. PERENNIAL
- A. Frequent
- B. Regular
- C. Lasting
- D. Rare

36. RARELY
- A. Hardly
- B. Definitely
- C. Frequently
- D. Periodically

37. STARTLED
- A. Amused
- B. Relaxed
- C. Endless
- D. Astonished

38. ADHERENT
- A. Detractor
- B. Enemy
- C. Alien
- D. Rival

39. QUIESCENT
- A. Indifferent
- B. Troublesome
- C. Weak
- D. Unconcerned

40. CONDENSE
- A. Expand
- B. Distribute
- C. Interpret
- D. Lengthen

41. BENIGN
- A. Malevolent
- B. Soft
- C. Friendly
- D. Unwise

42. OBSCURE
- A. Implicit
- B. Obnoxious
- C. Explicit
- D. Pedantic

43. HYPOCRITICAL
- A. Gentle
- B. Sincere
- C. Amiable
- D. Dependable

44. EVASIVE
- A. Free
- B. Honest
- C. Liberal
- D. Frank

45. INDUSTRIOUS
- A. Indifferent
- B. Indolent
- C. Casual
- D. Passive

46. EXTRICATE
- A. Manifest
- B. Palpable
- C. Release
- D. Entangle

47. LUCID
- A. Glory
- B. Noisy
- C. Obscure
- D. Distinct

48. INSIPID
- A. Tasty
- B. Stupid
- C. Discreet
- D. Feast

49. OBEYING
- A. Ordering
- B. Following
- C. Refusing
- D. Contradicting

50. VICTORIOUS
- A. Defeated
- B. Annexed
- C. Destroyed
- D. Vanquished

ANSWERS

1	2	3	4	5	6	7	8	9	10
B	B	D	A	B	D	D	C	B	D

11	12	13	14	15	16	17	18	19	20
C	C	B	C	D	A	C	C	D	A

21	22	23	24	25	26	27	28	29	30
A	C	D	A	C	C	C	C	D	B

31	32	33	34	35	36	37	38	39	40
D	C	D	C	D	D	B	B	A	C

41	42	43	44	45	46	47	48	49	50
A	C	B	B	B	D	C	A	A	A

One Word Substitutions

There are many words in English language which can be perfectly used for a number of words. These words help in expressing ideas in a short and correct manner for the right occasion. Such words not only enhance the vocabulary but also enable you to economise in the use of words to a great extent. Try to learn as many as you can.

Multiple Word Expression	Substitution
One who always looks towards the bright side of things	Optimist
One who always looks towards the dark side of things	Pessimist
The time when one develops from a child into an adult	Adolescence
The process of growing more plants in order to form a forest	Afforestation
The science which deals with farming	Agriculture
From some other country or place etc.	Alien
A term, etc. giving more than one meaning	Ambiguous
A vehicle which is used to carry sick persons	Ambulance
An animal which can live both in water and on land	Amphibian
A lawless situation when there is no government	Anarchy
Belonging to the history of thousands of years old	Ancient
Once a year	Annual
A very old object but still valuable	Antique
Words of opposite meanings	Antonyms
Words of similar meanings	Synonyms
Signatures of a famous person	Autograph
A government led by one person with absolute authority	Autocracy
A written work of one's own life history	Autobiography
A person who has never been married	Bachelor
A person usually having no hair on his head	Bald
A place where one can deposit money and get interest	Bank
A person who cuts our hair	Barber
A building/group of buildings where soldiers live	Barracks
A person who makes buns and biscuits	Baker
A person who lives by asking people for food and money without doing any useful job	Beggar
The crime of having married to two persons at the same time	Bigamy

Multiple Word Expression	*Substitution*
The branch of science which deals with the study of plants	Botany
Able to speak two languages	Bilingual
Able to speak more than two languages	Polyglot
The branch of science which deals with the living organisms	Biology
A powerful snow storm	Blizzard
A great successful book or movie	Blockbuster
A short news on the radio or TV	Bulletin
A system in which the most important works are organised by the government officials	Bureaucracy
A person who has no vision in his eyes	Blind
A page or a series of pages on which the information of days, weeks, months, etc. is given	Calendar
A person who eats human flesh	Cannibal
A complete list of items often arranged alphabetically	Catalogue
A sudden disaster	Catastrophe
A period of 100 years	Century
A branch of science which deals with chemicals	Chemistry
A printed leaf usually issued by banks that we sign to carry certain financial deal	Cheque
A person who makes or mends shoes	Cobbler
A group of people who has been chosen by others to make decisions on their own	Committee
A building in which nuns live	Convent
An animal which feeds on other animals	Carnivorous
A person who does criticism	Critic
A person who cannot hear	Deaf
A condition in which one loses a lot of water from one's body because of vomiting, etc.	Dehydration
A system of government in which the people cast their votes to elect their leaders	Democracy
The study of skin problems	Dermatology
A long piece of land covered with sand	Desert
The art of managing relationships between countries	Diplomacy
A piece of information about the words in a book form	Dictionary
A piece of information about the telephone numbers of the people in a book form	Directory
A person in charge of a newspaper, magazine etc.	Editor
A person who thinks he is better than the others	Egoist
To leave one's country and settle in some other country	Emigrate
A book or series of books giving almost all knowledge about an area or some persons etc.	Encyclopaedia
Study of insects	Entomology
Time when day and night are of the same duration	Equinox
To sell things out of the country	Export
To purchase things from some other country	Import
A plant or animal no longer in existence	Extinct
A situation when there is a shortage of food for a long period of time	Famine
An amount of money that we pay for some action or services	Fee
Related to women	Feminine

Multiple Word Expression	Substitution
An animal strong and aggressive	Ferocious
A piece of land where plants grow easily from the soil that is favourable to them	Fertile
A work of literature having some imaginary events	Fiction
A large amount of water covering certain area	Flood
A person who sells flowers	Florist
A religious ceremony for burying or cremating a dead person	Funeral
A substance which kills fungus	Fungicide
A person studying or having studied the diseases and the related things of female reproductory system	Gynaecologist
The murder of the person of the same group race or country	Genocide
A substance which kills germs	Germicide
A situation in which many people die because of fire during war	Holocaust
The act of killing a person deliberately	Homicide
A word having the pronunciation as the other one does but it differs in meaning	Homophone
A word having the same spelling as the other one does but it is pronounced in some other way	Homonym
A person who is attracted towards the person of the same sex	Homosexual
Go across and parallel to the ground	Horizontal
A substance which kills the insects	Insecticide
That cannot be corrected	Incorrigible
That cannot be defeated	Invincible
That cannot be eaten	Inedible
That cannot be seen	Invisible
A place in a school or college where books are kept for the benefit of students, teachers etc.	Library
A place in a school or college where scientific experiments are performed	Laboratory
An official who is a judge in the lowest court	Magistrate
A piece of music or a book before it is printed	Manuscript
Related to men	Masculine
One who believes in the existence of God	A theist
One who does not believe in the existence of good	An atheist
That can be believed	Credible
That cannot be believed	Incredible
That which dissolves in a solvent	Soluble
That which does not dissolves in a solvent	Insoluble
Handwriting that can be read	Legible
Handwriting that cannot be read	Illegible
A person who does jobs beneficial to mankind	Philanthropist
A person who goes on foot	Pedestrian
A person who fights for his own country	Patriot
An act of killing oneself	Suicide
A woman whose husband is dead	Widow
A man whose wife is dead	Widower
A person who eats vegetarian and non-vegetarian diets	Omnivorous
Something which is everywhere at the same time	Omnipresent

Multiple Word Expression	*Substitution*
One who knows everything	Omniscient
A child who does not have parents	Orphan
An award etc. given after the death of the person	Posthumous
The place where animals are kept for amusement and to increase the knowledge of the public	Zoo
The science which deals with the study of animals	Zoology

Multiple Choice Questions

Directions: *In questions given below, out of the four alternatives, choose the one which can be substituted for the given words/sentence.*

1. Something that relates to everyone in the world
   A. General
   B. Common
   C. Usual
   D. Universal

2. An expression of mild disapproval
   A. Warning
   B. Denigration
   C. Impertinence
   D. Reproof

3. One who is not easily pleased by anything
   A. Maiden
   B. Medieval
   C. Precarious
   D. Fastidious

4. Murder of a king
   A. Infanticide
   B. Matricide
   C. Genocide
   D. Regicide

5. A remedy for all diseases
   A. Stoic
   B. Marvel
   C. Panacea
   D. Recompense

6. A dramatic performance
   A. Mask
   B. Mosque
   C. Masque
   D. Mascot

7. Study of birds
   A. Orology
   B. Optology
   C. Ophthalmology
   D. Ornithology

8. Ready to believe
   A. Credulous
   B. Credible
   C. Creditable
   D. Incredible

9. Incapable of being seen through
   A. Ductile
   B. Opaque
   C. Obsolete
   D. Potable

10. One who eats everything
    A. Omnivorous
    B. Omniscient
    C. Irresistible
    D. Insolvent

11. A place where bees are kept is called
    A. An apiary
    B. A mole
    C. A hive
    D. A sanctuary

12. One who cannot be corrected
    A. Incurable
    B. Incorrigible
    C. Hardened
    D. Invulnerable

13. One who is in charge of a museum
    A. Curator
    B. Supervisor
    C. Caretaker
    D. Warden

14. Continuing fight between parties, families, clans, etc.
    A. Enmity
    B. Feud
    C. Quarrel
    D. Skirmish

15. A voice loud enough to be heard
    A. Audible
    B. Applaudable
    C. Laudable
    D. Oral

16. A paper written by hand
    A. Handicraft
    B. Manuscript
    C. Handiwork
    D. Thesis

17. Habitually silent or talking little
    A. Serville
    B. Unequivocal
    C. Taciturn
    D. Synoptic

18. To slap with a flat object
    A. Chop
    B. Hew
    C. Gnaw
    D. Swat

19. A person who speaks many languages
    A. Linguist
    B. Monolingual
    C. Polyglot
    D. Bilingual

20. A light sailing-boat built specially for racing
    A. Canoe
    B. Yacht
    C. Frigate
    D. Dinghy

21. A fixed orbit in space in relation to earth
    A. Geological
    B. Geo-synchronous
    C. Geo-centric
    D. Geo-stationary

22. A style in which a writer makes a display of his knowledge
A. Pedantic   B. Verbose
C. Pompous   D. Ornate

23. A religious discourse
A. Preach   B. Stanza
C. Sanctorum   D. Sermon

24. A place that provides refuge
A. Asylum   B. Sanatorium
C. Shelter   D. Orphanage

25. Detailed plan of a journey
A. Travelogue   B. Travelkit
C. Schedule   D. Itinerary

26. A person who insists on something
A. Disciplinarian   B. Stickler
C. Instantaneous   D. Boaster

27. A drawing on transparent paper
A. Red print   B. Blue print
C. Negative   D. Transparency

28. One who believes that all things and events in life are predetermined is a
A. Fatalist   B. Puritan
C. Egoist   D. Tyrant

29. A school boy who cuts classes frequently is a
A. Defeatist   B. Sycophant
C. Truant   D. Martinet

30. The act of violating the sanctity of the church is
A. Blasphemy   B. Heresy
C. Sacrilege   D. Desecration

31. A place where monks live as a secluded community
A. Cathedral   B. Diocese
C. Convent   D. Monastery

32. One who is fond of fighting
A. Bellicose   B. Aggressive
C. Belligerent   D. Militant

33. Tending to move away from the centre or axis
A. Centrifugal   B. Centripetal
C. Axiomatic   D. Awry

34. A person of good understanding, knowledge and reasoning power
A. Expert   B. Intellectual
C. Snob   D. Literate

35. One absorbed in his own thoughts and feelings rather than in things outside
A. Scholar   B. Recluse
C. Introvert   D. Intellectual

36. One who does not marry, especially as a religious obligation
A. Bachelor   B. Celibate
C. Virgin   D. Recluse

37. A person who tries to deceive people by claiming to be able to do wonderful things
A. Trickster   B. Impostor
C. Magician   D. Mountebank

38. To take secretly in small quantities
A. Robbery   B. Pilferage
C. Theft   D. Defalcation

39. Policemen riding on motorcycles as guards to a VIP
A. Outriders   B. Servants
C. Commandos   D. Attendants

40. The part of a government which is concerned with making of rules
A. Court   B. Tribunal
C. Bar   D. Legislature

ANSWERS

1	2	3	4	5	6	7	8	9	10
D	D	D	D	C	C	D	A	B	A

11	12	13	14	15	16	17	18	19	20
A	B	A	B	A	B	C	D	A	B

21	22	23	24	25	26	27	28	29	30
D	A	D	A	D	B	D	A	C	C

31	32	33	34	35	36	37	38	39	40
D	A	A	B	C	B	A	B	A	D

# Idioms and Phrases

Verbal Phrases

- **Act upon** (to follow)
  I acted upon my father's advice.

- **Act upto** (to perform within limits)
  He acted upto his conscience.

- **Act beyond** (to perform crossing limits)
  We should not act beyond our capacity.

- **Act for** (to perform in place of someone else)
  The vice principal acted for the principal.

- **Back up** (to make a queue)
  The vehicles began to back up.

- **Back down** (withdraw claim in the presence of opposition)
  The leader backed down from his previous statement.

- **Back off** (draw back some plan or action)
  They backed off from building a flyover.

- **Back out** (withdraw from a promise, etc.)
  The government backed out of its promise.

- **Break down** (stop working) My car broke down on the highway.

- **Break into** (enter in certain premises by breaking the door, etc.)
  Last night a thief broke into my neighbour's.

- **Break off** (stop all of a sudden)
  She broke off and began to think over about her/his hand.

- **Break out** (spread)
  Cholera has broken out in the town.

- **Break out of** (escape from)
  A prisoner broke out of the prison last night.

- **Break up** (disperse)
  The cloud of fog began to break up as the sun rose.

- **Break something up** (Cause something to break into small pieces)
  She broke up the chocolate to distribute it among the girls.

- **Break with** (Cut off connection after quarrelling with someone)
  He has broken with his brother.

- **Call on** (pay a visit to somebody)
  I'll call on Mohan's today.

- **Call out** (to start)
  The workers have called out a strike.

- **Call off** (to stop the strike etc.)
  The workers have called off the strike.

- **Call at** (to visit someone's house)
  I called at his house yesterday.

- **Call in** (send for)
  Please call in the doctor.

- **Carry on** (continue)
  Please carry on your work.

- **Carry something out** (perform a task)
  Our company is carrying out a big deal with a foreign company.

- **Carry something over** (postpone)
  The fancy dress competition had to be carried over till Monday)

- **Carry someone off** (kill somebody)
  Cancer carried her off on the day of her 20th birthday.

- **Come of age** (get established)
  As our company has come of age, so, there is no problem in selling our goods.

- **Come of** (belong to)
  She comes of a royal family.

- **Come over** (surmount)
  We at last came over all our problems.
- **Come off** (to take place)
  The marriage of my brother comes off in the next month.
- **Come round** (agree)
  At last he came round to my views.
- **Come under** (fall in the category of)
  All these animals come under the same species.
- **Come down with** (suffer from)
  She came down with whopping cough.
- **Come from** (be the nature of)
  She came from London.
- **Come about** (happen)
  The explosion came about when the worker struck the match to light a cigarette.
- **Cut off** (die)
  The princess was cut off in the prime of her life.
- **Cut down** (reduce)
  The prices of consumer goods should be cut down.
- **Cut someone out** (exclude someone)
  His father cut him out of his will.
- **Fall in**
  She fell in love with the prince.
- **Fall down** (fail)
  The deal fell down for lack of transparency.
- **Fall out** (quarrel)
  She fell out with his elder brother.
- **Fall through** (fail)
  The project fell through for lack of funds.
- **Get away** (escape)
  She got away with her life.
- **Get by** (to accomplish something with great difficulty)
  She is not rich. She has just enough to get by.
- **Get on** (perform)
  How are you getting on with your studies?
- **Get out** (become known)
  The news got out that the PM was paying a visit to Russia.

- **Get over** (overcome)
  At last I got over all obstacles.
- **Get up** (rise)
  When do you get up in the morning?
- **Give up** (stop)
  He gave up smoking.
- **Give out** (emit)
  Garlic gives out a pungent smell.
- **Give in** (collapse)
  The bridge gave in under the heavy load.
- **Give away** (distribute)
  The Principal gave away the prizes.
- **Give out** (announce)
  It was given out that the President of India would visit the place soon.
- **Go off** (explode)
  The gun went off suddenly.
- **Go on** (continue)
  She went on about how she flew the aeroplane.
- **Go through** (examine)
  I'll go through this book later on.
- **Go up** (be built)
  The construction of the house is going up.
- **Grind on** (continue for a long time in a tedious way)
  The discussion over political issues ground on.
- **Grind something out** (produce something a tedious way)
  She will grind some more short stories.
- **Look out** (be careful)
  Look out! there is a snake.
- **Look down upon** (hate)
  We should not look down upon the poor.
- **Look at** (watch)
  Look at the blackboard.
- **Look after** (take care of)
  We ought to look after our old parents.
- **Look into** (investigate)
  The new police inspector will look into the matter.

- **Look up** (rise)
  The prices of consumer goods are looking up.
- **Look back** (think of the past)
  It made her feel disolate when she looked back on things of the past.
- **Make up** (to fulfil)
  I'll make up my deficiency in Mathematics.
- **Make out** (understand)
  I could not make out what she said.
- **Make up one' mind** (to resolve)
  I have made up my mind to settle in the USA.
- **Make off** (leave hurriedly)
  She made off without informing anybody.
- **Make something over** (transfer)
  She should make her property over to her sons.
- **Make over** (hand over)
  He made over the charge of the file to Mr Robert.
- **Pull back** (retreat)
  The government has pulled back from its previous policy.
- **Pull something down** (demolish)
  The authorities concerned pulled down a few building which were illegally built on government land.
- **Pull out** (pluck)
  The child pulled out a few petals of the flower.
- **Pull through** (recover)
  The patient will pull through.
- **Push on** (continue a journey)
  It was getting darker but we pushed on.
- **Push at** (exert force)
  He pushed at the bell, but it did not ring.
- **Push for** (demand persistently)
  The workers have been pushing for the installation of new machines for five years.
- **Put out** (extinguish)
  She put out the light.
- **Put on** (wear)
  He put on an overcoat.
- **Put off** (postpone)
  The plan had to be put off.
- **Put by** (spare something for future)
  We must put by some money for future.
- **Put up with** (stay)
  Your aunt is out of town for a couple of days, you may put up with us till she comes.
- **Put something down** (record something)
  She put a new idea down on the paper.
- **Take after** (resemble)
  He takes after his father.
- **Take off** (remove)
  He took off his shoes.
- **Take something out** (obtain)
  You may take out some money from Rohit if you want to purchase this car.
- **Take to** (fall into the habit of)
  He took to gambling.
- **Turn something down** (reject something)
  The judge turned down his appeal.
- **Turn on** (attack)
  The thief turned on him with a knife.

Multiple Choice Questions

Directions: *Some idioms/phrases are given below with their probable meanings. Select the options with their correct meanings.*

1. **Carry out**
   A. To take from one place to another
   B. To continue
   C. To obey
   D. To make efforts

2. **In the same boat**
   A. A worn out choice
   B. Indifferent
   C. In identical circumstances
   D. Carry off

3. **In one's good book**
   A. A costly book
   B. A priceless treasure

C. In one's favour
D. An enchanting beauty

4. Keep a straight face
A. To do make up
B. To change clothes
C. Assume responsibility
D. To remain serious

5. To be above board
A. To have a good height
B. To be honest in any business deal
C. To have no debts
D. To try to be beautiful

6. On the face of it
A. To agree
B. From an action
C. More than enough
D. Apparently

7. Let the bygones be bygones
A. In one's favour
B. To pretend
C. To forget the past
D. Other choice

8. To split hairs
A. Major distinctions
B. Hair with two ends
C. To make minute distinction
D. Without distinction

9. Bread and butter
A. Both bread and butter
B. Something essential
C. Livelihood
D. Relevant things

10. To bell the cat
A. To catch a cat and tie a bell round its neck
B. To make an effort
C. To be quick
D. To face a risk

11. Hard and fast
A. Strict
B. Solid
C. Fast moving
D. Some hard surface

12. Part and parcel
A. The part of a parcel
B. An essential part
C. A missing parcel
D. Some part of a machine sent by parcel

13. Null and void
A. Something invalid
B. Something that can be avoided
C. Something that can be nullified
D. Something evil

14. To make clean breast of
A. To gain prominence
B. To praise oneself
C. To confess without reserve
D. To destroy before it blooms

15. Trump card
A. A powerful means of achieving an object
B. Resourcefulness
C. The best gamble to attain success
D. None of these

16. Tall talk
A. A discussion continued for a long time
B. A high sounding talk
C. A meaningful talk
D. A useless talk

17. Small talk
A. Gossip
B. A discussion carried on for a long time
C. A brief discussion
D. None of these

18. Throw out of gear
A. To replace
B. Hinder, disturb
C. To decide
D. Take up tune

19. To and fro
A. Back and forth
B. Puzzled
C. Amazed
D. Reprove

20. To bell the cat
A. To do an easy job
B. To be indifferent to
C. To undertake a difficult job
D. To clarify

21. To be under cloud
A. Puzzle
B. Enjoy the favour
C. Talk thoughtlessly
D. To be under suspicion

22. A labour of love
A. A tragic end
B. A funny thing
C. Not fruitful
D. Work done without payment

23. Follow suit
   A. Follow an example B. Wear a new dress
   C. Irrelevant   D. A gay person

24. Foul play
   A. Bad intentions
   B. A play not well acted
   C. A play not liked by the audience
   D. None of these

25. To pick holes
   A. To find some reason to quarrel
   B. To destroy something
   C. To criticise someone
   D. To cut some part of an item

26. To smell a rat
   A. To see signs of plague epidemic
   B. To get bad smell of a dead rat
   C. To suspect foul dealings
   D. To be in a bad mood

27. To put a spoke in one's wheel
   A. To encourage
   B. Act without restraint
   C. Risk something
   D. To obstruct one's progress

28. To pull one's leg
   A. To give up   B. Take care of
   C. To befool   D. To know

29. To play with fire
   A. Grasp the truth
   B. To handle something dangerous
   C. To ridicule
   D. To flee away

30. To reckon with
   A. Take up time
   B. Make an inventory
   C. To deal with
   D. Submit to punishment

31. To run short
   A. Talk until one is tired at
   B. Apply to oneself
   C. To get rid of
   D. To have or be too little

32. A man of letters
   A. A postman   B. A learned man
   C. A hypocrite   D. An ignorant man

33. A maiden speech
   A. A speech made in the parliament
   B. A speech made before unmarried girls
   C. A speech made by a political leader
   D. A speech made for the first time

34. Order of the day
   A. An order passed on a particular day
   B. A current law
   C. Something common or general
   D. None of these

35. To end in smoke
   A. To make completely understand
   B. To ruin oneself
   C. To excite great applause
   D. None of these

36. To give vent to
   A. To allow to flow forth
   B. To prove a failure
   C. To amass wealth
   D. To evade

37. To eat humble pie
   A. To apologise or confess
   B. To order
   C. To flatter
   D. To get rid of

38. A black sheep
   A. An unlucky person
   B. A negro
   C. An ugly person
   D. None of these

39. To catch a tartar
   A. To trap wanted criminal with great difficulty
   B. To catch a dangerous person
   C. To meet with disaster
   D. To deal with a person who is more than one's watch

40. Sit on fence
   A. To remain neutral
   B. To show contempt
   C. To enjoy the surroundings
   D. To become fond of

41. Pay off old scores
   A. To repay the debt
   B. To have revenge
   C. To invite
   D. Secretly

42. Turn turtle
  A. To cheat
  B. To be lopsided
  C. To frustrate
  D. To dance to the tune

43. Wash one's hands of
  A. To refuse   B. To assist
  C. To abuse   D. To refuse to be

44. Under duress
  A. Under compulsion
  B. Willing
  C. To elicit information
  D. To demand

45. To turn the tables
  A. To ruin someone
  B. To turn the situation to one's own side
  C. To reverse the situation
  D. To move from one point to another

46. On the cards
  A. Possibly   B. Probably
  C. Openly   D. Likely

47. To leave someone in the lurch
  A. To come to compromise with someone
  B. Constant source of annoyance to someone
  C. To put someone at ease
  D. To desert someone in his difficulties

48. To play second fiddle
  A. To be happy, cheerful and healthy
  B. To reduce importance of one's senior
  C. To support the role and view of another person
  D. To do back seat driving

49. To yearn for
  A. To weep for
  B. To remember
  C. To admire
  D. To long for intensely

50. Call off
  A. To finish
  B. To withdraw
  C. To postpone
  D. To cry

ANSWERS

1	2	3	4	5	6	7	8	9	10
C	C	C	D	B	D	C	C	C	D
11	**12**	**13**	**14**	**15**	**16**	**17**	**18**	**19**	**20**
A	B	A	C	C	B	A	B	A	C
21	**22**	**23**	**24**	**25**	**26**	**27**	**28**	**29**	**30**
D	D	A	A	C	C	D	C	B	C
31	**32**	**33**	**34**	**35**	**36**	**37**	**38**	**39**	**40**
D	B	D	C	D	A	A	D	B	A
41	**42**	**43**	**44**	**45**	**46**	**47**	**48**	**49**	**50**
B	B	D	A	C	D	D	C	D	B

❑ ❑ ❑

Narration

The exact words spoken by the speaker are known as Direct Speech. The words spoken by somebody and expressed by someone else with some modification are known as Indirect Speech.

Multiple Choice Questions

Directions (Qs. 1 to 13): *Select the correct Indirect Speech for the following sentences:*

1. I said to him, "I shall help you."
   A. I told him that I can help him.
   B. I told him that I would help him.
   C. I told him that I will help him.
   D. I told him that I shall be helping him.

2. My Teacher said to me, "The earth revolves round the sun."
   A. My teacher told me that the earth revolves round the sun.
   B. My teacher told me that the earth revolve round the sun.
   C. My teacher told me that the earth had been revolving round the sun.
   D. My teacher told me that the earth has been revolving round the sun.

3. I said to my friend, "My father daily goes for a walk."
   A. I told my friend that my father daily goes for a walk.
   B. I told my friend that my father daily went for a walk.
   C. I told my friend that my father has to go for a walk.
   D. I told my friend that my father had gone for a walk.

4. He said to me, "May God bless you!"
   A. He requested that God can bless me.
   B. He prayed that God can bless me.
   C. He prayed that God might bless me.
   D. He prayed that God will bless me.

5. The patient said, "Thank you, doctor."
   A. The patient thanked the doctor.
   B. The patient requested the doctor with thanks.
   C. The patient told the doctor thanks.
   D. The patient suggested the doctor thanks.

6. Satish said, "No, I shall not talk to him."
   A. Satish told that he should not talk to him.
   B. Satish suggested that he would not have talked to him.
   C. Satish exclaimed with sorrow that he would not talk with him.
   D. Satish refused to talk to him.

7. The child said, "What a lovely place!"
   A. The child exclaimed with sorrow that it was a lovely place.
   B. The child thought that the place was lovely.
   C. The child exclaimed with joy that the place was very lovely.
   D. The child suggested that the place was lovely.

8. He said, "What a fool I have been!"
   A. He told himself with sorrow that he was a fool.
   B. He confessed with regret that he had been a great fool.
   C. He said himself a fool.
   D. He suggested that he could be a fool.

9. He said, "Alas! I am ruined."
   A. He told me that he had been ruined.
   B. He exclaimed with joy that he had been ruined.
   C. He exclaimed with sorrow that he was ruined.
   D. He told me that he should not be ruined.

10. The accused said, "I am not guilty."
   A. The accused exclaimed with sorrow that I am not guilty.
   B. The accused exclaimed with joy that he was not guilty.
   C. The accused stated that he was not guilty.
   D. The accused told me that he has not been guilty.

11. My teacher said, "The earth is round".
   A. My teacher said that the earth was round.
   B. My teacher says that the earth is round.
   C. My teacher said that the earth is round.
   D. My teacher ordered that the earth is round.

12. He said, "What a place it is!"
   A. He said that it was a very fine place.
   B. He said that is a very fine place.
   C. He said that the place is fine.
   D. He exclaimed with joy/surprise that it was a very fine place.

13. Ria said, "Shall I thread the needle?"
   A. Ria asked if she should thread the needle.
   B. Ria asked if she shall thread the needle.
   C. Ria ordered if she should thread the needle.
   D. Ria says that if she would thread the needle.

Directions (Qs. 14 to 30): *Pick out the correct alternative that completes the incomplete sentence which is changed into Indirect Narration.*

14. She said to me, "I shall see you as soon as I get time."
   She told me:
   A. that she will see me as soon as she will get time.
   B. that she would see me as soon as she would get time.
   C. she would see me whenever she got time.
   D. that she would see me whenever she gets time.

15. My secretary said to me, "Your plane will leave if you do not go at once."
   My secretary told me that:
   A. her plane would leave if she did not go at that time.
   B. her plane would leave if I do not go at once.
   C. my plane would leave if I did not go at that very time.
   D. my plane will leave if I did not go at that time.

16. My mother said to me, "Don't quarrel among yourselves".
   My mother:
   A. forbade me to quarrel among ourselves.
   B. asked me not to quarrel among ourselves.
   C. asked me that not to quarrel among ourselves.
   D. asked me to quarrel not among ourselves.

17. Her father said to her mother, "Excuse the daughter."
   Her father:
   A. requested her mother to excuse the daughter.
   B. asked her mother to excuse the daughter.
   C. asked her mother to have excused the daughter.
   D. asked her mother to have been excused.

18. He said to his friend, "Wait here till father comes."
   He requested his friend:
   A. to wait here till father had come.
   B. that to wait there till his friend came.
   C. to wait there till father came.
   D. to wait here until his friend came.

19. She said to her maid, "Run and catch the thief."
   She ordered her maid:
   A. ran and catch the thief.
   B. that to run and to catch the thief.

C. ran and caught the thief.

D. to run and catch the thief.

20. Anita said to Sunita, "What are you doing?"
Anita asked Sunita:

A. what she will be doing.

B. that what she is doing.

C. that what she was doing.

D. what she was doing.

21. She said to me, "Are you meeting me today?"
She enquired of me:

A. whether I am meeting her that day.

B. whether I was meeting her today.

C. whether I was meeting her that day.

D. I was meeting her that day.

22. Nitish said to me, "When did you buy this pen?"
Nitish asked me:

A. when I was to buy that pen.

B. when I would buy that pen.

C. when I had bought that pen.

D. when I was buying that pen.

23. She said to me, "Are you going to market?"
She enquired of me:

A. I am going to market.

B. I was going to market.

C. if I was going to market.

D. if I had been going to the market.

24. Damini said, "Why did not you change your clothes?"
Damini asked me:

A. why I had not changed my clothes.

B. why I did not change my clothes.

C. why I would not change my clothes.

D. why I have not been changing my clothes.

25. Umesh said to me, "Have you read that novel?"
Umesh asked me:

A. if he was reading that novel.

B. if he had read that novel.

C. if I had read that novel.

D. if I was reading that novel.

26. She said to me, "I shall forgive you."
She told me:

A. that she will forgive me.

B. that she was going to forgive me.

C. that she will not forgive me.

D. that she would forgive me.

27. I said to her, "It was very hot last night."
I told her:

A. that it had been very hot the previous night.

B. that it was very hot the previous night.

C. that it has been very hot the last night.

D. that it had been very hot this night.

28. She said to me, "I thank you for the help you have given."
She:

A. told me that she thanked me for the help I had given.

B. thanked me for the help I have given.

C. thanked to me for the help I have given.

D. thanked me for the help I had given.

29. Mohini said to me, "Trust in God."
Mohini advised me:

A. that I should trust in God.

B. should trust in God.

C. trusted in God.

D. to trust in God.

30. I said to him, "Let us go to school."
I told him:

A. we would go to school.

B. we shall go to school.

C. that we would go to school.

D. that we should go to school.

ANSWERS

1	2	3	4	5	6	7	8	9	10
B	A	A	C	A	D	C	B	C	C
11	12	13	14	15	16	17	18	19	20
C	D	A	B	C	A	B	C	D	D
21	22	23	24	25	26	27	28	29	30
C	C	C	A	C	D	A	A	A	D

Voice

A sentence in active voice focuses on the person or thing doing the action. A sentence in passive voice focuses on the person or thing affected by the action.
e.g.,

The idol was built.	(Active voice)
Someone built the idol.	(Passive voice)

Transformation of Voice

- Voice and Tense are closely associated with each other.
- Tense plays an important role while transforming the voice.

On the basis of following points, voice can be transformed from active to passive voice.

The Present Indefinite Tense

Active voice: Subject + V_1 + Object
Passive voice: Subject + is, am, are + V_3 + by + Object

- **Active voice:** He sings sweet songs.
  Passive voice: Sweet songs are sung by him.

The Present Continuous Tense

Active voice: Subject + is/am/are + V_1 + ing + Object.
Passive voice: Subject + is/am/are + being + V_3 + by + Object.

- **Active voice:** She is cooking food.
  Passive voice: Food is being cooked by her.

The Present Perfect Tense

Active voice: Subject + has/have + V_3 + Object.
Passive voice: Subject + has/have + been + V_3 + by + Object.

- **Active voice:** I have written an essay.
  Passive voice: An essay has been written by me.

The Past Indefinite Tense

Active voice: Subject + V_2 + Object
Passive voice: Subject + was/were + V_3 + by + Object

- **Active voice:** He composed a new song.
  Passive voice: A new song was composed by him.

The Past Continuous Tense

Active voice: Subject + was/were + V_1 + ing + Object
Passive voice: Subject + was/were + being + V_3 + by + Object

- **Active voice:** The farmers were ploughing the fields.
  Passive voice: The fields were being ploughed by the farmers.

The Past Perfect Tense

Active voice: Subject + had + V_3 + Object.
Passive voice: Subject + had + been + V_3 + by + Object

- **Active voice:** He had issued me an import licence.
  Passive voice: I had been issued an import licence.

The Future Indefinite Tense

Active voice: Subject + will/shall + V_1 + Object.
Passive voice: Subject + will/shall + be + V_3 + by + Object.

- **Active voice:** He will remove the dust from the shelf.
  Passive voice: The dust from the shelf will be removed by him.

The Future Perfect Tense

Active voice: Subject + will/shall + have + V$_3$ + Object.

Passive voice: Subject + will/shall + have + been + V$_3$ + by + Object.

- **Active voice:** They will have sold their house by then.
  Passive voice: Their house will have been sold by them by then.

Imperative Sentences

- **Active voice:** Open the window.
  Passive voice: You are ordered to open the window.
  Or
  Let the window be opened.

Infinitives

- **Active voice:** It is time to open the shop.
  Passive voice: It is time for the shop to be opened.

Prepositional Verb

- **Active voice:** She laughed at the beggar.
  Passive voice: The beggar was laughed at by her.

Double Object

- **Active voice:** He gave me a pen.
  Passive voice: A pen was given to me by him.

Use of Preposition other than 'by'

- **Active voice:** The jug contains juice.
  Passive voice: Juice is contained in the jug.

Quasi Passive Verbs

- **Active voice:** Quinine tastes bitter.
  Passive voice: Quinine is bitter when tasted.

Implied Sentences

- **Active voice:** The driver drove the bus.
  Passive voice: The bus was driven.

Multiple Choice Questions

Directions (Qs. 1 to 20): *In the following questions, a sentence has been given in Active/Passive Voice. Out of the four alternatives suggested, select the one that Best Expresses the same sentence in Passive/Active Voice.*

1. Circumstances will oblige me to go.
   A. I will oblige the circumstances and go.
   B. I shall be obliged to go by the circumstances.
   C. Under the circumstances, I should go.
   D. I shall be obliged by the circumstances to go.

2. We waste much time on trifles.
   A. Much time was wasted on trifles.
   B. Much time will be wasted on trifles.
   C. Much time is wasted by us on trifles.
   D. Much time is wasted on trifles.

3. Mohan gave the beggar an old shirt.
   A. An old shirt was given to Mohan by the beggar.
   B. An old shirt was given to the beggar by Mohan
   C. The begger was gave an old shirt by Mohan.
   D. An old shirt was gave to the beggar by Mohan.

4. They have made him a king.
   A. A king has been made by him.
   B. He was made a king by them.
   C. They have been made kings by him.
   D. He has been made a king by them.

5. Who taught you English?
   A. By whom English was taught to you?
   B. By whom you were taught English?
   C. By whom was English taught to you?
   D. By whom are you taught English?

6. Was he knocking at the door?
   A. Was the door being knocked at by him?
   B. Was the door being knocked by him?

C. Was the door knocked by him?
D. Was the door knocking at him?

7. What was Rani doing?
  A. What was done by Rani?
  B. What was Rani being done?
  C. What was being done by Rani?
  D. What was being doing Rani?

8. Why were you wasting your time?
  A. Why was your time being wasted?
  B. Why was your time being wasted by you?
  C. Why was your time wasted by you?
  D. Why was your time wasted?

9. She has laid out a small garden.
  A. A small garden has been laid by her.
  B. A small garden has laid her.
  C. A small garden being laid by her.
  D. A small garden has been laid out by her.

10. She had already solved all the sums.
  A. All the sums had already been solved by her.
  B. All the sums have already been solved by her.
  C. All the sums have been solved by her.
  D. All the sums are solved by her.

11. He will have posted the letter.
  A. The letter has been posted by him.
  B. The letter will be posted by him.
  C. The letter will have been posted by him.
  D. The letter is posted by him.

12. They will have sold all the books by 4 P.M.
  A. All the books will be sold by 4 P.M.
  B. All the books will have been sold by 4 P.M.
  C. All the books were being sold by 4 P.M.
  D. All the books must be sold by 4 P.M.

13. Do you speak English?
  A. Is English spoken by you?
  B. Does English spoken by you?

C. Is English being spoken by you?
D. Does English being spoken by you?

14. Had they seen me before?
  A. Had myself been seen by them before?
  B. Had me being seen by them before?
  C. Had I been seen by them before?
  D. Had I being seen by them before?

15. May I take this pen?
  A. May this pen will be taken by me?
  B. May this pen shall be taken by me?
  C. May this pen should be taken by me?
  D. May this pen be taken by me?

16. Can we send it by air?
  A. Can this be sent by air?
  B. Can it be sent by air?
  C. Can it go by air?
  D. Can it be send by air?

17. Who wrote this book?
  A. By whom was this book written?
  B. By whom is this book written?
  C. By whom was this book being written?
  D. By whom is this book being written?

18. What did you buy?
  A. What is bought by you?
  B. What is being bought by you?
  C. What was bought by you?
  D. What was being bought by you?

19. Whom do you want?
  A. Who is wanted by you?
  B. Who is being wanted by you?
  C. You are wanted by whom?
  D. You are being wanted by whom?

20. When will you raise this question?
  A. When this question will be raised by you?
  B. When will this question be raised by you?
  C. When this question is being raised by you?
  D. When is this question being raised by you?

ANSWERS

1	2	3	4	5	6	7	8	9	10
D	C	B	D	C	A	C	B	D	A

11	12	13	14	15	16	17	18	19	20
C	B	A	C	D	B	A	C	A	B

> Filling the blanks is such an exercise that starts with the primary schools and continues at the highest level of competitive examinations. One must practise it regularly to score well.

Multiple Choice Questions

Directions: *Pick out the most effective word(s) from the given words to fill in the blanks and make the sentence meaningfully complete.*

1. One requires great .... to teach and handle little children who are restless.
   A. patience
   B. attitude
   C. determination
   D. knowledge

2. The researchers will .... some of the causes of increasing poverty in the state.
   A. fund
   B. investigate
   C. promote
   D. circulate

3. I usually perform .... when nobody is watching me.
   A. alone
   B. good
   C. better
   D. hard

4. It was .... to everyone that the minister had been drinking.
   A. observed
   B. known
   C. discovered
   D. realised

5. I would rather stay indoors .... the rain stops.
   A. so
   B. waiting
   C. until
   D. usually

6. The process should be completed as far as possible within a week, ... which the matter should be brought to notice of the officer concerned.
   A. following
   B. failing
   C. realizing
   D. referring

7. The officers are ..... to regular transfers.
   A. free
   B. open
   C. subject
   D. available

8. All letters received from Government should ..... be acknowledged.
   A. suddenly
   B. obviously
   C. immediately
   D. occasionally

9. Mumbai office ..... a meeting of senior officials to discuss the high incidence of frauds.
   A. attended
   B. convened
   C. reported
   D. registered

10. The note should be ..... to all the concerned departments for their consideration.
    A. regulated
    B. requested
    C. carried
    D. forwarded

11. Your present statement does not .... what you said last week.
    A. accord to
    B. accord in
    C. accord with
    D. accord for

12. I had a vague .... that the lady originally belonged to Scotland.
A. notion B. expression
C. imagination D. theory

13. The prisoner showed no .... for his crimes.
A. hatred B. obstinacy
C. remorse D. anger

14. It is inconceivable that in many schools children are subjected to physical .... in the name of discipline.
A. violation B. exercise
C. violence D. security

15. We have not yet fully realised the .... consequences of the war.
A. happy B. pleasing
C. grim D. exciting

16. Happiness consists in being .... what we have.
A. contented to B. contented with
C. contented for D. contented in

17. His rude behaviour is a .... his organization.
A. disgrace for B. disgrace on
C. disgrace upon D. disgrace to

18. No child is .... understanding. One has to wait and provide proper guidance.
A. dull to B. dull in
C. dull of D. dull for

19. I am fully .... the problems facing the industry.
A. alive with B. alive to
C. alive for D. alive on

20. The Romans were .... science.
A. bad in B. bad to
C. bad for D. bad at

21. Although I was .... of his plans, I encouraged him, because there was no one else who was willing to help.
A. sceptical B. remorseful
C. fearful D. excited

22. You have no business to .... pain on a weak and poor person.
A. inflict B. put
C. direct D. force

23. Her uncle died in a car accident. He was quite rich. She suddenly .... all her uncle's money.
A. succeeded B. caught
C. gave D. inherited

24. There was a major accident. The plane crashed. The pilot .... did not see the tower.
A. likely B. probably
C. scarcely D. hurriedly

25. The car we were travelling in .... a mile from home.
A. broke off B. broke down
C. broke into D. broke up

ANSWERS

1	2	3	4	5	6	7	8	9	10
A	B	C	A	C	B	C	C	B	D
11	12	13	14	15	16	17	18	19	20
C	A	C	C	C	B	D	B	B	D
21	22	23	24	25					
B	C	C	B	C					

Cloze Test

A cloze test is a procedure in which a person is asked to supply words that have been removed from a passage as a test of his ability to comprehend text. Practise it regularly to score well.

PASSAGES

Directions: *In each of the following passages some numbered blank spaces are given. For each numbered blank space four answer choices are given. Pick out the one which is the most appropriate for that blank space, keeping the trend of the passage in mind.*

Passage-1

Mankind's most ....(1).... treasure of thoughts is carefully preserved in the golden casket of books. The ....(2).... of books is as vast as the universe, for there is no corner of it which they have left ....(3).... . There is no ....(4).... of books on any topic, be it as simple as the composition of sodium nitrate or as ....(5).... as the mechanism of a spacecraft rocketing towards Mars. The ....(6).... of books is not only most easily available but is enlightened, dependable and lifelong. In times of distress they make us stoically ....(7).... of the object that causes uneasiness and we learn to ....(8).... with the sting of adversity.

Questions

1. A. costly   B. important
    C. valuable   D. vast

2. A. area   B. scope
    C. storage   D. kingdom

3. A. unexplored   B. unseen
    C. untouched   D. unapproached

4. A. lack   B. dearth
    C. shortage   D. insufficiency

5. A. extricate   B. intricate
    C. intrinsic   D. internecine

6. A. company   B. assistance
    C. friendship   D. companionship

7. A. defiant   B. defendant
    C. defensible   D. delusive

8. A. adapt   B. adopt
    C. exist   D. co-exist

Passage-2

Though the government has tried to ....(1).... Naxalism with all its might, much more needs to be done to totally root out the ....(2).... of Naxalism. The roots of Naxalism ....(3).... economic backwardness and social exploitation of the peasants and the weaker classes. Thus, the best way to ....(4).... Naxalism is to bring the naxals ....(5).... the mainstream. ....(6).... policies and schemes should be implemented effectively ....(7).... the Naxals economically stable. They should be ....(8).... to participate in democratic processes. The government has to ....(9).... the social upliftment of the Naxals. Use of force in ....(10).... Naxalism will yield little success.

Questions

1. A. crush B. handle C. tackle D. suppress
2. A. menace B. whole C. gamut D. stems
3. A. lies in B. are in C. abound in D. exist in
4. A. crash B. crush C. break D. defy
5. A. in B. on C. into D. within
6. A. Current B. Latest C. Occurring D. Existing
7. A. so that B. so as to make C. such that D. to make
8. A. insisted B. brought C. encouraged D. forced
9. A. assure B. insure C. guarantee D. ensure
10. A. countering B. defying C. banishing D. desecrating

Passage-3

We are living in very exciting ....(1).... . The ....(2).... change is dizzying and the impact this progress is having on our present and — more importantly — on our future is difficult to ....(3).... in its ...(4).... . This is the age of ....(5).... micro-processors, sophisticated software, new hardware technology and high bandwidth, high-speed networks. The PC gave us a new way to work, play and ....(6).... . In fact, it brought ....(7).... our desktops computing power, which until a few years ....(8).... had only been available to corporates. With the ....(9).... of the internet, the PC ....(10).... us the most convenient and flexible way to head on to the Net.

Questions

1. A. periods B. days C. phase D. times
2. A. phase B. pace C. sphere D. drastic

3. A. guess B. forecast C. comprehend D. approximate
4. A. whole B. entirety C. fruition D. fullness
5. A. strong B. changing C. powerful D. sonorous
6. A. convey B. communicate C. entertain D. enjoy
7. A. onto B. to C. on D. at
8. A. back B. earlier C. behind D. before
9. A. addendum B. adherence C. afoot D. advent
10. A. allowed B. privileged C. brought D. offered

Passage-4

What is required today in our country is ....(1).... of a new political culture based on full respect for human liberty, on pluralism and on a better social deal for all. The major ....(2).... facing us today is to carry out democratic transformation in all the ....(3)...., social, cultural, economic and political. The events of the 20th century ....(4).... one thing absolutely clear that human ....(5)...., everywhere, specially in countries whose political structures were ....(6).... to reflect the revolutionary aspirations of the people ....(7).... not only under stress and strain but are ....(8).... vast upheavals because of the ....(9).... of democracy. At the same time it has also to be understood that democracy cannot be ....(10).... into a static mould.

Questions

1. A. growing B. developing C. creating D. creation
2. A. development B. crisis C. challenge D. drawback
3. A. corners B. context C. realm D. spheres
4. A. have made B. has made C. had made D. made

5. A. travails   B. traverse
   C. traps   D. transverse
6. A. supposed   B. meant
   C. caused   D. forced
7. A. were   B. was
   C. are   D. have been
8. A. developing   B. evolving
   C. experiencing   D. faced with
9. A. denial   B. rebuff
   C. rebuttal   D. absence
10. A. shaped   B. flex
    C. frozen   D. caused

Passage-5

For centuries, women not only in India but all over the world ....(1).... treated as ....(2).... secondary position to men. ....(3).... human history men ....(4).... far greater power then women to name, classify, and order the worlds in which they both live. ....(5).... studies in various parts of the world point out to a wide ....(6).... in male and female roles ....(7).... cultures and demonstrate the possibility of change in these sex-determined roles. The 20th century in particular ....(8).... the cause of gender justice by internationalizing struggles for equality ....(9).... women and other oppressed people. Women's struggles against their ....(10).... were intertwined in ....(11).... degrees with ideologies and movements based on the values of freedom, self-determination, equality, democracy and justice.

Questions

1. A. has been   B. have been
   C. had been   D. were
2. A. occupying   B. taking
   C. possessing   D. serving
3. A. All through   B. Throughout
   C. Since   D. From
4. A. have   B. had
   C. have had   D. enjoy
5. A. Sociological   B. Anthropological
   C. General   D. Practical
6. A. concord   B. repulsion
   C. disagreement   D. variation
7. A. among   B. across
   C. between   D. of
8. A. developed   B. evolved
   C. promoted   D. entertained
9. A. for   B. to
   C. among   D. by
10. A. subsidiary   B. subsequent
    C. subservience   D. subordination
11. A. various   B. varying
    C. changing   D. differing

ANSWERS

Passage-1

1	2	3	4	5	6
C	D	A	B	B	D

7	8
A	D

Passage-2

1	2	3	4	5	6
C	A	A	B	C	D

7	8	9	10
B	C	D	A

Passage-3

1	2	3	4	5	6
D	B	C	B	C	B

7	8	9	10
A	D	D	D

Passage-4

1	2	3	4	5	6
D	C	D	A	A	B

7	8	9	10
C	C	A	C

Passage-5

1	2	3	4	5	6
B	A	B	C	B	D

7	8	9	10	11
B	C	D	D	B

PASSAGES

Directions: *Read the following passages and answer the questions given below each.*

PASSAGE-1

In the Roman times, defected enemies were generally put to death as criminals for having offended the emperor of Rome. In the middle ages, however, the practice of ransoming of returning prisoners in exchange for money became common. Though some saw this custom as a step towards a most humane society, the primary reasons behind it were economic rather than humanitarian.

In those times, rulers had only a limited ability to raise taxes. They could neither force their subject to fight nor pay them to do so. The promise of material compensation in the form of goods and ransom was therefore the only way of inducing combatants to participate in a war. In the middle ages, the predominant incentive for the individual soldiers was the expectation of spoils. Although collecting ransom clearly brought financial gain, keeping a prisoner and arranging for his exchange had its cost. Consequently, procedures were devised to reduce transaction costs.

One such device was a rule asserting that the prisoner had to assess his own value. This compelled the prisoner to establish a value *without too much distortion;* indicating too low a value would increase, the captive's chances of being killed, while indicating too high a value would either ruin him financially or create a prohibitively expensive ransom that would also result in death.

1. It can be inferred from the passage that a medieval soldier
   A. was less likely to kill captured members of opposing armies than was a soldier of the Roman Empire
   B. was similar to a 20th century terrorist in that he operated on a basically independent level and was motivated solely by economic incentives
   C. had few economic options and chose to fight because it was the only way to earn an adequate living
   D. was motivated to spare prisoners' lives by humanitarian rather than economic ideals

2. Which of the following best describes the change in policy from executing prisoners in Roman times to ransoming prisoners in the middle ages?
   A. The emperors of Rome demanded more respect than did medieval rulers and thus Roman subjects went to greater lengths to defend their nation
   B. It was a reflection of the lesser degree of direct control medieval ruler had over subjects
   C. It became a show of strength and honour warrior of the middles ages to be able to capture and return their enemies
   D. Medieval soldiers were not as humanitarian as their ransoming practices might have indicated

3. The primary purpose of the passage is to
   A. discuss the economic basis of the medieval practice of exchanging prisoners for ransom
   B. examine the history of the treatment of prisoner of war
   C. emphasize the importance of a warrior's code of honour during the middle ages
   D. explore a way of reducing the cost of ransom

4. The author uses the phrase *"without too much distortion"* in order to
   A. indicate that prisoners would fairly assess their worth
   B. emphasize the important role medieval prisoners played in determining whether they should be ransomed
   C. explain how prisoners often paid more than an appropriate ransom in order to increase their chances for survival
   D. suggest that captors and captives often had understanding relationships

PASSAGE-2

The world dismisses curiosity by calling it idle or mere idle curiosity—even though curious persons are seldom idle. Parents do their best to extinguish curiosity in their children because it makes life difficult to be faced everyday with a string of unanswerable questions about what makes fire hot or why grass grows. Children whose curiosity survives parental discipline are invited to join our university. With the university, they go on asking their questions and trying to find the answers. In the eyes of a scholar, that is what a university is for. Some of the questions which the scholars ask, seem to the world to be scarcely worth asking, let alone answering. They asked questions too minute specialised for you and me to understand without years of explanation. If the world inquires of one of them why he wants to know the answer to a particular question he may say especially if he is a scientist, that the answer will in some obscure way make possible a new machine or weapon or gadget.

He talks that way because he knows that the world understands and respects utility.

But to you who are now part of the university, he will say that he wants to know the answer simply because he does not know it, the way the mountain climber wants to climb a mountain, simply because it is there. Similarly a historian asked by an outsider why he studies history may come out with the argument that he has learnt to repeat on such occasions, something about knowledge of the past making it possible to understand the present and mould the future. But if you really want to know why a historian studies the past, the answer is much simpler, something happened and he would like to know what. All this does not mean that the answers which scholars find to their questions have no consequences. They may have enormous consequences but these seldom form the reason for asking the questions or pursuing the answers. It is true that scholars can be put to work answering questions for the sake of the consequences as thousands are working, now, for example, in search of a cure for cancer. But this is not the primary function of the scholars. For the consequences are usually subordinate to the satisfaction of curiosity.

1. According to the passage, the children make life difficult for their parents
   A. by their ceaseless curiosity
   B. by unceasing bombardment of questions
   C. by asking irrelevant questions
   D. by posing profound questions

2. The common people consider some of the questions that the scholars ask unimportant
   A. as they are too lazy and idle
   B. as they are too modest
   C. as it's beyond their comprehension
   D. as it is considered a waste of time

3. A historian really studies the past
   A. to comprehend the present and to reconstruct the future
   B. to explain the present and plan the future
   C. to understand the present and make fortune
   D. to understand the present and mould the future

4. Children whose curiosity survives parental discipline means
A. children retaining their curiosity in spite of being discouraged by their parents
B. children pursuing their mental curiosity
C. children's curiosity subdued due to parents' intervention
D. children being disciplined by their parents

5. According to the passage, parents do their best to discourage curiosity in their children
A. because they have no time
B. because they have no patience to answer them
C. because they feel that their children ask stupid questions continuously
D. because they are unable to answer all their questions

PASSAGE-3

The factor of geographical distribution is equally, possibly even more, significant that English is spoken as first or native language in at least four continents of the world, Russian in two, Chinese and the Indian languages in one. English is without question the closest approach to a world language today. It goes without saying that no two persons ever have an identical command of their common language. Certainly, they have not precisely the same vocabulary. There are at least minor differences in pronunciation, indeed the same individual will not pronounce his vowels and consonants in absolutely identical fashion everytime he utters them. Everyone possesses, in addition, certain individual traits of grammatical form and syntactical order, constituting that peculiar and personal quality of language which we term as style. All of this is implicit in the well-known phrase, 'Style is the man.' No men are identical, no two styles are the same. If this be true of but two persons, the potential of differences resident in a language spoken by more than 200 million truly staggers imagination.

1. The author argues that English is the closest approach to a world language because
A. there are more native speakers of English than of any other language
B. English has less number of mutually unintelligible dialects
C. the geographical distribution of English covers a much greater area
D. other languages are much too complex to be world languages

2. The fact that the same individual will not pronounce his vowels and consonants identically everytime shows that
A. literary style varies from person to person
B. mutual intelligibility is a myth
C. vocabulary varies from individual to individual
D. no two persons speak the same language exactly the same way

3. It is evident from the passage that style is
A. a strange type of language
B. a language where one does not have to be particular about correctness and grammar
C. language used in a particular way by an individual
D. a question of grammatical and syntactic correctness

4. According to some authorities
A. more people speak Chinese dialect than English
B. more people speak English as an auxiliary language than as a first language
C. more people speak English in the UK than in England
D. about one-fourth of the world's population speaks English

5. The overall implication of the passage is that
A. to suppose that 230 million people speak English as a native language would certainly be an underestimate
B. the 55 million inhabitants of the British Isles speak like the 30 million inhabitants of the dominions and colonies
C. a little less than half the native English speakers in the world live in the US
D. about one-tenth of the total English-speaking world population lives in British dominions and colonies

PASSAGE-4

What is the future which awaits our children? The underlying assumption of the question, that Indian children have a common future, is itself dubious. It can legitimately be asked whether a student who is well-fed, attending a boarding school in the salubrious climate of the hills and learning to use computers has any future in common with a malnourished child who goes to a school with no blackboards, if indeed he does go to school. The latter may have no worthwhile future at all. And it might be worthwhile to analyse the significance of this marginalisation of more than 75 per cent of the children of this country.

The failure to provide an infrastructure for primary education in the villages of India more than 40 years after independence is in sharp contrast with the sophisticated institutions, for technical institutes of higher education are funded by the government, which essentially means that the money to support them comes from taxes. And, since indirect taxation forms a substantial part of the taxes collected by the government, the financial burden is borne by all the people. L.K. Jha put it graphically when he observed that 25 paise of every rupee spent on educating an IIT student comes from the pockets of men and women whose children may never enter a proper classroom.

1. The author is trying to highlight which of the following?
   A. Faulty system of direct taxes
   B. The greatness of L.K. Jha
   C. Need of sophisticated education for rural poor
   D. Need to have common future for Indian children

2. Which of the following pairs have been termed as 'sharp contrast' by the author?
   (i) Infrastructure for technical education
   (ii) Lack of infrastructure for rural primary schools
   (iii) 25 paise of every rupee earned by Government is spent on education
   (iv) The financial burden of higher technical education is borne by all people
   (v) 75% of children have limited opportunities
   A. (ii) and (iv)   B. (ii) and (iii)
   C. (iii) and (iv)   D. (i) and (ii)

3. Which of the following statements is not true?
   (i) The author welcomes Govt.'s initiative on primary education
   (ii) 75% of the children have a bright future
   (iii) 25% cost of educating a technocrat comes from poor people
   A. Only (i)   B. Only (ii)
   C. Only (iii)   D. Only (i) and (ii)

4. According to the author, who among the following does not have a hopeful and prosperous future?
   (i) All students from technical institutes
   (ii) All students financially supported by the Government
   A. Only (i)   B. Only (ii)
   C. Both (i) and (ii)   D. Neither (i) nor (ii)

5. What seems to be the likely answer of the author to the question posed by him in the first sentence of the passage?
   (i) There is no common future for the Indian children
   (ii) The future is worthwhile for majority of Indian children
   (iii) The majority may never enter a proper classroom
   A. Only (i)   B. Only (ii)
   C. Only (iii)   D. Both (i) and (ii)

6. What seems to be the purpose of the author in writing this passage?
   A. Setting goals for children of upper middle class
   B. Questioning the legitimacy of public schools
   C. Highlighting lack of infrastructural facilities for primary education
   D. Focusing on inequality in educational opportunities

PASSAGE-5

Cyber crime is the branded stigma defacing the culture and magnanimity of computer technology. It is upkeeping the flag with indomitable triumph against developing computer technology worldwide.

Modern age is striding with marching steps of technology revolution beating the past decade of ancestral belief with ultimate care. Computer invention has unfolded the mystery of quick access with the objective of minimum manpower and cutting the time consumption parameters.

As each coin has dual face of its portrait, likewise computer technology is sick of creeping virus. Synthetic man-made dilemma of site hackers activation is causing setback to the expanding anchor of revolutionary device with great loss of time, economy and data profile as suffered by consumers. A recent report from Internet security firm Websense estimates that 85.6 per cent of all the unwanted e-mails contained links to spam sites. The company's data suggests that the number of malicious sites grew 233 per cent in the last six months and saw 671 per cent growth in the number of malicious sites during the last year. In June alone, the total number of e-mails detected as containing viruses increased by 600 per cent compared to May.

Chat rooms, blogs and message-boards where the users post comments have been identified as the top targets of hackers and spammers due to the high traffic these attract. According to Websense, 95 per cent of user-generated comments to blogs, chat rooms and message-boards during the first half of the year were malicious.

It is advisable not to click on spurious links and stay away from keying in passwords at unknown sites as they are most likely to be spammed. Hackers can steal your passwords and log in to your account and access critical information like account numbers and contact details among other things.

1. The above passage is:
   A. an advisory for the computer users.
   B. an advisory for the Internet users.
   C. a warning against possible threat to the Internet users.
   D. related to chat rooms, blogs and message boards.

2. People who use chat rooms and blogs,
   A. are safe and have no threats from spam.
   B. are more prone to malicious e-mails.
   C. create virus and hack the accounts of others.
   D. are unsafe.

3. According to the writer, it is not safe to:
   A. log on to spurious links.
   B. access one's own account frequently.
   C. have essential information stored in a computer.
   D. include data-stealing code.

4. Hackers and spammers, according to the writer, are:
   A. a new threat to the Internet users and the economy.
   B. only pranksters and not serious threat to the system.
   C. trained, professional technocrats who are an asset.
   D. not expert professionals.

5. Which word in the passage is synonym of *weblog*?
   A. blog   B. password
   C. site   D. e-mail

6. Which agency has assessed the data record with spam sites?
   A. Microsoft
   B. Internet security from Google
   C. Websense
   D. Spammers

7. Which month dominates the e-mails detection data record?
   A. May   B. June
   C. Last six months   D. Last year

ANSWERS

PASSAGE-1

1	2	3	4
A	B	A	A

PASSAGE-2

1	2	3	4	5
A	C	D	A	D

PASSAGE-3

1	2	3	4	5
A	D	C	D	A

PASSAGE-4

1	2	3	4	5	6
D	A	D	A	A	D

PASSAGE-5

1	2	3	4	5	6	7
A	D	A	A	A	C	B

Jumbled Words

Different words form a sentence and convey their meaning only when arranged in a proper order. A Paragraph is formed from sentences, it will convey its true meaning and purpose only when the sentences are arranged in a proper manner. Try and practise it in this exercise.

Multiple Choice Questions

Directions: *In the following questions, some parts of the sentence have been jumbled up. You are required to rearrange these parts which are labelled P, Q, R and S to produce the correct sentence. Choose the option with proper sequence.*

1. We are doing
   P : to the people
   Q : to give relief
   R : all we can
   S : but more funds are needed
   The correct sequence should be
   A. P Q R S   B. R Q P S
   C. Q P R S   D. S P Q R

2. The man
   P : when he was
   Q : in the office last evening
   R : could not finish
   S : all his work
   The correct sequence should be
   A. P Q R S   B. Q R S P
   C. R Q P S   D. R S P Q

3. The people decided
   P : they were going
   Q : how much
   R : to spend
   S : on the construction of the school building
   The correct sequence should be
   A. Q P R S   B. P Q R S
   C. P R Q S   D. S Q P R

4. The man said that
   P : those workers
   Q : would be given a raise
   R : who did not go on
   S : strike last month
   The correct sequence should be
   A. P Q R S   B. P R S Q
   C. Q P R S   D. R S P Q

5. I think
   P : the members
   Q : are basically in agreement
   R : of the group
   S : on the following points
   The correct sequence should be
   A. R Q P S   B. S Q R P
   C. P R Q S   D. P Q S R

6. While it was true that
   P : I had
   Q : to invest in industry
   R : some lands and houses
   S : I did not have ready cash

The correct sequence should be
A. P Q R S   B. P R S Q
C. S Q P R   D. Q P R S

7. P : But for your help
   Q : to finish this work
   R : it would not have been possible
   S : in time
   The correct sequence should be
   A. P R Q S   B. S P Q R
   C. R P Q S   D. P Q R S

8. The boy
   P : in the competition
   Q : who was wearing spectacles
   R : won many prizes
   S : held in our college
   The correct sequence should be
   A. P Q R S   B. R P S Q
   C. Q R P S   D. Q P S R

9. About 200 years ago,
   P : in the south of India
   Q : an old king
   R : ruled over a kingdom
   S : called Rajavarman
   The correct sequence should be
   A. Q S R P   B. P Q R S
   C. Q P S R   D. Q S P R

10. P : his land
    Q : a wooden plough
    R : the Indian peasant still uses
    S : to cultivate
    The correct sequence should be
    A. R Q P S   B. Q P S R
    C. S R Q P   D. R Q S P

11. He was a man,
    P : even if he had to starve
    Q : who would not beg
    R : borrow or steal
    S : from anyone
    The correct sequence should be
    A. P Q R S   B. P R Q S
    C. Q R S P   D. Q P R S

12. P : in the progress of
    Q : universities play a crucial role
    R : our civilization

S : in the present age
The correct sequence should be
A. S Q P R   B. Q R S P
C. Q R P S   D. S Q R P

13. P : far out into the sea
    Q : for the next two weeks there were further explosions
    R : which hurled
    S : ashes and debris
    The correct sequence should be
    A. Q R P S   B. R S P Q
    C. Q R S P   D. S R P Q

14. William Shakespeare,
    P : in his lifetime
    Q : the great English dramatist
    R : wrote thirty-five plays
    S : and several poems
    The correct sequence should be
    A. P Q R S   B. R S P Q
    C. Q S R P   D. Q R S P

15. Whenever I am,
    P : with an old friend of mine
    Q : in New Delhi
    R : to have dinner
    S : I always try
    The correct sequence should be
    A. S Q P R   B. Q S R P
    C. R P S Q   D. P R Q S

16. P : I don't know
    Q : must have thought
    R : what people sitting next to me
    S : but I came away
    The correct sequence should be
    A. R S Q P   B. R Q S P
    C. P Q R S   D. P R Q S

17. P : in estimating the size of the earth
    Q : but they were hampered by the lack of instruments of precision
    R : ancient astronomers
    S : used methods which were theoretically valid
    The correct sequence should be
    A. R P Q S   B. P R Q S
    C. R S Q P   D. R P S Q

18. P : It is a pity that
    Q : by offering a handsome dowry
    R : a number of parents think that
    S : they will be able to ensure the happiness
          of their daughters
    The correct sequence should be
    A. S Q R P   B. P R S Q
    C. P S R Q   D. P R Q S

19. The common man
    P : in nurturing
    Q : a more active role
    R : communal harmony
    S : should play
    The correct sequence should be
    A. P R S Q   B. S Q P R
    C. S Q R P   D. P R Q S

20. The doctor
    P : able to find out
    Q : what has caused
    R : the food poisoning
    S : has not been
    The correct sequence should be
    A. S P R Q   B. P R Q S
    C. P R S Q   D. S P Q R

21. P : was suspended
    Q : the officer being corrupt
    R : before his dismissal
    S : from service
    The correct sequence should be
    A. Q P S R   B. Q P R S
    C. R S Q P   D. R S P Q

22. With an unsteady hand
    P : on my desk
    Q : from his pocket
    R : he took an envelope
    S : and threw it
    The correct sequence should be
    A. Q R P S   B. Q R S P
    C. R Q P S   D. R Q S P

23. P : she gave her old coat
    Q : to a beggar
    R : the one with the brown fur on it
    S : shivering with cold
    The correct sequence should be
    A. S Q R P   B. S P R Q
    C. P R Q S   D. P S Q R

24. It is a privilege
    P : to pay tax
    Q : of every citizen
    R : as well as the duty
    S : who is well-placed
    The correct sequence should be
    A. R P S Q   B. S P R Q
    C. R Q S P   D. S Q R P

25. It is not good
    P : of the wicked persons
    Q : to overthrow
    R : to accept the help
    S : the righteous persons
    The correct sequence should be
    A. R S Q P   B. Q S R P
    C. R P Q S   D. Q P R S

ANSWERS

1	2	3	4	5	6	7	8	9	10
B	D	A	B	C	C	A	C	A	D
11	12	13	14	15	16	17	18	19	20
C	A	C	D	B	D	C	B	B	D
21	22	23	24	25					
B	D	C	C	B					

Essay Writing

In a short essay, you can deal with a very few points only. It is of no use to write down a lot of things that have nothing to do with the subject. Write down facts that will help you in your essay. Write down your own ideas. Find the main idea of your essay. Choose the most important point you are going to present. Organise your facts and ideas in a way that develops your main idea. Once you have chosen the most important point of your essay, you must find the best way to tell your reader about it. Develop each supporting paragraph and make sure to follow the correct paragraph format. Write simple sentences to express your meaning. Use simple words; be clear as well as brief. Focus on the main idea of your essay. Check your essay for mistakes and correct them. Make sure that your handwriting is clear and legible. The examiner may not have enough time to take pains to read each and every word carefully. An illegible handwriting might only put off his interest in reading your essay even though it might be good. An essay can be written just about anything, even a poem. Hence it will be difficult to predict which essay you may be asked to write about in your exam. Here are a few selected essays for your study.

HEALTH IS WEALTH

There is a well-known saying : If wealth is lost, nothing is lost. If health is lost, something is lost. If character is lost, everything is lost.

It can be reasonably believed that no person in a sound mind would like to lose something even.

A healthy man can work hard and earn wealth, whereas an unhealthy man can't do this. Moreover, it is said and that rightly so, that a sound mind lives only in a sound body. In the modern world brain is everything to get all that man desires, but health is a prerequisite for having a good brain.

A student who works hard throughout the year has to bring out his knowledge on the paper on the day of examination. But if he does not enjoy good health, he may fall ill on the day of examination and thus all the labour done by him the whole year may just go down the drain.

In normal case, even to pursue one's studies in a sustained manner may not be possible for one who doesn't enjoy good health.

It is for this reason that it is said that students and all young people should take part in sports and games and have regular walks and exercise on daily basis.

Those people who run after money excessively and lose their health, are no gainers in any way. A man having a lot of money, may not even be able to enjoy the fruits of his labour because death and disease can overpower him any time. So, the first and foremost thing for us is to take care of our health. Wealth-earning and other motives must take only a secondary place in our scheme of things.

BETTER LATE THAN NEVER

In life, we sometimes come across some late bloomers in our own family or elsewhere. Such were

Einstein, Churchill, Gandhiji and several others. Modern scientists tell us that they or at least some of them, suffered from dyslexia. It means that even though they were really intelligent, they could not express their intelligence in their speech or on the paper.

It does not mean that if a person has once missed the bus, he will always miss it. If a student once fails in an examination, he should try once again. He may pass the examination the next time. He may get even very high marks which a renewed study of curricula can ensure him.

If any of the members of our family or anybody in our social circle falls in evil ways, he may not be shunned and treated as a pariah. Instead, he should be given a chance to improve his ways of life. We ourselves can come to his rescue and help him in changing the course of his life for the better. The famous film actor Sanjay Dutt had got addicted to drugs. With the help of de-addiction specialists and through sheer will power, he came over it. Others can take a cue from him and again become useful members of society.

CHILD IS THE FATHER OF MAN

The statement 'Child is father of the Man' may seem strange-but these are the words of the celebrated Romantic poet of England, William Wordsworth, and are full of meaning and truth of life. If we think a little deeply, we'll realize that child is a man-in-the making and man is only a grownup child. In other words, the growth from childhood to manhood is continuous, symmetrical, spontaneous and natural.

This in simple words means that the traits of childhood continue in manhood. In other words, if we want to have better men, we must first have better children. If we pay no attention to the child, he grows into a worthless youth and equally or even more worthless man.

A child's mind is like a clean slate. Whatever is written on it, its imprint continues on his mind for ever in life. A child is greatly influenced by the milieu and environment in which he lives. If his parents are quarrelsome and aggressive by nature, he grows almost like them. If they are religiously minded, he acquires the same traits.

Some children suffer from want, lack of affection and neglect. Such children cannot develop a good and lovable personality. We may read carefully the words Anant Waraich on child psychology as given below: "Child is the father of man" is a common proverb which literally explains the practical importance of child psychology. A nation depends upon the care and upbriging of children. The future of tomorrow's society depends upon the physiological and psychological development of today's children.

Child psychology therefore assumes importance for all those who are interested in the healthy development of a child's personality."

WORK IS WORSHIP

It is rightly said that an idle man's brain is the devil's workshop. A man who is lazy can achieve nothing in life. The story of the ant and the cricket is well-known. The cricket had laid by nothing for winter. When he went for help and advice to the ant, she asked him, 'What did you do in summer ?' He replied ; 'I kept singing during summer.' Then the ant retorted 'Now, dance winter away.'

An idle man is always thinking of something mischievous and destructive. Those who are shirkers, become dullards and these dullards mostly end as dropouts and then as they grow up, they become thieves, pickpockets, burglars and even murderers.

Our mind is like a constantly running stream. It cannot be controlled easily. The best way out is to keep it busy and direct it to some constructive work.

A man who is always busy, has no time to think of anything wrong. He kills two birds with one stone. On the one hand, he keeps himself safe from going on any wrong path and on the other hand, he ultimately reaps the fruit of his hard work.

A student who takes a keen interest in his studies, rises to some good position in life. A farmer who pays full attention to his work, reaps a bumper crop at the and of the season. A soldier who learns martial arts studiously, wins the battle in the long run. A businessman can be successful only if he works steadily and meticulously.

It is rightly said that Rome was not built in a day. So, to complete any project there is need for patience and constant, hard work. Thus, worship of God is possible not just in the temple but it is possible also in the field of life. We can say without any doubt that work is worship.

LIVE AND LET LIVE

Man has to live on this planet only for a number of decades. This span of man's life is less than a moment in the infinite span of cosmic life. Man is less than a grain of sand or a bubble on the ocean of existence. He is not one of the most important objects in the universe.

Surprisingly, man thinks too highly of himself. Even more curiously, he deems others of no significance.

The net result of this line of thinking is man's crass and stark materialism, selfishness and even dehumanization. Man is basically an animal and has several traits of a wild beast in his mental make-up.

Fortunately for mankind, there have emerged off and on some highly enlightened great men who have exhorted man to realize the oneness of humanity, universal brotherhood, world peace and mutual goodwill, help, aid and cooperation. Among such men there have been Jesus Christ, Lord Rama, Krishna, the Buddha, Socrates, Guru Nanak, Kabir, Mahatma Gandhi and others.

It is in this context that India while believe in non-violence, universal love and mutual respect for each other, signed the Panchsheel with China. It is another matter that China stabbed India in the back.

Later, perhaps China too realized the value of the policy 'Live and Let Live' and now China and India have both been trying for quite some time to enhance the scope for friendship between two countries even when the boundary dispute is still there. India has tried her best to follow the policy of 'Live and Let Live' and it is hoped that in spite of numerous failures, India will finally succeed in her efforts.

Thus, it can be said conclusively that the policy 'Live and Let Live' is a sound policy that must be followed by all nations, countries and all communities and all sections of society.

KNOWLEDGE IS POWER

The main difference between a man and an animal is that man has some knowledge but an animal has no knowledge of anything.

Knowledge is hardly ever inborn. Most of the knowledge is acquired by man. As man gains more and more knowledge, he becomes more and more powerful, as knowledge is power the acquisition of which increases man's physical as well as intellectual capacity and capability.

Knowledge is the godmother of all discoveries, explorations and inventions. Mostly man gains knowledge through observation and experimentation : At first man starts with certain hypothesis or theory and some times even without any premeditation, prerequisite or predetermination. In other words, he embarks upon a project just at random and the results are startlingly positive or negative. Einstein, for instance, was actually not working for discovering the atom when he stepped upon it just by chance. Even Newton's sight of the falling apple and the thoughts that it generated in his mind which led to the discovery of the theory of gravitation were not foreconceived by him.

All the modern technology which has made certain nations so powerful economically and militarily is all based on knowledge. In countries like the USA research in all fields of science is done on regular basis and that is one of the underlying secrets of her success and matchlessness and invulnerability as a nation in the world, at least not to the extent of a crippling effect.

India has also done great research in certain fields, as for instance, in the fields of information technology and telecommunications and she is now reaping rich harvest for this.

So, in a nutshell we shall have to agree to what Bacon said four centuries ago that knowledge is power. All human progress and perhaps even man's very existence on the globe depends upon his retention and growth of knowledge in various fields for positive and constructive purposes because if knowledge is used for negative purposes, it can play havoc with our life and existence on earth.

BETTER ALONE THAN IN BAD COMPANY

It need not be stressed here that man is a social animal and that he cannot live without some sort of company. It is rightly said that one who can live without company cannot be a human being. He must be either an animal or a divine being.

All such reflections may be based on stark realities of life. But it is also possible that these may be just philosophical musings. The fact that sometimes circumstances take such a turn in man's life that he has to shun all company and live a secluded life. Certainly, a hermit or a recluse who leads a cloistered life cannot be termed as an insane person. Many of our great philosophers, saints, seers and wise men have, indeed, risen from ashrams and 'maths' where they could get ample time for brooding over various intricate philosophical questions and riddles of life.

In life sometimes we find ourselves surrounded by cheats, thugs, swindlers, terrorists, fanatics and other such anti-social elements such that we feel that we could do better than live and work among such people. It is said that a single black sheep infests the whole flock. So, we don't want to get infested and infected while living and working among such people.

In such circumstances, if we are honest and thus want to lead a segregated life and steer our own course of life, there should be nothing wrong with such a compulsive decision.

A FRIEND IN NEED IS A FRIEND INDEED

The world is full of fair weather friends. A friend is tested in time of need only. It is rightly said prosperity makes friends and adversity tries them.

The story of two friends and the bear is well-known to be related here. The crucial point in the story is the words of the helpless friend which he spoke to the fair-weather friend : "The bear said to me in my ears; 'Never trust a fair-weather friend.'"

Man is social animal. He cannot live without company. He has to choose the company of some friends. At least one of these friends must be a highly reliable one in whom all the secrets of life can be confided. However, in the modern world sometimes one feels cheated when at the moment of crisis one is ditched even by one's best friend who becomes a model of betrayal.

In such moments, one feels lonely, abandoned and ignored. He has the realization that even his best friend has left him in the lurch. Then, the only company possible for him is God and that is how he is able to maintain his balance of mind philosophically. So, we should always try to avoid the company of a fair weather friend.

THE SECRET OF HAPPINESS

It is commonly said that happiness is a state of mind. Real happiness does not depend upon the amount of wealth and items of luxury one has but upon one's state of mind. It is said that Alexander was unhappy even after conquering major part of the world since he felt that there was no more world to be conquered. Great generals and rulers like Julius Caesar, Napoleon, Changez Khan, Timur, Hitler and others had an insatiable desire for land and they could not be said to be quite happy even after winning so many battles and conquering country after country.

In spite of all this, it has to be admitted that man's need for money in the modern age cannot be summarily dismissed. Every man needs some luxuries to lead a comfortable life. He needs money to buy food, clothes and other necessary articles.

The most important thing is that man should earn money through honest means only. Corrupt and underhand methods to earn money only demean and dehumanize a man and peace of mind eludes such a man.

So, if a man leads a simple, honest life, and is hardworking, he can really live a happy life. Hard work is rightly said to be the key to success. One can find real happiness in work and nowhere else. One must be truthful, honest and brave. That is also essential for a happy, healthy life.

STORY OUTLINE

Boy set to guard sheep—told to cry "Wolf!" if he sees a wolf near the flock—watches the sheep for several days—gets tired of the monotonous work—so one day shouts "Wolf!" as a joke—all the villagers hasten to his help—they find no wolf—boy laughs at them—villagers angry—plays the same joke a few days later—some villagers take no notice-some come running—finding nothing, they beat the boy—at last wolf really comes—boy is terrified and shouts "Wolf! Wolf"—villagers take no notice—wolf kills several sheep.

THE STORY : THE BOY WHO CRIED "WOLF!"

One of the boys in a village was sent out into fields to look after the sheep.

"Mind you take care of them and don't let them stray", said the villagers to him.. "And keep a good look out for wolves. Don't go far away: and if you see a wolf coming near the sheep, shout out "Wolf!" as loudly as you can, and we will come at once to help you."

"All right!" said the boy, "I will be careful."

So every morning he drove his sheep out to the hillside and watched them all day. And when evening came, he drove them home again.

But after a few days he got rather tired of this lonely life. Nothing happened and no wolves came. So one afternoon he said to himself: "These villagers have given me a very stupid job. I think I will play a trick on them just for fun."

So he got up and began shouting as loudly as he could, "Wolf! Wolf!"

The people in the village heard him, and at once they came running with sticks.

"Wolf! Wolf!" shouted the boy; and they ran faster. At last they came up to him, out of breath.

"Where is the wolf?" they panted. But the boy only laughed and said: "There is no wolf. I only shouted in fun. And it was fun to see you all running as hard as you could!"

The men were very angry.

"You young rascal!" they said. "If you play a trick like that again, we will beat you instead of the wolf."

And they went back to their work in the village.

For some days the boy kept quiet. But he got restless again, and said to himself: "I wonder if they will come running again if I cry 'Wolf!' once more. It was such fun the last time."

So once more he began shouting, "Wolf! Wolf!"

The villagers heard him. Some said, "That boy is up to his tricks again." But others said, "It may be true this time; and if there really is a wolf, we shall lose some of our sheep."

So they seized their sticks, and ran out of the village to the hillside.

"Where is the wolf?" they cried, as they came up.

"Nowhere!" said the boy laughing. "It was fun to see you running up the hill as fast you could."

"We will teach you to play jokes," shouted the angry men; and they seized the boy and gave him a good beating, and left him crying instead of laughing.

A few days later a wolf really did come. When the boy saw it, he was very frightened and began shouting "Wolf! Wolf! Help!" as loudly as he could.

The villagers heard him, but they took no notice.

"He is playing his tricks again," they said. "We don't be made fools for a third time. You can't believe a boy after you have caught him lying twice."

So no one went to his help, and the wolf killed several sheep and frightened the boy nearly out of his wits.

STORY OUTLINE

A farmer had many sons—they often quarrelled among themselves—farmer's advice proved useless—he placed a bundle of sticks before them—asked each to break it—all tried but failed—he untied the bundle—sticks now easily broken—farmer's advice.

THE STORY : A FARMER AND HIS SONS

There lived a farmer in a village. He had many sons who used to fight and quarrel among themselves quite often. He would advise them saying, "You fight quite often. It's not good as it will weaken you." But his advice had no effect on them. His sons continued fighting among themselves on very silly things. The farmer decided to teach them a good thing through a practical. One day he brought a bundle of sticks before them and asked each of them to break that. All of them tried to break it but they failed. The farmer untied the bundle and said to them, "Now break the sticks one by one." The sons didn't face any problem and burst out easily, "This was very easy." The farmer said, "Do you get any lesson out of it?" The sons declined. Then he said that his purpose behind the story was that union is strength. His sons understood everything and promised not to fight among themselves.

STORY OUTLINE

Two friends travelling through a forest—agree to help each other in danger—suddenly a bear appears—one at once climbs up a tree—the other lies down on the ground and holds his breath—the bear comes up to him—smells his face—thinks he is dead—goes away—the first man now comes down—asks the other what the bear said in his ear—answers : "Beware of a friend who runs away in time of danger."

THE STORY : TWO FRIENDS AND A BEAR

Once upon a time there were two friends. They were travelling through a forest. They had agreed that they would help each other in danger. Suddenly there appeared a bear before them. One friend saw the bear and to save himself climbed up a tree to escape. The other couldn't do so. But he understood everything. At once, to escape from the bear he lay down on the ground and held his breath. Soon the bear came upon him and smelled his face. He thought him dead and went away without doing anything to him. It is said that bears do not attack the dead ones. The friend who had climbed up the tree came down and asked him what the bear said in his ear. The other told him that the bear said, "Beware of a friend who runs away in time of danger."

STORY OUTLINE

A merchant riding home from a fair—a large sum of money with him—sudden heavy rainfall—merchant gets wet—grumbles—shortly after attacked by a robber—robber's attempt to shoot—failure—powder damp—the merchant escapes.

THE STORY : A MERCHANT AND A ROBBER

Once upon a time there was a rich merchant. He was riding home from a fair. He had a large sum of money with him. All of a sudden, the weather became bad. Soon it started raining and within minutes there was a very heavy rainfall. The merchant got wet and all his money was also wet. He started grumbling as he valued money more than anything. He tried his best to keep himself and the money safe from every danger. But what was destined to happen happened. Shortly after it there came a robber. The robber understood everything. He realized that the merchant had plenty of money. So the robber attacked him with his gun. But his gun didn't fire as the gun powder had become wet. Meanwhile, the merchant found a chance to escape and within no time he escaped. Thus the rain which he had called bad had saved his life and money.

STORY OUTLINE

A thirsty crow—in search of water—sees a jug half filled with water—beak can't reach it—sees pebbles—puts them into the jug-water level comes up—drinks—flies away.

THE STORY : A THIRSTY CROW

There was a crow. He was very thirsty as it was very hot. So he had been flying for some time in search of water. At last he saw a jug and got down to see if he could quench his thirst. He was disappointed to see that it didn't have enough water. It had water at its bottom. His beak couldn't reach that water level. He was sad for a few seconds. But he started investing how be could get the water. He mused, "I must think to do something so that the water comes up. I think if some pebbles are put into it, the water will come up."

He thought to put this into practice and flew in search of pebbles. He saw some pebbles nearby and picked them up one by one. He put these pebbles into the jug. Soon the water level in the jug came up. He quenched his thirst and flew away satisfied.

STORY OUTLINE

A man has a hen which lays a golden egg everyday—the man collects ten eggs in ten days—is happy at this sudden fortune—hopes to become rich soon—then he gets impatient—wants to become rich overnight—kills the hen.

THE STORY : A GREEDY MAN

Once upon a time there lived a man in a village. He had a hen which laid a golden egg daily. Thus the man had collected ten golden eggs in ten days. He was very happy at this sudden fortune as he was now growing richer day by day. But he didn't seem satisfied with it. He wanted to be rich very quickly due to the greed. But soon the greed in him comes up on the fore. He said to himself, "If I have all the eggs together, I shall be very rich and happy." He wanted many golden eggs. So he started thinking how to get the golden eggs. The man felt that it would be better if he killed the hen. He would be rich overnight by selling all the golden eggs in its abdomen. So he grew impatient and one day killed the hen. There was no golden egg daily as the hen had died. He wept and wept at his foolish act. But whatever had happened had happened. He repented but nothing could be done.

STORY OUTLINE

A slave runs away from his cruel master—a lion in the forest—crying in pain—the slave takes out a thorn from his foot—a few months later—the slave caught by his master's men—ordered to be thrown before a hungry lion—the lion rushes at him—licks his feet—remembers his old kindness—the slave and the lion set at liberty.

THE STORY : THE SLAVE AND THE LION

Once upon a time there was a slave. He worked very hard for his master. But his master used to treat him badly. So the slave thought how to escape from him.

Fortunately, he escaped from his cruel master. While crossing the forest he saw a lion. The lion was crying in pain. The slave wanted to know the reason and went near him. He saw that the lion had a thorn in his foot which couldn't come out. The slave took out the thorn from his foot. The lion stopped crying in pain and went his way. The slave also went his way but he was caught again by the master's men a few months later. The master beat him much and finally ordered him to be thrown before a hungry lion. This hungry lion was the same whose thorn had been taken out by the slave. The lion rushed at him, smelled him and started licking his feet. He remembered the slave's old kindness. The master understood the whole truth and set the lion and the slave at liberty.

STORY OUTLINE

A good boy—disobeys his parents—gets into bad company—father gives him some good apples—tells him to lay them aside for a few days—places a rotten apple among them—the rotten-apple spoils the good ones—a lesson on bad company.

THE STORY : A BAD BOY AND HIS PARENTS

Once upon a time there was a very good boy of his loving parents. They were a happy family as everything went good. But soon he started disobeying his parents as he got into a bad company. He would shout at his parents and abuse them. Also he demanded money the other day as he wasted it in gambling. His parents tried all methods to bring him on the right path of life but it was of no use. Then one day, his father brought him some good quality apples. He asked him to lay them aside for a few days. Then he gave him a rotten apple and asked him to keep this rotten apple among the good ones. He asked his son to bring all the apples to him after two days. When his son brought him all the apples, he asked him to see these. The son understood that one rotten apple had rotten (spoilt) all the other good ones. He understood the meaning and promised to be a good son to his parents.

The following points should be borne in mind while writing a letter.

1. A letter should contain all the necessary parts which normally and formally it is required to contain.
2. It should follow the pattern according to the nature of the letter whether it is personal, impersonal, to the editor, to some official, customer, etc.
3. It should contain no irrelevant matter.
4. Normally it should indicate the date of writing.
5. In English most of the letters start in a direct way and there is not much scope for introductory words except in letters of particular nature.

Read the following examples of different kinds of letters carefully:

1. Write a letter to your father requesting him to allow you to join an educational tour.

65, Balaji Boy's Hostel
Grace Public School
Nagpur

10 October ....

My dear Father,

You have often advised me to join an educational tour whenever I get an opportunity. Now, here is a good opportunity for me.

The educational tour of our school is leaving for a visit to various historical and religious places of India in the first week of coming November. It will be a two week tour and will be led by our famous teacher of history, Ms Susheilla Nayyar, who is a renowned historian and has been recognized as such even by NCERT.

Surprisingly, each student joining the tour has to pay only a small amount, that is, two thousand rupees only. This amount includes boarding, lodging, travelling and all other expenses. It is because it'll be a highly subsidized one as the Railways and the school authorities have decided to pay the major part of the expenses.

I hope you'll not allow me to miss this chance. As a sum of two thousand rupees has to be deposited in the school office by 31 October of this month. I'll be grateful if you send me the required sum as early as possible.

Love to mamma and little naughty Kittu
Yours affectionately
Somesh

2. Write a letter to your father requesting him to increase your monthly allowance.

12, Girls Hostel
Porbander

15 November ....

My dear Father,

You'll be glad to learn that I've done well in my first home Test. However, I'm now facing a problem.

The problem which I'm facing is financial in nature and has arisen out of a variety of reasons. First, our school authorities have now prescribed a new dress code which I've to purchase within a fortnight. Secondly, a number of teachers of my class have recommended some text books which I must purchase within ten days or so. Also tuition fees and mess charges in the hostel have been increased by twenty per cent. The washerwoman has also increased her rates.

I'll, therefore, request you, papa, to send me five thousand rupees immediately and also increase my monthly allowance by at least one thousand rupees. Dear papa, I'm aware of your greatly limited resources but there is no escape from the expenses referred to above.

Love to mamma and little naughty Bittu.
Your loving daughter
Rashmi

3. Write a letter to your father, who has gone abroad, giving him home news.

31, Deep Andheri,
Mumbai
December 16 ....
My dear Father,

I was overjoyed to read your letter which I received yesterday. Even more than the news that your business tour has been a grand success, what gladdened me most was that you are hale and hearty and are enjoying yourself a lot there visiting museums, exhibitions and historical buildings.

Now, news from here Papa, it'll please you a lot to learn that we're all quite well here, though, of course, we miss you most and sometimes feel your absence strongly.

Here, I give you some detail.

Mummy is visiting the lepers' colony regularly and is doing whatever she can for the helpless souls. She does not care for her own health, as usual, but I can assure that she is fit as fiddle except that she is dead tired when she returns in the evening.

I'm attending school and also my tuition classes as usual. I won the first prize at the drawing contest yesterday.

Tinu is playing with his chess all the time during the day. He studies little but, as we know, he has a sharp learning skill and can pick up his studies in a short period near the examination. Still, I advise him to work hard but he doesn't listen to me. Day before yesterday when he was playing, his ball hit a by-stander and we had to listen to some unpleasant words from the victim, but we kept our cool and the matter was soon over.

Yours affectionately
Kiran Bale

4. Write a letter to your mother describing the Prize Distribution function at your school.

22, Girls Hostel II
Bikaner Public School,
Bikaner

21 February ....

My dear Mother,

Yesterday the Prize Distribution function of our school was held in the school hall. Mrs Savitri Loomba, the D.C. of Bikaner was the chief guest.

The hall had already been tastefully decorated. The function started at 10 am sharp. The chief guest was punctual to the minute.

The President of the managing committee welcomed the chief guest. Then a cultural show started. Everybody liked it. The hall resounded with loud clapping by students and teachers.

The chief guest gave away the prizes. I got the first prize in aggregate and the second prize in English. The chief guest was greatly impressed by the large number of prizes won by students not only in the house examinations but also in Board examination and inter-school contests. This point she stressed in particular in her brief speech which she made after distribution of prizes.

The principal in her speech highlighted the achievements of the school in the matter of studies and other activities during the year. I, as the head girl, thanked the chief guest.

The function came to an end at about 1pm with the chanting of the National Anthem.

Convey my love to papa and dear Shibu.
Yours affectionately
Shalini

5. Write a letter to your younger brother advising him to give more attention to studies.

75, Deshbandhu Gupta Road
Krishna Mohalla,
Bareilly
12 September ....

Dear Mukesh,

I have just received the report of your first House Test. I'm shocked to learn that you have failed in every subject. It is clear that you are not taking any interest in studies. I've also learnt that you are always moving in bad company. You're fond of seeing movies and have developed certain bad habits like drinking, smoking and perhaps drug-taking.

Dear Mukesh, if you waste your prime of life in idle pursuits, you'll have to repent in the long run. I, as your elder brother, want to advise you to leave bad company and give up bad habits. Start working hard right from now. I expect good results from you in your next examinations.

I hope you'll act upon my advice.

Love from Papa and Mamma

Yours affectionately

Lokesh

6. Write a letter to your uncle thanking him for a birthday gift.

32, Ghumar Mandi

Suranassi

(Jalandhar)

19 August ....

My dear Uncle,

Yesterday was my fourteenth birthday. It was celebrated in the usual simple but decent way. My all friends had come. My other relatives, including uncle Mr Shakeel, were there. I missed you very much.

A day earlier I had received the wonderful gift of a pocket PC from you. I showed it to all present at the function and they appreciated it very much.

Uncle, I thank you very much for the gift. Only I wish you yourself had been there at the function to present me the gift. I hope you will make it a point to be present in person on the occasion of my next birthday.

Convey my love to Aunty and Summu.

Yours affactionately

Akbar

7. Write a letter to your friend congratulating him on her grand success in the examination.

20, Sathara Street

Kashmere Gate

Delhi

15 April ....

My dear Priya,

I'm very glad to learn from today's newspaper that you have passed the Matriculation Examination in the first division. Not only this, your name appears in the Merit list.

This is the hard-earned fruit of your strenuous work done during the year and is, thus, well-deserved. Please accept my heartiest congratulations and convey the same to your revered parents also. I'm sure you'll continue with this progress in your next class also.

I'm, however, waiting for a grand party from you. When should I expect it? Please remember I'm very impatient and can't wait for long.

Yours sincerely

Sunita

8. Write a letter to a friend inviting him to a hill station.

32, Curzon Street

Sundernagar,

Mussoorie

30 May ....

My dear Hemant,

You'll be glad to know that I've reached this hill station today along with my uncle who is a Hostel Manager here. As we started the uphill journey from Dehradoon, the thrill started. I loved not only the scenic beauty of dense forests and snow capped peaks at some distance but also enjoyed the cool breeze and refreshing, pollution-free atmosphere.

I hereby invite you to come and join me at your earliest. We'll gain good health here and also study a lot as it is a calm and quiet place where the concentration of the mind is a natural outcome. The sights of sailing clouds and springs are an added charm. Morever, there are many places worth-seeing here in and around Mussoorie.

Convey my compliments to your parents.

Yours ever

S. Nagarajan

HONOUR KILLING

To be young and in love has proved fatal for many young girls and boys in parts of North India as an intolerant and bigoted society refuses to accept any violation of its rigid code of decorum, especially when it comes to woman. Honour killing is an euphemism for doing away with anyone seen as spoiling the family's reputation. Many such killings are happening with regularity in Punjab, Haryana and Western UP. These are socially sanctioned by caste Panchayats and carried out by mobs with the connivance of family members. In many cases, the victims who run away with 'unsuitable' partners are lured back home only to be put to death by their relatives and fellow villagers. Yet, pre-emptive action to protect them is never taken. Undoubtedly, the virus of caste and class that affects those carrying out such crimes affects the police in the area too. But that can be no excuse to sanction murder. The usual remedy to such murders is to suggest that society must be prevailed upon to be more gender-sensitive and to shed the prejudices of caste and class. Efforts should be made to sensitise people as to the need to do away with social biases. The collection of evidence becomes tricky and the eye-witnesses are never forthcoming. Active policing combined with serious penal sanctions is the only antidote to this most dishonourable practice.

CRIMES BY JUVENILES IN INDIA

Over the past few years juvenile delinquency has increased considerably. Young school students and college students have been indulging in petty offences like chain-snatching, pick-pocketing and automobile-lifting. On a few occasions they have been found committing serious crimes like robbery, murder and rape. Many young people loiter around in parks and public places either taking drugs or indulging in eve-teasing. In addition to these offences, there is the bitter issue of MMS scandals that are created and proliferated by children, especially the juveniles. Thus the problem of 'juveniles delinquency' confronts us with its dreadful consequences. Presumably, the chief culprit is 'improper upbringing.' Parents, nowadays, especially the working ones do not devote quality time to their children who are left to their own devices. As a result they end up getting trapped in bad company. Quite often they commit crimes for fun and for the sake of adventure. Loneliness and emotional depravity pushes them into drug addiction and recklessness. Failure of the school as alma mater and destruction of the joint family system has further aggravated this problem. Young boys and girls have started undertaking dangerous experiments with their lives including sexual adventurism. This is not an ordinary problem. It will endanger the entire future generation, if allowed to spread like a contagion. Taming this shrew is not possible without parents' participation and affirmative action by the schools. Focus on cultural conditioning of children is necessary so that they imbibe strong moral values.

EDUCATIONAL REFORMS

Education is always in need of reforms because the world is always growing, evolving itself, and such reforms are urgently needed in a country like India. The British rulers left an educational system in

India which was suited to their needs for purposes of communication with the natives. It was heavily arts-based. It was realised after Independence that scientific education was indispensable for India to enable her to progress rapidly. The lacunae was removed to a great extent and India has certainly progressed rapidly, though not as rapidly as she should have. India has made tremendous progress in nuclear, space and software techniques, but much remains to be done, particularly at the grass-root level. The primary education and the female education, specifically in the rural areas, need a quick boosting. It is good that much attention is now being paid to medicine, engineering, commerce, management, administration, chemicals, textile, agriculture, power, etc., but what is urgently needed in education for the poorest is that education should be employment-oriented. It should be vocational and technical without ignoring the humanities. There should be more primary schools and teachers should be better trained and informed. Teacher-student ratio should be reduced. Education must be result-oriented and answerable to those who pay their wards's fees.

THE SECRET OF HAPPINESS

Happiness is a relative term. We cannot give an absolute answer if somebody asks : "What is happiness?" A child possessing nothing and not caring to possess anything is happy. A billionaire may not be happy. Money and luxuries do not necessarily bring happiness. This, however, does not mean that we do not need money. Money is essential for existence and a decent living. The absence of it can obstruct the smooth flow of life and cause us tension, worry and lack of happiness. A holy man who does not work with his own hands may still be happy because of his spiritual way of life and his freedom from burden of life in a family, but he has to depend on the doles and donations or alms of others and to this extent, at least, his happiness gets curtailed. Hence, work is essential to make life worth-living and provide us real happiness. One must, however, live within one's means and not make running after money the be-all and end-all of life. One must find joy and contentment in work which should lie to one's taste. This alone can give true happiness.

LIVE AND LET LIVE

There are certain truths of life which are evergreen. "Live and Let Live" is one of them. It is not difficult to understand the telling importance of this saying. In a family, we adjust ourselves to accommodate the views of other members. This is true in society as well as in the whole world. Our earth has only a limited space and limited resources. All the human beings living in any country have to live in this limited space. They have to make use of the limited resources available on the earth. If all these resources are shared and equitably distributed, there can be no or very little conflict. So many wars in the history of mankind over the centuries evince that man has not learned to share these resources and does not still know the art of leading a peaceful, carefree life. We can lead such a life only if we let others also lead such a life. It is foolish to be greedy, covetous, avaricious, rapacious and envious. Others can also get such facilities and this can lead to hostility. Many nations are imperialistic or expansionist by nature. This becomes the cause of war sooner or later. The golden rule for all individuals, religions and nations is to live and let live.

POPULATION EXPLOSION

In an overpopulated country like India, if there is anything which is more scaring than the atom bomb, it is the population explosion. It is indeed, shameful for the Indians that a dictatorial country like China should steal a march over the democratic India in the matter of population control. The main point is that China has given much more attention to the spread of literacy than India. A vast majority of the Indian people is illiterate. Female illiteracy is still more prevalent. These illiterate people have no knowledge of the advantages of population control and they know nothing or not much about the means of population control. Particularly in the rural areas most of the people do not seem to be aware of the family planning methods. Many poor people also think that they need more hands to have extra earnings. Certain people say that population control is against their religious faith. All concerned should be well-educated about the merits and advantages of family planning. This baby boom causes several problems in the matters of food, health, prices, houses, etc., and can spell disaster. It can be tackled through joint efforts of the people and the government.

PRICE RISE

Frequent rise in prices has made the life of a common man a veritable hell. It is, indeed, very difficult for the poor men to make both ends meet. The salaried people with fixed income are also greatly hit. There are several reasons for this price rise. The first and foremost is the rapid increase in population. It is very important to spread literacy so that people realise the significance of population control. Population control devices should be distributed free of cost. Those with small families should be given incentives. Another reason for price rise is shortfall in production. All out steps should be taken to increase production. Latest scientific instruments should be used for this purpose. Some restrictions should be imposed on strikes and lock-outs. Precious foreign exchange should not be wasted on import of luxury items. Even otherwise, wastage of all kinds should be avoided. Exports should be increased and imports should be decreased. There should be rapid industrialisation in villages and cottage and small scale industries should also be promoted. Taxation system should be streamlined. The hoarders and stockists who cause scarcity in the market should be severely dealt with.

UNEMPLOYMENT

Of all the agonies a man has to suffer, joblessness is perhaps the worst. A philosopher has said that the people should be asked to dig up holes and then fill them up and dig them up again and so on instead of keeping them unemployed. Unemployment is one of the major causes of frustration and depression and even of use of drugs and committing crimes among the youth. A young man, as he comes out of the portals of an institution, expects some decent treatment which is manifested in nothing better than a decent job. But instead of this, what do we see? We see an army of the unemployed youth with arts, science, engineering and other degrees in their hands moving from one office or concern to the other in search of jobs and those who can do nothing, just stand in queues before the employment exchanges. Those more talented leave the shores of our country and then we all lament the brain-drain. It is essential that there should be a comprehensive long-term policy to tackle this ticklish problem. We should realise that keeping millions of youth unemployed, is a great national loss. The youth should preferably be taught to start their own units for which low-interest loans should be provided to them.

SCARCITY AND RESOURCES

There are two important factors on earth for human beings— on the one hand, resources available to us are limited, on the other hand, our capacity to tap all the resources is limited. So, we can avail ourselves of resources only upto a limited extent. As such, we are always liable to feel a scarcity of resources. Since, we cannot get all we want, the only way for us is to keep our wants under control. If we are excessively ambitious, we have to suffer the pangs of frustration and depression. Despite all this, tremendous progress has been made to tap various resources and fulfil many of man's wishes for comfort and luxury and decent living and maintain life for a longer and healthier period. It is mainly because science has proved so handy to man. Man has probed the levels of the earth and brought out metals and minerals. He has tapped the utility of various plants to produce the means of medicine and food. The use of atomic power for useful purposes and electricity have enabled him to have products in abundance. Still, since man's wants will ever remain unlimited and his skill and resources scarce relatively, he will have to maintain the spirit of contentment along with high ambition.

THE ART OF LIVING

As man appears on this earth not of his own accord, he has to live somehow. But he can make this living delectable or miserable according to his own whims and ways. It is, indeed, pitiable that many people just drag their lives. They never try to realise that our life is as we make it. We cannot only make our tenure on this earth longer but also pleasure-some. First of all, we must have a positive and optimistic outlook. We should not always be grumbling and moping. We should develop a healthy outlook. It is better to give up hatred and malice and bad habits like those of back-biting and betraying our friends than to feel depressed and forlorn in the arena of life. It is imperative for us to make friends with good people and avoid the company of those who have dubious character and nature. It is beneficial to develop the habit of working hard and that most sincerely. Money is not everything. Money is nothing before good health, character and satisfaction obtained through doing some good to others. We should have a daily routine in the matter of getting up early, going out for a walk, taking regular exercise, taking light but nourishing meals at fixed hours, studying regularly and doing some social service and pursuing some hobby to our taste. We should never indulge in smoking, drinking, gambling, etc. We should develop a taste for music to make our life complete.

MORALS AND MANNERS

In the present curricula, the teaching of morals virtually means teaching about God or religions or just mannerism. Morals as taught in the schools, do not just leave the sphere of manners to touch, much less enter, the sphere of real morality. For instance, it is not taught if a choice has to be made between manners and morals, which should be preferred? Manners to morals or morals to manners? It is for the man of prudence to decide whether a child has the right to ask his parents. "Is the car in which I'm taken to school bought with money earned through honest means? Is the big house in which we are living built with money earned through fair means? Are my hefty fees and pocket money paid from honest earnings?" And can he refuse to accept such money if he finds it tainted? It is for the field experts to decide. Then it will be for the educationists to decide whether, the child can be taught to put such questions to his parents? Since parents adopt dishonest means to earn money mainly for their children, if the latter refuse to accept such money, the problem of dishonesty may probably be solved to some extent. But who is to teach such morals to students—parents or teachers? May be, the proposition needs a lot of discussion, as no conclusion is possible in haste.

EASY LIFE BUT ENDANGERED LIFE

Scientific advancements have considerably contributed to the growth of our civilization. Scientist have improved the quality of our lives immeasurably, for example, computers, telephones, televisions, airplanes, etc. Science is man's only hope against diseases which were incurable in the past. But science has also produced problems—problems that are inherently hazardous and detrimental to the very human existence. For example, pollution. Global warming and the fear of global inundation are the fallouts of pollution. Nuclear weapons have led to a constant apprehension of annihilating warfares. There is also the scare of an obnoxious biological warfare that might lead to painful destruction of our race. On a less hazardous front, we see that people have become lethargic and obese because of the conveniences in excess. A mechanised lifestyle has led to the break down of human communication. People are becoming distant islands—indifferent towards each other and without tender emotions. Excess dependance on science could bring a cataclysmic end of our earth.

GENERAL KNOWLEDGE

INDIA : AT A GLANCE

- **Population (2011) :** 1,21,08,54,977
- **Capital :** New Delhi ● **Area :** 32,87,263 sq km
- **Geographic Location :** Between 8⁰4' and 37⁰6' north latitudes; Between 68⁰7' and 97⁰25' east longitudes
- **Coastline Length :** 7,516.6 km including the coastline of Lakshadweep, Andaman & Nicobar Islands.
- **Number of States :** 28 (After reorganisation of Jammu- & Kashmir in 2019)
- **Number of Union Territories :** 9
- **Major Languages :** 22
- **National Anthem :** Jana Gana Mana
- **National Currency :** Rupee (₹)
- **National Animal :** Tiger
- **National Aquatic Animal :** Dolphin
- **National Bird :** Peacock
- **National River :** Ganga
- **Characteristics of Indian Constitution :** Socialist, Secular, Democratic, Republic
- **Legislature :** Bicameral Legislature at the Centre Uni/Bicameral Legislatures in States
- **Executive :** President, Vice-President and Council of Ministers at the Centre; Governor and Council of Ministers in States
- **Judiciary :** Independent from Executive with Supreme Court at the apex of the hierarchy
- **Total Road Length :** 5.6 million kilometres at Present

INDIA: STATES & UNION TERRITORIES

States & U/T	Capital & Language
Andhra Pradesh	Amaravati—*Telugu*
Arunachal Pradesh	Itanagar—*Nyishi, Dafla, Miji, Wancho etc.*
Asom	Dispur—*Assamese*
Bihar	Patna—*Hindi, Maithili*
Chhattisgarh	Raipur—*Hindi*

States & U/T	Capital & Language
Goa	Panji—*Marathi and Konkani*
Gujarat	Gandhinagar—*Gujarati*
Haryana	Chandigarh—*Hindi*
Himachal Pradesh	Shimla—*Hindi and Pahari*
Jharkhand	Ranchi—*Hindi, Santhali*
Karnataka	Bengaluru—*Kannada*
Kerala	Thiruvananthapuram —*Malayalam*
Madhya Pradesh	Bhopal—*Hindi*
Maharashtra	Mumbai—*Marathi*
Manipur	Imphal—*Manipuri*
Meghalaya	Shillong—*Khasi, Garo and English*
Mizoram	Aizawl—*Mizo and English*
Nagaland	Kohima—*Sema, English*
Odisha	Bhubaneswar—*Odiya*
Punjab	Chandigarh—*Punjabi*
Rajasthan	Jaipur—*Hindi and Rajasthani*
Sikkim	Gangtok—*Bhutia, Nepali, Lepcha and Limbu*
Tamil Nadu	Chennai—*Tamil*
Telangana	Hyderabad—*Telugu*
Tripura	Agartala—*Bengali, Kakborak, Manipuri*
Uttar Pradesh	Lucknow—*Hindi and Urdu*
Uttarakhand	Dehradun—*Hindi*
West Bengal	Kolkata—*Bengali*
Andaman & Nicobar Island	Port Blair—*Bengali, Hindi,* Nicobarese, *Tamil, Telugu, and Malayalam*
Chandigarh	Chandigarh—*Hindi, Punjabi*
Dadara and Nagar Haveli	Silvassa—*Gujarati and Hindi*
Daman and Diu	Daman—*Gujarati*
Delhi	Delhi—*Hindi, Punjabi & Urdu*
Lakshadweep	Kavaratti—*Malayalam*
Puducherry	Puducherry—*Tamil, Telugu, Malayalam, English and French*
Jammu & Kashmir	Srinagar (Summer)—*Kashmiri, Urdu, Dogri* Jammu (Winter)
Ladakh	Leh—*Ladakhi*

POPULATION

Second Largest Nation : In terms of the size of population, India is the second largest country in the world, next only to China. China tops the list with 1341.0 million people. India's population constitutes nearly 17.5 per cent of the total world population while her geographical area is only 2.42 per cent of the world area. With such a huge population to support on so small an area, the country finds herself in great difficulty in making any significant dent on its poverty and economic backwardness. India's national income, which is barely 2 per cent of the total global income, clearly shows the tremendous strain of population on her economy.

2011 Census Highlights

Population of India–Total Indian population is 17.5% of total world population	:	1,21,08,54,977 (Male: 62,32,70,258; Female: 58,75,84,719)
Decadal Growth (2001-2011)	:	17.7 per cent (Males: 17.1 per cent; Females: 18.3 per cent)
Hightest Decadal Growth (State-wise)	:	Meghalaya (27.9 per cent)
Lowest Decadal Growth (State-wise)	:	Nagaland (–0.6 per cent)
Most populous State	:	Uttar Pradesh
Density of population	:	382 persons per sq. km.
Most densly populated State	:	Bihar : 1106 per sq. km
Sex Ratio	:	943 females per 1000 males
Total Literacy Rate	:	73% (Males – 80.9%), (Females – 64.6%)
Highest Literacy (State-wise)	:	Kerala (94%)
Lowest Literacy (State-wise)	:	Bihar (61.8%)

Other Details

(a) Population of India

1951	36,10,88,090	1961	43,92,34,771
1971	54,81,59,652	1981	68,33,29,097
1991	84,64,21,039	2001	102,87,37,436
2011	1,21,08,54,977		

(b) Density of Population (Persons per square kilometre)

1951	113	1961	138
1971	177	1981	216
1991	267	2001	324
2011	382		

(c) Annual Compound Rate of Growth

1941-1951	1.25 per cent	1951-1961	1.96 per cent
1961-1971	2.22 per cent	1971-1981	2.20 per cent
1981-1991	2.14 per cent	1991-2001	1.95 per cent
2001-2011	1.64 per cent		

India's Population At A Glance : 2011 (Final Data)

S.I. No.	State/UTs	Area (sq. km)	Population	Sex Ratio	Density	Literacy Rate	(%) Decadel Growth Rate (2001-2011)
1.	Jammu & Kashmir*	222,236.00	1,25,41,302	889	124	67.2	23.6
2.	Himachal Pradesh	55,673.00	68,64,602	972	123	82.8	12.9
3.	Punjab	50,362.00	2,77,43,338	895	551	75.8	13.9
4.	Chandigarh	114.00	10,55,450	818	9258	86.0	17.2
5.	Uttarakhand	53483.00	1,00,86,292	963	189	78.8	18.8
6.	Haryana	44212.00	2,53,51,462	879	573	75.6	19.9
7.	Delhi	1483.00	1,67,87,941	868	11320	86.2	21.2
8.	Rajasthan	342,239.00	6,85,48,437	928	200	66.1	21.3
9.	Uttar Pradesh	240,928.00	19,98,12,341	912	829	66.7	20.2
10.	Bihar	94,163.00	10,40,99,452	918	1106	61.8	25.4
11.	Sikkim	7,096.00	6,10,577	890	86	81.4	12.9
12.	Arunachal Pradesh	83,743.00	13,83,727	938	17	65.4	26.0
13.	Nagaland	16,579.00	19,78,502	931	119	79.6	−0.6
14.	Manipur	22,327.00	28,55,794	985	128	79.2	31.79
15.	Mizoram	21,081.00	10,97,206	976	52	91.3	23.5
16.	Tripura	10,486.00	36,73,917	960	350	87.2	14.8
17.	Meghalaya	22,429.00	29,66,889	989	132	74.4	27.9
18.	Assam	78,438.00	3,12,05,576	958	398	72.2	17.1
19.	Pachim Banga	88752.00	9,12,76,115	950	1028	76.3	13.8
20.	Jharkhand	79714.00	3,29,88,134	949	414	66.4	22.4
21.	Odisha	155,707.00	4,19,74,218	979	270	72.9	14.0
22.	Chhattisgarh	135,191.00	2,55,45,198	991	189	70.3	22.6
23.	Madhya Pradesh	308,245.00	7,26,26,809	931	236	69.3	20.3
24.	Gujarat	196,024.00	6,04,39,692	919	308	78.0	19.3
25.	Daman & Diu	112.00	2,43,247	618	2191	87.1	53.8
26.	Dadra & Nagar Haveli	491.00	3,43,709	774	700	76.2	55.9
27.	Maharashtra	307,713.00	11,23,74,333	929	365	82.3	16.0
28.	Andhra Pradesh	160,205.00	4,93,86,799	993	308	67.0	11.0
29.	Karnataka	191,791.00	6,10,95,297	973	319	75.4	15.6
30.	Goa	3,702.00	14,58,545	973	394	88.7	8.2
31.	Lakshadweep	32.00	64,473	947	2149	91.8	6.3
32.	Kerala	38863.00	3,34,06,061	1084	860	94.0	4.9
33.	Tamil Nadu	130,058.00	7,21,47,030	996	555	80.1	15.6
34.	Puducherry	479.00	12,47,953	1037	2546	85.8	28.1
35.	Andaman & Nicobar Island	8249.00	3,80,581	876	46	86.6	6.9
36.	Telangana	114,840.00	3,51,93,978	993	310	66.5	11.0
37.	Ladakh	—	—	—	—	—	—
	India	**3,287,263.00**	**1,21,08,54,977**	**943**	**382**	**73.0**	**17.7**

* Data of Ladakh is also included in Jammu & Kashmir.

NATIONAL SYMBOLS

National Emblem: State emblem of India is an adaptation from the Sarnath Lion Capital of Ashoka. It was adopted by the Government of India on January 26, 1950. In the adapted form, only three lions are visible, the fourth being hidden from the view. The wheel (Dharma Chakra) appears in relief in the centre of the abacus with a bull on the right and a horse on the left. The bell-shaped lotus has been omitted. The words "Satyameva Jayate" meaning "Truth alone triumphs" are inscribed below the Emblem in Devanagari script.

National Flag: The National Flag of India is a horizontal tricolour of deep saffron (Kesari), white and dark green in equal proportion. In the centre of the white band there is a wheel in navy blue colour. It has 24 spokes. The ratio of the length and the breadth of the flag is 3 : 2. Its design was adopted by the Constituent Assembly of India on July 22, 1947.

National Anthem: Rabindranath Tagore's song 'Jana-gana-mana' was adopted by the Constituent Assembly as the National Anthem of India on January 24, 1950.

Jana-gan-mana-adhinayaka jaya he,
Bharata-bhagya-vidhata
Punjab-Sindh-Gujarat-Maratha-Dravida-
Utkala-Banga
Vindhya-Himachala-Yamuna-Ganga Uchhala-
jaladhi-taranga.

Tava subha name jage, Tava subha asisa mange,
Gahe tava jaya gatha,
Jana-gana-mangala-dayak, jaya he Bharata
bhagya vidhata,
Jaya he, jaya he, jaya he, Jaya jaya jaya,
jaya he.

National Song: Bankim Chandra Chatterji's 'Vande Mataram' which was a source of inspiration to the people in their struggle for freedom, has been adopted as National Song. It has an equal status with the National Anthem.

Vande Mataram
Sujalam, suphalam, malayaja-shitalam,
Shasya shyamalam, Mataram
Shubhrajyotsna, pulkita yaminim,
Phulla kusumita drumadalashobhinim,
Subhasinim sumadhura—bhashinim,
Sukhadam, Varadam, Mataram.

National Bird and Animal of India: Peacock and Tiger; **National Aquatic Animal:** Dolphin; **National Flower:** Lotus; **National Game:** Hockey; **National Calendar:** It was adopted on March 22, 1957. It has 365 days in the year and the first month of the year is Chaitra.

Months of the National

Calendar: (1) Chaitra, (2) Vaishakha, (3) Jaishtha, (4) Ashadha, (5) Shravan, (6) Bhadra, (7) Ashvina, (8) Kartika, (9) Marga-Shirsha, (10) Pausha, (11) Magha, (12) Phalguna.

The Universe 

The Solar System: Some Facts

Number of Planets: 8—Mercury, Venus, Earth, Mars, Jupiter, Saturn, Uranus and Neptune.

Largest most

Massive planet	Jupiter
Brightest planet	Venus
Brightest star	Sirius
Fastest orbiting planet	Mercury
Longest (Synodic) day	Mercury
Most moons	Jupiter-79
Planet with largest moon	Jupiter
Greatest average density	Jupiter
Tallest mountain	Earth
Strongest magnetic fields	Jupiter
Most circular orbit	Venus
Shortest (synodic) day	Jupiter
Hottest planet	Venus
No moons	Mercury, Venus
Planet with moon with most eccentric orbit	Neptune
Lowest average density	Saturn
Greatest amount of liquid on the surface	Earth

The Earth: Facts and Data

Composition of the Earth: Aluminium (0.4%), Sulphur (2.7%), Silicon (13%), Oxygen (28%), Calcium (1.2%), Nickel (2.7%), Magnesium (17%), Iron (35%)

- **Surface area :** 510100500 sq km
- **Land Surface :** 148950800 sq km (29.1%)
- **Ocean Surface :** 361149700 sq km (70.9%)
- **Type of water :** 97% salt, 3% fresh
- **Total area of water :** 382672000 sq km
- **Equatorial diameter :** 12753 km
- **Equatorial Circumference :** 40066 km
- **Polar Circumference :** 39992 km
- **Polar diameter :** 12710 km
- **Equatorial radius :** 6376 km
- **Polar radius :** 6335 km
- **Mass (estimated weight) :** 594×10^{19} metric tons
- **Mean distance from the Sun :** 149407000 km
- **Earth's orbit speed (around sun) :** 107320 kmph
- **Period of Revolution (round the sun) :** 365 days 5 hrs; 48 min. 45.51 seconds
- **Time of Rotation (on its axis) :** 23 hrs 56 min.; 4.09 seconds
- **Inclination of the axis (to the plane of the eclipitc) :** 23°27'

Solar Statistics

- **Distance from the Earth :** 149.8 million km
- **Absolute Visual Magnitude :** 4.75
- **Diameter Core :** 13,84,000 km
- **Temperature :** 15000000 K
- **Photosphere Temperature :** 5770 K
- **Rotation as seen from the Earth** (at the equator) **:** 25.38 days
- **Rotation as seen from the Earth** (near the poles) **:** 33 days
- **Chemical Composition :** Hydrogen 71%; Helium 26.5%; Other elements 2.5%
- **Age :** About 4.5 billion years
- **Expected lifetime of a normal star :** About 10 billion years

Longest Rivers

Name	Country/ Continent	Length in Kilometres
Nile	Africa	6650
Amazon	S. America	6437
Mississippi-Missouri	USA	6020
Yangtze-Kiang	China	5494
Ob-Irtysh	Russia	5410
Lena	Russia	4400
Hwang Ho	China	4344
Niger	Africa	4180
St. Lawrence	Canada (USA)	4023
Murray-Darling	Australia	3780
Volga	Russia	3690
Indus	Asia	2900
Danube	Europe	2850
Orinoco	S. America	2575

Major Riverside Cities

City	River	Country
Alexandria	Nile	Egypt
Amsterdam	Amsel	Netherland
Ankara	Kizil	Turkey
Baghdad	Tigris	Iraq
Bangkok	Menam	Thailand
Belgrade	Danube	Yugoslavia
Berlin	Spree	Germany
Budapest	Danube	Hungary
Cairo	Nile	Egypt
Chittagong	Karnaphuli	Bangladesh
Karachi	Indus	Pakistan
Khartoum	Blue & White Nile	Sudan
Lahore	Ravi	Pakistan
Lisbon	Tagus	Portugal
Liverpool	Mersey	England
London	Thames	England
Moscow New	Moskva	Russia
Orleans	Mississipi	USA
New York	Hudson	USA
Paris	Seine	France
Rangoon (Yangon)	Irawadi	Myanmar
Rome	Tiber	Italy

Oceans of the World

- Pacific .... 16,62,41,000 sq km
- Atlantic .... 8,65,57,000 sq km
- Indian .... 7,34,27,000 sq km
- Arctic .... 94,85,000 sq km

Major Gulfs of the World

Names	*Areas (Sq. Km.)*
Gulf of Mexico	15,44,000
Gulf of Hudson	12,33,000
Arabian Gulf	2,38,000
Gulf of St. Lawrence	2,37,000
Gulf of California	1,62,000
English Channel	89,900

Major Mountain Ranges of the World

Range	*Location*	*Length (km)*
Andes	South America	7,200
Himalayas-Karakoram-Hindukush	South Central Asia	5,000
Rockies	North America	4,800
Great Dividing Range	East Australia	3,600
Atlas	North West Africa	1,930
Western Ghats	Western India	1,610
Caucasus	Europe	1,200
Alaska	USA	1,130
Alps	Europe	1,050

Largest Deserts of the World

Subtropical

Sahara, North Africa	94,00,000 sq. km.
Kalahari, Southern Africa	9,00,000 sq. km.
Thar, India/Pakistan	2,00,000 sq. km.
Great Sandy, Australia	4,00,000 sq. km.

Cool Coastal

Atacama, Chile S.A.	1,40,000 sq. km

Cool Winter

Gobi, China	13,00,000 sq. km.
Colorado, Western USA	3,37,000 sq. km.

(also called the painted desert)

Atmosphere

Composition of Gases in Atmosphere

Nitrogen 78.03%	Oxygen 20.99%
Argon 0.93%	Carbon dioxide ... 0.03%
Hydrogen 0.01%	Neon 0.0018%
Helium 0.0005%	Crypton 0.0001%
Xenon 0.000,005%	Ozone 0.000,0001%

World Important Local Winds

- **Chinoon:** A warm day wind frequently experienced on the eastern side of the Rocky Mountains.
- **Fohn:** A warm dry wind descending a mountain, as on the north side of the Alps.
- **Haboob:** A sand storm or a dust storm in north and north-east Sudan near Khartoum.
- **Bagrrio:** It is the tropical cyclone of the Philippine Island.
- **Loo:** A hot wind which blows in summer season in Indian sub-continent.
- **Papasago:** A cold northerly wind sometimes felt on the Mexico plateau.
- **Bora:** It is the name given to the cold dry wind experienced particularly in winter along the eastern coast of the Atlantic Ocean and in northern Italy.
- **Black Toller:** A hot dust wind which blows in the vast plain of North America.

Types of World Agriculture

- **Viticulture:** The cultivation of the vine for production of grapes and wine.
- **Pisciculture:** The breeding, rearing and transplantation of fish by artificial means.
- **Sericulture:** The raising of silk worms for the production of raw silk.
- **Horticulture:** To grow flower front, vegetables on small plots.
- **Apiculture:** Bee keeping on a commercial scale for the sale of honey.
- **Floriculture:** The cultivation of flowers or flowering plants.
- **Mariculture:** Sea farming, or the cultivation of marine plants and animals for commercial purposes.
- **Olericulture:** The cultivation of vegetables and kitchen herbs.

Principal Mountain Peaks of the World

Mountains	*Height in Metres*	*Range*	*Date of First Ascent*
1. Mount Everest	8,848	Himalayas	May 29, 1953
2. K-2 (Godwin Austen)	8,611	Karakoram	July 31, 1954
3. Kanchenjunga	8,597	Himalayas	May 25, 1955
4. Lhotse	8,511	Himalayas	May 18, 1956
5. Makalu I	8,481	Himalayas	May 15, 1955
6. Dhaulagiri I	8,167	Himalayas	May 13, 1960
7. Mansalu I	8,156	Himalayas	May 9, 1956
8. Chollyo	8,153	Himalayas	Oct. 19, 1954
9. Nanga Parbat	8,124	Himalayas	July 3, 1953
10. Annapurna I	8,091	Himalayas	June 3, 1950
11. Gasherbrum I	8,068	Karakoram	July 5, 1958
12. Broad Peak I	8,047	Karakoram	June 9, 1957
13. Gasherbrum II	8,034	Karakoram	July 7, 1956
14. Shisha Pangma (Gosainthan)	8,014	Himalayas	May 2, 1964
15. Gasherbrum III	7,952	Karakoram	Aug. 11, 1975

Famous Straits of the World

Strait	*Between*	*Country*
Malacca Strait	Andaman Sea and South China Sea	Indonesia
Palk Strait	Mannar and Bay of Bengal	India-Sri Lanka
Magellan Strait	Pacific and South Atlantic Ocean	Chile
Dover Strait	English Channel and North Sea	England-France
Berring Strait	Berring Sea and Chukasi Sea	Alaska-Russia
Sugaroo Strait	Japan Sea and Pacific Ocean	Japan
Sunda Strait	Java and Indian Ocean	Indonesia
Gibralter Strait	Mediterranean Sea and Atlantic Ocean	Spain
Harmuj Strait	Persia and Bay of Oman	Oman-Iran
Hudson Strait	Bay of Hudson and Atlantic Ocean	Canada

Famous Newspapers of the World

Newspaper	*Place of Publishing*	*Language*	*Newspaper*	*Place of Publishing*	*Language*
Daily News	New York	English	Hindu, Hindustan		
Guardian	London	English	Times, Times of India,		
Pravada	Moscow	Russian	Tribune, Statesman,		
Al-Ahram	Cairo (Egypt)	Arabic	Indian Express,		
Merdeca	Jakarta	Indonesian	Economic Times	India	English
Times	London	English	Hindustan, Nav Bharat		
People's Daily	Beijing	Chinese	Times, Rashtriya Sahara,		
New Statesman	Britain	English	Dainik Jagaran,		
Daily Mirror	Britain	English	Punjab Kesari	India	Hindi

World's Famous Official Documents

White Paper: India; **Orange Book:** Netherlands; **Yellow Book:** France; **Green Book:** Italy and Iran; **White Book:** Portugal, China and Germany; **Grey Book:** Japan and Belgium.

Important Boundary Lines

Boundary Line	Countries
Hindenberg Line	Germany-Poland
Maginot Line	France and Germany
Mannerhein Line	Russia-Finland
Mc Mahon Line	India and China
Order Niesse Line	Germany-Poland
Radcliff Line	India-Pakistan
Seigfrid Line	Germany-France
Durand Line	Pakistan and Afghanistan
17th Parallel	The line which defined the boundary between North Vietnam and South Vietnam before the two were united.
38th Parallel	North Korea and South Korea
49th Parallel	U.S.A. and Canada

Areawise 10 Big and Small Countries

10 Big Countries

S. No.	Country	(Total Portion) Sq. km	Area (Thousand sq. km)
1.	Russia (Europe-Asia)	17,098,242	16889
2.	Canada (N. America)	99,84,670	9221
3.	China (Asia)	95,96,961	9327
4.	U.S.A. (N. America)	93,72,614	9159
5.	Brazil (S. America)	85,14,877	8457
6.	Australia (S. Pacific)	77,41,220	7682
7.	India (Asia)	32,87,263	2973
8.	Argentina (S. America)	27,80,400	2737
9.	Kazakhstan (Europe-Asia)	27,24,900	2671
10.	Algeria (Africa)	23,81,741	2381

10 Small Countries

S. No.	Country	Area (Sq. km)
1.	Vatican City (Europe)	0.44
2.	Monaco (Europe)	1.95
3.	Nauru (Southern Pacific)	21.10
4.	Tuvalu	26.00
5.	San Marino (Europe)	62.00
6.	Liechtenstein (Europe)	160.00
7.	Marshall Island (Central Pacific)	181.00
8.	St. Kitts and Nevis (Eastern Caribbean)	269.00
9.	Maldives	298.00
10.	Malta	316.00

Populationwise Big and Small Countries

10 Big Countries

S. No.	Country	Population (2019)
1.	China	1,433,783,686
2.	India	1,366,417,754
3.	United States	329,064,917
4.	Indonesia	270,625,568
5.	Pakistan	216,565,318
6.	Brazil	211,049,527
7.	Nigeria	200,963,599
8.	Bangladesh	163,046,161
9.	Russia	145,872,256
10.	Mexico	127,575,529

10 Small Countries

S. No.	Country	Population (2019)
1.	Vatican City (Holy See)	799
2.	Nauru	10,756
3.	Tuvalu	11,646
4.	Palau	18,008
5.	San Marino	33,860
6.	Liechtenstein	38,019
7.	Monaco	38,964
8.	Saint Kitts & Nevis	52,823
9.	Marshall Islands	58,791
10.	Dominica	71,808

Signals/Signs and Meaning

Signal/Sign	Meaning
Red Triangle	Family Planning
Red Cross	Medical Help
Red Light	Danger, 'Stop' for the movement of vehicles
Green Light	Go
Olive Branch	Peace
White Pigeon or Dove	Peace
Black Strip on Arm	(i) Opposition (ii) Sorrow
Black Flag	Opposition
Red Flag	(i) Danger (ii) Revolution
White Flag	Treaty or Surrender
Yellow Flag	Vehicles with patients of contagious diseases
Two Bones across with a Skull	Danger of electricity
Half mast flown Flag	National mourning
Lotus	Sign of civilization and culture
Wheel (Chakra)	Sign of Progress
A blind folded woman with scale in hand	Sign of Justice
Reversed flown	National calamity flag

National Emblems of Important Countries

Country	National Emblem
America	Golden Rod
Australia	Kangaroo
Ireland	Shamrock
Italy	White Lily
Israel	Candelabrum
Iran	Rose
Canada	White Lily
Great Britain	Rose
Chile	Candor and Huemul
Germany	Corn Flower
Japan	Chrysanthemum
Zimbabwe	Zimbabwe Bird
Turkey	Crescent and Star
The Netherlands	Lion
New Zealand	Kiwi, Fern Southern Cross
Norway	Lion
Nepal	Kukri
Pakistan	Crescent
Poland	Eagle
France	Lily
Belgium	Lion
Bangladesh	Water Lily
Russia	Double headed eagle
Lebanon	Cedar Tree
Sudan	Secretary Bird
Syria	Eagle
India	Lioned Capital

The Continents of the World

Name	Area (In sq. km.)	Population (2016) (In million)	Per cent of the World's Population
Asia	3,18,45,872	4,436	59.69
Africa	3,01,95,394	1,216	16.36
Europe	2,30,64,084	738	9.94
North America	2,43,98,475	579	7.79
South America	1,78,08,695	422	5.68
Australia	85,25,391	39.9	0.54
Antarctica	1,42,00,000	—	—

International Date Line

It roughly corresponds to 180°E or W meridian of longitude which falls on the opposite side of the Greenwich meridian and the date changes by one day (i.e. 24 hours), as this line is crossed. On crossing this line from east to west a day is added, and a day is subtracted on crossing it from west to east.

Indian Constitution is a comprehensive document and it is the lengthiest written Constitution in the World.

The Preamble of the Constitution: "We the people of India, having solemnly resolved to Constitute India into a Sovereign, Socialist, Secular Democratic Republic and to secure to all its citizen."

Justice: Social, economic and political.

Liberty: Of thought, expression, belief, faith and worship.

Equality: Of status and of opportunity, and to promote among them all.

Fraternity: Assuring the dignity of the individual and the unity and integrity of the nation. In our Constituent Assembly this twenty-sixth day of November, 1949, do hereby adopt, enact and give to ourselves this Constitution.

SCHEDULES TO THE CONSTITUTION

The Constitution of India originally contained only eight schedules. Presently there are 12 schedules in the constitution.

First Schedule: It consists the list of the States and Union territories. *Second Schedule:* This Schedule is related to salary and allowances of the President, Governors, Speaker, Supreme Court and High Court Judges etc. *Third Schedule:* Contains forms of oath and affirmation. *Fourth Schedule:* Contains allocation of seats to each State and Union territory in the Council of States. *Fifth Schedule:* Provides for administration and control of scheduled areas and scheduled tribes. *Sixth Schedule:* Provides for administration of Tribal Areas in Assam, Meghalaya and Mizoram. *Seventh Schedule:* Distribution of powers and functions between the centre and state governments under three lists. *Eighth Schedule:* The languages recognised by Parliament. *Ninth Schedule:* It contains laws passed by the Union or States which cannot be taken to courts. *Tenth Schedule:* Provisions as to disqualification on the ground of political defection. *Eleventh Schedule:* Provisions regarding powers, authority etc. of Panchayati Raj institutions.

Twelfth Schedule: Provisions regarding powers, authority etc. of Municipalities etc.

Foreign Sources of Indian Constitution

Foreign Sources	Subject
Britain	Parliamentary system, collective responsibilities of Cabinet
America	Fundamental right, Citizenship, Independent Judiciary, Judicial review
Canada	Division of powers
Ireland	Directive principles
Germany	Emergency provisions
Russia	Fundamental duties
Australia	Concurrent list

THE SUPREME COURT

Supreme Court of India, the highest Court of the country, consists of a Chief Justice and not more than 33 Judges appointed by the President. The Judges hold office till the age of 65. For appointment as a Judge of the Supreme Court, a person must be a citizen of India and must have been for at least five years as Judge of a High Court or Advocate of a High Court for at least ten years or he must be, in the opinion of the President, a distinguished jurist. The Supreme Court normally sits in New Delhi.

FUNDAMENTAL RIGHTS

Following fundamental rights are enjoyed by every Indian citizen, irrespective of caste, colour, creed and sex:

1. Right to Equality: No special privileges, no distinction on grounds of religion, caste, creed and sex.

2. Right to Freedom: The right to freedom of expression and speech, the right to choose one's own profession, the right to reside in any part of the Indian Union.

3. Right to Freedom to Religion: Except when it is in the interest of public order, morality, health or other conditions, everybody has the right to profess, practice and propagate his religion freely.

4. Cultural and Educational Rights: The Constitution provides that every community can run its own institutions to preserve its own culture and language.

5. Right against Exploitation: Traffic in human beings and forced labour and the employment of children under 14 years in factories or mines, are punishable offences.

6. Rights to Constitutional Remedies: When a citizen finds that any of his fundamental rights has been encroached upon, he can move the Supreme Court, which has been empowered to safeguard the fundamental rights of a citizen (Article 32).

PARLIAMENT

Parliament is the national legislature of the Indian Union. It consists of two Houses known as the Council of States or the Rajya Sabha and the House of People or Lok Sabha. The President is an integal part of Parliament.

Rajya Sabha: The Rajya Sabha is the Upper House of the Parliament and it is constituted of representatives from the States or the Constituent units of the Indian Union. It is a permanent body, one third of its members retiring after every two years. Its maximum strength is 250. Out of these, twelve members are nominated by the President from well-known personalities in the realm of Science, Art, Literature and Social Service. Rest of 238 representatives of the States and Union Territories are elected.

Lok Sabha: The Lok Sabha whose life is five years, is the Lower House of Parliament and comprises of members directly elected by the people. The House of the people (Lok Sabha) at present consists of 545 members of these, 530 members are directly elected from the states and 13 from Union Territories while 2 are nominated by the President from Anglo-Indian community. The House of the People shall continue for five years (unless sooner dissolved) from the date of its meeting and no longer and the expiry of the said period of 5 years shall operate as dissolution of the House.

Parliamentary Committees: There are several Parliamentary Committees to assist the Parliament in its deliberations. These are appointed or elected by the respective Houses of Lok Sabha and Rajya Sabha on a motion made or are nominated by their presiding officers, i.e., the Speaker of Lok Sabha and the Chairman of Rajya Sabha respectively. Broadly, Parliamentary Committees are of two kinds—standing committees and ad-hoc committees. Among the Standing Committees, three are financial Committees: (i) Public Account Committee; (ii) Estimate Committee; (iii) Public undertaking Committee. Ad-hoc Committees are appointed as the need arises and cease to exist when the work is over.

Speaker of Lok Sabha: Speaker is elected by the Lok Sabha from among its members. The Speaker will have the final power to maintain order within the House of the People and to interpret its rules of procedure. Speaker decides whether a bill is a money bill or a non-money bill.

PRESIDENT

The President of India is the constitutional head of India. To be eligible for the office of the President, a person must be : (i) a citizen of India; (ii) should be more than 35 years of age; (iii) should be eligible for membership of Lok Sabha; (iv) should not suffer from any prescribed disqualifications.

The Election Procedure: The President is elected through an electoral college consisting of elected members of Parliament and elected members of state Legislative Assemblies. The President holds office for 5 years. He can resign earlier or can be removed through impeachment before the expiry of his term. He is eligible for a re-election. He draws a fix salary per month besides various other allowances. In case of a vacancy in the office of the President due to his resignation, death or removal, the Vice-President acts as the president. In case the Vice-President is also not available, the Chief Justice of India discharges duties of the office of President. The Vice-President can hold this office for a maximum period of six months and in the mean time, a new President is elected.

The Powers: The Constitution has vested the President with the following powers : (*i*) *Executive powers :* executive authority is exercised in his name. He is the supreme commander of armed forces and declares war and makes peace. He appoints all important executive officials, like Prime Minister, Governors etc.; (*ii*) *Legislative Powers :* The President is a part of the Parliament; he summons and prorogues both the Houses jointly and separately; he nominates 12 members in Rajya Sabha and 2 in Lok Sabha. His assent to the bills is essential; money bills are introduced with his recommendation; (*iii*) *Financial Powers :* He acts as a custodian of contingency Fund; appoints Finance Commission; (*iv*) *Judicial powers :* He appoints Chief Justice and other judges of the Supreme Court— he can seek the advice of the Chief Justice on any matter of public importance; he can grant pardon and reprieve, commute or suspend sentence; he is not answerable before any court; (*v*) *Diplomatic powers :* He enjoys the right to represent India in international sphere; he has power to receive and send envoys, conclude international treaties etc.; (*vi*) *Emergency Powers :* He enjoys extensive powers, dealing with three types of emergencies : (a) emergency due to war or external aggression or internal rebellion; (b) emergency due to the failure of constitutional machinery in the state; and (c) emergency due to financial instability. During emergencies, the President assumes extraordinary powers. The position of the President has been finally determined by 42nd Amendment. It has made it obligatory on the part of the President to act on the advice of the Council of Ministers.

VICE-PRESIDENT

The Vice-President is elected by the elected members of the both Houses of the Parliament. A candidate for the office of Vice-President should be : (i) above 35 years of age; (ii) citizen of India; (iii) eligible for election as a member of Rajya Sabha; (iv) should not hold any office of profit; (v) should not be a member of parliament; and (vi) should not be of unsound mind.

Vice-President holds office for 5 years and can be removed from office earlier through a resolution passed by a two-third majority of Rajya Sabha agreed to by the Lok Sabha.

The Presiding Officer : Vice-President is the ex-officio chairman of Rajya Sabha and presides over the sessions of the Upper House. He performs all the duties of the president when the office of the President falls vacant due to the death, resignation or absence of the President. He draws a fix salary in his capacity of being the Chairman of the Rajya Sabha.

PRIME MINISTER

The Prime Minister is the leader of the majority party in the Parliament and the President cannot exercise his discretion in the appointment of the Prime Minister. He stays in office till the majority of the members of Lok Sabha has confidence in him. He occupies an important position in relation to the council of Ministers. He recommends the names of the persons to be included in the Council of Ministers. He allocates portfolios among them and can ask any minister to tender resignation. He can drop a minister while reshuffling the ministry. He coordinates the administration of various departments. He is the chief link between the President and the Council. He is the leader of the majority party and so, he has a great influence on the Parliament and the party. The Prime Minister enjoys such extensive powers as have been described as the virtual ruler of the country.

THE ELECTION COMMISSION

For supervising the entire procedure and machinery of elections, a commission called Election Commission has been set up. It comprises a chairman and a few members. All are appointed by the president but they can be removed only through impeachment. Its main functions are to supervise, direct and control elections to the Parliament, state legislatures and also to the office of the President and Vice-President. Doubts and disputes concerning elections are decided by the commission. It can suspend an election if it feels that proper conditions for that election are or were not prevailing.

INVENTIONS AND DISCOVERIES

Important Inventions

Name of Invention	Inventor	Nationality	Year
Aeroplane	Orville & Wilbur Wright	U.S.A.	1903
Ball-Point Pen	John J. Loud	U.S.A.	1888
Barometer	Evangelista Torricelli	Italy	1644
Bicycle	Kirkpatrick Macmillan	Britain	1839-40
Bifocal Lens	Benjamin Franklin	U.S.A.	1780
Car (Petrol)	Karl Benz	Germany	1888
Celluloid	Alexander Parkes	Britain	1861
Cinema	Nicolas & Jean Lumiere	France	1895
Clock (mechanical)	I-Hsing & Liang Ling-Tsan	China	1725
Diesel Engine	Rudolf Diesel	Germany	1895
Dynamo	Hypolite Pixii	France	1832
Electric Lamp	Thomas Alva Edison	U.S.A.	1879
Electric Motor (DC)	Zenobe Gramme	Belgium	1873
Electric Motor (AC)	Nikola Tesla	U.S.A.	1888
Electro-magnet	William Sturgeon	Britain	1824
Electronic Computer	Dr. Alan M. Turing	Britain	1943
Film (moving outlines)	Louis Prince	France	1885
Film (musical sound)	Dr. Le de Forest	U.S.A.	1923
Fountain Pen	Lewis E. Waterman	U.S.A.	1884
Gramophone	Thomas Alva Edison	U.S.A.	1878
Helicopter	Etienne Oehmichen	France	1924
Jet Engine	Sir Frank Whittle	Britain	1937
Laser	Charles H. Townes	U.S.A.	1960
Lift (Mechanical)	Elisha G. Otis	U.S.A.	1852
Locomotive	Richard Trevithick	Britain	1804
Machine Gun	James Puckle	Britain	1718
Microphone	Alexander Graham Bell	U.S.A.	1876
Microscope	Z. Janssen	Netherlands	1590
Motor Cycle	G. Daimler	Germany	1885
Photography (on film)	John Carbutt	U.S.A.	1888
Printing Press	Johann Gutenberg	Germany	c.1455
Razor (safety)	King C. Gillette	U.S.A.	1895
Refrigerator	James Harrison & Alexander Catlin	U.S.A.	1850
Safety Pin	Walter Hunt	U.S.A.	1849
Sewing machine	Barthelemy Thimmonnier	France	1829
Ship (steam)	J.C. Perier	France	1775

Name of Invention	Inventor	Nationality	Year
Ship (turbine)	Hon. Sir C. Parsons	Britain	1894
Skyscraper	W. Le Baron Jenny	U.S.A.	1882
Slide Rule	William Oughtred	Britain	1621
Steam Engine (condenser)	James Watt	Britain	1765
Steel Production	Henry Bessemer	Britain	1855
Steel (stainless)	Harry Brearley	Britain	1913
Submarine	David Bushnell	U.S.A.	1776
Tank	Sir Ernest Swinton	Britain	1914
Telegraph	M. Lammond	France	1787
Telegraph Code	Samuel F.B. Morse	U.S.A.	1837
Telephone (perfected)	Alexander Graham Bell	U.S.A.	1876
Television (mechanical)	John Logie Baird	Britain	1926
Television (electronic)	P.T. Farnsworth	U.S.A.	1927
Thermometer	Galileo Galilei	Italy	1593
Transformer	Michael Faraday	Britain	1831
Transistor	Bardeen, Shockley & Brattain	U.S.A.	1948
Washing Machine (elec.)	Hurley Machine Co.	U.S.A.	1907
Zip-Fastener	W.L. Judson	U.S.A.	1891

Important Discoveries

Discovery	Discoverer	Nationality	Year
Aluminium	Hans Christian Oerstedt	Denmark	1827
Atomic number	Henry Moseley	England	1913
Atomic structure of matter	John Dalton	England	1803
Chlorine	C.W. Scheele	Sweden	1774
Electromagnetic induction	Michael Faraday	England	1831
Electromagnetic waves	Heinrich Hertz	Germany	1886
Electromagnetism	Hans Christian Oersted	Denmark	1920
Electron	Sir Joseph Thomson	England	1897
General theory of relativity	Albert Einstein	Switzerland	1915
Hydrogen	Henry Cavendish	England	1766
Law of electric conduction	Georg Ohm	Germany	1827
Law of electromagnetism	Andre Ampere	France	1826
Law of falling bodies	Galileo	Italy	1590
Laws of gravitation & motion	Isaac Newton	England	1687
Laws of planetary motion	Johannes Kepler	Germany	1609-19
Magnesium	Sir Humphry Davy	England	1808
Neptune (Planet)	Johann Galle	Germany	1846
Neutron	James Chadwick	England	1932
Nickel	Axel Cronstedt	Sweden	1751
Nitrogen	Daniel Rutherford	England	1772

Discovery	Discoverer	Nationality	Year
Oxygen	Joseph Priestly C.W. Scheele	England Sweden	1772
Ozone	Christian Schonbein	Germany	1839
Pluto (Planet)	Clyde Tombaugh	U.S.A	1930
Plutonium	G.T. Seaborg	U.S.A	1940
Proton	Ernest Rutherford	England	1919
Quantum Theory	Max Planck	Germany	1900
Radioactivity	Antoine Bacquerel	France	1896
Radium	Pierre & Marie Curie	France	1898
Silicon	Jons Berzelius	Sweden	1824
Special theory of relativity	Albert Einstein	Switzerland	1905
Sun as centre of solar system	Copernicus	Poland	1543
Uranium	Martin Klaproth	Germany	1789
Uranus (Planet)	William Herschel	England	1781
X-rays	Wilhelm Roentgen	Germany	1895

Geographical Explorations/Discoveries

Place	Explorer/Discoverer	Nationality	Year
America	Christopher Columbus	Italy	1492
Hawaii Islands (Sandwich Islands)	Captain James Cook	England	1778
Newfoundland	John Cabot	England	1497
New Zealand	Abel Janszoon Tasman	Holland	1642
North Pole	Robert Peary	USA	1909
Sea Route to India (via Cape of Good Hope)	Vasco da Gama	Portugal	1498
South Pole	Roald Amundsen	Norway	1911

Scientific Instruments

Name of Instrument	Used for
Altimeter	measuring altitude
Ammeter	measuring strength of an electric current
Anemometer	measuring the velocity of wind
Audiometer	measuring level of hearing
Barometer	measuring atmospheric pressure
Callipers	measuring the internal and external diameters of tubes
Calorimeter	measuring quantity of heat
Compass	finding out direction
Dynamo	converting mechanical energy into electrical energy
Eudiometer	measuring volume changes during chemical reactions between gases
Galvanometer	detecting and determining the strength of small electric currents
Hydrometer	measuring specific gravity of a liquid
Hygrometer	measuring the humidity in the atmosphere
Lactometer	measuring the purity of milk
Manometer	measuring the gaseous pressure
Micrometer	measuring minute distances, angles, etc.

Name of Instrument	Used for
Microscope	seeing magnified view of very small objects
Periscope	with the help of this instrument an observer in a submarine can see what is going on the surface of the sea
Photometer	measuring intensity of light from distant stars
Pyrometer	measuring high temperatures
Radar	detecting and finding the presence and location of moving objects like aircraft, missile, etc.
Radiometer	measuring the emission of radiant energy
Rain Gauge	measuring the amount of rainfall
Seismograph	measuring and recording the intensity and origin of earthquake shocks
Sextant	measuring altitude and angular distances between two objects or heavenly bodies
Spectrometer	measuring the refractive indices
Spherometer	measuring the curvature of spherical objects/surface
Sphygmomanometer	measuring blood pressure
Stethoscope	ascertaining the condition of heart and lungs by listening to their function
Stroboscope	viewing objects that are moving rapidly with a periodic motion as if they were at rest
Tachometer	measuring the rate of revolution or angular speed of a revolving shaft
Telescope	viewing magnified images of distant objects
Theodolite	measuring the horizontal and vertical angles
Thermocouple	measuring the temperature inside furnaces and jet engines
Thermometer	measuring human body temperature
Thermostat	regulating constant temperature
Ultrasonoscope	measuring utrasonic sounds
Viscometer	measuring the viscosity of a fluid
Voltmeter	measuring potential difference between two points.

Diseases and the Parts of Body they Affect

Disease	Part of body affected	Disease	Part of body affected
AIDS	Immune system of body	Jaundice	Liver
Arthritis	Inflammation of joints	Meningitis	Brain or spinal cord
Asthma	Lungs	Pleurisy	Pleura (inflammation of)
Cataract	Eyes	Polio	motor neurons
Conjunctivitis	Eyes	Pneumonia	Lungs
Diabetes	Pancreas	Pyorrhoea	Sockets of teeth
Diphtheria	Throat	Tuberculosis	Lungs
Glaucoma	Eyes	Typhoid	Intestine
Eczema	Skin	Malaria	Spleen
Goitre	Front of the neck (due to enlargement of thyroid gland)	Leukaemia	Blood
		Rickets	Bones
Gout	Joints of bone		

United Nations Organisation ▶▶

- **Origin:** UN Charter was signed by 50 members on June 26, 1945. It officially came into existence on October 24, 1945.
- **UN Charter:** The Charter is the Constitution of the UNO and contains its aims and objectives and rules and regulations for its functioning.
- **Aims and Objectives:** They are security, welfare and human rights.
- **Headquarters:** New York.
- **Flag:** The flag is light blue in colour, and emblazoned in white, in its centre is the UN symbol—a polar map of world embraced by twin olive branches open at the top.
- **Official Languages:** The official languages of the UN are: English, French, Chinese, Russian, Arabic and Spanish. However, working languages are English & French only.

Secretary General of the U.N.O.

Name	Country	Tenure
Trygve Lie	Norway	(1946-53)
Dog Hammarsk-joeld	Sweden	(1953-61)
U. Thant	Myanmar	(1961-71)
Kurt Waldheim	Austria	(1972-81)
Javier Perez de Cuellar	Peru	(1982-91)
Dr. Boutros Ghali	Egypt	(1992-96)
Kofi Annan	Ghana	(1997-2006)
Ban Ki-moon	South Korea	(2007-2017)
Antonio Guterres	Portugal	(2017- .....)

- **Main Organs of the UNO:** There are six main organs:
  1. General Assembly
  2. Security Council
  3. Economic and Social Council
  4. Trusteeship Council
  5. International Court of Justice, and (6) Secretariat.

1. **General Assembly:** It consists of representative of all members of the UN. Each member country has only one vote. It meets once a year and passes UN Budget.
2. **Security Council:** It is the Executive body of the UN and is mainly responsible for maintaining international peace and security. It has 15 members, 5 of which (USA, UK, France, Russia and China) are permanent members. The 10 non-permanent members are elected by General Assembly for two-year term and are not eligible for immediate re-election.
3. **Economic and Social Council:** It has 54 members elected by General Assembly.
4. **Trusteeship Council:** It looks after interest of the people in areas not yet independent and leads them towards self-government.
5. **International Court of Justice:** It has 15 judges, no two of whom may be nationals of the same state. They are elected by General Assembly and Security Council for a term of 9 years. The Court elects its President and Vice-President for a 3-year term.
6. **Secretariat:** It is the Secretariat of the UN and is headed by the Secretary General.

Famous International Organisations, Headquarters and Year of Establishment

International Organisations	Headquarters	Year of Establishment
United Nations Organisations (U.N.O.)	New York	1945
International Monetary Fund (I.M.F.)	Washington	1945
World Health Organisation (W.H.O.)	Geneva	1948
Food & Agricultural Organisation (FAO)	Rome	1943
International Labour Organisation (ILO)	Geneva	1919

International Organisations	Headquarters	Year of Establishment
UNESCO	Paris	1946
International Court of Justice	The Hague	—
Universal Postal Union (UPU)	Berne	1874
International Civil Aviation Organisation (ICAO)	Montreal	1947
UNIDO	Vienna	1967
International Atomic Energy Agency (IAEA)	Vienna	1957
International Finance Corporation (IFC)	Washington	1956
United Nations Development Programme (UNDP)	New York	—
UNICEF	New York	1946
International Maritime Organisation (IMO)	London	1948
World Meteorological Organisation (WMO)	Geneva	1951
International Telecommunication Union (ITU)	Geneva	1947
Arab League	Cairo	1945
Commonwealth of Nations	London	1949
World Trade Organisation (WTO)	Geneva	1995
International Development Association (IDA)	Washington D.C.	1960
International Bank for Reconstruction and Development (IBRD)	Washington D.C.	1946
World Intellectual Property Organisation (WIPO)	Geneva	1967
Organisation of Islamic Conference (OIC)	Mecca (Saudi Arabia)	1971
European Union (EU)	Brussels	1958
Red Cross	Geneva	1863
Interpol	Lyons	1923
Asian Development Bank (ADB)	Manila	1966
North Atlantic Treaty Organisation (NATO)	Brussels	1949
Association of South East Asian Nations (ASEAN)	Jakarta	1967
South Asian Association for Regional Cooperation (SAARC)	Kathmandu	1985
Asia-Pacific Economic Cooperation (APEC)	–	1989
Organisation for Economic Cooperation and Development (OECD)	Paris	1961
Organisation of Petroleum Exporting Countries (OPEC)	Vienna	1960
Common Wealth of Independent States (CIS)	Belarus	1991
International Olympic Committee (IOC)	Switzerland	1894
Amnesty International (AI)	London	1961
Shanghai Cooperation Organisation (SCO)	—	2002
BRICS Bank	Shanghai	2014

FIRST IN THE WORLD

- *First Chinese visitor to India* : Fahien
- *First foreign invader of India* : Alexander, the Great (Greek)
- *First person to climb Mt. Everest* : Tenzing Norgay (India) and Edmund Hillary (New Zealand) (1953)
- *First atom bomb dropped at* : Hiroshima (Japan)
- *First man in the space* : Yuri Gagarin (former USSR)
- *First woman in the space* : Valentina Tereshkova (former USSR)
- *First person to walk in the space* : Alexei Leonov (former USSR)
- *First person to land on the moon* : Neil Armstrong (USA)
- *First and the only woman to have climbed Mt. Everest twice* : Santosh Yadav (Indian; May 12, 1992; May 10, 1993)
- *First person on Mt. Everest without oxygen* : Phu Dorjee (Indian; May 9, 1984)
- *First person to climb Mt. Everest twice* : Nawang Gombu
- *First person to climb Mt. Everest maximum times* : Chhewang Nima Sherpa (19 times)
- *First President of the USA* : George Washington
- *First woman Prime Minister* : Sirimavo Bandaranaike (Sri Lanka)
- *First person to swim across English Channel* : Mathew Webb
- *First woman to swim across English Channel* : Gertrude Caroline Ederle
- *First woman to climb Mt. Everest* : Junko Tabei (Japan)
- *First woman to climb Mt. Everest alone and without oxygen supplies* : Alison Hargreaves (Briton: May 13, 1995)
- *First Aeroplane to fly around the world without refuelling* : Voyager (Dec. 1986)
- *First test-tube Baby* : Louise Brown (UK; 1978)
- *First all-talking Film* : Jaz Singer (1927)
- *First Secretary-General of the UN* : Trygve Lie (Norway: 1946-53)

- *First woman President of the UN General Assembly* : Vijayalakshmi Pandit (India: 1953)
- *First woman to reach North Pole* : Ann Bancroft (1986)
- *First person to reach North Pole* : Robert Peary
- *First person to reach South Pole* : Amundsen (1911)
- *First woman to command Spacecraft in space* : Ellin Collins

POPULAR NAMES

- *Badshah Khan* : Abdul Ghaffar Khan
- *Bapu, Father of Nation* : M.K. Gandhi
- *Bard of Avon* : William Shakespeare
- *Chachaji or Panditji* : Jawaharlal Nehru
- *Desert Fox* : Gen. Rommel (Germany)
- *Desh Bandhu* : C.R. Das
- *Father of English Poetry* : Geoffrey Chaucer
- *Fuhrer* : Adolf Hitler
- *Grand Old Man of India* : Dadabhai Naoroji
- *Grand Old Man of Britain* : W.E. Gladstone
- *Gurudev* : Rabindra Nath Tagore
- *Guruji* : M.S. Golwalkar
- *Grand Commoner* : Pitt, the younger
- *Iron Man of India* : Sardar Patel
- *Lady with the Lamp* : Florence Nightingale
- *Lal, Bal, Pal* : Lala Lajpat Rai, Bal Gangadhar Tilak, Bipin Chandra Pal
- *Li-Kwan* : Pearl Buck
- *Little Corporal or Man of Destiny* : Napoleon Bonaparte
- *Lokmanya* : Bal Gangadhar Tilak
- *Lok Nayak* : Jayaprakash Narain
- *Mahamana* : Pt. Madan Mohan Malaviya
- *Maid of Orleans* : Joan of Arc
- *Maiden Queen* : Queen Elizabeth I
- *Man of Blood and Iron* : Prince Bismark
- *Netaji* : Subhash Chandra Bose
- *Nightingale of India* : Sarojini Naidu
- *Priyadarshini* : Indira Gandhi
- *Punjab Kesari* : Lala Lajpat Rai
- *Wizard of the North* : Walter Scott

GEOGRAPHICAL SURNAMES

- *Bengal's Sorrow* : Damodar River
- *Blue Mountains* : Nilgiri Hills
- *China's Sorrow* : Hwang-Ho
- *City of Palaces* : Kolkata
- *City of Skyscrapers or Empire City* : New York
- *City of Dreaming Spires* : Oxford
- *Cockpit of Europe* : Belgium
- *Dark Continent* : Africa
- *Emerald Isle* : Ireland
- *Eternal City* : Rome
- *Forbidden City* : Lhasa (Tibet)
- *Gateway of India* : Mumbai
- *Gate of Tears* : Strait of Bab-el-mandab
- *Gift of the Nile* : Egypt
- *Granite City* : Aberdeen (Scotland)
- *Hermit Kingdom* : Korea
- *Holy Land* : Jerusalem (Palestine)
- *Island of Pearls* : Bahrain (Persian Gulf)
- *Island of Cloves* : Zanzibar
- *Key to the Mediterranean* : Gibraltar
- *Land of Five Rivers* : Punjab
- *Land of Golden Pagoda* : Myanmar (Burma)
- *Land of Kangaroo* : Australia
- *Land of Maple Leaf/Lillies* : Canada
- *Land of Midnight Sun* : Norway
- *Land of Morning Calm* : Korea
- *Land of the Rising Sun* : Japan
- *Land of Thousand Lakes* : Finland
- *Land of Thunderbolt* : Bhutan
- *Land of the White Elephants* : Thailand
- *Manchester of the Orient* : Osaka (Japan)
- *Pearl of the Antilles or Sugar Bowl of the World* : Cuba
- *Pink City* : Jaipur
- *Playground of Europe* : Switzerland
- *Queen of the Adriatic* : Venice (Italy)
- *Roof of the World* : Pamirs
- *Sick Man of Europe* : Turkey
- *Venice of the North* : Stockholm (Sweden)
- *Windy City* : Chicago
- *Whiteman's Grave* : Guinea Coast of Africa
- *World's Loneliest Island* : Tristan de Cunha

Countries'/Cities' Names—Old and New

Old Name	New Name
Abyssinia	Ethiopia
Basutoland	Lesotho
Bechuanaland	Botswana
British Honduras	Belize
Burma	Myanmar
Ceylon	Sri Lanka
Zaire	Congo
Constantinople	Istanbul
Dahomey	Benin
Dutch East Indies	Indonesia
East Pakistan	Bangladesh
Formosa	Taiwan
Gold Coast	Ghana
Leningrad	St. Petersburg
Leopoldville	Kinshasa
Mesopotamia	Iraq
North Rhodesia	Zambia
Nyasaland	Malawi
Peking	Beijing
Persia	Iran
Rangoon	Yangon
Salisbury	Harare
Siam	Thailand
South West Africa	Namibia
Southern Rhodesia	Zimbabwe

IMPORTANT RESIDENCES

- **Buckingham Palace (London):** King/Queen of Britain
- **10, Downing Street (London):** Prime Minister, Britain
- **Elysee Palace (Paris):** President, France
- **Rashtrapati Bhawan (New Delhi):** President, India
- **White House (Washington):** President, USA
- **Vatican (Rome):** Pope

Important towns situated on the River Banks

Town	River
Agra	Yamuna
Ahmedabad	Sabarmati
Allahabad	Confluence of the Ganga and the Yamuna
Ayodhya	Saryu
Baghdad	Tigris

Town	River
Berlin	Spree
Cairo	Nile
Kolkata	Hooghly
Cuttack	Mahanadi
Delhi	Yamuna
Dibrugarh	Brahmaputra
Dublin	Liffey
Hardwar	Ganga
Hyderabad	Musi
Jabalpur	Narbada
Kanpur	Ganga
Karachi	Indus
Lahore	Ravi
Leh	Indus

Town	River
London	Thames
Lucknow	Gomati
Nasik	Godavari
New York	Hudson
Paris	Seine
Patna	Ganga
Rome	Tiber
Srinagar	Jhelum
Surat	Tapti
Sydney	Murray-Darling
Varanasi	Ganga
Vienna	Danube
Washington	Potamac
Yangon	Irawadi

BOOKS AND AUTHORS

FOREIGN

Book	Author
Aesop's Fables	Aesop
Adventure of Robinson Crusoe	Daniel Defoe
Adventures of Sherlok Holmes	Arthur Conan Doyle
Alice in Wonderland	Lewis Carrol
Apple Cart	G.B. Shaw
Arabian Nights	Sir Richard Burton
As You Like It	William Shakespeare
A Tale of Two Cities	Charles Dickens
A Tale of Two Gardens	Octavio Paz
A Thousand Suns	Dominique Lapierre
August Coup	Mikhail S. Gorbachev
Ben Hur	Lewis Wallace
Candida	G.B. Shaw
Das Kapital	Karl Marx
David Copperfield	Charles Dickens
Divine Comedy	A. Dante
Doctor's Dilemma	G.B. Shaw
Freedom From Fear	Aung San Suu Kyi
Hamlet	William Shakespeare
Iliad	Homer
Inferno	A. Dante
In Memoriam	Lord Tennyson
Ivanhoe	Walter Scott

Book	Author
Julius Caesar	William Shakespeare
Lady Chatterley's Lover	D.H. Lawrence
Lajja	Taslima Nasreen
Les Miserable	Victor Hugo
Leviathan	Thomas Hobbes
Lycidas	John Milton
Mein Kampf	Adolf Hitler
Merchant of Venice	William Shakespeare
Midnight's Children	Salman Rushdie
Moor's Last Sigh	Salman Rushdie
Mother	Maxim Gorky
Ninteen Eighty Four	George Orwell
Origin of Species	Charles Darwin
Othello	William Shakespeare
Paradise Lost	John Milton
Paradise Regained	John Milton
Path to Power	Margaret Thatcher
Pickwick Papers	Charles Dickens
Pride and Prejudice	Jane Austen
Republic	Plato
Romeo and Juliet	William Shakespeare
Round the World in Eighty Days	Jules Verne
Rubaiyat-i-Omar Khayyam	Edward Fitzgerald (Translator)

Book	Author
Shape of Things to Come	H.G. Wells
The Satanic Verses	Salman Rushdie
The Social Contract	Rousseau
The Tempest	William Shakespeare
Time Machine	H.G. Wells
Twelfth Night	William Shakespeare

Book	Author
Uncle Tom's Cabin	H.B. Stowe
Unto This Last	John Ruskin
Universe Around Us	James Jeans
Vicar of Wakefield	Oliver Goldsmith
War and Peace	Leo Tolstoy
Wealth of Nations	Adam Smith

INDIAN

Book	Author
Abhigyan Shakuntalam	Kalidas
Ain-i-Akbari	Abul Fazal
Anand Math	Bankim Chandra Chatterjee
Arthashastra	Kautilya
A Suitable Boy	Vikram Seth
Chidambara	Sumitranandan Pant
Devdas	Sarat Chandra Chatterjee
Diwan-i-Ghalib	Mirza Ghalib
Discovery of India	Jawaharlal Nehru
Essays on Gita	Aurobindo Ghosh
Eternal India	Indira Gandhi
Geet Govind	Jaya Dev
Geetanjali	R.N. Tagore
Godaan	Prem Chand
Gul-e-Nagma	Firaq Gorakhpuri
Gunahon ka Devta	Dharmveer Bharti
Harsh Charita	Bana Bhatta
Hindu View of Life	S. Radhakrishnan
Idols	Sunil Gavaskar
India Divided	Dr. Rajendra Prasad
The Judgement	Kuldip Nayyar
Juhi ki Kali	Surya Kant Tripathi 'Nirala'
Justice of Peace ke Aansu Chand ka Munh Terha Hai	Janardan Prasad Singh Muktibodh
Kadambari	Bana Bhatta
Kagaz Te Kanwas	Amrita Pritam
Kamayani	Jai Shankar Prasad
Kitni Nawon	S.H. Vatsyayan
Kumar Sambhav	Kalidas
Mahabharata	Ved Vyas
Malgudi Days	R.K. Narayan

Book	Author
Manvini Bhavai	Pannalal Patel
Mati Matal	Gopi Nath Mohanty
Meghdoot	Kalidas
Meri Ekyavan Kavitain	Atal Bihari Vajpayee
Meri Sansadiya Yatra	Atal Bihari Vajpayee
Mudrarakshasa	Vishakhadatta
My Experiments with Truth	M.K. Gandhi
My Own Boswell	M. Hidayatullah
My Presidential Years	R. Venkataraman
Nisheeth	Uma Shankar Joshi
'No, Sir'	P.G. Mavlankar
One Day Wonders	Sunil Gavaskar
Panchtantra	Vishnu Sharma
Passage to England	Nirad C. Chaudhuri
Prison Diary	Jaya Prakash Narayan
Raghuvansha	Kalidas
Rajtarangini	Kalhana
Ramcharit Manas	Tulsidas
Satyarth Prakash	Swami Dayanand
Sur Sagar	Surdas
The Guide	R.K. Narayan
The Insider	P.V. Narasimharao
The Post Office — *Dak Ghar*	Rabindra Nath Tagore
The God of Small Things	Arundhati Roy
Urvashi	Ram Dhari Singh 'Dinkar'
Yama	Mahadevi Verma
My Country : My Life (Autobiography)	L.K. Advani
The Test of My Life	Yuvraj Singh
Twenty Years in a Decade	Shah Rukh Khan

FIRST IN INDIA

- *Nobel Prize for Literature (1913)* : Rabindra Nath Tagore
- *Nobel Prize for Physics (1929)* : C.V. Raman
- *Nobel Prize for Peace (1979)* : Mother Teresa
- *Nobel Prize for Economics (1998)* : Amartya Sen
- *Special Oscar award winner (1992)* : Satyajit Ray
- *Governor-General of free India (Last also)* : C. Rajagopalachari
- *Woman Governor of the State* : Smt. Sarojini Naidu
- *Indian Chief of the Army Staff* : General K.M. Cariappa
- *Woman Chief Minister of a State* : Smt. Sucheta Kripalani
- *Woman President of United Nations General Assembly (1954)* : Smt. Vijaylakshmi Pandit
- *President of International Court of Justice* : Dr. Nagendra Singh
- *Woman to swim across the English Channel* : Ms. Aarti Saha
- *Miss Universe* : Miss Sushmita Sen
- *Miss World* : Reita Faria
- *Indian to swim across the English Channel* : Mihir Sen
- *Field Marshal* : S.H.F.J. Manekshaw
- *Indian recipient of Victoria Cross* : Khudadad Khan
- *Indian to conquer Mt. Everest* : Sherpa Tenzing, May 29, 1953
- *Indian male cosmonaut (1984)* : Rakesh Sharma
- *Indian female cosmonaut* : Kalpana Chawla (19 Nov., 1997)
- *Woman to climb Mt. Everest* : Miss Bachendri Pal, May 23, 1984
- *Woman to get Olympic Medal* : Karnam Malleswari
- *Indian to address the UN General Assembly in Hindi* : Atal Bihari Vajpayee
- *Newspaper* : Bengal Gazette, Jan 27, 1780
- *Postage Stamp issued* : In 1852
- *Telegraph line laid* : In 1851, Kolkata; Diamond Harbour
- *Railways run* : April 16, 1853; Bombay-Thana
- *Electric Train run* : 1925: Bombay-Kurla
- *Atomic Power Station* : Tarapore (Maharashtra)
- *Passenger-cum-cargo ship made in India* : Harshavardhan
- *Satellite* : Aryabhatta (1975)
- *Rocket* : Rohini (1967)
- *Atomic Reactor* : Apsara (1956)
- *Climb Everest without oxygen* : Phu Dorjee (1987)
- *First film (movie)* : Raja Harishchandra (1913)
- *First film (talkie)* : Alam Ara (1931)
- *Metro Railway* : Kolkata Metro Railway
- *Test-tube baby, scientifically documented* : Born on August 6, 1986 at K.E.M. Hospital, Mumbai
- *TV Centre* : At Delhi
- *Indian to get an Oscar* : Bhanu Athaiya
- *Woman pilot in IAF* : Ms Harita Kaur Deol
- *Cellular Phone* : Kolkata, August 1, 1995
- *Women president of Indian National Congress* : Smt. Annie Besant
- *President of Indian National Congress* : W.C. Banerjee (1885)
- *Indian who passed in I.C.S. Examination* : Satendra Nath Tagore
- *Woman chief justice of High Court* : Lila Saith (Himachal Pradesh)
- *Woman Foreign Secretary* : Chokila Iyyar

FIRST IMPORTANT OFFICIALS OF INDIA

- *The Governor-General of free India* : Lord Mountbatten
- *President* : Dr. Rajendra Prasad
- *President (Female)* : Pratibha Patil
- *Vice-President* : Dr. S. Radhakrishnan
- *Prime Minister* : Jawahar Lal Nehru
- *Prime Minister (Female)* : Indira Gandhi
- *Deputy Prime Minister* : Sardar Vallabhbhai Patel
- *Chief Justice* : Harilal J. Kania
- *First Female Judge in Supreme Court* : Smt. Meera Sahib Fatima Bibi
- *Speaker, Lok Sabha* : Ganesh Vasudeo Mawlankar
- *Woman Speaker of Lok Sabha* : Meira Kumar
- *Chief Election Commissioner* : Sukumar Sen
- *Commander-in-Chief* : General Sir Roy Bucher
- *Chief of Army Staff* : General Maharaj Rajendra Sinhji
- *Chief of Air Staff* : Air Marshal Sir Thomas Elmhirst
- *Chief of Naval Staff* : Vice Admiral Ramdas Katari
- *Female Minister* : Raj Kumari Amrit Kaur (Health Minister)
- *Female Governor* : Sarojini Naidu (U.P.)
- *Female Chief Minister* : Sucheta Kripalani (U.P. 1963)
- *Finance Commissioner* : K.C. Niyogi
- *Leader of Opposition in Lok Sabha (Recognised)* : Y.V. Chavan (Congress)
- *Leader of Opposition in Rajya Sabha (Recognised)* : Kamalapati Tripathi (Congress)

HIGHEST, BIGGEST, LARGEST & LONGEST IN INDIA

- *Award for Gallantry, Highest* : Param Vir Chakra
- *Award, highest civilian* : Bharat Ratna
- *Bank with largest number of branches* : State Bank of India (24,000 branches till April, 2017)
- *River bridge, Longest* : Bhupen Hazarika Setu (across Lohit River : Assam 9.15 km)
- *Cantilever Span Bridge, Largest* : Howrah Bridge (Kolkata)
- *Cattle Fair, Largest* : Sonepur Fair (Bihar)
- *City, Most Populous* : Mumbai
- *Corridor, Longest* : Ramanathaswamy Corridor, Tamil Nadu (1,220 mt.)
- *Desert, Largest* : Thar (Rajasthan)
- *Dam, Longest* : Hirakud Dam (Odisha)
- *Dam, Highest* : Tehri Dam on Bhagirathi river in Uttarakhand (855 ft.)
- *Delta, Largest* : Sunderban (12,872 Sq. km.)
- *Dome, Largest* : Gol Gumbaz (Bijapur)
- *Gateway, Highest* : Buland Darwaja at Fatehpur Sikri (54 m.)
- *Lake, Largest (Fresh Water)* : Wular Lake (Kashmir)
- *Literacy, Highest* : Kerala
- *Museum, Largest* : Indian Museum (Kolkata)
- *Mosque, Biggest* : Jama Masjid (Delhi)
- *Peak, Highest* : K-2 (8,611 mt.)
- *Railway Platform, Longest* : Gorakhpur, NE, Railway (1335.4 mtrs.)
- *Railway Bridge, Largest* : Vembanad Rail Bridge, Kerala
- *River, Longest* : The Ganga river (2,525 km.)
- *Rainfall, Highest (annual mean)* : Mowsynram near Cherrapunji (1,080 mm) (Meghalaya)
- *Road, Longest* : Grand Trunk Road
- *Rock-cut Temple, Largest* : Kailash Temples, Ellora (Maharashtra)
- *State, maximum percentage of forest cover* : Mizoram (cover 86.27% area)
- *State, Largest (area)* : Rajasthan (3,42,239 sq.km.)
- *State, Most Populous* : Uttar Pradesh (19,98,12,341)
- *State with Maximum density of population* : Bihar (1106 persons per sq. km.)
- *Tunnel, Longest (Road)* : Chenani-Nashri Tunnel (J & K—9.28 km)
- *Tunnel, Longest (Railway)* : Banihal-Qazigund Railway Tunnel (J&K, 11.21 km)
- *Tower, Highest* : Qutub Minar (Delhi, 72.5 mt.)
- *Waterfall, Highest* : Gersoppa Waterfall, Mysuru (290 m.)
- *Zoo, Largest* : Zoological Gardens, Kolkata
- *Man-made Lake, Largest* : Govind Sagar (Bhakra)

AKADEMIES

There are three akademies for promotion of creative art.

1. **Lalit Kala Akademi, New Delhi:** Established in 1954, the Lalit Kala Akademi strives for the popularisation of Indian art within the country and in various countries of the world through exhibitions, publications, workshops and camps. Every three year it organises the Triennale India, an international exhibition. It publishes research papers on Indian arts. Besides organising seminars, it honours eminent artists. The Akademi has set up regional centres called Rashtriya Lalit Kala Kendras at Lucknow, Kolkata, Chennai and Bhubaneswar and a small office at Mumbai.

2. **Sangeet Natak Akademi, New Delhi:** The Sangeet Natak Akademi, set-up in 1953, aims at the promotion and development of dance, drama and music. It holds seminars and festivals, presents awards to the eminent artists and extends financial assistance to traditional teachers and scholarships to students. It also operates a scheme of exchange of troupes.

3. **Sahitya Akademi, New Delhi:** The Sahitya Akademi, established in 1954, has the main functions of development of Indian letters, setting up high literary standards, translation of literary works of one Indian language into other Indian languages, publication of books on history of literature and criticism, bibliographies and reference books. The Akademy has regional offices at Mumbai, Kolkata, Bengaluru and Chennai.

4. **National School of Drama:** It is one of the top theatre training institutes in the world and only one of its kind in India. It was set up in 1959 under Sangeet Natak Akademi but was later made autonomous organisation in 1975.

SCULPTURE

Archaeological Survey of India, set up in 1861, is responsible for preservation and maintenance of sculptures and historical monuments and manages a number of archaeological museums.

National Archives of India, established in 1891, it is the official custodian of all non-current records of permanent value of the Government of India and its predecessor bodies.

DANCE

Classical Dance

Dance	State	Famous Artists
Bharat Natyam	Tamil Nadu	Yamini Krishnamurthy, Rukmini Devi Arundale, Swapna Sundari, Sonal Mansingh, Vaijanti Mala, Mrinalini Sarabhai, Chandralekha, Indrani, Ram Gopal, Bal Saraswati
Kathakali	Kerala	Gopinath, K.K. Nayar, Kunju-Kurup, T.K. Chandu
Kuchipudi	Andhra Pradesh	Sapna Sundari, Raja Reddy, Shobha Nayar, Radha Reddy, Vedantam Satyanarayan, Vimpanti Chinna Satyam.
Kathak	North India	Birju Maharaj, Gopi Krishna, Shambhu Maharaj, Sitara Devi, Vishnu Sharma, Durga Lal, Shobhana Narayan
Odissi	Odisha	Kelucharan Mahapatra, Indrani Rehman, Madhavi Mudgal, Protima Bedi, Samyukta Panigrahi, Sonal Mansingh, Debudas
Manipuri	Manipur	Uday Shankar, Bipin Singh, Suryamukhi, Darohra Jhaveri

MUSIC

Main Schools of Classical Music: There are two main schools of classical music, namely, the Hindustani and the Carnatic. The Hindustani school of classical music is in vogue in north-western India, eastern India and northern parts of the South India.

Musical Instruments: They are: Tabla, Mridangam, Pakhawaj, Chandai, Dholak, Veena, Sitar, Sarod, Gootuvadhyam, Sarangi, Flute, Nadaswaram, Shehnai, Shringi and Turahi.

Musical Instruments and Artists

Musical Instrument	Artists
Flute	Hari Prasad Chaurasia, Panna Lal Ghosh, T.R. Mahalingam, N. Ramani, Vijaya Raghava Rao
Tabla	Allah Rakha, Gudai Maharaj, Latif Khan, Zakir Hussain
Violin	Lalgudi Jayaraman, L. Subramaniam, M.S. Gopal Krishnan, S. Subrahmaniam, V.G. Jog, N. Rajan
Shehnai	Bismilla Khan, Imrat Khan Ali Akbar
Sarod	Khan, Amjad Ali Khan, Alauddin Khan, Saren Rani, Brij Narayan
Sitar	Pandit Ravishankar, Vilayat Khan
Santur	Shiv Kumar Sharma
Rudraveena	Zia Mohiuddin Dagar
Pakhawaj	Govind Rao, Anokhe Lal, Kanthi Maharaj
Mridanga	Palghat R. Raghu, U.S. Burman
Harmonium	Purushottam Walawakar, M. Dhaulpuri
Guitar	Pt. Vishnu Mohan Bhatt, Brij Bhushan Kalra
Ghatam	T.H. Vinayakaram
Janjira	V. Nagarajan
Symphony	Jubin Mehta

WILD LIFE PARKS & SANCTUARIES IN INDIA

India is rich in flora and fauna. However, due to increasing population and industrial and commercial activities, there has been acute pressure on forests. The Government has taken several steps to check the sharp fall in the number of these species. Among the measures are declaration of certain habitats as national parks and sanctuaries. 103 national parks and 544 sanctuaries have been established so far, important ones being given below:

- **Assam:** Kaziranga National Park (know for one-horn Rhinoceroses); Manas Sanctuary.
- **Jharkhand:** Hazaribagh National Park; Betla Tiger Reserve Palamau.
- **Gujarat:** Valvadar National Park, Bhavnagar; Marine National Park, Gir Forests.
- **Himachal Pradesh:** Rohla National Park; Motichur Sanctuary.
- **Jammu & Kashmir:** Dachigam Sanctuary.
- **Karnataka:** Bandipur National Park; Bannargheta National Park, Bangalore; Nagorhole National Park, Coorg; Ranganthitto Bird Sanctuary.
- **Kerala:** Eravikulam Rajmallay National Park, Idduki; Periyar Game Sanctuary.
- **Madhya Pradesh:** Kanha National Park; Bandhavgarh National Park, Shahdol; Shivpuri National Park.
- **Maharashtra:** Taloba National Park, Chandrapur; Panch National Park, Nagpur; Borivali National Park, Mumbai; Nawagaon National Park, Bandara; Melghat National Park.
- **Manipur:** Reibul Lamjao National Park.
- **Odisha:** Simlipal, Tiger Sanctuary.
- **Rajasthan:** Sariska Sanctuary; Ghana Bird Sanctuary, Ranthambhor Sanctuary.
- **Sikkim:** Khangchandzenda National Park, Gangtok.
- **Tamil Nadu:** Vedanthangal Bird Sanctuary; Guindy National Park, Chennai; Mudumalai Sanctuary; Kalakad-Munden Thurai Reserve.
- **Uttar Pradesh:** Chandraprabha Sanctuary; Dudhwa National Park, Lakhimpur.
- **West Bengal:** Jaldapara Sanctuary; Sunderbans.
- **Uttarakhand:** Corbett National Park; Nainital.

NATIONAL AWARDS

1. Bharat Ratna: This is India's highest civilian award. It is given for exceptional work on art, literature, science and recognition of public service of the highest order. Government servants are not eligible for it. The table shows the recipients of the award:

Bharat Ratna Award Winners:

1.	Dr. S. Radhakrishnan	1954
2.	C. Rajagopalachari	1954
3.	Dr. C.V. Raman	1954
4.	Dr. Bhagwan Das	1955
5.	Dr. M. Visvesvaraya	1955
6.	Jawahar Lal Nehru	1955
7.	Govind Ballabh Pant	1957
8.	Dr. D.K. Karve	1958
9.	Dr. Bidhan Chandra Roy	1961
10.	Purushottam Das Tandon	1961
11.	Dr. Rajendra Prasad	1962
12.	Dr. Zakir Hussain	1963
13.	Dr. Pandurang Vaman Kane	1963
14.	Lal Bahadur Shastri	1966
15.	Indira Gandhi	1971
16.	V.V. Giri	1975
17.	K. Kamraj	1976
18.	Mother Teresa	1980
19.	Acharya Vinoba Bhave	1983
20.	Khan Abdul Ghaffar Khan	1987
21.	M.G. Ramachandran	1988
22.	Dr. B.R. Ambedkar	1990
23.	Dr. Nelson R. Mandela	1990
24.	Rajiv Gandhi	1991
25.	Sardar Vallabhbhai Patel	1991
26.	Morarji R. Desai	1991
27.	Maulana Abul Kalam Azad	1992
28.	Jehangir Ratanji Dadabhai Tata	1992
29.	Satyajit Roy	1992
30.	Shri Gulzari Lal Nanda	1997
31.	Mrs. Aruna Asaf Ali	1997
32.	Dr. A.P.J. Abdul Kalam	1998
33.	M.S. Subbalakshmi	1998
34.	C. Subramaniam	1998
35.	Jaya Prakash Narayan	1999
36.	Prof. Amartya Sen	1999
37.	Pt. Ravi Shankar	1999
38.	Gopinath Bardoloi	1999
39.	Lata Mangeshkar	2001
40.	Bismillah Khan	2001
41.	Bhimsen Joshi	2008
42.	C.N.R. Rao	2014
43.	Sachin Tendulakar	2014
44.	Pt. Madan Mohan Malaviya	2015
45.	Atal Bihari Vajpayee	2015
46.	Nanaji Deshmukh	2019
47.	Bhupen Hazarika	2019
48.	Pranab Mukherjee	2019

2. Padma Vibhushan: This award is given for exceptional and distinguished service in any field, including service rendered by Govt. servants.

3. Padma Bhushan: This award is given for distinguished service of a high order in any field, including service rendered by Govt. servants.

4. Padma Shri: This award is given for distinguished service in any field, including service rendered by Government servants.

GALLANTRY AWARDS

1. Param Vir Chakra: The highest award for bravery or some daring and pre-eminent act of valour or self-sacrifice in the presence of the enemy, whether on land, at sea or in the air.

2. Mahavir Chakra: It is the second highest decoration and is awarded for acts of conspicuous gallantry in the presence of the enemy, whether on land, at sea or in the air.

3. Vir Chakra: It is the third in order of awards given for acts of gallantry in the presence of enemy, whether on land, at sea or in the air.

4. **Ashok Chakra:** This medal is awarded for the most conspicuous bravery or some daring or pre-eminent act of valour or self-sacrifice on land, at sea or in the air but not in the presence of enemy.

5. **Vishishta Sewa Medal:** It is awarded to personnel of all the three Services in class I, II and III in recognition of distinguished service of the "most exceptional" and "exceptional" and a "high" order respectively. Prefixes *Parma* and *Ati* are added before first two categories of medals respectively.

6. **Jeewan Raksha Padak:** Awarded for meritorious acts or a series of acts of a human nature displayed in saving life from drowning, fire and rescue operations in mines etc.

Dada Saheb Phalke Award Winners:

Mrs Devika Rani Roerich	1969
B.N. Sirkar	1970
Prithvi Raj Kapoor	1971
Pankaj Mallick	1972
Mrs Ruby Myers	1973
B.N. Reddy	1974
Dhiren Ganguly	1975
Mrs Kanan Devi	1976
Nitin Bose	1977
R.C. Boral	1978
Sohrab Modi	1979
P. Jai Raj	1980
Naushad Ali	1981
L.V. Prasad	1982
Mrs. Durga Khote	1983
Satyajit Roy	1984
V. Shantaram	1985
B. Nagi Reddy	1986
Raj Kapoor	1987
Ashok Kumar	1988
Lata Mangeshkar	1989
A. Nageshwar Rao	1990
Bhalji Pendharkar	1991
Bhupen Hazarika	1992
Majrooh Sultanpuri	1993
Dilip Kumar	1994
Dr Raj Kumar (Kannada actor)	1995
Sivaji Ganesan (Tamil Actor)	1996
Pradeepji (Poet, lyricist)	1997
B.R. Chopra	1998
Hrishikesh Mukherjee	1999
Asha Bhonsle (Playback singer)	2000
Yash Chopra	2001
Devanand	2002
Mrinal Sen	2003
Ador Gopala Krishnan	2004
Shyam Benegal	2005
Tapan Sinha	2006
Manna Dey	2007
V.K. Murthy	2008
D. Ramanaidu	2009
K. Balachander	2010
Soumitra Chatterjee	2011
Pran	2012
Gulzar	2013
Shashi Kapoor	2014
Manoj Kumar	2015
Kasinathuni Vishwanath	2016
Vinod Khanna	2017
Amitabh Bachchan	2018

Highest Honours of Some Countries

Country	*Highest Honour*
India	Bharat Ratna
Pakistan	Nishan-e-Pakistan
Kuwait	Mubarak-Al-kabir Medal
Saudi Arabia	Shah Abdul Aziz Medal
Argentina	The Order of Sona Martin
Nicaragua	Augusto-Caesar Sandino Order
Vietnam	The order of the Golden Star
Hungary	The Order of Banner
Britain	Member of British Empire, Victoria Cross
Japan	Order of Moulovenice Sun
Denmark	Order of Diana Brog
France	Legend of Honour
America	Presidential Medal of Freedom
Germany	Pore Lee Merit Iron Cross
The Netherlands	Netherlands Lion

IMPORTANT CUPS & TROPHIES

International

• *American Cup*	:	Yacht Racing
• *Ashes*	:	Cricket
• *Benson and Hedges*	:	Cricket
• *Canada Cup*	:	Golf
• *Colombo Cup*	:	Football
• *Corbitton Cup*	:	Table Tennis (Women)
• *Davis Cup*	:	Lawn Tennis
• *Derby*	:	Horse Race
• *Grand National*	:	Horse Streple Chase Race
• *Jules Rimet Trophy*	:	World Soccer Cup
• *King's Cup*	:	Air Races
• *Merdeka Cup*	:	Football
• *Ryder Cup*	:	Golf
• *Swaythling Cup*	:	Table Tennis (Men)
• *Thomas Cup*	:	Badminton
• *Uber Cup*	:	Badminton (Women)
• *U. Thant Cup*	:	Tennis
• *Walker Cup*	:	Golf
• *Westchester Cup*	:	Polo
• *Wightman Cup*	:	Lawn Tennis
• *World Cup*	:	Cricket
• *World Cup*	:	Hockey
• *Reliance Cup*	:	Cricket
• *Rothman's Trophy*	:	Cricket
• *William's Cup*	:	Basketball
• *European Champions Cup*	:	Football
• *Eisenhower Cup*	:	Golf
• *Essande Champions Cup*	:	Hockey
• *Rene Frank Trophy*	:	Hockey
• *Grand Prix*	:	Table Tennis
• *Edgbaston Cup*	:	Lawn Tennis
• *Grand Prix*	:	Lawn Tennis
• *World Cup*	:	Weightlifting

National

• *Agarwal Cup*	:	Badminton
• *Agha Khan Cup*	:	Hockey
• *All India Women's Guru Nanak Championship*	:	Hockey
• *Bandodkar Trophy*	:	Football
• *Bangalore Blues Challenge Cup*	:	Basketball
• *Barna-Bellack Cup*	:	Table Tennis
• *Beighton Cup*	:	Hockey
• *Bombay Gold Cup*	:	Hockey
• *Burdwan Trophy*	:	Weightlifting
• *Charminar Trophy*	:	Atheletics
• *Chadha Cup*	:	Badminton
• *C.K. Naidu Trophy*	:	Cricket
• *Chakola Gold Trophy*	:	Football
• *Divan Cup*	:	Badminton
• *Deodhar Trophy*	:	Cricket
• *Duleep Trophy*	:	Cricket
• *D.C.M. Cup*	:	Football
• *Durand Cup*	:	Football
• *Dhyan Chand Trophy*	:	Hockey
• *Dr. B.C. Roy Trophy*	:	Football (Junior)
• *Ezra Cup*	:	Polo
• *F.A. Cup*	:	Football
• *G.D. Birla Trophy*	:	Cricket
• *Ghulam Ahmed Trophy*	:	Cricket
• *Gurmeet Trophy*	:	Hockey
• *Guru Nanak Cup*	:	Hockey
• *Gyanvati Devi Trophy*	:	Hockey
• *Holkar Trophy*	:	Bridge
• *Irani Trophy*	:	Cricket
• *I.F.A. Shield*	:	Football
• *Indira Gold Cup*	:	Hockey

- *Jawaharlal Challenge* : Air Racing
- *Jaswant Singh Trophy* : Best Services Sportsman
- *Kuppuswamy Naidu Trophy* : Hockey
- *Lady Rattan Tata Trophy* : Hockey
- *MCC Trophy* : Hockey
- *Moinuddaula Gold Cup* : Cricket
- *Murugappa Gold Cup* : Hockey
- *Modi Gold Cup* : Hockey
- *Narang Cup* : Badminton
- *Nehru Trophy* : Hockey
- *Nixan Gold Cup* : Football
- *Obaidullah Gold Cup* : Hockey
- *Prithi Singh Cup* : Polo
- *Rani Jhansi Trophy* : Cricket
- *Ranji Trophy* : Cricket
- *Rangaswami Cup* : Hockey
- *Ranjit Singh Gold Cup* : Hockey
- *Rajendra Prasad Cup* : Tennis

- *Ramanujan Trophy* : Table Tennis
- *Rene Frank Trophy* : Hockey
- *Radha Mohan Cup* : Polo
- *Raghbir Singh Memorial* : Football
- *Rohinton Baria Trophy* : Cricket
- *Sanjay Gold Cup* : Football
- *Santosh Trophy* : Football
- *Sir Ashutosh Mukherjee* : Football
- *Subroto Cup* : Football
- *Scindia Gold Cup* : Hockey
- *Sahni Trophy* : Hockey
- *Sheesh Mahal Trophy* : Cricket
- *Todd Memorial Trophy* : Football
- *Tommy Eman Gold Cup* : Hockey
- *Vittal Trophy* : Football
- *Vizzy Trophy* : Cricket
- *Vijay Merchant Trophy* : Cricket
- *Wellington Trophy* : Rowing
- *Wills Trophy* : Cricket

SPORTS MEASUREMENTS

- *Badminton Courts:* 44 ft. by 20 ft. (doubles) 44 ft. by 17 ft. (singles)
- *Boxing Ring:* 12 ft. by 28 ft. Sq.
- *Cricket Pitch:* 22 yards (distance)
- *Derby Course:* 1½ miles. (2.4 km)
- *Football Field:*
  (a) Length : 100 – 120 yards.
     Breadth: 50 – 56 yards.
  (b) Rugby : 100 yards by 75 yards
- *Hockey Ground:* 100 yards by 55 to 60 yards
- *Lawn Tennis Court:* 78 ft. by 36 ft. (double), 78 ft. by 28 ft. (single)
- *Marathon Race:* 26 miles, 385 yards
- *Polo Ground:* 300 yards by 200 yards (if boarded)
- *Golf:* Hole 4½ inches in diameter.

SPORTS TERMS

- **Badminton:** Mixed doubles; Deuce; Drop; Smash; Let; Foot work; Setting.
- **Base Ball:** Pitcher; Put out, Strike; Home; Bunt.
- **Billiards:** Cue; Jigger; Pot; Break; In Baulk; In Off; Cannons.
- **Boxing:** Upper cut; Round; Punch; Bout; Knock down; Hitting below the belt; Ring.
- **Bridge:** Finesse; Dummy; Revoke; Grand Slam; Little Slam; No Trump; Rubber.
- **Chess:** Bishop, Gambit; Checkmate; Stalemate.
- **Cricket:** L.B.W. *(leg before wicket)*; Creases, Popping-creases; Stumped; Bye; Leg-Bye; Googly; Hattrick; Maiden over; Drive; Bowling; Duck; Follow-on; No ball; Leg Break; Silly point; Cover point; Hit-wicket; Late-cut; Slip; Off-spinner; In-swing.
- **Football:** Off Side; Block; Drop-kick; Penalty-kick (or *goal kick*); Corner-kick; Free-kick; Dribble; Thrown-in; Foul.
- **Golf:** Boggy; Foursome; Stymic; Tee; Put; Hole; Niblic; Caddie; Links; The green; Bunker.
- **Hockey:** Carried; Short Corner; Bully; Sticks;

Off side; Roll in; Striking Circle; Under-cutting; Dribble.

- **Horse racing:** Jockey; Punter.
- **Polo:** Bunker; Chukker; Mallet.
- **Tennis:** Back hand drive; Volley; Smash; Half-volley; Deuce; Service; Let; Grand Slam.

Name of Playing Compound of Different Games

Name of Compound	Related Sports
Court	Lawn Tennis, Badminton, Netball, Hand ball, Volleyball, Squash, Kho-Kho, Kabaddi
Diamond	Baseball
Ring	Boxing, Skating, Wrestling, Circus, Riding display
Course	Golf
Board	Table Tennis
Pool	Swimming
Alley	Bowling
Mat	Judo, Karate II
Arena	Horse Riding
Vellodrum	Cycling
Field	Polo, Football, Hockey
Track	Athletics
Pitch	Cricket, Rugby
Rink	Ice Hockey

National Sports and Games of Some Countries

Country	Sports & Games
Australia	Cricket
Canada	Ice Hockey
England	Cricket and Rugby Football
India	Hockey
Japan	Ju-Jitsu
Russia	Chess
Scotland	Rugby Football
Spain	Bull Fighting
USA	Baseball
China	Table Tennis
Malaysia	Badminton
Pakistan	Hockey

Number of Players in Some Games/Sports

Sports	No. of Players
Badminton	1 or 2
Baseball	9
Basketball	5
Billiards (Snooker)	1
Boxing	1
Bridge	2
Chess	1
Cricket	11
Croquest	13 or 15
Football (Soccer)	11
Hockey	11
Lacrosse	12
Netball	7
Polo Rugby	4
Football (Rugby)	15
Table	1 or
Tennis	2
Lawn	1 or
Tennis	2
Volleyball	6
Water Polo	7

OLYMPIC GAMES

First of all these games were held by the Greeks in 776 B.C. on Mount Olympus in honour of the Greek God Zeus. In this way, the history of Olympic Games is about twenty eight hundred years old. These games continued to be held every four years until 394 A.D. When these games were stopped by a royal order of the emperor of Rome. The modern Olympic Games which started in Athens in 1896, are the result of the devotion and dedication of a French educator Baron Pierre de Coubertin and the first Olympic meet in the modern series was held in 1896 in Athens, the Capital of Greece. Since then, they are being held every four years except for breaks during world wars. The Olympic flag is white in colour with five coloured rings, each ring symbolic of a continent. Summer as well as winter Olympics are held in the same year.

Olympic Games (Venues & Dates)

Year	Venue	Organising	Participating Countries
1896	Athens	6–15 April	13
1900	Paris	20th May to 28th Oct.	22
1904	St. Louis	1st July to 23rd Nov.	13
1908	London	27th April to 31st Oct.	22
1912	Stockholm	5th May to 22nd July	28
1916	Berlin	Cancelled due to World War	—
1920	Antwerp	20th April to 12th Sept.	29
1924	Paris	4th May to 27th July	44
1928	Amsterdam	17th May to 12 Aug.	46
1932	Los Angeles	30th July to 14th Aug.	47
1936	Berlin	1st May to 16th Aug.	49
1940	Tokyo (Helsinki)	Cancelled due to Wold War	—
1944	London	Cancelled due to World War	—
1948	London	29th July to 14th Aug.	59
1952	Helsinki	19th July to 3rd Aug.	69
1956	Melbourne	22nd November to 8th December	71
1960	Rome	25th Aug. to 11th Sept.	83
1964	Tokyo	10th to 24th October	93
1968	Mexico City	12th to 27th October	112
1972	Munich	26th August to 10 September	122
1976	Montreal	17th July to 1st Sep-	88
1980	Moscow	19th July to 3rd Aug.	81
1984	Los Angeles	28th July to 12th Aug.	140
1988	Seoul	17th Sept. to 2nd Oct.	160
1992	Barcelona	25th July to 9th Aug.	170
1996	Atlanta	19th July to 4th Aug.	197
2000	Sydney	15th Sept. to 1st Oct.	199
2004	Athens	14th to 29th August	202
2008	Beijing	8th to 24th August	204
2012	London	27th July to 12 August	204
2016	Rio de Janeiro	5th to 21st August	206
2020	Tokyo	(to be held)	

Note: Games not held in 1916, 1940, and 1944.

ASIAN GAMES

After the Second World War, most of the Asian Countries gained independence. On the lines of Olympic Games, Asian Games were planned every four years. India hosted the first Asian Games in 1951.

Asian Games: An Overview

Year	Venues	Participating Countries	No. of Games	First Position
1951	New Delhi	11	6	Japan
1954	Manila	18	7	Japan
1958	Tokyo	20	13	Japan
1962	Jakarta	16	13	Japan
1966	Bangkok	18	14	Japan
1970	Bangkok	18	13	Japan
1974	Teheran	25	16	Japan
1978	Bangkok	25	19	Japan
1982	New Delhi	33	21	China
1986	Seoul	34	25	China
1990	Beijing	37	27	China
1994	Hiroshima	42	34	China
1998	Bangkok	41	36	China
2002	Busan	44	38	China
2006	Doha	46	43	China
2010	Guangzhou	45	42	China
2014	Incheon	45	36	China
2018	Jakarta	45	40	China
2022	Hangzhou	(to be held)		

COMMONWEALTH GAMES

The Commonwealth Games are held every four years. All the Commonwealth Countries (former colonies of Britain) can take part in it.

Venues of Commonwealth Games

Venues	Year	Countries	Events
Hamilton, (Canada)	1930	11	6
London, (U.K.)	1934	16	6
Sydney, (Australia)	1938	15	7
Auckland, (New Zealand)	1950	12	7
Vancouver, (Canada)	1954	24	9
Cardiff, (U.K.)	1958	35	9
Perth, (Australia)	1962	35	9
Jamaica, (West Indies)	1966	34	9
Edinburgh, (U.K.)	1970	42	9
Christchurch, (New Zealand)	1974	39	9
Edmonton, (Canada)	1978	48	10
Brisbane, (Australia)	1982	47	10
Edinburgh, (U.K.)	1986	26	10
Auckland, (New Zealand)	1990	55	10
Victoria, (Canada)	1994	64	
Kuala Lumpur, (Malaysia)	1998	70	16
Manchester, (U.K.)	2002	72	17
Melbourne, (Australia)	2006	71	16
Delhi, (India)	2010	71	17
Glasgow, (Scotland)	2014	71	18
Gold Coast (Aus.)	2018	71	19
Birmingham (England)	2022	(Scheduled)	

National/International Days

JANUARY

Infant Protection Day	: January 7
African National Congress Foundation Day	: January 8
NRI Day (India)	: January 9
World Laughter Day	: January 10
National Youth Day (India)	: January 12
Army Day (India)	: January 15
Indian Tourism Day	: January 25
Republic Day (India); International Customs Day	: January 26
Martyrs' Day (India); World Leprosy Eradication Day	: January 30

FEBRUARY

World Wetlands Day	: February 2
World Marriage Day	: Second Sunday of February
Valentine Day (World)	: February 14
Mother Tongue Day (World)	: February 21
National Science Day (India)	: February 28

MARCH

International Women's Day;	: March 8
World Disabled Day : World Consumer Rights Day	: March 15
World Forestry Day; International Day for Elimination of Racial Discrimination	: March 21
World Day for Water	: March 22
World Meteorological Day	: March 23
World TB Day	: March 24

APRIL

National Maritime Day (India)	: April 5
World Health Day	: April 7
World Aviation and Cosmonautics Day	: April 12
World Haemophilia Day	: April 17
World Heritage Day,	: April 18
Earth Day (World)	: April 22
World Book and Copyright Day	: April 23

MAY

Workers' Day (International Labour Day)	: May 1
Press Freedom Day; World Asthma Day	: May 3
World Red Cross Day	: May 8
World Mother's Day (2nd Sunday of May)	: May 8
World Thalassaemia Day	: May 9
National Technology Day	: May 11
International Nurses Day	: May 12
International Day of the Family	: May 15
World Telecommunication Day	: May 17
Anti-Terrorism Day	: May 21
Commonwealth Day	: May 24
Anti-Tobacco Day	: May 31

JUNE

International Day of Innocent Children Victims of Aggression	: June 4
World Environment Day	: June 5
Father's Day (3rd Sunday of June)	: June 19
International Yoga Day	: June 21
International Day Against Drug Abuse & Illicit Trafficking	: June 26

JULY

Doctors' Day	: July 1
American Independence Day	: July 4
World Zoonosis Day	: July 6
World Population Day	: July 11

AUGUST

World Breast Feeding Week	: August 1-7
International Friendship Day	: August 3

Hiroshima Day	: August 6
World Senior Citizen's Day	: August 8
Quit India Day; Nagasaki Day	: August 9
Indian Independence Day	: August 15
International Day of the World's Indigenous People	: August 18
Sadbhavna Divas (India)	: August 20
National Sports Day (India)	: August 29

SEPTEMBER

Teachers' Day	: September 5
World (International) Literacy Day	: September 8
Hindi Day (India)	: September 14
All India Flag Day	: September 15
World Ozone Day	: September 16
Alzheimer's Day (World)	: September 21
Day for Peace & Non-Violence (UN)	: September 21
Rose Day (Welfare of Cancer Patients) World Heart Day	: September 22
International Tiger Day	: September 25
World Tourism Day	: September 27

OCTOBER

International Day for the Elderly People	: October 1
Gandhi Jayanti, International Day of Non-Violence	: October 2
World Animal Day	: October 2
World Vegetarian Day	: October 2
World Habitat Day	: October 3
World Animal Welfare Day	: October 4
World Post Office Day	: October 9
National Post Day (India)	: October 10
World Allergy Awareness Day	: October 11
UN International Day for Natural Disaster Reduction	: October 13
World Standards Day	: October 14
World Food Day	: October 16
International Day for the Eradication of Poverty	: October 17
UN Day	: October 24
World Development Information Day	: October 24
Infants Day	: October 27
World Thrift Day	: October 30
National Integration Day (India)	: October 31

NOVEMBER

Legal Services Day	: November 9
Children's Day (India)	: November 14
Diabetes Day	: November 14
National Epilepsy Day	: November 17

DECEMBER

World AIDS Day	: December 1
World Disabled Day	: December 3
International Volunteer Develompent Day	: December 5
Armed Forces Flag Day (India)	: December 7
Human Rights Day (World)	: December 10
National Energy Conservation Day	: December 14
Farmer's Day	: December 23

✳ ✳ ✳ ✳ ✳

History

1. Where is the Indus Civilization city Lothal?
   A. Gujarat
   B. Rajasthan
   C. Punjab
   D. Haryana

2. Mohenjodaro is situated in—
   A. Sindh Province of Pakistan
   B. Gujarat
   C. Punjab
   D. Afghanistan

3. Which deity was *not* worshipped by the Vedic Aryans?
   A. Indra
   B. Marut
   C. Varun
   D. Pashupati

4. The Vedanga consists of the—
   A. Kalp, Shiksha, Nirukta, Vyakaran, Chhanda, Jyotish
   B. Kalp, Shiksha, Brahman, Vyakaran, Chhandra, Jyotish
   C. Kalp, Shiksha, Nirukta, Aranyak, Chhanda, Jyotish
   D. Kalp, Upanishad, Nirukta, Vyakaran, Chhanda

5. The Mahavir belonged to the clan—
   A. Kalams
   B. Bhaggas
   C. Lichhivis
   D. Bulis

6. The Jain text which contains the biographies of the Tirthankaras is known as—
   A. Bhagwatisutra
   B. Uvasagadasao
   C. Adi Purana
   D. Kalpasutra

7. The first Buddhist Sangeeti (conference) was held at—
   A. Vaishali
   B. Pataliputra
   C. Rajgriha
   D. Ujjain

8. The battle between Alexander and Porus took place on the bank of river—
   A. Sutlej
   B. Ravi
   C. Jhelum
   D. Ganga

9. Who of the following was *not* a patron of Jainism?
   A. Bimbisara
   B. Kharvela
   C. Kanishka
   D. Chandragupta Maurya

10. The last king of Mauryan empire was—
    A. Devavarman
    B. Brihadrath
    C. Kunala
    D. Shalishuk

11. The writer of the 'Kalpasutra' was—
    A. Simuka
    B. Panini
    C. Bhadrabahu
    D. Patanjali

12. Guru Govind Singh was killed in 1708 at—
    A. Amritsar
    B. Keeratpur
    C. Nanded
    D. Anandpur

13. Swaraj Party was formed by—
    A. C.R. Das
    B. Motilal Nehru
    C. Jawaharlal Nehru
    D. C.R. Das and Motilal Nehru

14. 'Lucknow Pact' was concluded between—
    A. Congress and the British Government
    B. Muslim League and the British Government
    C. Congress and the Muslim League
    D. Congress, the Muslim League and the British Government

15. Who among the following participated in all the three Round Table Conferences?
    A. Madan Mohan Malviya
    B. B.R. Ambedkar
    C. Sardar Patel
    D. None of these

16. Which of the following pairs is *correct*?
    A. Ramprasad Bismil—Second Lahore Conspiracy Case

B. Surya Sen—Chatgaon Case
C. Bhagat Singh—Kakori Conspiracy Case
D. Chandrashekar Azad—Delhi Bomb Case

17. Subhash Chandra Bose inaugurated the government of Free India at—
A. Burma   B. Japan
C. Germany   D. Singapore

18. Which of the following pairs is *correct*?
A. Chuar Revolt—Orissa
B. Sanyasi Revolt—Bihar
C. Parlakhemundi Revolt—Orissa
D. Rampa Revolt—Karnatak

19. Who said, "You give me blood, I will give you freedom"?
A. Mahatma Gandhi
B. Bal Gangadhar Tilak
C. Subhash Chandra Bose
D. Bhagat Singh

20. 6th April, 1930 is well known in the history of India because this date is associated with ....
A. Dandi March by Mahatma Gandhi
B. Quit India Movement
C. Partition of Bengal
D. Partition of India

21. The concept of 'Din-e-Elahi' was founded by which king?
A. Dara Shikoh   B. Akbar
C. Shershah Suri   D. Shahjahan

22. The central point in Ashoka's Dharma was—
A. Loyalty to kings
B. Peace and non-violence
C. Respect to elders
D. Religious toleration

23. Mahatma Gandhi for the first time practised his Satyagraha in India at—
A. Chauri-Chaura   B. Ahmedabad
C. Champaran   D. Nauokhali

24. 'Do or Die' was one of the most powerful slogans of India's freedom struggle. Who gave it?
A. Gandhiji

B. J.L. Nehru
C. Balgangadhar Tilak
D. Subhash Chandra Bose

25. Who among the following formed a party named as 'Forward Block'?
A. Subhash Chandra Bose
B. Sardar Bhagat Singh
C. Chandrashekhar Azad
D. J.L. Nehru

26. Who was the first Indian lady to preside over the Congress?
A. Rajkumari Amrit Kaur
B. Annie Besant
C. Vijayalakshmi Pandit
D. Amrita Shergill

27. When was 'Purna Swaraj' day first celebrated?
A. August 15, 1947   B. August 15, 1930
C. January 26, 1950   D. January 26, 1930

28. The only Sultan of Delhi who exempted his subject from nearly 24 taxes was—
A. Mubarak Shah Khalji
B. Ghiyasuddin Tughlaq
C. Firoz Tughlaq
D. Sikandar Lodi

29. Who edited 'Harijan Patrika'?
A. Aurobindo Ghosh
B. Mahatma Gandhi
C. Bal Gangadhar Tilak
D. Bipin Chandra Pal

30. Who launched the Non-Cooperation Movement in 1920?
A. Frontier Gandhi
B. Surendranath Banerjee
C. Woomesh Chandra Banerjee
D. None of these

31. 'Subsidiary Alliance' system was introduced by—
A. Lord Dalhousie   B. Lord Curzon
C. Lord Hastings   D. Lord Wellesley

32. The famous Ilbert Bill Controversy arose during the tenure of—
A. Lord Mayo   B. Lord Lytton
C. Lord Dufferin   D. Lord Ripon

33. The Tattvabodhini Sabha was founded by—
A. H.V. Derozio
B. Rammohan Roy
C. Debendranath Thakur
D. Swami Vivekananda

34. Which of the following laid the foundation of the image worship in the country?
A. Jainism   B. Buddhism
C. Ajivikas   D. Vedic religion

35. Which one of the following is *not* associated with the Court of Kanishka?
A. Ashvaghosha   B. Charaka
C. Nagarjuna   D. Patanjali

36. Kalsi is famous for—
A. Buddhist Chaityas
B. Persian Coins
C. Rock-edicts of Ashoka
D. Temples of Gupta Period

37. Which dynasty of rulers is associated with the construction of famous Kailasha Temple of Ellora?
A. Chalukyas   B. Cholas
C. Pallavas   D. Rashtrakutas

38. Who of the following was associated with the collection of revenue in Mauryan Mantriparishad?
A. Samaharta   B. Vyabharika
C. Annapala   D. Pradeshta

39. Who wrote Dashkumaracharita?
A. Bharavi   B. Bilhana
C. Dandin   D. Somadeva

40. Which of the following places was the capital of Satvahanas?
A. Pratisthan
B. Nagarjuna Konda
C. Shakald or Syalkot
D. Patliputra

41. A bomb was thrown on the occasion of his State entry into Delhi at—
A. Lord Curzon   B. Lord Mayo
C. Lord Minto   D. Lord Hardinge

42. Aurobindo Ghosh wrote—
A. Extremist movement
B. Moderate movement
C. Kesari
D. The Divine Life

43. Sarnath Stambh was built by—
A. Harshvardhan
B. Ashoka
C. Gautam Buddha
D. Kanishka

44. Which Urdu newspaper was started by Lajpat Rai from Lahore in 1920?
A. Bande Mataram
B. People
C. Tribune
D. Vir Arjun

45. Who called the Indian National Congress as a 'Begging Institute'?
A. B.C. Pal
B. Tilak
C. Aurobindo Ghosh
D. None of them

46. Who had established 'India Independence League'?
A. Subhash Chandra Bose
B. Ras Behari Ghosh
C. Surendranath Bannerjee
D. Ras Behari Bose

47. Which of the following Indian leaders did not support the Khilafat movement?
A. Jawahar Lal Nehru
B. Madan Mohan Malviya
C. Mohammad Ali
D. Swami Shraddhanand

48. Saddler Commission was associated with—
A. Judiciary
B. Revenue Administration
C. Education
D. Police Administration

49. Who of the following helped Humayun in recovering his kingdom?
A. Bahadur Shah of Gujarat
B. Shah Husain Arghun of Sind
C. Shah Tahmasp of Persia
D. Maldeo of Bikaner

50. Who was the Governor-General of the East India Company when the Revolt of 1857 took place?
A. Lord Bentinck
B. Lord Hastings
C. Lord Dalhousie
D. Lord Canning

51. During the Indian freedom struggle, what was the purpose of the Simon Commission?
A. To inquire into events related to Jallianwala Bagh Massacre
B. To look into the working of the Government of India Act, 1919
C. To suggest strategies for promoting Western education in India
D. To design a Constitution for India within the framework of 'Dominion Status'

52. Who of the following brought the Sikh Kingdom of Punjab under direct British rule by an official proclamation?
A. Lord Hastings   B. Lord Cornwallis
C. Lord Minto   D. Lord Dalhousie

53. Who of the following wrote the book *Precepts of Jesus*?
A. Raja Rammohan Roy
B. Devendranath Tagore
C. Ishwarchandra Vidyasagar
D. Keshab Chandra Sen

54. Who among the following was sent by Lord Hardings to South Africa to plead the cause of Indians led by the young Gandhi?
A. B.G. Tilak   B. G.K. Gokhle
C. M.G. Ranade   D. Motilal Nehru

55. The efforts of whom of the following led to the "Age of Consent Act, 1891"?
A. Rabindranath Tagore
B. M.G. Ranade
C. Surendranath Benerjee
D. Mulbari

56. What was the name of the party formed by Subhash Chandra Bose after leaving Indian National Congress?
A. Congress Socialist Party
B. Forward Bloc
C. Indian National Conference
D. Swaraj Party

57. Among the following who was a prominent leader of Khilafat Movement?
A. Jawaharlal Nehru B. Mahatma Gandhi
C. Rajendra Prasad   D. Vallabhbhai Patel

58. Who was the architect of the 'Drain Theory' and the author of the book *Poverty and Un-British Rule in India*?
A. Dadabhai Naoroji
B. Gopal Krishna Gokhale
C. Abul Kalam Azad
D. Ramesh Chandra Dutt

ANSWERS

1	2	3	4	5	6	7	8	9	10
A	A	D	A	C	D	C	C	A	B
11	**12**	**13**	**14**	**15**	**16**	**17**	**18**	**19**	**20**
C	C	D	C	B	B	D	B	C	A
21	**22**	**23**	**24**	**25**	**26**	**27**	**28**	**29**	**30**
B	D	C	A	A	B	D	C	B	D
31	**32**	**33**	**34**	**35**	**36**	**37**	**38**	**39**	**40**
D	D	C	D	D	C	D	A	C	A
41	**42**	**43**	**44**	**45**	**46**	**47**	**48**	**49**	**50**
D	D	B	A	C	D	B	C	C	D
51	**52**	**53**	**54**	**55**	**56**	**57**	**58**		
B	D	A	B	D	B	B	A		

1. When a Governor reserves a bill passed by the State Legislature?
   A. He may be impeached
   B. He sends it to the President
   C. He may help the bill pending indefinitely
   D. He may give assent to the bill later

2. Match the following features of Indian Constitution and their sources—

   List-I
   (*a*) Bill of Right and Judicial Review.
   (*b*) Parliamentary System of Democracy.
   (*c*) Directive Principles.
   (*d*) Residuary Powers with Centre.

   List-II
   1. England
   2. Ireland
   3. U.S.A.
   4. Canada

   Codes:

	(a)	(b)	(c)	(d)
A.	4	1	2	3
B.	1	2	3	4
C.	3	4	2	1
D.	3	1	2	4

3. A uniform civil code has been recommended in the Directive Principles to ensure—
   A. Economic equality
   B. National security
   C. National integration
   D. Support for weaker sections of society

4. Indian Institute of Public Administration is situated at—
   A. Delhi
   B. Chennai
   C. Kolkata
   D. Mumbai

5. Which of the following News-paper is not associated with Gandhiji?
   A. The Statesman
   B. Harijan
   C. Young India
   D. Indian Opinion

6. Which Article of Indian Constitution guarantees constitutional protection to our civil servants?
   A. 311
   B. 312
   C. 313
   D. 315

7. Which Constitutional Amendment is related to Panchayati Raj?
   A. 52nd
   B. 62nd
   C. 72nd
   D. 73rd

8. In which year, the National Commission for Scheduled Caste and Scheduled Tribe was created?
   A. 1989
   B. 1990
   C. 1991
   D. 1996

9. In India, the power of Judicial review is enjoyed by the—
   A. High Court only
   B. Supreme Court only
   C. Supreme Court and High Court only
   D. Parliament

10. What are the essential elements of the State?
    A. Population, Territory, Constitution, Power
    B. Population, Territory , Government, Sovereignty
    C. Population, Territory, Political Party, Sovereignty
    D. Population, Power, Authority, Sovereignty

11. In the Indian Constitution the word secularism means—
    A. State has a religion of its own
    B. State has nothing to do with religion
    C. State has irreligious
    D. State tolerates religion without professing any particular religion

12. Who presides over the Joint Session of the two Houses of the Parliament?
A. President of India
B. Speaker of Lok-Sabha
C. Prime Minister
D. Leader of Ruling Party

13. The minimum age for becoming President of India is—
A. 25 years B. 21 years
C. 35 years D. 18 years

14. Who was the Chairman of the "Drafting Committee in the Constituent Assembly"?
A. Dr. Rajendra Prasad
B. Dr. B. R. Ambedkar
C. J. L. Nehru
D. B. N. Rao

15. Through which Amendment was the word 'Socialism' added to the Constitution?
A. 42nd Amendment
B. 43rd Amendment
C. 44th Amendment
D. 45th Amendment

16. The number of Judges in International Court of Justice are—
A. 15 B. 10
C. 11 D. 14

17. In India, the work of Budget forming is performed by—
A. NITI Aayog
B. Public Service Committee
C. Finance Minister
D. Finance Commission

18. Which one of the following Commissions was constituted to examine the Centre-State relations?
A. Sarkaria Commission
B. Shah Commission
C. Bachhavat Commission
D. Jain Commission

19. The first State where the Panchayati Raj System was implemented?
A. Madhya Pradesh
B. Andhra Pradesh
C. Rajasthan
D. Uttar Pradesh

20. The slogan 'Swaraj is my Birth Right' was given by—
A. Mahatma Gandhi
B. Lala Lajpat Rai
C. Lokmanya Tilak
D. Bipin Chandra Pal

21. Which one of the following is not a fundamental Right?
A. Right of Life
B. Right to Liberty
C. Right to Property
D. Right to Freedom of Expression

22. Indian system is—
A. Federal
B. Quasi-federal
C. Unitary
D. Federal with unitary bias

23. 'Panchayati Raj' Amendment Act is known as—
A. 73rd Amendment B. 74th Amendment
C. 75th Amendment D. 76th Amendment

24. Regarding the re-election of the Vice-President our—
A. Constitution prescribes re-election only once
B. Constitution places a clear ban
C. Constitution is absolutely silent
D. Constitution prescribes re-election for a maximum, period of two terms

25. National Development Council was established in—
A. August 1951 B. August 1947
C. August 1952 D. August 1950

26. The Fundamental Duties of Indian citizens are contained in—
A. Part I of the Constitution
B. Part III of the Constitution
C. Part IV of the Constitution
D. None of the above

27. Which article of our Constitution empowers the Comptroller and Auditor-General to submit report relating to the accounts of a State Government?
A. Article 149 B. Article 150
C. Article 151(1) D. Article 151(2)

28. The President can dismiss any member of the Union Council of Ministers—
A. On recommendation of the Prime Minister
B. With the consent of the Speaker
C. At his discretion
D. None of the above

29. Which article of our Constitution declares that "The property and income of a State shall be exempt from Union taxation"?
A. Article 287   B. Article 288
C. Article 289   D. Article 290

30. If the Speaker of the Lok Sabha decides a bill as a money bill—
A. It can be challenged by the Supreme Court
B. It can be challenged by the Opposition Leader
C. It is final and cannot be challenged
D. It can be challenged by any member of Lok Sabha

31. A money bill is introduced in the Lok Sabha of Parliament with the prior recommendations of—
A. The Speaker of Lok Sabha
B. The Prime Minister
C. The Union Finance Minister
D. The President of India

32. Which article of our Constitution provides for exemption of property of the Union Government from taxation by any State—
A. Article 282   B. Article 283
C. Article 284   D. Article 285

33. Which article of our Constitution provides for a Proclamation of financial emergency by the President?
A. Article 357   B. Article 358
C. Article 359   D. Article 360

34. Which statement among the following is inapplicable during the period of a financial emergency?
A. President can issue directions to reduce salaries and allowances of any class of Union and State Government employees
B. President can issue directions to reduce salaries and allowances of Judges of the Supreme Court and High Courts
C. President may direct all Money Bills passed by State Legislatures be kept reserved for his consideration
D. President may issue directions to nationalize any industry

35. Which amendment of the Constitution of India provided constitutional status of Municipalities?
A. 42nd   B. 52nd
C. 60th   D. 74th

36. Provisions relating to Panchayati Raj can be found in which Schedule of the Indian Constitution?
A. 7   B. 9
C. 10   D. 11

37. In India, who appoints the Chief Election Commissioner?
A. Prime Minister   B. President
C. Vice-President   D. None of the above

38. Who generally acts as Chairman of the Public Accounts Committee of Union Parliament?
A. Comptroller and Auditor-General
B. Prime Minister
C. A member of Lok Sabha who is not a member of the ruling party
D. None of the above

39. The Comptroller and Auditor-General can be given further appointment after retirement as—
A. Finance Minister of India
B. Governor of any State
C. Ambassador to any country
D. None of the above

40. Who was the first Chairman of Planning Commission?
A. J.B. Kripalani
B. Ashok Mehta
C. Prasanta Mahalanobis
D. Jawaharlal Nehru

41. Which article of the Constitution of India deals with the composition of Finance Commission?
A. Article 277   B. Article 278
C. Article 279   D. Article 280

42. 'Vote on Account' is related to which of the following?
A. Government Expenditure
B. Government Revenue
C. Both Revenue and Expenditure in a Budget
D. None of the above

43. The Chairman of the National Development Council is—
A. The Commerce Minister of the Union Government
B. The Finance Minister of the Union Govt.
C. The Prime Minister
D. The Union Minister for Planning

44. The President's rule in an Indian State is declared under—
A. Article 368 of the Constitution of India
B. Article 362 of the Constitution of India
C. Article 352 of the Constitution of India
D. Article 356 of the Constitution of India

45. Who appoints the Comptroller and Auditor-General of India?
A. President
B. Prime Minister
C. Chief Justice of India
D. Union Public Service Commission

46. On what basis the seats of Lok Sabha are distributed among the States?
A. Area and Resources
B. Population
C. Area, Resources and Population
D. None of the above

47. Which article of our Constitution empowers the Comptroller and Auditor-General to submit report relating to the accounts of the Union Government?
A. Article 149   B. Article 150
C. Article 151(1)   D. Article 151(2)

48. A Bill referred to a 'Joint Sitting' of the two Houses of the Parliament is required to be passed by—
A. A simple majority of the members present
B. Absolute majority of the total member-ship
C. 2/3rd majority of the members present
D. 3/4th majority of the members

49. Who is the constitutional head of the Government of India?
A. President
B. Prime Minister
C. Chief Justice of India
D. Attorney-General

50. Who certifies a Bill to be a Money Bill in India?
A. Finance Minister
B. President
C. Speaker of the Lok Sabha
D. Prime Minister

51. By which Amendment were 'Fundamental Duties' added to the Constitution?
A. 40th Amendment B. 42nd Amendment
C. 44th Amendment D. 45th Amendment

⊢ANSWERS⊣

1	2	3	4	5	6	7	8	9	10
B	D	C	A	A	A	D	B	B	B
11	**12**	**13**	**14**	**15**	**16**	**17**	**18**	**19**	**20**
D	B	C	B	A	A	C	A	C	C
21	**22**	**23**	**24**	**25**	**26**	**27**	**28**	**29**	**30**
C	D	A	C	C	C	D	A	B	C
31	**32**	**33**	**34**	**35**	**36**	**37**	**38**	**39**	**40**
D	D	D	B	D	D	B	C	B	D
41	**42**	**43**	**44**	**45**	**46**	**47**	**48**	**49**	**50**
D	C	C	D	A	C	C	A	A	C
51									
B									

1. Consider the following statements with reference to doldrums—
1. Dolrums comprise the equatorial belt of low atmospheric pressure.
2. The trade winds converge at doldrums.
3. There is strong upward movement of air in doldrums.
4. Doldrums are characterized by turbulent weather.

Which of the statements given above are correct?
A. 1 and 2 only
B. 3 and 4 only
C. 1, 2 and 3 only
D. 1, 2, 3 and 4

2. Which one among the following is nearest to the Tropic of Cancer?
A. Patna   B. Ranchi
C. Rourkela   D. Varanasi

3. Match List-I (Type of Rocks) with List-II (Example) and select the correct answer using the code given below the lists—

List-I (Type of Rocks)	List-II (Example)
(a) Igneous Rocks	1. Basalt and Granite
(b) Metamorphic Rocks	2. Limestone and Sandstone
(c) Sedimentary Rocks	3. Marble and Quartzite

Codes:

	(a)	(b)	(c)
A.	1	2	3
B.	1	3	2
C.	2	3	1
D.	3	1	2

4. Match List-I (Volcano) with List-II (Country) and select the correct answer using the codes given below the lists—

List-I (Volcano)	List-II (Country)
(a) Semeru	1. Indonesia
(b) Cotopaxi	2. Ecuador
(c) Etna	3. Italy
(d) Kilimanjaro	3. Kenya
	5. India

Codes:

	(a)	(b)	(c)	(d)
A.	1	2	3	4
B.	3	4	5	2
C.	1	4	3	2
D.	3	2	5	4

5. The 'Agulhas' water current flows through which one of the following oceans?
A. South Atlantic Ocean
B. North Atlantic Ocean
C. Indian Ocean
D. North Pacific Ocean

6. Consider the following statements—
1. Rainfall in the doldrums is of convectional type.
2. In China type climate, rainfall occurs throughout the year.

Which of the statements given above is/are correct?
A. 1 only   B. 2 only
C. Both 1 and 2   D. Neither 1 nor 2

7. In which one of the following regions of the world, are the grasslands called Campo found?
A. Brazil   B. China
C. Eurasia   D. North America

8. In India, in which one of the following areas are the tropical evergreen forests found?
A. The Western Ghats
B. The Eastern Ghats
C. The Western Himalaya
D. The Central Himalaya

9. Match List-I (Location) with List-II (Industry) and select the correct answer using the codes given below the lists—

List-I	List-II
(Location)	**(Industry)**
(a) Moradabad	1. Cotton Textile Industry
(b) Mathura	2. Iron and Steel Industry
(c) Salem	3. Oil Refinery
(d) Coimbatore	4. Copper and Brass Industry

Codes:

	(a)	(b)	(c)	(d)
A.	4	3	2	1
B.	4	2	3	1
C.	1	3	2	4
D.	1	2	3	4

10. Match List-I (Atomic Power Plant) with List-II (State) and select the correct answer using the codes given below the lists—

List-I	List-II
(Atomic Power Plant)	**(States)**
(a) Kalpakkam	1. Karnataka
(b) Narora	2. Madhya Pradesh
(c) Rawatbhata	3. Maharashtra
(d) Tarapur	4. Rajasthan
	5. Tamil Nadu
	6. Uttar Pradesh

Codes:

	(a)	(b)	(c)	(d)
A.	1	6	4	2
B.	1	4	6	2
C.	5	6	4	3
D.	5	4	6	3

11. Match List-I (Place of Economic Importance) with List-II (State) and select the correct answer using the code given below the lists—

List-I	List-II
(Place of Economic Importance	**(State)**
(a) Alwaye	1. Gujarat
(b) Kaiga	2. Jharkhand
(c) Giridih	3. Karnataka
(d) Kakrapar	4. Kerala

Codes:

	(a)	(b)	(c)	(d)
A.	1	2	3	4
B.	1	3	2	4
C.	4	2	3	1
D.	4	3	2	1

12. Match List-I (Town) with List-II (Factory/Plant) and select the correct answer using the codes given below the lists—

List-I	List-II
(Town)	**(Factory/Plant)**
(a) Namrup	1. Aluminium Plant
(b) Vishakhapatnam	2. Steel Plant
(c) Perambur	3. Fertilizer Plant
(d) Renukoot	4. Integral Coach Factory

Codes:

	(a)	(b)	(c)	(d)
A.	1	2	4	3
B.	1	4	2	3
C.	3	2	4	1
D.	3	4	2	1

13. Which one of the following towns is well-known for its aluminium industry?

A. Coimbatore   B. Koraput
C. Ranchi   D. Rourkela

14. At which one of the following towns do National Highway Nos. 6 and 7 cross each other?

A. Bhopal   B. Gwalior
C. Jhansi   D. Nagpur

15. Which one of the following pairs is not correctly matched?

Town		River
A. Bharuch	:	Narmada
B. Surat	:	Tapi
C. Vijayawada	:	Krishna
D. Vishakhapatnam	:	Krishna

16. In which one of the following States is Zojila Pass located?

A. Arunachal Pradesh
B. Jammu and Kashmir
C. Himachal Pradesh
D. Sikkim

17. Match List-I (Town) with List-II (River) and select the correct answer using the code given below the lists—

List-I		**List-II**
(Town)		*(River)*
(a) Nanded	1.	Godavari
(b) Nellore	2.	Tungbhadra
(c) Hospet	3.	Musi
(d) Hyderabad	4.	Penneru

Codes:

	(a)	*(b)*	*(c)*	*(d)*
A.	1	4	2	3
B.	1	2	4	3
C.	3	4	2	1
D.	3	2	4	1

18. Which one of the following pairs is/are correctly matched?

1. Hirakud Reservoir : Sambalpur
2. Ukai Reservoir : Amravati
3. Tawa Reservoir : Pachmarhi

Select the correct answer using the codes given below:

Codes:

A. 1 only   B. 1 and 3 only
C. 1 and 2 only   D. 1, 2 and 3

19. Chaurabari glacier is located towards—
A. South of Kedarnath temple
B. West of Kedarnath temple
C. North of Kedarnath temple
D. East of Kedarnath temple

20. Which one of the following is not correctly matched?
A. Bailadila – Madhya Pradesh
B. Kemangundi – Karnataka
C. Singhbhum – Jharkhand
D. Mayurbhanj – Odisha

21. Arrange the following States in descending order of their length of National Highways. Use the codes given below to select the correct answer.
(a) Arunachal Pradesh
(b) Mizoram
(c) Nagaland
(d) Sikkim

A. *(b)*   *(b)*   *(c)*   *(d)*
B. *(a)*   *(b)*   *(c)*   *(d)*
C. *(d)*   *(c)*   *(b)*   *(a)*
D. *(c)*   *(d)*   *(a)*   *(b)*

22. Which one of the following is not the leading producer of petroleum in India?
A. Uttar Pradesh   B. Gujarat
C. Maharashtra   D. Assam

23. In which country is 'Takla Makan' desert situated?
A. Kazakhstan   B. Russia
C. USA   D. China

24. Which one of the following States does not produce Mica?
A. Jharkhand   B. Madhya Pradesh
C. Rajasthan   D. Andhra Pradesh

25. Which one of the following rivers does not pass through Uttar Pradesh?
A. Ganga   B. Yamuna
C. Ramganga   D. Jhelum

26. Sarnath is in the State of—
A. Kerala   B. Maharashtra
C. Gujarat   D. Uttar Pradesh

27. Which one of the following is not correctly matched?
A. Ramagundam – Fertilizer
B. Chittaranjan – Locomotive
C. Korba – Aluminium
D. Pimpri – Pesticides

28. Which one of the following is correctly matched?
A. Wet winter dry summer – Italy
B. Wet throughout the year – Sudan
C. Wet summer dry winter – Iran
D. Dry throughout the year – Chile

29. Mount Titlis is in—
A. Germany   B. France
C. Switzerland   D. U.S.A.

30. Which one of the following is correctly matched?
A. Hamburg – Elbe river
B. Belgrade – Seine river
C. Kiev – Don river
D. Lahore – Sutlej river

31. Which State of U.S.A. is also known as the 'Blue Grass State'?
   A. California
   B. Kentucky
   C. Montana
   D. Texas

32. Which one of the following is not correctly matched?
   A. Donbas Basin – Coal
   B. Mesabi Range – Copper
   C. Mosul – Petroleum
   D. Transvaal – Gold

33. Which of the following pairs does not match?
   A. Trans Siberian Railway – Moscow to Vladivostok
   B. Canadian Pacific Railway – Halifax to Vancouver
   C. Orient Express Railway – Paris to Istanbul
   D. Cape Cairo Railway – Warsaw to Madrid

34. Which is the newer mountain range?
   A. Aravali
   B. Satpura
   C. Vindhyachal
   D. Himalaya

35. Which of the following are connected by Suez canal?
   A. Red Sea and Dead Sea
   B. Red Sea and Arabian Sea
   C. Red Sea and Mediterranean Sea
   D. Red Sea and Black Sea

36. Which of the following ports is *not* situated at Pacific coast?
   A. Vancouver
   B. Los Angeles
   C. San Francisco
   D. Miami

37. Which of the following airports is not situated at New York-Tokyo air route?
   A. London
   B. Paris
   C. Rome
   D. Panama

38. In which region of the world are nights the winters?
   A. Tundra region
   B. Mediterranean region
   C. Tropical desert region
   D. Equatorial region

39. Which of the following is not the most developed part of the world?
   A. Most of the Western Europe
   B. Japan
   C. Nepal
   D. South-East Australia

40. How much is the area of India?
   A. 32,87,263 sq. km
   B. 99,76,140 sq. km
   C. 95,97,000 sq. km
   D. 31,40,200 sq. km

41. Which is the southern-most point of India?
   A. Kanyakumari
   B. Goa
   C. Indira point
   D. Rameshwaram

42. From economic point of view, the most important rocks are—
   A. Dharwar
   B. Gondwana
   C. Vindhyan
   D. Cuddapah

43. Which river is known as the 'Sorrow of Bihar'?
   A. Kosi
   B. Chambal
   C. Gandak
   D. Sone

44. In which state are the Mahadeo hills located?
   A. Bihar
   B. Rajasthan
   C. Madhya pradesh
   D. Chhttisgarh

45. The 'Kalabaisakhis' originate during—
   A. Winter season
   B. Rainy season
   C. Period of retreating monsoon
   D. Summers

46. What type of forests are the 'Sunderbans'?
   A. Tidal forests
   B. Monsoon forests
   C. Tropical Evergreen forests
   D. Temperate Evergreen forests

47. The 'Regur' soil is—
   A. Red soil
   B. Black soil
   C. Alluvial soil
   D. None of these

48. Which river basin has the maximum amount of water available for irrigation?
   A. The Ganga
   B. The Indus
   C. The Brahmaputra
   D. Mahanadi

49. Which state of India is the largest producer of Iron ore?
   A. Karnataka
   B. Odisha
   C. Jharkhand
   D. Madhya Pradesh

50. Which mineral is known as 'Black Gold'?
A. Iron ore　　　　　　B. Bauxite
C. Coal　　　　　　　　D. Manganese

51. Which food grain occupies the largest cropped area in India?
A. Maize　　　　　　　B. Wheat
C. Rice　　　　　　　　D. Sugarcane

52. Which of the following states is the largest producer of wheat?
A. Punjab　　　　　　　B. Uttar Pradesh
C. Haryana　　　　　　D. Madhya Pradesh

53. The leading jowar (Sorghum) producing state in India is—
A. Maharashtra　　　　B. Andhra Pradesh
C. Karnataka　　　　　D. Bihar

54. Which of the following is a cash crop?
A. Rice　　　　　　　　B. Wheat
C. Jowar　　　　　　　D. Sugarcane

55. Which of the following states is the leading producer of sugarcane in India?
A. Uttar Pradesh　　　B. Madhya Pradesh
C. Punjab　　　　　　　D. Bihar

56. Which Indian state has the highest per hectare production of cotton?
A. Haryana　　　　　　B. Maharashtra
C. Tamil Nadu　　　　D. Punjab

57. Which state is the largest producer of tea in India?
A. Assam　　　　　　　B. West Bengal
C. Kerala　　　　　　　D. Karnataka

58. In India, the local name of shifting cultivation is—
A. Jhum　　　　　　　B. Kumari
C. Penda　　　　　　　D. All of these

59. Which of the following is called the 'Cottonopolis' of India?
A. Kanpur　　　　　　　B. Agra
C. Mumbai　　　　　　D. Ahmedabad

60. Which of the following states does ***not*** have common boundary with Madhya Pradesh?
A. Gujarat　　　　　　B. Rajasthan
C. Jharkhand　　　　　D. Bihar

61. Which state of India is the largest producer of diamond?
A. Madhya Pradesh　　B. Chhattisgarh
C. Jharkhand　　　　　D. Rajasthan

62. Which of the following landforms is formed by glacier?
A. Tarn　　　　　　　　B. Lagoon
C. Lappies　　　　　　D. Doline

▰ ANSWERS ▰

1	2	3	4	5	6	7	8	9	10
D	B	B	A	C	A	A	A	A	C

11	12	13	14	15	16	17	18	19	20
D	C	B	D	D	B	A	A	C	A

21	22	23	24	25	26	27	28	29	30
A	A	D	B	D	D	D	A	C	A

31	32	33	34	35	36	37	38	39	40
B	B	D	D	C	D	D	C	C	A

41	42	43	44	45	46	47	48	49	50
C	A	A	C	D	A	B	B	B	C

51	52	53	54	55	56	57	58	59	60
C	B	A	D	A	D	A	D	C	D

61	62
A	A

1. Trade in invisible refers to—
   A. Unrecorded trade
   B. Smuggling
   C. Trade in military goods
   D. Trade in services

2. The maximum number of people in India work in the—
   A. Primary sector
   B. Secondary sector
   C. Tertiary sector
   D. None of the above

3. Investment in public works is known as—
   A. Revenue expenditure
   B. Current expenditure
   C. Capital expenditure
   D. Both B and C

4. Who appoints the Finance Commission in India?
   A. President
   B. Prime Minister
   C. Finance Minister
   D. Governor of Reserve Bank of India

5. Which of the following is direct tax?
   A. Sales tax
   B. Excise duty
   C. Custom duty
   D. None of the above

6. The merit of zero-based budgeting is that—
   A. Tax liability is reduced
   B. Profit goes up
   C. Deficit financing becomes zero
   D. Expenditure is rationalised

7. Misery Index represents—
   A. Product of rate of inflation and rate of unemployment
   B. Proportion of very poors to poors living below poverty line
   C. Sum of rate of inflation and rate of unemployment
   D. Both A and B

8. Which one of the following is *not* an objective of fiscal policy?
   A. Economic growth
   B. Economic stability
   C. Maximisation of employment level
   D. Regulation of financial institutions

9. 'National Development Council' in India was constituted in the year—
   A. 1945   B. 1948
   C. 1952   D. 1965

10. Which of the following *does not* form a part of the foreign exchange reserves in India?
    A. Gold
    B. Special Drawing Rights
    C. Foreign currency assets
    D. Foreign currency and securities held by the bank and corporate bodies

11. Which Five-Year Plan had 'poverty-alleviation' as one of its objects?
    A. First Plan   B. Third Plan
    C. Fifth Plan   D. Seventh Plan

12. The 'Repo rate' is—
    A. Share brokerage rate
    B. Short-term interest rate
    C. Bond discount rate
    D. The spread between foreign currency buying and selling prices

13. Which one of the following statements is correct with regard to tax?
    A. Tax is a compulsory payment
    B. Tax and fee both are compulsory payments
    C. Tax is a voluntary payment
    D. Tax and fee both are voluntary payments

14. GNP can be defined as—
   A. NNP + Direct taxes
   B. NNP + Export
   C. NNP + Indirect taxes
   D. NNP + Depreciation

15. Open market operations are a part of—
   A. Monetary Policy
   B. Fiscal Policy
   C. Foreign Trade Policy
   D. Industrial Policy

16. NABARD is—
   A. An Autonomous Public Sector Institution
   B. A Subsidiary of SBI (State Bank of India)
   C. A Nationalised Public Sector Bank
   D. An Apex Agricultural Sector Bank

17. Fiscal Policy is concerned with—
   A. Export and Import
   B. Public Revenue and Expenditure
   C. Issue of Currency
   D. Population Control

18. One among the following is not a Central Government tax.
   A. Income tax
   B. Custom tax
   C. Land revenue
   D. Central excise

19. MUDRA Bank has been set-up with the corpus of .... crore.
   A. ₹ 25,000   B. ₹ 20,000
   C. ₹ 50,000   D. ₹ 1,00,000

20. Foreign Exchange Reserves of India are kept in the custody of—
   A. International Bank for Reconstruction and Development
   B. International Monetary Fund
   C. Government Treasury
   D. Reserve Bank of India

21. Which of the following terms is not used in Banking World?
   A. Credit   B. Absolute Zero
   C. Rate   D. Discount

22. Out of the following, which country is dependent on others for the raw material for its Iron-Steel industry?
   A. England   B. Australia
   C. Japan   D. Turkey

23. Which of the following industries are the major beneficiaries of the Mumbai port?
   A. Iron and Steel industry
   B. Sugar and Cotton textile industry
   C. Cotton textile and Petrochemical industry
   D. Engineering and Fertilizer industry

24. In the law of demand, the statement 'Other things remain constant' means—
   A. Income of consumer should not change
   B. Price of other goods should not change
   C. Taste of consumer should not change
   D. All of the above

25. A firm is in equilibrium when its—
   A. Marginal cost equals the marginal revenue
   B. Total cost is minimum
   C. Total revenue is maximum
   D. Average revenue and marginal revenue are equal

26. The World Trade Organisation (WTO) was earlier known as—
   A. GATT   B. UNICEF
   C. UNCTAD   D. FAO

27. Given the money wages, if the price level in an economy increases, then the real wages will—
   A. Increase   B. Decrease
   C. Remain constant D. Become flexible

28. The difference between visible exports and visible imports is defined as—
   A. Balance of trade
   B. Balance of payment
   C. Balanced terms of trade
   D. Gains from trade

29. What is Value Added Tax (VAT)?
   A. A simple, transparent, easy to pay tax imposed on consumers

B. A new initiative taken by the Government to increase the tax-burden of high income groups

C. A single tax that replaces State taxes like, surcharge, turnover tax, etc.

D. A new tax to be imposed on the producers of capital good

30. The outcome of 'devaluation of currency' is—
A. Increased export and improvement in balance of payment
B. Increased export and foreign reserve deficiency
C. Increased import and improvement in balance of payment
D. Increased export and import

31. In India, 'yellow revolution' is associated with—
A. Production of paddy
B. Production of oilseeds
C. Production of tea
D. Production of flower

32. Which of the following is considered a cash crop in India?
A. Maize   B. Gram
C. Onion   D. Wheat

33. The term 'Green GNP' emphasizes—
A. Rapid growth of GNP
B. Increase in per capita income
C. Economic development
D. Sustainable development

34. The common currency which has been introduced among many European Nations is known as—
A. Euro Pound   B. Euro
C. Euro Dollar   D. None of these

35. What is referred to as 'Depository Services'?
A. A new scheme of fixed deposits
B. A method regulating stock exchanges
C. An agency for safe-keeping of securities
D. An advisory service to investors

36. A meeting of the shareholders held only once during the life time of the company is known as—

A. Meeting of the Directors
B. Meeting of the Creditors
C. Extraordinary General Meeting
D. Statutory Meeting

37. The first Stock Exchange in India was established in—
A. Calcutta   B. Delhi
C. Bombay   D. Madras

38. Blue Chips Shares mean—
A. Those shares which are listed in Stock Exchange
B. Those shares whose guarantee is given by Government
C. Those shares on shown dividend is paid at higher rate regularly
D. Those shares which are issued at first time

39. FEMA stands for—
A. Foreign Exchange Management Act
B. Funds Exchange Management Act
C. Finance Enhancement Monetary Act
D. Future Exchange Management Act

40. Which of the following is false about WTO?
A. It is the main organ for implementing the Multilateral Trade Agreement
B. It is global in its membership
C. It has far wider scope than GATT
D. Only countries having more than prescribed level of total GDP can become its member

41. Convertibility of the rupee implies—
A. Being able to convert rupees notes into gold
B. Allowing the value of the rupee to be fixed by market-forces
C. Freely permitting the conversion of rupee to other major currencies and *vice versa*
D. Developing an international market for currencies in India

42. .... has been founded to act as permanent watchdog on the international trade.
A. ISRD   B. ADS
C. WTO   D. DIMF

43. Which of the following statement is correct?
   A. The disinvestment programme has been successfully carried out in India
   B. Privatisation up to 100% has been carried out in all the PSU in India
   C. Under strategic sale method of disinvestment, the government sells a major share to a strategic partner
   D. None of the above

44. Which, institution is known as the 'Soft Loan Window' of World Bank?
   A. IFC (International Financial Corporation)
   B. IDA (International Development Association)
   C. IMF (International Monetary Fund)
   D. Indian Development Forum

45. Which is not a insurable risk?
   A. Accident Risk
   B. Loss of Crops Risk
   C. The Risk of Trading in New Market
   D. The Risk of Sinking of a Ship

46. The Life Insurance in India was nationalised in the year—
   A. 1870   B. 1956
   C. 1960   D. 1966

47. Fire Insurance is based on the principle of—
   A. Utmost Good faith
   B. Insurable Interest
   C. Indemnity
   D. Cooperation

48. Heroin is obtained from—
   A. Indian hemp   B. Opium poppy
   C. Tobacco   D. Arecanut

49. 'Varuna' is a variety of—
   A. Mustard   B. Linseed
   C. Sunflower   D. Sesamum

50. Farming of cloves is done in—
   A. Kerala   B. Karnataka
   C. Tamil Nadu   D. Uttar Pradesh

51. In India, the largest area under rice cultivation lies in the State of—
   A. Andhra Pradesh   B. Odisha
   C. Uttar Pradesh   D. West Bengal

52. The most popular sport goods come from—
   A. Ludhiana   B. Jalandhar
   C. Kanpur   D. Agra

53. After the merger of Air India and Indian Airlines, the new entity is now known as—
   A. Air India   B. India Airlines
   C. Indian Airways   D. Inod-Air

54. Which sector got high rate of growth in its cooperative units?
   A. Sugar   B. Cotton textile
   C. Jute   D. Cement

◄ ANSWERS ►

1	2	3	4	5	6	7	8	9	10
D	A	C	A	D	C	B	D	C	D

11	12	13	14	15	16	17	18	19	20
C	B	A	D	A	B	B	C	B	D

21	22	23	24	25	26	27	28	29	30
B	C	D	B	C	A	C	C	A	D

31	32	33	34	35	36	37	38	39	40
B	C	D	B	C	D	C	C	A	D

41	42	43	44	45	46	47	48	49	50
C	C	C	B	C	B	C	B	A	A

51	52	53	54
C	B	A	B

1. Carbon dating is used to determine the age of—
   A. Fossils   B. Plants
   C. Rocks   D. None of the above

2. The function of haemoglobin in body is—
   A. Transport of Oxygen
   B. Destruction of Bacteria
   C. Prevention of Anaemia
   D. Utilisation of Iron

3. What is measured in cusecs?
   A. Purity of water   B. Depth of water
   C. Flow of water   D. Quality of water

4. What is the mineral composition of diamond?
   A. Carbon   B. Nitrogen
   C. Nickel   D. Zinc

5. The stars receive their energy from which of the following?
   A. Nuclear fusion   B. Nuclear fission
   C. Chemical reaction   D. Gravitational pull

6. Ozone layer of atmosphere absorbs—
   A. Cosmic rays   B. Infra red rays
   C. Ultraviolet rays   D. All radiations

7. The fuel used in Fast Breeder Test Reactor at Kalpakkam is—
   A. Enriched Uranium   B. Thorium
   C. Plutonium   D. Tungsten

8. Chemical energy is coverted into Electrical energy by—
   A. Electrolysis   B. Photosynthesis
   C. Respiration   D. Transpiration

9. In integrated circuit the chip of semi-conductor used is made up of—
   A. Beryllium   B. Carbon
   C. Silicon   D. Zircon

10. When kidneys fail to function, there is accumulation of—
    A. Fats in the body
    B. Proteins in the body
    C. Sugar in the blood
    D. Nitrogenous waste products in the blood

11. Chemical composition of pearl is—
    A. Calcium Carbonate
    B. Calcium Carbonate and Magnesium Carbonate
    C. Calcium Chloride
    D. Calcium Sulphate

12. Which of the following disease is hereditary?
    A. Haemophillia   B. Tuberculosis
    C. Cancer   D. Dysentery

13. Acid rain is caused by pollution of environment by—
    A. Carbon monoxide and Carbon dioxide
    B. Carbon dioxide and Nitrogen
    C. Ozone and Carbon dioxide
    D. Nitrous oxide and Sulphur dioxide

14. Which of the following proteins is found in milk?
    A. Aglutinin   B. Casein
    C. Myosin   D. Haemoglobin

15. Blood grouping was discovered by—
    A. Landsteriner   B. William Harvey
    C. Robert Koch   D. Louis Pasteur

16. Jaundice affects the—
    A. Pancreas   B. Stomach
    C. Liver   D. Intestine

17. When a person becomes older, his blood pressure generally—
    A. Decreases   B. Increases
    C. Remains the same   D. Varies widely

18. The fourth dimension in Physics was introduced by—
    A. Newton   B. Einstein
    C. Galileo   D. Neil Bohr

19. The hormone insulin which is used in treating diabetes was discovered by—
A. F.G. Banting
B. Schleiden and Schwann
C. Brown
D. Hooke

20. In Pathology excess of white corpuscles in the blood is called—
A. Anoxia   B. Leukaemia
C. Anaemia   D. Septicemia

21. Doctors recommend that we should cook our food in oil rather than in Vanasapti ghee because—
A. Oil contains unsaturated fats
B. Oil contains saturated fats
C. Oil is easier to store
D. Oil is cheaper

22. What is meant by energy crisis?
A. Shortage of hydro electricity
B. Mal nutrition leading to short supply of energy in the body
C. Shortage of thermal power
D. Danger of extinction of fossil fuel like coal and petrol

23. Pyrometers are used to measure—
A. Depth   B. Humidity
C. Temperature D. Altitudes

24. Cholesterol is a—
A. Type of chlorophyll
B. Derivative of chloroform
C. Fatty alcohol found in animal fat
D. Chromium salt

25. In a normal healthy man rate of heart beat per minute is—
A. 60 times   B. 78 times
C. 120 times   D. 72 times

26. Normally how many pairs of chromosomes are there in the human body?
A. 46   B. 43
C. 23   D. 24

27. Which of these metals is the best conductor of electricity?
A. Lead   B. Silver
C. Copper   D. Aluminium

28. Who was the first Man to set foot on the Moon?
A. Yuri Gagarin   B. Amundson
C. Roben Pears   D. Neil Armstrong

29. Light from the Sun takes so much time to reach the Earth—
A. 8 seconds
B. 12 minutes
C. 8 minutes (Approximately)
D. 4 minutes

30. pH of pure water is—
A. 14   B. 2
C. 7   D. 9

31. Haemophilia is a genetic disease which is caused by—
A. Fall in Haemoglobin level
B. Rheumatic heart
C. Absence of clotting of blood
D. Fall in number of white blood cells

32. How much percentage of protein is present in Soyabean?
A. 30%   B. 40%
C. 50%   D. 60%

33. Which gas is used in preparation of Soda Water?
A. Carbon Monoxide
B. Chlorine
C. Carbon Dioxide
D. Carbon

34. Mammals which can fly, is—
A. Whale   B. Bat
C. Emu   D. Kangaroo

35. How much %age of nitrogen is present in the Atmosphere?
A. 10%   B. 33%
C. 50%   D. 78%

36. Steel ball floats on mercury because—
A. nothing can sink in mercury
B. density of mercury is higher than steel
C. density of steel is higher than mercury
D. ball cannot float

37. Enzymes are made of mostly the following—
A. fats   B. proteins
C. carbonic acid D. carbohydrate

38. What is an atomic reactor?
 A. A reservoir of heavy water
 B. Atomic Bhatti in which nuclear fission produces heat
 C. A chemical reservoir
 D. An atom bomb

39. Who invented Polio-vaccine?
 A. Neil Bohr
 B. Jonas Salk
 C. Homi Bhabha
 D. Lord Chelmsford

40. 'Decibel' is used to measure—
 A. Haemoglobin in blood
 B. Sugar in urine
 C. Sound in atmosphere
 D. Particles in air

41. Match List-I with List-II and select the correct answer using the codes given below the lists—

List-I	List-II
(a) Retinol	1. Vitamin-E
(b) Ascorbic acid	2. Vitamin-C
(c) Calciferol	3. Vitamin-A
(d) Tocopherol	4. Vitamin-D

Codes:

	(a)	(b)	(c)	(d)
A.	3	2	1	4
B.	3	2	4	1
C.	2	3	4	1
D.	2	3	1	4

42. Match List-I with List-II and select the correct answer using the codes given below the lists—

List-I (Vitamin)	List-II (Deficiency Disease)
(a) Vitamin-A	1. Scurvy
(b) Vitamin-C	2. Pallagra
(c) Vitamin-B_1	3. Xerophthamia
(d) Vitamin-B_5	4. Beri-beri

Codes:

	(a)	(b)	(c)	(d)
A.	3	1	2	4
B.	1	3	4	2
C.	3	1	4	2
D.	1	3	2	4

43. Arrange the following colours of light in increasing order of their wavelength—
 1. Violet 2. Green
 3. Yellow 4. Red
 A. 1, 2, 3, 4 B. 1, 3, 2, 4
 C. 4, 3, 2, 1 D. None of these

44. Which part of the cell is called its power house?
 A. Nucleus B. Centrosome
 C. Mitochondria D. Plastics

45. The only source of Nitrogen in human body which is essential for replacement of body cells is—
 A. Amino-acids B. Carbohydrates
 C. Mineral salts D. Lipids

46. Which of the following vitamins is essential for the formation of prothrombin which is essential for normal clotting of blood?
 A. Vitamin-D B. Vitamin-E
 C. Vitamin-K D. Vitamin-B

47. Match the following

List-I	List-II
(a) Carborundum	1. Chlorophicrin
(b) Gammexane	2. Sodium Aluminium, Silicon
(c) Lapis Lazuli	3. Benzene Hexachloride
(d) Tear Gas	4. Silicon Carbide

Codes:

	(a)	(b)	(c)	(d)
A.	4	3	1	2
B.	4	3	2	1
C.	3	4	2	1
D.	3	4	1	2

48. Match the following—

List-I	List-II
(a) Capacity	1. coloumb
(b) Charge	2. farad
(c) Potential	3. volt
(d) Power	4. watt

Codes:

	(a)	(b)	(c)	(d)
A.	1	2	4	3
B.	1	2	3	4
C.	2	1	3	4
D.	2	1	4	3

49. Different forms of a chemical element are called—
- A. isotopes
- B. allotropes
- C. isotones
- D. None of these

50. In a simple pendulum the force acting on the bob—
- A. is maximum when the bob is passing through its initial equilibrium position
- B. is maximum when the bob is at its maximum displacement position
- C. is constant throughout the motion of the bob
- D. becomes zero as soon as the bob starts moving

51. Any substance capable of affecting the rate of chemical reaction without changing itself is called—
- A. Reachant
- B. Oxidiser
- C. Catalyst
- D. Reducer

52. Acid rain is caused due to emission of which of the following into the atmosphere?
- A. oxides of nitrogen and sulphur
- B. carbon-di-oxide and carbon mono-oxide
- C. ozone and carbon-di-oxide
- D. nitrogen and carbon-mono-oxide

53. Which one of the following diseases is caused through the wound or injury or surfaces of unsterilised surgical instruments?
- A. Kala Azar
- B. Chancroid
- C. Diphtheria
- D. Tetanus

54. Which of the following organs of the human body breaks down the old red blood cells and stores iron from them?
- A. Kidney
- B. Gall bladder
- C. Pancreas
- D. Spleen

55. What is the correct sequence in the increasing order of heat energy received per unit area from the sun as measured on Earth, Mars and Jupiter?
- A. Jupiter > Mars > Earth
- B. Earth > Mars > Jupiter
- C. Jupiter > Earth > Mars
- D. Earth > Jupiter > Mars

56. Urea is a—
- A. Sodium fertilizer
- B. Phosphatic fertilizer
- C. Nitrogenous fertilizer
- D. Potassium fertilizer

57. Which one of the following spices is obtained from flower buds?
- A. Clove
- B. Cardamom
- C. Turmeric
- D. Coriander

58. Which climate is required for better growth and production of crops?
- A. Hot dry
- B. Cold dry
- C. Cold-moist
- D. Hot moist

■ANSWERS■

1	2	3	4	5	6	7	8	9	10
A	A	C	A	A	C	A	A	C	D
11	**12**	**13**	**14**	**15**	**16**	**17**	**18**	**19**	**20**
A	A	D	B	A	C	A	B	A	B
21	**22**	**23**	**24**	**25**	**26**	**27**	**28**	**29**	**30**
A	D	C	C	D	C	B	D	C	C
31	**32**	**33**	**34**	**35**	**36**	**37**	**38**	**39**	**40**
C	D	C	B	D	B	B	B	B	C
41	**42**	**43**	**44**	**45**	**46**	**47**	**48**	**49**	**50**
B	C	A	C	A	C	B	C	B	B
51	**52**	**53**	**54**	**55**	**56**	**57**	**58**		
C	A	D	D	B	C	A	B		

1. The Pulitzer Prize is associated with which one of the following?
   A. Environmental Protection
   B. Olympic Games
   C. Journalism
   D. Civil Aviation

2. Dada Saheb Phalke Awards are given for showing excellence in the field of—
   A. Journalism
   B. Literature
   C. Sports
   D. Cinema

3. Who among the following scientists has been conferred upon 'Bharat Ratna'?
   A. C.N.R. Rao
   B. K.L. Mashelker
   C. G.P. Rao
   D. Hariharan Parthsarthi

4. 'BAFTA' award is associated with—
   A. Banking Sector
   B. Cinema
   C. Insurance Sector
   D. Tourism

5. Who among the following Pakistani national was awarded 'Bharat Ratna' by the Indian Government?
   A. Khan Abdul Ghaffar Khan
   B. Liaqat Ali Khan
   C. M. A. Jinnah
   D. Muhammad Iqbal

6. Which of the following awards is given for excellence in the field of Literature?
   A. N. Borlaug Award
   B. Kalinga Prize
   C. Kishor Kumar Award
   D. Saraswati Samman

7. Which of the following awards is given for excellence in the field of sports?
   A. Kalidas Samman
   B. Shanti Swarup Bhatnagar Award
   C. Jananpith Award
   D. Arjun Award

8. 'Booker Prize' is given in the field of—
   A. Literature
   B. Social Service
   C. Films
   D. Science

9. Dronacharya Awards are given to a person associated with—
   A. Education
   B. Social service
   C. Journalism
   D. Sports

10. Padma Bhushan Award is—
    A. Gallantry Award
    B. Bravery Award
    C. Civilian Award
    D. Literary Award

11. Saraswati Samman is an award given for excellence in the field of—
    A. Sports
    B. Social Service
    C. Literature
    D. Science and Technology

12. Which of the following is known as the Nobel Prize in architecture?
    A. Pulitzer Prize
    B. Abel Prize
    C. Pritzker Prize
    D. None of the above

13. International Merlin Award is given in the field of—
    A. Architecture
    B. Magic
    C. Literature
    D. Music

14. Vyas Samman is given for excellence in the field of—
    A. Literature
    B. Science
    C. Dance
    D. Economics

15. Which is the highest civilian award in India?
    A. Padam Shri
    B. Padam Bhushan
    C. Padam Vibhushan
    D. Bharat Ratna

16. Which among the following awards is given to sportspersons by the Government of Madhya Pradesh?
    A. Arjuna Award
    B. Vikram Award
    C. Dronacharya Award
    D. Khel Ratna Award

17. Who among the following is a Nobel Prize winner?
A. M.K. Gandhi
B. J.L. Nehru
C. Kailash Satyarthi
D. Sardar Patel

18. With reference to the Government of India's various programmes what is Nirmal Gram Puraskar?
A. It is an incentive scheme of scholarships for the single girl child in families in villages
B. It is an incentive scheme of scholarship for female sportspersons from villages, who represent their states in any game
C. It is an incentive scheme for schools in the villages for computer education
D. It is an incentive scheme for Panchayati Raj institutions

19. In which country is the committee which selects winners for Nobel Peace Prize located?
A. Norway
B. Sweden
C. Finland
D. Denmark

20. 'Jnanpith Award' is given for the excellence in the field of—
A. Music
B. Politics
C. Literature
D. Sports

21. 'National Kabir Samman' is given by the Govt. of—
A. Madhya Pradesh
B. Uttar Pradesh
C. Rajasthan
D. Odisha

22. Which among the following awards is associated with the field of dancing?
A. Rukmini Devi Award
B. Shankar Puraskar
C. Aga Khan Award
D. Prem Bhatia Award

23. Amartya Sen was awarded the Nobel Prize for his contribution to—
A. Development Economics
B. Welfare Economics
C. Monetary Economics
D. Econometrics

24. For a Sri Lankan national the highest civilian honour is—
A. Sri Lanka Bhushan
B. Sri Lanka Ratna
C. Sri Lanka Vibhushan
D. Sri Lanka Bhimanya

25. Which of the following is not a Civilian Award?
A. Bharat Ratna
B. Ashok Chakra
C. Padma Shri
D. Borloug Award

26. Nobel Prize is not awarded in the field of—
A. Medicine
B. Economics
C. Peace
D. Music

27. Who amongst the following is a Nobel Prize winner?
A. Jimmy Carter
B. George Bush
C. Bill Clinton
D. Richard Nixon

28. The Ist recipient of Nehru Award for International Understanding was—
A. Martin Luther King
B. Mother Teresa
C. U. Thant
D. Dr. Jonas Salk

29. Which of the following awards is instituted by the UNESCO?
A. Nehru Award
B. Kalinga Prize
C. Arjuna Award
D. Nobel Prize

30. Oscar awards are associated with—
A. Literature
B. Films
C. Science
D. Sports

31. Consider the following statements—
1. The Nobel Prize Awarding Ceremony takes place on December 10 of every year.
2. The Nobel Prize for Literature was added later on to the other five areas—Physics, Chemistry, Physiology or Medicine, Peace and Economics.

Which of the statements given above is/are correct?
A. 1 only
B. 2 only
C. Both 1 and 2
D. Neither 1 nor 2

32. Dhyan Chand Awards for Lifetime Achievement are given for excellence and life time achievement in the field of—
A. Economics   B. Science
C. Sports   D. Journalism

33. Who amongst the following is not a recipient of Bharat Ratna?
A. A.P.J. Abdul Kalam
B. Satyajit Ray
C. Amartya Sen
D. Rahul Bajaj

34. First Indian who got Nobel Prize was—
A. R.N. Tagore   B. Mother Teresa
C. C.V. Raman   D. Manmohan Singh

35. Which of the following pair about the Indian recipient and their field of Nobel Prize is wrong?
A. R.N. Tagore (1913)—Literature
B. C.V. Raman (1930)—Physics
C. Mother Teresa (1979)—Literature
D. Amritya Sen (1998)—Economics

36. Highest gallantry award of our nation is—
A. Bharat Ratna   B. Mahavir Chakra
C. Paramvir Chakra   D. Vir Chakra

37. Who was the first recipient of Bharat Ratna Award?
A. C. Rajgopalachari
B. B. R. Ambedkar
C. Subhash Chandra Boss
D. Morarji Desai

38. Which of the following pair is wrong about award and their field?
A. Arjun Award   — Sports
B. Dronacharya   — Coaches of Sports
C. Dada Sahib Falke — Film
D. Bhartiya Jnanpith — Medicine

39. Magsysay award for International peace and Understanding is given by the which country?
A. India   B. Russia
C. Philipines   D. Japan

40. Who among the following has won the Nobel Prize at least twice?
A. Winston Churchill
B. Madam Curie
C. Octavio Paz
D. Robert A. Mundell

41. In which of the following years Nobel Prizes were instituted?
A. 1910   B. 1901
C. 1911   D. 1903

42. The writer who refused the Nobel Prize for literature was—
A. Winston Churchill   B. Jcan Paul Sartre
C. Boris Pasternak   D. Prem Chand

43. In which year was the Nobel Prize for Economics announced for the first time?
A. 1901   B. 1919
C. 1969   D. 1970

44. Which country awards the Nobel Prize?
A. USA   B. UK
C. Russia   D. Sweden

45. In how many disciplines or fields Nobel Prizes are awarded?
A. Four   B. Five
C. Six   D. Nine

46. Name the first Arabic writer be awarded Nobel Prize for Literature?
A. Salman Rushdie   B. Gen. Gaddafi
C. Yasser Arafat   D. Naguib Mah Fouz

47. Who among the following was the first recipient of the Rajiv Gandhi Khel Ratna award?
A. Dhanraj Pillai
B. Homi Matiwala
C. Vishwanathan Anand
D. Bahadur Prasad

48. What is the highest award of National distinction for exceptional work in the field of art, literature, science, Sport and public service in India?
A. Nehru Award
B. Jnanpith Award
C. Magsaysay Award
D. Bharat Ratna Award

49. Arjuna Awards are given to individuals for—
   A. outstanding contribution to Indian literature
   B. outstanding contribution towards promotion of international understanding, goodwill and friendship among the people of the world
   C. showing bravery in the face of enemy attack
   D. outstanding contribution for enhancing the glory of the game

50. In which of the following years Arjuna Award were instituted?
   A. 1961   B. 1971
   C. 1951   D. 1965

51. In which year Nehru Award for International Understanding was instituted?
   A. 1965   B. 1969
   C. 1984   D. 1964

52. 'Victory Medal' is awarded in—
   A. the UK   B. the USA
   C. Russia   D. France

53. In which year Indira Gandhi Peace Prize was instituted?
   A. 1985   B. 1984
   C. 1986   D. 1987

54. On which day every year National Awards for Teachers are announced?
   A. November 14   B. November 19
   C. August 15   D. September 5

55. R.D. Birla National Award is given annually for—
   A. outstanding Social Welfare Services
   B. progress and innovation in industry
   C. high productivity
   D. outstanding research work in medical and related fields

56. Kabir, Kalidasa and Tansen Sammans are given by—
   A. Lalit Kala Akademi B. Sahitya Akademi
   C. MP Government   D. Govt of India

57. National film awards were instituted in the year—
   A. 1950   B. 1954
   C. 1961   D. 1969

58. Famous 'Oscar Awards' are presented by the—
   A. American Motion Pictures Association
   B. World Film Society
   C. American Film Society
   D. Academy of Motion Pictures, Arts and Sciences

59. In how many fields, Magsaysay Awards, to commemorate the memory of Ramon Magsaysay, the former President of the Philippines, are awarded?
   A. Four   B. Five
   C. Six   D. Seven

60. In which year was Pulizer Prize instituted?
   A. 1917   B. 1907
   C. 1901   D. 1900

◼ ANSWERS ◼

1	2	3	4	5	6	7	8	9	10
C	D	A	B	A	D	D	A	D	C
11	**12**	**13**	**14**	**15**	**16**	**17**	**18**	**19**	**20**
C	C	B	A	D	B	C	D	A	C
21	**22**	**23**	**24**	**25**	**26**	**27**	**28**	**29**	**30**
A	A	B	D	B	D	A	C	B	B
31	**32**	**33**	**34**	**35**	**36**	**37**	**38**	**39**	**40**
A	C	D	A	C	C	A	D	C	B
41	**42**	**43**	**44**	**45**	**46**	**47**	**48**	**49**	**50**
B	B	C	D	C	D	C	D	D	A
51	**52**	**53**	**54**	**55**	**56**	**57**	**58**	**59**	**60**
D	B	C	D	D	C	B	D	C	A

1. 'Derbi' is associated with the game—
   A. Cricket
   B. Football
   C. Horse riding
   D. Badminton

2. Ranga Swami Cup is awarded in—
   A. Hockey
   B. Football
   C. Horse riding
   D. Volleyball

3. The weight of a Basketball is—
   A. 400-500 ounce
   B. 500-600 gm
   C. 567-650 ounce
   D. 567-650 gm

4. The length and width of a volleyball court is—
   A. 17 × 9 metre
   B. 18 × 9 metre
   C. 19 × 10 metre
   D. 20 × 10 metre

5. Name the first Indian woman who won the Gold Medal in Asian games—
   A. P.T. Usha
   B. Sunita Rani
   C. Shayni Abrahim
   D. Kamaljit Sandhu

6. Which of the following game's playground has 'bonus line'?
   A. Basketball
   B. Hockey
   C. Kabaddi
   D. Volleyball

7. Davis Cup is associated with—
   A. Hockey
   B. Volleyball
   C. Baseball
   D. Lawn Tennis

8. In test cricket, how many bouncers can be bowled in one over?
   A. 1
   B. 2
   C. 3
   D. 4

9. Olympia city is situated in which country of the world?
   A. Greece
   B. Germany
   C. Italy
   D. China

10. 'Set Shot' is related to—
    A. Snooker
    B. Squash
    C. Basketball
    D. Golf

11. The weight of Javelin for women is—
    A. 600 gm
    B. 800 gm
    C. 825 gm
    D. 700 gm

12. Strategy 'Fast break' is related with the game—
    A. Athletics
    B. Basketball
    C. Swimming
    D. Boxing

13. The first National Marathon Race was organized at—
    A. Allahabad
    B. Pune
    C. Kolkata
    D. New Delhi

14. Rovers Cup is associated with the game—
    A. Basketball
    B. Chess
    C. Boxing
    D. Football

15. The highest sports award of India is—
    A. Arjuna Award
    B. Dronacharya Award
    C. Rajeev Gandhi Khel Ratna
    D. Padam Vibhushan

16. The term 'Double Fault' is related with—
    A. Bridge
    B. Golf
    C. Cricket
    D. Lawn Tennis

17. Strategy 'Double Nelson' is related to the game—
    A. Hockey
    B. Athletics
    C. Wrestling
    D. Kho Kho

18. Maulana Azad Trophy is awarded for overall games championship at—
    A. State level
    B. Inter-university level
    C. National games level
    D. International level

19. Which cricketer is known as 'palm tree hitter'?
    A. Kapil Dev
    B. Hanumant Singh
    C. Virendra Sehwag
    D. Polly Umrigar

20. The length of cricket bat is—
  A. 38 inch   B. 39 inch
  C. 37 inch   D. 40 inch

21. Who was the first Indian to win an award in Wimbleldon?
  A. Ramnathan Krishnan
  B. Ramesh Krishnan
  C. Vijay Amritraj
  D. Jaideep Mukherjee

22. The length and width of Badminton court is—
  A. 40 × 25 feet   B. 44 × 20 feet
  C. 35 × 15 feet   D. 44 × 22 feet

23. In which game you can see Antenna—
  A. Basketball   B. Football
  C. Volleyball   D. Tennis

24. According to rules, the colour of football goal post is—
  A. Light yellow   B. Green
  C. Light blue   D. White

25. Which of the following line is related to vollyball?
  A. Bonus line   B. Baulk line
  C. Attack line   D. Service line

26. Which of the following game's team consists of both men and women players?
  A. Corfball   B. Netball
  C. Softball   D. Handball

27. The types of swimming in competitions are—
  A. 10   B. 6
  C. 4   D. 2

28. When did Cricket World Cup start?
  A. 1970   B. 1975
  C. 1979   D. 1973

29. What was the Mascot of first Asian games held at New Delhi?
  A. Jantar Mantar   B. Kutub Minar
  C. Lotus flower   D. Appu

30. The weight of a hockey ball approximately is—

  A. $5\frac{1}{2}$ ounce to $5\frac{3}{4}$ ounce

  B. 5 ounce to $5\frac{1}{2}$ ounce

  C. 6 ounce to $6\frac{1}{2}$ ounce

  D. $5\frac{3}{4}$ ounce to 6 ounce

31. How many events are there in Heptathlan?
  A. 5   B. 6
  C. 7   D. 9

32. 'Pele' is related to which game?
  A. Cricket   B. Horse Riding
  C. Swimming   D. Football

33. Who declares the 'Olympic games close'?
  A. Chairman IOC
  B. President IOC
  C. Secretary IOC
  D. Prime Minister of the country

34. The width of a lane in an athletic track is—
  A. 1.20 mt   B. 1.21 mt
  C. 1.19 mt   D. 1.22 mt

35. The landing arena of High Jump will be—
  A. 5 × 4 mts   B. 5 × 5 mts
  C. 5 × 3 mts   D. 5 × 6 mts

36. The total time limit in Kho-Kho is—
  A. 45 minutes   B. 49 minutes
  C. 55 minutes   D. 59 minutes

37. How many events are there in Decathlon?
  A. 7   B. 8
  C. 9   D. 10

38. The term 'Long Horse' is related with the game—
  A. Horse riding   B. Gymnastics
  C. Polo   D. Show Jumping

39. The height of a hurdle in women 100 metre hurdle race is—
  A. 0.80 metre   B. 0.91 metre
  C. 0.76 metre   D. 0.84 metre

40. The organisation of Olympic games is given to—
  A. City   B. Country
  C. District   D. Capital

41. The length of a standard swimming pool is—
A. 60 metre   B. 50 metre
C. 70 metre   D. 80 metre

42. The skill 'Forward Defence' is related to the game of—
A. Wrestling   B. Judo
C. Cricket   D. Boxing

43. Inner diameter of shot put (Throwing) circle is—
A. 2.50 metre   B. 2.135 metre
C. 1.067 metre   D. 1.076 metre

44. The first woman player got Arjuna Award is—
A. Merry Stephi D'Souza
B. Kamaljit Sandhu
C. P.T. Usha
D. Bala Shambha

45. The length of a cricket pitch is (App.)—
A. 66 feet   B. 68 feet
C. 70 feet   D. 72 feet

46. Modern Olympic Games were started in the year—
A. 1886   B. 1896
C. 1906   D. 1916

47. Shivaji Stadium in Delhi is related with the game of—
A. Football   B. Cricket
C. Hockey   D. Boxing

48. The distance of exchange zone in relay race is—
A. 10 metre   B. 15 metre
C. 20 metre   D. 22 metre

49. Who is the first Indian women cricketer to hit sixer?
A. D. Iduljee
B. Anjali Mehta
C. Asha Agrawal
D. Shanta Rangaswami

50. The total distance of Marathon race is—
A. 42.260 km   B. 42.105 km
C. 42.195 km   D. 42.294 km

51. Rolland Garros is associated with—
A. Badminton   B. Football
C. Tennis   D. Rowing

52. Keenan stadium is located at—
A. Jamshedpur   B. Cuttack
C. Patna   D. Ranchi

53. Dola Banerjee is associated with the game of—
A. Chess   B. Archery
C. Swimming   D. Rifle Shooting

54. 'LBW' is a term related to the game of—
A. Badminton   B. Cricket
C. Hockey   D. Football

55. Which of the following cups/trophies is not given for excellence in the game of Badminton?
A. Uber Cup   B. Thomas Cup
C. Aros Junior Cup   D. Merdeka Cup

■ANSWERS■

1	2	3	4	5	6	7	8	9	10
C	A	D	B	D	C	D	B	A	C
11	12	13	14	15	16	17	18	19	20
A	B	C	D	C	D	C	B	D	A
21	22	23	24	25	26	27	28	29	30
A	B	C	D	D	C	C	B	A	A
31	32	33	34	35	36	37	38	39	40
C	D	A	D	C	C	D	B	D	A
41	42	43	44	45	46	47	48	49	50
B	C	B	A	A	B	C	C	D	C
51	52	53	54	55					
C	A	B	B	D					

Books and Authors ▶▶

1. Who amongst the following is the author of the book 'Freedom From Fear"?
   A. Boris Yeltsin
   B. Shobha De
   C. Peter Carcy
   D. Aung San Suu Kyi

2. Who amongst the following is the author of the book 'The Last Moghul'?
   A. Vikram Seth
   B. A.P.J. Abdul Kalam
   C. Salman Rushdie
   D. William Darlymple

3. Who wrote the best-selling book 'The Road Ahead'?
   A. Bill Clinton
   B. I.K. Gujral
   C. Bill Gates
   D. T.N. Seshan

4. Who translated the novel 'Nil Darpan' in English?
   A. Rabindranath Tagore
   B. Madhushudan Dutta
   C. Dinabandhu Mitra
   D. Bankim Chandra Chatterjee

5. In which of the following languages the book entitled 'Hind Swaraj' was written?
   A. Hindi
   B. Urdu
   C. Gujarati
   D. English

6. Which one of the following pairs is not correctly matched?
   A. Jawahar Lal Nehru—Hind Swaraj
   B. Maulana Abdul Kalam Azad—India Wins Freedom
   C. Subhash Chandra Bose—Indian Struggle
   D. Lala Lajpat Rai—Unhappy India

7. Tamil and Malayalam languages belong to ....linguistic family.
   A. Aryan
   B. Dravidian
   C. Austric
   D. Mongolean

8. Who was the author of 'India wins Freedom'?
   A. J. L. Nehru
   B. Maulana Abul Kalam Azad
   C. M.K. Gandhi
   D. None of them

9. The author of the book 'My Truth' is—
   A. Sarojini Naidu
   B. R.K. Narayan
   C. Mahatma Gandhi
   D. Indira Gandhi

10. Who amongst the following is the author of the book 'Faith and Compassion'?
    A. Arun Gandhi
    B. Kuldeep Nayyar
    C. Amit Chaudhary
    D. Navin Chawla

11. 'Tale of Two Cities' was written by—
    A. D.H. Lawrence
    B. R.L. Stevenson
    C. Charles Dickens
    D. Khushwant Singh

12. 'Oliver Twist' was written by—
    A. E.M. Forster
    B. Nathaniel Hawthorne
    C. Charles Dickens
    D. Victor Hugo

13. The author of 'Chaturanga' is—
    A. Humayun Kabir
    B. Rabindranath Tagore
    C. Annadasankar Roy
    D. Sunil Gangopadhyay

14. Who was the author of the book 'Geet Govinda'?
    A. Chandidas
    B. Jayadeva
    C. Jadu Bhatt
    D. Shri Chaitanya

15. Which of the following is the book written by Kiran Desai?
    A. Higher than Everest
    B. A Passage to England
    C. Affluent Society
    D. The Inheritance of Loss

16. 'Between the Assassinations' is a book written by—
    A. Chetan Bhagat
    B. Kiran Desai
    C. Shobha De
    D. Arvind Adiga

17. 'The Universe in a Single Atom' is a book by—
 A. Dr. Subhash C. Kashyap
 B. Dalai Lama
 C. A.P.J. Abdul Kalam
 D. M.S. Swaminathan

18. The Book 'Mother India' was written by—
 A. Catherine Mayo
 B. Lala Lajpat Rai
 C. Bal Gangadhar Tilak
 D. Bipin Chandra Pal

19. Who wrote the drama 'Malati Madhav'?
 A. Bhas
 B. Kalidas
 C. Bhavabhuti
 D. Banbhatt

20. Who is the author of the book 'Two Lives'?
 A. Vikram Seth
 B. Anita Nair
 C. Upmanyu Chatterji
 D. Stephen King

21. Who amongst the following is the author of the book "The Algebra of Infinite Justice"?
 A. Kiran Desai
 B. Anita Desai
 C. Arundhati Roy
 D. Anita Nair

22. Who amongst the following is the author of the book "No Full Stops in India"?
 A. B.K. Nehru
 B. D.R. Mankekar
 C. R.K. Narayan
 D. Mark Tully

23. Who wrote the 'Discovery of India'?
 A. Jawahar Lal Nehru
 B. Lala Lajpat Rai
 C. Dada Bhai Naoroji
 D. Moti Lal Nehru

24. Who wrote 'Anand Math'?
 A. Subhash Chandra Bose
 B. Sarat Chandra Chattopadhyaya
 C. Rabindra Nath Tagore
 D. Bankim Chandra Chatterji

25. Which of the following books was known as the 'Bible of Bengali Patriotism'?
 A. Geetanjali
 B. Anand Math
 C. Devdas
 D. Gora

26. Who wrote the book 'Life Divine'?
 A. Mulk Raj Anand
 B. Abul Kalam Azad
 C. Aurobindo Ghosh
 D. J.L. Nehru

27. Who is the author of the book 'Argumentative Indian'?
 A. V.S. Naipaul
 B. Vikram Seth
 C. Shashi Tharoor
 D. Amartya Sen

28. Who is the author of the book 'Amitabh—The Making of a Superstar?
 A. Tushar Raheja
 B. Vijay Singhvi
 C. Susmita Das Gupta
 D. Raj Kamal Jha

29. The book 'Zafar Nama' was written by—
 A. Guru Gobind Singh
 B. Aurangzeb
 C. Guru Angad
 D. Guru Tegh Bahadur

30. 'Why I am an Atheist' was written by—
 A. Bhagat Singh
 B. Sardar Udham Singh
 C. Subhash Chandra Bose
 D. Captain Shahnawaz

ANSWERS

1	2	3	4	5	6	7	8	9	10
D	D	C	B	C	A	B	B	D	D
11	12	13	14	15	16	17	18	19	20
C	C	B	B	D	D	B	A	C	A
21	22	23	24	25	26	27	28	29	30
C	D	A	D	B	C	D	C	A	A

1. Which is the part of Computer System?
   A. Hardware
   B. Accounting system
   C. Note-book
   D. Tools

2. Which is the part of Computer Hardware?
   A. Input devices   B. CPU
   C. Output devices   D. All of these

3. Which is main part of Computer System?
   A. Input   B. CPU
   C. Output   D. All of the above

4. Which is the brain of computer?
   A. CPU
   B. Input Devices
   C. Auxiliary Memory Devices
   D. LAN

5. Which is the steps of data processing?
   A. Recording of data
   B. Classification
   C. Sorting
   D. All of the above

6. Ascending of data is related with—
   A. Recording of data
   B. Sorting
   C. Summarising
   D. Calculating

7. The Calculator was developed by—
   A. Franc Boldwin
   B. Jacards Loom
   C. J. Betty
   D. Howard Aiken

8. Hybrid computer is a combination of—
   A. Analog Computer and Digital Computer
   B. Calculator and Laptop
   C. Laptop and Abacus
   D. Punch Card and Analog Computer

9. Which is the counting devices?
   A. Abacus
   B. Written Manual
   C. Mechanical Calculator
   D. All of the above

10. Java is—
    A. Programming Language
    B. Network
    C. Calculating devices
    D. All of these

11. Which is a Programming Language(s)?
    A. COBOL   B. FORTRAN IV
    C. Java   D. All of the above

12. Voltage meter is—
    A. Analog Computer
    B. Digital Computer
    C. Language
    D. LAN

13. Who is known as father of computer?
    A. Bill Gates   B. Charles Babege
    C. Alen Euning   D. Johan Euring

14. Electricity meter is a .... computer.
    A. Microcomputer
    B. Hybrid Computer
    C. Analog Computer
    D. Digital Computer

15. Which is the Microcomputer?
    A. Watch   B. Calculator
    C. Written Manual   D. Palm Top

16. Who made the first computer programme?
    A. Bil Gates   B. Lady Loveless
    C. New lman   D. Einstine

17. What is disk storage capacity of Mini Computer?
    A. 20 GB   B. 40 GB
    C. 100 GB   D. 1000 GB

18. Laptop is a—
A. Microcomputer
B. Hybrid Computer
C. Analog Computer
D. Digital Computer

19. CPU stand for—
A. Control Processing Unit
B. Central Processing Unit
C. Common Processing Unit
D. All of these

20. Which is the part of CPU?
A. Control Unit   B. ALU
C. Main Memory   D. All of the above

21. ALU stand for¡
A. Arithmetic and Logical Unit
B. Art Logical Unit
C. Apple Log Unit
D. Access Logical Unit

22. Which is the part of structure of Micro Processor?
A. ALU   B. Register
C. Control Unit   D. All of these

23. Keyboard is a—
A. Input device   B. Output device
C. LAN   D. Network

24. Which is input device?
A. Mouse   B. Punch Card
C. Scanner   D. All of these

25. Number Keys are—
A. 0, 1 and 3   B. F1 to F12
C. Enter   D. Shift

26. Which of the following are Control Keys?
A. Enter   B. Shift
C. Esc   D. All of these

27. Match the following—

List-I	**List-II**
(Keyboard)	**(Type of Keys)**
(a) Number Keys	1. O
(b) Alphabet Keys	2. B
(c) Edit Keys	3. Page down
(d) Control Keys	4. Lock
	5. %

Codes:

	(a)	(b)	(c)	(d)
A.	1	2	3	4
B.	3	1	2	4
C.	3	1	4	2
D.	1	4	3	2

28. Which is Editing Key of Computer?
A. Page up   B. Page down
C. Delete   D. All of these

29. Which is the Symbol Keys of Keyboard?
A. ?   B. %
C. @   D. All of these

30. Which is the eye of the Computer?
A. Scanner   B. Punch Card
C. Mouse   D. All of these

31. OMR is—
A. Option Multiple Report
B. Optical Mark Reader
C. Open Mark Reader
D. All of these

32. The Bar Coding has the—
A. 10 digit   B. 100 digit
C. 1000 digit   D. 1 digit

33. Plotter is a—
A. Input device   B. LAN
C. Language   D. Output device

34. Which is the output device?
A. Printer   B. VDV
C. Plotter   D. All of these

35. The plotter may be used in—
A. Graphics and Artists
B. Accounting
C. Recording
D. Sorting

36. RAM is a—
A. Computer Memory
B. Network
C. Language
D. Programme

37. Which is the Primary Memory of the Computer?
A. RAM   B. ROM
C. PROM   D. All of these

38. Which is the full form of ROM?
A. Read only Memory
B. Read on Memory
C. Roal only Memory
D. Role on Memory

39. The Personal Computer is—
A. Desktop Mode
B. Notebook Computer
C. Plam Computer
D. All of the above

40. Which is the component of Computer System?
A. Hardware   B. Software
C. Users   D. All of these

41. Which is the Hardware of Personal Computer?
A. Input and Output Device
B. Processor
C. Memory
D. All of these

42. Which is the output device of Personal Computer?
A. Speaker   B. Monitor
C. Printer   D. All of the above

43. Which is the input device of Personal Computer?
A. Microphone   B. Digital Camera
C. Touch Pad   D. All of these

44. Control bus is an—
A. Electronic Path B. Computer
C. Network   D. Memory

45. Which is a Semiconductor Memory of Computer?
A. Cache Memory   B. RAM
C. ROM   D. All of these

46. Which is the Secondary Memory of Computer?
A. RAM   B. ROM
C. Cache Memory   D. Magnetic

47. Bus is a—
A. Network Topology
B. Memory
C. Cost
D. Planning

48. Which is the short form of Local Areal Network?
A. LAN   B. MAN
C. WAN   D. RAM

49. LAN Topology contains—
A. Bus   B. Star
C. Ring   D. All of these

50. Which is the feature of Internet?
A. www   B. Telenet
C. Channels   D. All of these

51. System Unit
A. coordinates the input and output devices
B. is a container consisting of electronic components
C. is a combination of hardware and software
D. control and manipulates data

ANSWERS

1	2	3	4	5	6	7	8	9	10
A	D	B	A	D	B	A	A	D	A
11	**12**	**13**	**14**	**15**	**16**	**17**	**18**	**19**	**20**
D	A	B	C	D	B	A	A	B	D
21	**22**	**23**	**24**	**25**	**26**	**27**	**28**	**29**	**30**
A	D	A	D	A	D	A	D	D	A
31	**32**	**33**	**34**	**35**	**36**	**37**	**38**	**39**	**40**
B	A	D	D	A	A	D	A	D	D
41	**42**	**43**	**44**	**45**	**46**	**47**	**48**	**49**	**50**
D	D	D	A	A	D	A	A	D	D
51									
B									

1. Match List-I with List-II and select the correct answer using the codes given below the Lists :

List-I	List-II
(a) Visakhadatta	1. Mrichhakatika
(b) Shudraka	2. Ritusamhara
(c) Kalidasa	3. Kamasutra
(d) Vatsyayana	4. Devichandraguptam

Codes :

	(a)	(b)	(c)	(d)
A.	1	4	2	3
B.	4	1	3	2
C.	1	4	3	2
D.	4	1	2	3

2. In which one of the following langauges is the *Dalit* writing more conspicuous?
   A. Punjabi
   B. Assamese
   C. Marathi
   D. Odiya

3. The first writer to use Urdu as the medium of poetic expression was:
   A. Amir Khusrau
   B. Mirza Ghalib
   C. Bahadur Shah Zafar
   D. Faiz

4. The religious text of the Zoroastrians is named as:
   A. Torah
   B. The Analects
   C. Tripatika
   D. Zend Avesta

5. The film 'The Making of the Mahatma' has been directed by:
   A. Shyam Benegal
   B. Peter Ustinov
   C. Richard Attenborough
   D. Mira Nair

6. Raja Harishchandra, an early Indian film, was produced by :
   A. D.G. Phalke
   B. Ashok Kumar
   C. Ardeshir Irani
   D. None of the above

7. All films are certificed by .... before they are publicly exhibited.
   A. Films Division
   B. National Film Development Corporation (NFDC)
   C. Directorate of Advertising and Visual Publicity (DAVP)
   D. Central Board of Film Certificate (CBFC)

8. What name is given to the designs drawn by the women of Tamil Nadu on their floors and thresholds, using pastes and powders?
   A. Madna
   B. Alpana
   C. Kalam
   D. Rangoli

9. Who directed the all time famous movie called 'Mother India':
   A. Yash Chopra
   B. Ramesh Sippy
   C. Mehboob Khan
   D. Prithvi Raj Kapoor

10. The film 'Train to Pakistan' is based on the novel of the same name, written by:
    A. Bhishma Sahani
    B. Khushwant Singh
    C. Amrita Pritam
    D. Khwaja Ahmed Abbas

11. Which of the following is a folk dance form of Jharkhand?
    A. Pali
    B. Jhumar
    C. Nati
    D. Chhau

12. The first feature film (talkie) to be produced in India was:
    A. Hatimtai
    B. Alam Ara
    C. Pundalik
    D. Raja Harishchandra

13. Who directed the film "Bombay"?
    A. Shyam Benegal
    B. Meera Nair
    C. Shekhar Kapoor
    D. Mani Ratnam

14. Late Iftekhar Ahmad was famous in which of the following fields?
    A. Acting
    B. Singing
    C. Music
    D. Literature

15. The Hozagiri Dance belongs to which state?
    A. Mizoram
    B. Sikkim
    C. Nagaland
    D. Tripura

16. During whose reign did the 'Mughal Painting' flourish?
A. Aurangzeb B. Akbar
C. Jahangir D. Shahjahan

17. A popular Hindi film-based on the famous Sanskrit play *Mrichhakatika*, was titled:
A. Meghadoot B. Amrapali
C. Utsav D. Shakuntala

18. Who composed the song 'Zara Yad Karo Kurbani'?
A. Javed Akhtar
B. Pradeep
C. Nusrat Fateh Ali Khan
D. Raghupati Sahay 'Firaq'

19. Who was the producer of the serial 'Mahabharat'?
A. Shyam Benegal B. B.R. Chopra
C. Ramanand Sagar D. Mani Ratnam

20. Which of the following is a folk dance of Rajasthan?
A. Garba B. Dandya
C. Jhumar D. Kathak

21. The famous dancer Mamata Sankar is the daughter of :
A. Ravi Sankar B. Sachin Sankar
C. Uday Sankar D. Moni Sankar

22. Which is Maharashtra's well-known folk form of musical theatre?
A. Lavni B. Nautanki
C. Tamasha D. Goatha

23. The classical Indian Music has its origin in which of the following :
A. Atharvaveda B. Rigveda
C. Samaveda D. Yajurveda

24. Teratali is the folk dance of:
A. Kerala B. Rajasthan
C. Madhya Pradesh D. Tamil Nadu

25. 'Karagam', a religious folk dance is associated with:
A. Tamil Nadu B. Kerala
C. Andhra Pradesh D. Karnataka

26. Consider the following statements regarding the Chakiarkoothu form of dance :
1. It is performed by Chakiar caste.
2. It cannot be traditionally witnessed by the higher caste Hindus.

3. Mizhavu is the accompanying instrument.
4. Its theatre form is called Koothambalam.
Which of these statements are correct?
A. 1, 3 and 4 B. 1, 2 and 3
C. 2, 3 and 4 D. 1, 2 and 4

27. Which of the following is a classical dance form of Kerala?
A. Kathak B. Kuchipudi
C. Bharat Natyam D. Kathakali

28. The Shore Temple at Mahabalipuram was built by the:
A. Yadavas B. Kakatiyas
C. Hoysalas D. Pallavas

29. Maestro Kishan Maharaja is associated with :
A. Shehnai B. Tabla
C. Santoor D. Flute

30. Sitar, Sarangi and Tabla became popular from the period of:
A. The Mughals B. The Delhi Sultanate
C. The Vardhanas D. The Guptas

31. The Rashtrakutas built the:
A. Kailash Temple, Ellora
B. Brihadeshwara Temple, Tanjore
C. Keshava Temple, Somanathapura
D. Kailashnatha Temple, Kanchipuram

32. The *Talkappiyam* is a book of:
A. music and dance
B. grammar and rhetoric
C. poems
D. devotional songs

33. Which one of the following is essentially a solo dance?
A. Kuchipudi B. Kathak
C. Manipuri D. Mohiniattyam

34. Which one of the following dance forms is associated with Samyukta Panigrahi?
A. Kathakkali B. Mohini Attam
C. Kathak D. Odissi

35. The Lingaraja Temple was dedicated to:
A. Vishnu B. Krishna
C. Shiva D. Brahma

36. Kuchipudi is a dance drama of which of the following States?
A. Andhra Pradesh B. Kerala
C. Karnataka D. Tamil Nadu

37. Who built the Mahabodhi Temple at Bodh Gaya?

A. Gopala   B. Devapala
C. Dharmapala   D. Mahipala

38. Which one of the following pairs is *not* correctly matched?

A. Bharatanatyam   :   Tamil Nadu
B. Mohiniattam   :   Odisha
C. Kuchipudi   :   Andhra Pradesh
D. Bhangra   :   Punjab

39. Who is considered the founder of the Sufi cult in India?

A. Sheikh Ismail
B. Sheikh Hussain
C. Sheikh Ali-Bin-Usman-al-Hujwaisi
D. Sheikh Ali Hassan

40. This Sikh guru built the Golden Temple (Harimandir) :

A. Guru Angad   B. Guru Tegh Bahadur
C. Guru Arjan Dev   D. Guru Gobind Singh

41. Geeta Chandran is well known as a/an:

A. Bharatnatyam dancer
B. Classical Carnatic Vocalist
C. Film director
D. Exponent of Violin

42. Whose philosophy is called the Advaita?

A. Ramanujacharya
B. Shankaracharya
C. Nagarjuna
D. Vasumitra

43. Match List-I with List-II and select the correct answer using the code given below the Lists:

List-I (Person)	List-II (Knowns As)
(a) Bhajan Sopori	1. Bharatnatyam dancer
(b) Birju Maharaj	2. Exponent of Santoor
(c) Priyadarsini Govind	3. Mridangam Maestro
(d) T. V. Gopalakrishnan	4. Kathak dancer

Codes :

	(a)	(b)	(c)	(d)
A.	2	1	4	3
B.	3	1	4	2
C.	2	4	1	3
D.	3	4	1	2

44. Where is the famous Vijaya Vittala temple having its 56 carved pillars emitting musical notes located?

A. Belur   B. Bhadrachalam
C. Hampi   D. Srirangam

ANSWERS

1	2	3	4	5	6	7	8	9	10
D	C	A	D	A	A	D	C	C	B
11	**12**	**13**	**14**	**15**	**16**	**17**	**18**	**19**	**20**
D	B	D	A	D	C	C	B	B	C
21	**22**	**23**	**24**	**25**	**26**	**27**	**28**	**29**	**30**
C	C	C	B	C	B	D	D	B	B
31	**32**	**33**	**34**	**35**	**36**	**37**	**38**	**39**	**40**
A	B	D	D	C	A	B	B	C	C
41	**42**	**43**	**44**						
A	B	C	C						

1. The first state in India which was created on linguistic basis—
   A. Andhra Pradesh   B. Gujarat
   C. Haryana   D. Kerala

2. 'Kiwi' means players from—
   A. Australia   B. New Zealand
   C. West Indies   D. The UK

3. Who among the following is popularly known as 'Nightingale of India'?
   A. Lata Mangeshkar
   B. Asha Bhosle
   C. Suchitra Mitra
   D. Maya Sen

4. 'David Copperfield' is the name of a—
   A. Novel   B. Drama
   C. Poem   D. Short story

5. The First Statistics Day was observed on—
   A. July 7, 2007
   B. July 11, 2007
   C. June 12, 2007
   D. June 29, 2009

6. CTBT stands for—
   A. Continued Test Ban Treaty
   B. Continued Test Based Treatments
   C. Comprehensive Test Ban Treaty
   D. Commercial Test Based Tariff

7. 'CDMA'—technology used in mobile phones stands for—
   A. Computer Developed Management Application
   B. Code Division Multiple Application
   C. Code Division Multiple Access
   D. Code Division Mobile Application

8. Which English poet is known as the 'Singer of Sorrow'?
   A. Keats   B. Yeats
   C. Shelley   D. Wordsworth

9. Fakir Mohan Senapati is the famous literary figure of—
   A. Manipuri   B. Odia
   C. Maithili   D. Telugu

10. The first radio-programme in India was broadcast by Radio Club of Bombay in—
    A. 1924   B. 1923
    C. 1926   D. 1927

11. In India, the first state to institute a Human Rights Commission is—
    A. Andhra Pradesh B. Kerala
    C. West Bengal   D. Rajasthan

12. The first film actor to be nominated to Rajya Sabha was—
    A. Ashok Kumar   B. Dilip Kumar
    C. Jeevan   D. Prithviraj Kapoor

13. Commonwealth Day is observed by Member Countries on—
    A. 26th August   B. 24th May
    C. 27th December   D. 29th January

14. Glasgow is famous for—
    A. Ship building   B. Aircraft
    C. Automobile   D. Textiles

15. Rose is the national emblem of—
    A. Italy   B. Iran
    C. Israel   D. Iraq

16. The man first landed on the moon in—
    A. 1969   B. 1968
    C. 1970   D. 1958

17. The oldest monarchy in the world is that of—
    A. Nepal   B. UK
    C. Spain   D. Japan

18. Which is called the 'Tiger State'?
    A. Rajasthan   B. Madhya Pradesh
    C. Uttar Pradesh   D. Jammu & Kashmir

19. Which state of India has the largest area under forest?
   A. Assam
   B. Uttar Pradesh
   C. Himachal Pradesh
   D. Madhya Pradesh

20. The place Sabarimala is situated in which of the following states?
   A. Andhra Pradesh   B. Tamil Nadu
   C. Kerala   D. Karnataka

21. Paul Krugman is a/an—
   A. Scientist   B. Sportsman
   C. Banker   D. Economist

22. 'Dabbawala' is located at—
   A. Bhopal   B. New Delhi
   C. Kolkata   D. Mumbai

23. World Environment Day is observed on—
   A. June 1   B. June 5
   C. June 15   D. None of these

24. World Deafness Day is observed on—
   A. September 24   B. September 16
   C. September 2   D. September 27

25. World Standards Day is celebrated on—
   A. October 12   B. October 14
   C. October 24   D. October 19

26. Sun Temple is situated at—
   A. Puri   B. Khajuraho
   C. Konark   D. Gaya

27. Jaduguda is famous for—
   A. Iron ore   B. Manganese
   C. Gold   D. Uranium

28. Aung San Suu Kyi is a leader of—
   A. Vietnam   B. Myanmar
   C. Thailand   D. China

29. Which of the following days is observed as 'National Sports Day' in India?
   A. July 29   B. August 29
   C. September 29   D. October 29

30. What is the name of the first woman space tourist?
   A. Jullian Moore   B. Paula Radcliffe
   C. Namira Salim   D. Anousheh Ansari

31. World Consumer Rights Day is on—
   A. 15th March   B. 21st March
   C. 22nd March   D. 24th March

32. Whose theory is the 'struggle for existence'?
   A. Darwin   B. Lamarck
   C. De Vries   D. Mendel

33. "Man is born free and every where he is in Chains", is said by—
   A. Isaac Newton   B. Horace
   C. J.J. Rousseau   D. Galileo

34. Which is the last month of National Calendar of India?
   A. Chaitra   B. Phalguna
   C. Ashadha   D. Bhadra

35. Indian Naval Academy is located at—
   A. Panjim   B. Visakhapattnam
   C. Chennai   D. Cochin

36. Where is the National Industrial Security Academy of the CISF located?
   A. Hyderabad   B. Mount Abu
   C. Tekanpur   D. Gwaldam

37. The United Arab Emirates is a federation of how many Emirates?
   A. 6   B. 7
   C. 8   D. 9

38. Rabi Crops are sown in—
   A. Spring   B. Summer
   C. Autumn   D. Winter

39. 'World Savings Day' is celebrated on—
   A. October 31   B. November 9
   C. December 24   D. January 14

40. 'Legal Service Day' is celebrated on—
   A. November 9   B. October 20
   C. December 24   D. January 10

41. 'National Consumers Day' is observed on—
   A. December 10   B. December 24
   C. September 10   D. April 24

42. 'World Laughter Day' is observed on—
   A. January 14   B. February 14
   C. March 14   D. April 14

43. What is 'Super 301'?
A. A British anti-aircraft
B. An American trade law
C. A French News Channel
D. None of these

44. 'WAN' means—
A. Wide Area Network
B. Wide Allen Network
C. Woll Area Network
D. Wine Area Network

45. 'National Press Day' is observed on—
A. November 12   B. November 16
C. November 26   D. December 1

46. National Broadcasting Day' is observed on—
A. October 12   B. November 12
C. November 16   D. November 26

47. 'National Law Day' is observed on—
A. September 1   B. October 10
C. November 26   D. December 1

48. In which year Family Planning Programme was started in India?
A. 1950 AD   B. 1951 AD
C. 1952 AD   D. 1955 AD

49. The word 'Actuaries' is related to—
A. Banking   B. Insurance
C. Share-market   D. None of the above

50. Who was the speaker of the first Lok sabha?
A. Hukum Singh   B. G.V. Mavalankar
C. K.M Munshi   D. U.N. Dhebar

51. 'Oh Fatherland never shall we forget' is the national anthem of—
A. Angola   B. Andorra
C. Mali   D. Sierra Leone

52. The symbol of World Wildlife Fund is—
A. Polar Bear   B. White Bear
C. Red Panda   D. Cheeta

53. Tirupati is in—
A. Andhra Pradesh   B. Karnataka
C. Tamil Nadu   D. Kerala

54. NASA refers to—
A. National Aeronautics and Space Administration

B. North Atlantic Space Agency
C. North Airbase and Space Agency
D. None of the above

55. ISO 9000 is a—
A. Quality Standard Mark
B. Space Project
C. Trade Technique
D. None of these

56. Which is the longest sea bridge in the country?
A. Vidyasagar Setu, Kolkata
B. Bandra-Worli Sea Link, Mumbai
C. Bhakra-Nangal Project
D. None of these

57. Dr. Rajendra Pachauri is a/an—
A. Banker   B. Industrialist
C. Environmentalist   D. Scientist

58. Which city is known as the 'City of Joy'?
A. Delhi   B. Mumbai
C. Kolkata   D. Chennai

59. Which of these animals is not shown in the National Emblem of India?
A. Lion   B. Horse
C. Bull   D. Elephant

60. The name of India's first aircraft carrier is—
A. INS Vikrant   B. INS Nilgiri
C. INS Kukri   D. INS Himgiri

61. Which of the following is associated with the manufacture of guided missiles?
A. Bharat Earth Movers Limited
B. Bharat Dynamics Limited
C. Hindustan Aeronautics Limited
D. Bharat Electronics Limited

62. National Highway No. 3 runs from—
A. Delhi to Chennai
B. Amritsar to Kolkata
C. Delhi to Ahmedabad
D. Agra to Mumbai

63. The first nuclear test was conducted in India in the year—
A. 1973   B. 1974
C. 1975   D. 1976

64. Who said "Give me somewhere to stand, and I will move the world"?
A. Archimedes   B. Galileo
C. Edison   D. Newton

65. Jain temple of Abu is made of—
A. Sandstone   B. Lime Stone
C. Granite   D. Marble

66. Where is the Wild ass sanctuary?
A. Uttar Pradesh   B. Assam
C. Gujarat   D. Rajasthan

67. 'Project Arrow' is concerned with the modernisation of which of the following?
A. Airports   B. Post offices
C. Road Transport   D. Railways

68. Who is known as the father of Sanskrit Grammar?
A. Panini   B. Patanjali
C. Kalidas   D. None of the above

69. Who among the following is known as the morning star of Indian Renaissance?
A. Swami Vivekanand
B. Raja Rammohan Roy
C. Acharya Vinoba Bhave
D. Rabindra Nath Tagore

70. National Youth Day is observed on—
A. January 15   B. January 12
C. January 20   D. January 28

71. Which of the following is known as 'Queen of the Adriatic'?
A. Stockholm   B. Chicago
C. Venice   D. Strait of Gibralter

72. National Library, the largest in India is located at—
A. Chennai   B. Mumbai
C. Delhi   D. Kolkata

73. Which of the following states has the highest production of coffee in India?
A. Karnataka   B. Tamil Nadu
C. Kerala   D. Andhra Pradesh

74. Which one of the following is full form of ICC?
A. International Cricket Council
B. Indian Cricket Council
C. International Cost Camp
D. Indian Coast Cup

75. Sigma is a term of—
A. Accounting   B. Maths
C. Science   D. Arts

ANSWERS

1	2	3	4	5	6	7	8	9	10
A	B	A	A	D	C	C	C	B	B
11	**12**	**13**	**14**	**15**	**16**	**17**	**18**	**19**	**20**
C	D	B	A	B	A	D	B	D	C
21	**22**	**23**	**24**	**25**	**26**	**27**	**28**	**29**	**30**
D	D	B	A	B	C	D	B	B	D
31	**32**	**33**	**34**	**35**	**36**	**37**	**38**	**39**	**40**
A	A	C	B	D	A	B	D	A	A
41	**42**	**43**	**44**	**45**	**46**	**47**	**48**	**49**	**50**
B	A	B	A	B	B	C	C	B	B
51	**52**	**53**	**54**	**55**	**56**	**57**	**58**	**59**	**60**
A	C	A	A	A	B	C	C	D	A
61	**62**	**63**	**64**	**65**	**66**	**67**	**68**	**69**	**70**
B	D	B	A	D	C	B	A	B	B
71	**72**	**73**	**74**	**75**					
C	D	A	A	B					